A Roman settlement and bath house at Shadwell:

Excavations at Tobacco Dock
and Babe Ruth restaurant, The Highway, London

Published by Pre-Construct Archaeology Limited

ISBN 978-0-9563054-2-8

Edited by Victoria Ridgeway and Peter Rowsome

Typeset by Cate Davies

Index by Sue Vaughan

Printed by Henry Ling Limited, The Dorset Press

Front cover: reconstruction showing the bath house, service yard and ancillary buildings as they may have appeared in the late third and early fourth centuries.

Back cover: gold earring with filigree decoration and green glass bead (left); the bath house during excavation, looking east (top right); *pilae* stacks in the north-east corner of the *caldarium* (bottom right).

A Roman settlement and bath house at Shadwell:

Excavations at Tobacco Dock and Babe Ruth restaurant, The Highway, London

Alistair Douglas, James Gerrard and Berni Sudds

Pre-Construct Archaeology Limited: Monograph No. 12

Shadwell Excavations Volume 1

PCA Monograph Series

1   Excavations at Hunt's House, Guy's Hospital, London Borough of Southwark
    By Robin Taylor-Wilson, 2002
    ISBN   0-9542938-0-0

2   Tatberht's Lundenwic: Archaeological excavations in Middle Saxon London
    By Jim Leary with Gary Brown, James Rackham, Chris Pickard and Richard Hughes, 2004
    ISBN   0-9542938-1-9

3   Iwade: Occupation of a North Kent Village from the Mesolithic to the Medieval period
    By Barry Bishop and Mark Bagwell, 2005
    ISBN   0-9542938-2-7

4   Saxons, Templars & Lawyers in the Inner Temple: Archaeological excavations in Church Court & Hare Court
    By Jonathan Butler, 2005
    ISBN   0-9542938-3-5

5   Unlocking the Landscape: Archaeological Excavations at Ashford Prison, Middlesex
    By Tim Carew, Barry Bishop, Frank Meddens and Victoria Ridgeway, 2006
    ISBN   0-9542938-4-3

6   Reclaiming the Marsh: Archaeological Excavations at Moor House, City of London 1998-2004
    By Jonathan Butler, 2006
    ISBN   0-9542938-5-1

7   From Temples to Thames Street – 2000 Years of Riverside Development: Archaeological excavations at the Salvation Army International Headquarters
    By Timothy Bradley and Jonathan Butler, 2008
    ISBN   978-0-9542938-6-4

8   A New Millennium at Southwark Cathedral: Investigations into the first two thousand years
    By David Divers, Chris Mayo, Nathalie Cohen and Chris Jarrett, 2009
    ISBN   978-0-9542938-7-1

9   On the Boundaries of Occupation: Excavations at Burringham Road, Scunthorpe and Baldwin Avenue, Bottesford, North Lincolnshire
    By Peter Boyer, Jennifer Proctor and Robin Taylor-Wilson, 2009
    ISBN   978-0-9542938-8-6

10 The Sea and the Marsh: The Medieval Cinque Port of New Romney revealed through archaeological excavations and historical research
    By Gillian Draper and Frank Meddens, 2009
    ISBN   978–0–9542938–9–5

11 Pegswood Moor, Morpeth: A Later Iron Age and Romano-British Farmstead settlement
    By Jennifer Proctor, 2009
    ISBN   978–0–9563054–0–4

Contributors

Principal authors	Alistair Douglas, James Gerrard and Berni Sudds
Volume editors	Victoria Ridgeway and Peter Rowsome
Academic adviser	Martin Millett
Project manager	Peter Moore
Post-excavation managers	Victoria Ridgeway and Frank Meddens
Graphics	Josephine Brown
Finds illustrations	Adrian Bailey, Cate Davies and Dave Hopkins
Reconstruction drawings	Jake Lunt-Davies and Sarah Kensington
Photography	Alistair Douglas, Strephon Duckering and Richard Young
Roman pottery	James Gerrard with Malcolm Lyne
Samian	Joanna Bird
Mortaria	Kay Hartley
Amphorae	David Williams
Inscriptions and graffiti	Roger Tomlin, Yves Pierre Lambert and Berni Sudds
Building material	Berni Sudds
Painted wall plaster	Berni Sudds
Small finds	James Gerrard
Glass	Sarah Carter and John Shepherd
Coins	James Gerrard
Timber studies	Damian Goodburn
Dendrochronology	Ian Tyers
Animal bone	Philip Armitage
Environmental analysis	Nick Branch
French translation	Nathalie Barrett
German translation	Sylvia Butler
Series editor	Victoria Ridgeway

Contents

Figures

Tables

xii

Foreword

Prior to the last quarter of the twentieth century, our knowledge of Romano-British Shadwell largely comprised a handful of geographically isolated high-status burials strung along a presumed east–west road. The destination of this thoroughfare was somewhat perplexing. There is no archaeological evidence for it beyond the eastern cemetery and its destination is not immediately apparent. Whatever its exact trajectory, it ultimately ends up approaching the Thames somewhere in the vicinity of Ratcliffe.

Against this backdrop the discovery in the 1970s of substantial masonry remains alongside other mid to late third-century AD buildings, drains, tanks, burials and butchery evidence, sparked a debate about the nature of this area in the later Roman period. This presumed settlement was located immediately south of the modern street, The Highway, a route leading from Ratcliffe into the City and possibly reflecting the course of the conjectured earlier route. But what was the nature of this settlement and why was it located here, close to *Londinium* but very definitely beyond the City walls? And what were the masonry foundations? Could they be the remains of a signalling station, an interpretation originally propounded by Johnson (1975; 1979), and one which continues to be favoured by some (eg Bird 2008), or are they perhaps a mausoleum as Lakin (2002) has suggested?

This monograph details the results of investigations conducted by Pre-Construct Archaeology in the late 1990s and early 2000s, which have transformed our understanding of this area in the Roman period. Initial investigations at Tobacco Dock, some 50m west of the earlier excavations added to the emerging picture of Romano-British settlement in Shadwell, providing more evidence of third- and fourth-century occupation with clay-and-timber buildings, drains and water tanks, protected by substantial revetting put in place to terrace and consolidate the escarpment between the road and the river. Within a few months of these excavations finishing PCA returned to Shadwell where, beneath the former Babe Ruth restaurant, located between Tobacco Dock and the 1970s excavations, was a large hypocausted building. Occupying a gravel terrace overlooking the Thames, it had heated rooms, an apse and ready access to fresh spring water; all the hallmarks of a bath house. Yet it fails to readily conform to known examples, falling between public and private baths in terms of its size, and with an uncomfortably high number of heated rooms. Furthermore, the presence of such a monumental building raises fresh questions concerning the nature and status of Romano-British Shadwell. Who were the inhabitants of this settlement and what brought them to Shadwell? Why are such enigmatic but evidently impressive buildings found in this outlying enclave of *Londinium*? Who was responsible for building the bath house and why? Some have even questioned if this was a bath house at all.

In our opinion, this building seems most likely to be a stand-alone bath house which forms part of a wider settlement, the extent of which remains unknown. A well-appointed clay-and-timber building to the north may have provided accommodation or other services for the bathers, whilst buildings to the west appear more domestic in character. Whatever the current shortfalls in our knowledge, there are some things we can state with confidence: the third century AD saw the establishment of a settlement at Shadwell, one which thrived and apparently prospered. Over time the bath house was modified and extended, and the ancillary buildings frequently upgraded. The settlement and its associated baths were, for a while at least, a commercial success.

It has been suggested that, following the apparent demise of the quays and docks of *Londinium* in the mid third century due to falling sea levels and tidal regression, Shadwell and the Lea mouth may have become the focus of smaller 'ports' or beachmarkets (Brigham 1990). We still do not fully understand the relationship between the Shadwell settlement and the river and have no proof that it functioned as a port, but the existence of such facilities would certainly accord well with the pottery and coin evidence and the presence of significant masonry structures, the suggested road and other amenities. Developer-funded excavations provide us with keyhole glimpses into our past, but the location and timing of these interventions remain largely beyond our control. The constraints of excavation are imposed by concerns that largely lie beyond archaeological interests. Many questions remain and it is only through further research and excavation that these will be answered. However, PCA's excavations in Shadwell have contributed greatly to our knowledge and transformed our understanding. In this volume we attempt to present the evidence, to put it into a wider context and to offer some interpretations of what it might represent. We do this in order that the data might be available for reinterpretation in the future, and fully realising that some of these interpretations will be challenged and possibly even disproved by new theories and through future work.

It is therefore very apposite that as this volume goes to press in late October 2010 PCA is returning once more to excavate the western half of the site at Tobacco Dock; an opportunity which promises to extend our existing knowledge and perhaps even provide new avenues for exploring Romano-British Shadwell.

Victoria Ridgeway

Editor

Summary

Seven periods of prehistoric and Roman activity were identified at two adjacent excavations in Shadwell in 2002, on the north bank of the Thames just to the east of the City of London and the site of *Londinium*. The redevelopment sites lay to the south of The Highway and on either side of Wapping Lane; Tobacco Dock to the west (Site A; site code TOC02) and Babe Ruth restaurant to the east (Site B; HGA02). Excavations had taken place just to the northeast of Site B in the 1970s (LD74/LD76) and uncovered evidence of Roman activity that includes a large masonry structure near the crest of the hillside and originally identified as a military signal tower but more recently reinterpreted as a mausoleum.

Following a general introduction to the overall work at Shadwell (Chapter 1) the chronological narrative for Sites A and B is presented as a single land-use sequence (Chapter 2). Prehistoric activity on the steeply sloping ground, where the surface level dropped from *c.* 7m OD in the north to 1.6m OD in the south, was restricted to a small flint assemblage and evidence for a north–south aligned palaeochannel, the latter located between the two sites (Period 1; to AD 50). Early Roman activity (Period 2; *c.* AD 50–230) included external quarrying, rubbish pits, surface drainage and terracing of the escarpment. A timber building was established in the southwest and may have been a barn or granary (B1). This first and second-century activity was generally small scale and sporadic.

In the early to mid third century AD a step change in development took place at both sites, as new land divisions were established and buildings constructed on the lower terraces to the south, adjacent to the conjectured line of the river (Period 3; *c.* AD 230–275). A large stone-built bath house (B4), constructed on the southern part of Site B, contained at least ten rooms in its primary phase, including two bathing suites of warm (*tepidaria*) and hot rooms (*caldaria*) reached from a shared vestibule and changing area (*apodyterium*) or cold room (*frigidarium*). The bath house can be described as an axial row or angular row type, with its long axis aligned east–west and a south-central riverside entrance. A service yard, to the north of the bath building, was bounded on the west and north by the wings of a clay-and-timber accommodation block (B3). A small timber building (B2) was recorded to the south of a terrace on Site A to the west.

There was further intensive activity during Period 4, between *c.* AD 275–325, and this has been divided into five individual phases, based on the most detailed stratigraphic sequence, to the north of the bath house, where the accommodation block was repeatedly modified (B3a–3e; Period 4.1–4.5). The bath house itself was the subject of extensive alteration and expansion, with new rooms added to its north-western side (B4) and the under-floor hypocausts modified (Period 4.1). To the west of the bath house on Site A, contemporary external activity, a new timber building (B5) and ovens for food preparation were found. Further remodelling of the baths involved the removal of sub-floor dividing walls and extension of the entranceway southwards (Period 4.2) but the hypocausts were subsequently flooded and filled with silt, indicating a hiatus in use towards the end of Period 4. Hillside erosion and fragmentary building evidence (B6) on Site A may be roughly contemporary to the flood episode (Period 4.5).

In Period 5, between *c.* AD 325–375, the bath house (B4) returned to use and was extended, whilst a new structure (B7) was built to the north of its service yard. To the west of the baths a major new terracing revetment was established, with a new timber building (B8) to its south (Period 5.1). Occupation continued into the late fourth century, represented by a new building (B9) and drains to the west and the continued use of the bath complex in the east (Period 5.2).

The bath house was abandoned in the late fourth century and was probably quickly stripped of valuable materials for salvage (Period 6; *c.* AD 375–410). The service yard to the north of the ruined baths also fell out of use and was cut by drainage ditches (OA13), though a post-built structure (B10) was built to its north. To the west on Site A a relatively large masonry building (B11) was established and the external slope included a well and pitting (OA12). The latest evidence for activity at Shadwell cannot be dated accurately due to the relatively few finds recovered, but is likely to have continued until the early fifth century. Extensive robbing of the superstructure of the bath house, including the removal of walls and foundations, may have taken place later, though it cannot be dated (Period 7; *c.* AD 410+)

The Shadwell excavations also produced important assemblages of finds, particularly from the Later Roman periods. Chapter 3 includes specialist reports on the Roman pottery, coins, small finds, building materials, inscriptions, glass, and timber, some of which provided dendrochronological dating (3.1–3.8). The pottery includes groups of unusual samian and amphorae which are of both local and national significance, given their late date. Items of personal decoration include not only jewellery but a large number of hair pins that might be associated with use of the baths. There are also important collections of animal bone and significant archaeobotanical evidence for the local environment and economy (3.9–3.10).

Chapter 4 presents various thematic discussions including alternative interpretations of the bath house (4.1), its reconstruction, probable appearance and layout (4.2) and a consideration of the sites in relation to the river. Broader discussion of the status of Romano-British Shadwell is presented in Chapter 5.

The report is supported by appendices, including tabulated data, and the full site archive is available for study at the LAARC.

Peter Rowsome

Editor

Acknowledgements

Pre-Construct Archaeology would like to thank Messila House Ltd. (Bisley Properties SA) for funding and Wates Construction for commissioning the excavation at Tobacco Dock through Wates Construction. Thanks are extended to Dan Smith, SLLB Architects, Trevor Clifton and Mike Platt of Wates Construction, Tim Chapman, Joelle Chaubeau of ArupGeotechnics, for their help in setting up the excavation at Tobacco Dock. For their assistance and help during the excavation we want to thank Bob Williams (Wates Construction), Jan Windle (ArupGeotechnics) and all the site staff from Bittins Construction. We are especially grateful to archaeological consultant Richard Hughes of ArupGeotechnics and Jon Wardle of Wates Construction for all their support throughout the project.

Pre-Construct Archaeology would like to thank George Wimpey Central London Ltd. for their funding of and CgMs Consulting Ltd. for commissioning the excavation at 172–176 The Highway. Thanks are extended to archaeological consultant Duncan Hawkins of CgMs for helping to set up the project and his guidance and advice throughout the project. We would like to thank Blakedown Plant Hire and their operators for their professionalism in machining the site.

Special thanks are extended to Nick Truckle of English Heritage (Greater London Archaeology Advisory Service) for his monitoring of both sites and his support and encouragement throughout the project.

Pre-Construct Archaeology would very much like to thank all the field team for their hard work and commitment, at times in difficult and adverse conditions: R. Archer, S. Aylward, E. Bailey, H. Baxter, K. Bazley, T. Baxter, R. Bartkowiak, S. Bickelmann, K. Bradley, S. Burney, S. Byrne, H. Clough, C. Cross, L. Darton, R. Dave, S. Deeves, S. Duckering, R. Duckworth, C. Dunscomb, D. Eddisford, G. Evans, C. Forcey, I. Grosso, N. Hawkins, A. Haslam, S. Holden, M. House, K. Hulka, W. Johnston, D. Killock, F. Keith-Lucas, S. Keller, J. Langthorne, R. Lythe, A. Lord, J. Lord, A. Lask, S. Maher, R. Mattinson, G. Maurice, D. McLellan, P. McNulty, R. Meager, V. Osborn, C. O'Neill, S. Ouin, D. Quevillon, Q. Quinteros, C. Reese, G. Rees, J. Roberts, F. Sadarangani, E. Sayer, R. Shepard, R. Thorne, J. Taylor, A. Turner, D. Walker, S. Wallis, D. Waterfall, K. Wheaton, J. Wiles, E. Wragg, W. Valentine, A.M. Vandendriesche, M. Vinnels, T. Vitali, J. Vuolteenaho, and L. Yeomans. Thanks to Dave Dobson for logistics, Richard Young for the on-site photography, and Giles Hammond for surveying. Thanks also to the finds and environmental team K. Roberts, D. Dobson, J. Mitchell and G. Sherwood and to K. Sabel and J. Brown for their work both and post-excavation and on site identifying the ceramic building material.

The authors would like to thank Peter Moore the Project Manager, for his support throughout the project. Thanks also to Frank Meddens and Victoria Ridgeway for their management of the post-excavation programme. Märit Gaimster and Rob Nicholson are commended for their management of the finds. A special thanks to Francis Grew, John Shepherd and Jenny Hall from the Museum of London for their interest and encouragement, and to Paul Roberts of the Department of Greek and Roman Antiquities, British Museum for his advice. Thanks are also extended to Kevin Hayward for his petrological identification, Ian Betts for his identification and specialist knowledge of the ceramic building material, John Brown for assessing the Tobacco Dock building material, Richard Reece and Mike Hammerson for their help with the Roman coins, Hilary Major, Hilary Cool and Lynne Keys for their assistance with the small finds, and Ralph Jackson for his specialist knowledge of Roman surgical implements.

The authors are greatly indebted to Peter Rowsome for editing, comments and revisions to the text and for providing the summary, to Steve Roskams and Colin Wallace for their helpful comments, and to Josephine Brown for all her work on the graphics for this publication. Particular thanks are extended to David Bird for allowing us to view his paper discussing the Shadwell 'tower' (Bird 2008) in advance of publication.

Special thanks to Martin Millett for agreeing to be the academic adviser for the project and for all his support, advice and encouragement and especially the tea and sandwiches.

Chapter 1 Introduction

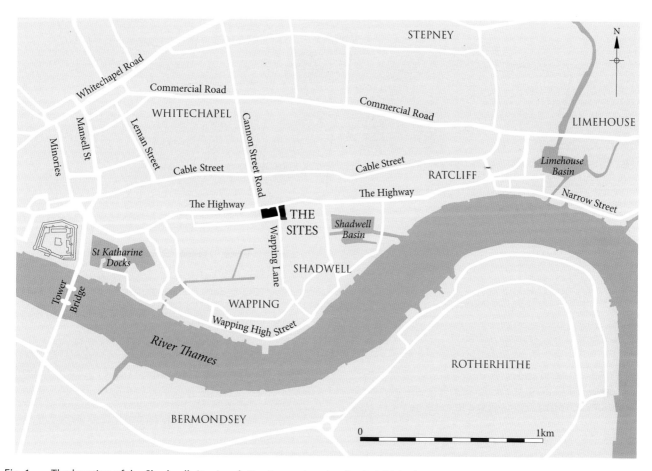

Fig. 1   The location of the Shadwell sites in relation to east London (scale 1:20,000)

This volume presents the results of archaeological investigations undertaken by Pre-Construct Archaeology Ltd. (PCA) on the edge of the Thames floodplain at Shadwell, London Borough of Tower Hamlets, East London (Fig. 1).

Two separate excavations were carried out by PCA at Shadwell, adding to information recovered from sites excavated in the 1970s immediately to the northeast and published elsewhere (Fig. 2; Lakin 2002; Johnson 1975). The Shadwell excavations revealed evidence of a complex sequence of human activity, ranging from prehistoric land use to the substantial remains of a Roman settlement and historically-documented nineteenth- and twentieth-century structures. This report presents findings related to the prehistoric and Roman phases.

1.1 Circumstances of the fieldwork

The first of the PCA excavations encompasses an area formerly used as the car park for the Tobacco Dock Factory Shops development (Site A) and forms a rectangular shaped piece of land 3600m², bounded by The Highway to the north, Chigwell Hill to the west, Wapping Lane (formerly Old Gravel Lane) to the east and Pennington Street to the south (NGR: TQ 3745 8070). Following its identification as an area of archaeological potential (Ove Arup and Partners 1994), Messila House Ltd. (Bisley Properties SA) commissioned PCA, through their archaeological consultant Richard Hughes of Ove Arup and Partners, to evaluate the site in 1996 and 1997 (Bishop 1996, Douglas 1997). Substantial evidence of Roman and post-medieval

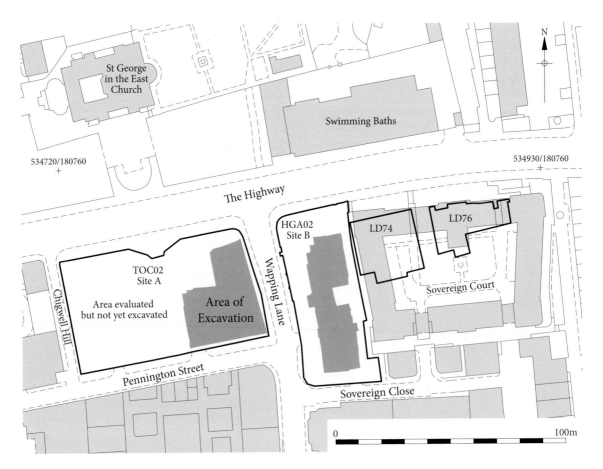

Fig. 2   Site and trench locations for the excavations at Tobacco Dock (Site A; TOC02), Babe Ruth restaurant (Site B; HGA02) and the 1970s investigations at the 'tower' site (LD74 and LD76) (scale 1:1,600)

activity was revealed and these interventions were given the Museum of London site code CYD96. Subsequently, a programme of works was designed to mitigate the impact of the proposed development of the site (Arup Geotechnics 2001; Brown and Moore 2001) and an open area excavation in the eastern half of the site was commissioned by Jon Wardle of Wates Construction on behalf of Messila House Ltd. (Bisley Properties SA). The excavations, supervised by Alistair Douglas, took place between March and May 2002. They were assigned the Museum of London site code TOC02 (Fig. 2). The western half of the site, though evaluated, has at the time of writing not been subject to controlled archaeological excavation.

The second site (Site B) was located to the east of Site A on land previously occupied by Babe Ruth restaurant at the corner of the junction of Wapping Lane and The Highway; NGR: TQ 34836 80702). Site B covered an area of approximately 2190m². Following a desktop assessment by CgMs Consulting (Hawkins and Meager 2002) an evaluation of the site was carried out by PCA in 2002 and revealed significant archaeological deposits. To further understand these deposits Duncan Hawkins of CgMs Consulting commissioned an open area excavation on behalf of George Wimpey Central London Ltd. This excavation revealed extensive Roman remains including a large late Roman building interpreted as a bath house

(Fig. 4). The excavation was supervised by Alistair Douglas of PCA between September 2002 and March 2003. The archaeological interventions at Site B were assigned the Museum of London site code HGA02.

1.2 Topographic and archaeological background

Sites A and B are located *c.* 1.2km east of the City of London on the north side of the River Thames and 4.7km west of the confluence of the Thames and the Lea. The course of the Thames now lies some 0.65km south of the site but probably ran closer to the site in the Roman period (see below). Both sites sit on the boundary formed by the Taplow, Mucking and Kempton Park gravels (Gibbard 1994) and overlook the alluvial deposits of the Thames floodplain. At Site A undisturbed Taplow/Mucking Gravel was encountered at 6.42m OD (Ordnance Datum) and was found to end at a sharply defined terrace edge. The lowest level recorded on the extant gravel surface was 2.95m OD. At Site B, Kempton Park Gravel was encountered in boreholes at 0.92–1.68m OD, 0.48–2.28m OD and 1.35–1.75m OD. Further to the north the interface of the terrace gravels with the underlying London Clay forms a natural spring line that would have formed an attractive source of fresh water (Williams 1993, 6).

The sites' Thameside location places them not only within the City of London's immediate hinterland but also within the Greater Thames Estuary. This is an area that has been recognised as being of national significance archaeologically for both the prehistoric and historic periods (Fulford *et al.* 1997; Williams and Brown 1999). However, the Sites and Monuments Record lists few finds from the immediate vicinity, probably a reflection of the densely urbanised nature of the modern landscape and the relative lack of archaeological investigation as a result. Prehistoric finds are restricted to a few scattered lithics assemblages that may indicate little more than occasional activity on the fringes of the Thames wetlands. There are slightly more Roman sites and finds and these are considered below.

The Romano-British activity in the vicinity of the sites is heavily influenced by the close geographical proximity of *Londinium*. Founded at the lowest fordable point on the Thames in the immediate aftermath of the Claudian invasion, *Londinium* quickly developed into a major trading centre and eventually the provincial capital (Perring 1991). As such the city stood at the hub of the Roman road network in Britain. The major Roman road linking London and Colchester was constructed approximately 1km north of the site shortly after the conquest. The road crossed the River Lea at Old Ford where evidence for late Roman roadside activity is concentrated (Sheldon 1971; 1972; Brown 2008, 83–87). A further route was laid out in *c.* AD 70–80 and appears to have run from *Londinium* towards the Thames at Ratcliff (Barber and Bowsher 2000, 51–52; Lakin 2002, 3), its extrapolated course would pass a little over 100 metres to the north of the sites reported on here (Fig. 5), though Merrifield's (1983) speculation that it roughly followed the line of The Highway would place it even closer to the northern boundaries of the site.

In common with most Roman cities, *Londinium* was ringed by cemeteries laid out beyond the city's boundaries and along the arterial roads. The cemeteries formed an important symbolic division between the urban settlement and its rural hinterland. Extensive excavations have investigated a large number of burials in the eastern cemetery (Barber and Bowsher 2000), which lies to the west of the site. This may suggest that Shadwell should be seen as separate from (although intimately connected with) *Londinium*.

Roman evidence from the Shadwell and Ratcliff area includes a scattering of stray finds and the occasional feature thought to indicate low density riverside activities such as ship building and fishing (Merrifield 1983). Antiquarian records include a number of high status burials east of the site. An east–west inhumation in a lead coffin was found in 1858 on the northern side of Shadwell basin "at no great distance from the south-west corner of the church yard of St Paul's" (Cuming 1858, 356; RCHM(E) 1928, 163) and several cremations and inhumations were found in *c.* 1615 in Sun Tavern Fields, now King David Lane (RCHM(E) 1928, 163–164).

The latter group of finds included a burial in a stone sarcophagus and lead coffin, as well as an inhumation accompanied by two 'sceptres', a small white stone figurine of Cupid, two jet-like 'nails' and coins of Pupienus (AD 238) and Gordian (*c.* AD 238–244). These high status burials may be particularly significant, given their distance from the eastern cemetery.

The most significant Roman evidence from Shadwell is the 'tower' and associated activity recorded during excavations in the 1970s (Museum of London site codes LD74 and LD76). The 'tower' structure was originally interpreted as a military signal station or watchtower connecting *Londinium* with the 'Saxon Shore' (Johnson 1975; Johnson 1979, 128). The tower site lies adjacent to Sites A and B (Fig. 2) and is crucial to the understanding of the present excavations.

The recent publication of the excavations at LD74 and LD76 has cast doubt on the military interpretation of the site, with the lack of military artefacts leading to the reinterpretation of the foundations for the 'tower' structure as a mausoleum. During the mid to late third century the site was the focus of intense activity, including utilitarian buildings, drainage ditches, timber-lined tanks and evidence for butchery (Lakin 2002). The site included some aspects that might suggest a military association, most notably an unusual assemblage of East Gaulish samian, and some commentators continue to prefer a military interpretation (Bird 2008). The primary site archive is short on detail and a definitive interpretation of the site remains elusive (Lakin 2002).

On the south side of the Thames, a late Roman site at Greenwich was located at *c.* 43m OD, overlooking the river and close to the projected route of Watling Street. Greenwich has produced a number of high status Roman finds, including statuary, *opus signinum* flooring and wall plaster as well as a large late Roman pottery assemblage, procuratorial tiles and coins. The Greenwich site has been interpreted as a Romano-Celtic temple (Sheldon and Yule 1979) or a *mansio*, territorial office or other type of official wayside complex that may have included a religious function (Wallower 2002a; 2002b).

Dated regional changes in relative sea level

Many Roman period foreshore sites have been systematically studied in the London region. On most of these sites foreshore structures and associated 'generally dry' surface layers have been closely dated using tree-ring dating or indirectly through finds groups (Brigham 1990a). Although some details remain to be further investigated a pattern of rapid fall in relative sea level of *c.* 1.5m from the first to late third century AD is clear (Brigham 1990a, 143; 2001, 26). In response urban quaysides in *Londinium* were built out further towards the deeper Thames channel until the mid third century AD by which time long distance trade through the port seems to have declined. The building of the riverside defensive

Fig. 3   General view of the Shadwell sites, looking south from the tower of St George in the East, with The Highway running east–west in the foreground and the Tobacco Dock warehouse in the background. Machine ground-reduction is taking place at the Tobacco Dock site in advance of archaeological excavation. To the left is Babe Ruth restaurant, prior to demolition

wall a little later effectively cut off the City from the easy handling of bulk cargoes in any case. Moving downstream to establish a new commercial port for larger seagoing trading vessels would have been an obvious solution for those administering *Londinium*'s port by the third century.

Prior to these excavations at Shadwell the find of a very late group of imported Samian pottery flagged up the area as a possible location for the lost late Roman port (Brigham 1990a, 160). Apart from proximity to navigable water a port location in a complex trading economy requires many service facilities for the ships, merchants and sailors using the settlement. One might suggest that just off the quay front, behind the warehouses, facilities such as bath houses, inns, eating places and brothels would be required. It is perhaps in this kind of context that we might set the later Roman archaeology found at Sites A and B at Shadwell. At a practical level the level of the ground water must have been affected by the tidal action a little to the south of the site. By the end of the Middle Saxon period we know relative sea levels had reached early Roman levels once again (Goodburn *et al.* in prep.).

The exact position of the Thames in relation to the sites remains unknown. Various models have been proposed for this area and that which seems to best fit the available evidence here follows closely that proposed in Barber and Bowsher (2000, fig 3). This shows a subsidiary channel of the Thames, approximately 70m wide, running

Fig. 4   Exposing the remains of the bath house at the Shadwell Babe Ruth site in January 2003; view looking north. In the background St George's Pools, the modern swimming baths

roughly east–west approximately 200m south of the site with the main channel of the Thames a further 400m to the south of this (see Fig. 5). Such a channel would roughly follow the line of the London Docks, constructed during the nineteenth century and now partly infilled, and which have removed any archaeological evidence for this area. This proposal is explored further below (see Chapter 4.3) and the evidence of contemporary

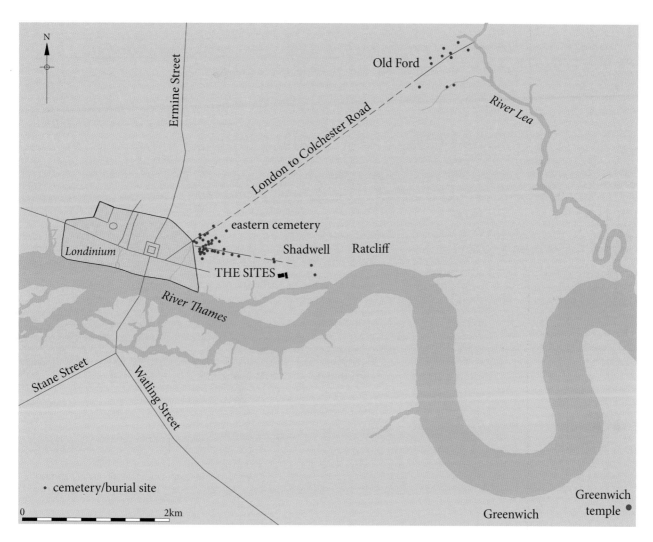

Fig. 5   The location of the Shadwell sites shown in relation to *Londinium* and its immediate hinterland, including main Roman roads, the extramural eastern cemetery and roadside settlement at Old Ford, with associated burials (scale 1:50,000)

geological sources seems to corroborate the theory that a river channel existed in this area. The location of the later docks along the alignment of a proposed channel may not be coincidental.

Shadwell, London and the Thames estuary: some research questions

The publication of the Shadwell 'tower' site in 2002 (Lakin 2002) included the reinterpretation of the 'tower' structure as a mausoleum, a controversial view given that site had become widely accepted as a military installation. The 2002 publication also highlighted some unusual aspects of ceramic supply to the site, most notably the prominence of third-century East Gaulish samian.

New excavations in the vicinity have the potential to shed further light on the interpretation of the settlement's status and function. Analysis of the structures and finds found at Sites A and B allows further review of interpretations of the 'tower' site and the surrounding area (Lakin 2002; Bird 2008).

The new findings also address key research priorities

for Roman London set out in *A research framework for London Archaeology*, particularly understanding the role of the Roman military in the defence of London and its socio-economic impact on the city (Nixon *et al.* 2002, 39). Other research priorities relevant to the Shadwell investigations include the relationship of *Londinium* to its hinterland, late Roman trade, the importance of public buildings and amenities, and the different experiences of the inhabitants of *Londinium* and its environs (Nixon *et al.* 2002, 30–43). The nature and scale of the bath house and associated buildings recorded at Sites A and B, as well as the associated finds assemblage, all contribute to these areas of research.

Shadwell is located near the head of the Greater Thames Estuary, which has been recognised as a nationally important landscape (Fulford *et al.* 1997; Williams and Brown 1999). The Thames played a significant role in the life of riverside communities. Evidence from Sites A and B contributes to the study of the economic exploitation of the river and its margins, whilst also providing evidence for the role of the Thames estuary in linking and dividing communities during the late Roman period (Williams and Brown 1999).

Period	Date	Site A	Site B	LD74/LD76
7	AD410+	Soil formation OA12 continued in use.	Demolition and robbing of B4 remains and external soil formation OA13 continued in use.	Demolition and robbing of 'tower' structure; inhumation burials; dark earth (phases 9 and 10).
6	AD375-410	OA12 dumping, well, ritual pitting and drainage; construction of B11.	Abandonment and stripping of baths B4; drainage ditches in OA13; fragmentary structure B10 to north.	
5.2	AD325-375	External activity and drainage OA11; construction of B9.	Period 5.1 activity continues.	
5.1		Terrace revetment and dumping OA10; construction of B8.	Extension and use of baths B4; OA5 and OA6 retained; new structure B7; OA7 retained.	Timber-lined cisterns and drains (phase 8).
4.5	AD275-325	Hill-slip and drainage OA9; construction of B6 (not illustrated).	B3e further changes to accommodation block; disuse of bath house B4? OA5, OA6 and OA7 continued.	Disuse of 'tower' structure; disuse of barn building and new external boundaries (phase 7).
4.4		Period 4.1 activity continues?	B3d further modifications to accommodation block; disuse of bath house B4? OA5, OA6 and OA7 continued.	
4.3		Period 4.1 activity continues?	Flooding and temporary disuse of bath house B4? OA5 and OA6 retained; B3c alterations; OA7 retained.	
4.2		Period 4.1 activity continues?	Further modification and expansion of bath house B4; OA5 and OA6 retained; B3b alterations; OA7 retained.	
4.1		B5 and associated yard and oven; drainage ditches in OA8.	Alterations to bath house B4; OA5 and OA6 retained; new wing B3a; OA7 retained to the north.	
3	AD230-275	B2; terracing and drainage OA4.	Construction and use of bath house B4; OA5 to south; service yard OA6 to north; accommodation block B3; OA7 external area and boundary to far north.	Boundary divisions; 'tower' retained; buildings, including a 'barn' and other structures (phases 4 to 6).
2	AD50-230	B1; OA2 quarrying and pitting; infilled channel.	OA3 quarrying and pitting; Thames foreshore.	Quarrying; cremation burials; construction of 'tower' structure (phases 2 and 3).
1	Before AD50	Open Area 1.	Open Area 1.	Open Area 1 (phase 1).

Fig. 6   Land-use diagram for Shadwell Sites A and B and the 'tower' site

1.3 Organisation of the report

Chapter structure

The integration of stratigraphic, finds and environmental data is an underlying principle of this report, which is organised as follows: a chronological narrative presenting the archaeological sequence recorded at the sites (Chapter 2), specialist reports (Chapter 3), thematic aspects (Chapter 4), discussion and conclusions (Chapter 5) specialist appendices (Chapter 6), followed by French and German summaries, bibliography and index.

Period and land-use numbering

The archaeological data presented in the chronological narrative is organised into dated periods. These are unique to the Shadwell site sequence and generally based on a combination of stratigraphic interpretation and dating evidence, particularly pottery. Divisions between periods are defined by major topographic change, such as the effects of a widespread fire or the construction of new buildings. A total of 7 periods, numbered 1–7, cover the evidence for pre-Roman activity through to post-Roman abandonment. The archaeological periods are supported by plans showing buildings and major features. Where appropriate these periods have been further subdivided into phases, eg Period 4 phase 1 (abbreviated to Period 4.1).

Within the period structure, land uses have been identified and uniquely numbered. Roman land uses are Buildings B1–B11 and Open Areas OA1–OA13. In some cases, individual land-uses may have more than one phase of use and span more than a single period. Land-use numbering is not always sequential. A simple diagram showing the relative chronological and spatial position of land uses is presented as an additional navigation aid for the reader (Fig. 6).

The research archive

Analysis of the stratigraphic sequence, finds and environmental material has involved the creation of further research unsuitable for publication in this volume, including detailed descriptions, matrices, and the identification, quantification, measurement and description of the various assemblages.

The research archive for the sites has been deposited with the Museum of London. The evaluation work established the potential for excavation, but was superceded by the excavation reported on here. The site records, finds and environmental archives are organised under the individual site codes TOC02 and HGA02, and CYD96 for the evaluation at Tobacco Dock. The archive may be consulted by prior arrangement with the archive manager at the London Archaeological Archive and Research Centre (LAARC), Mortimer Wheeler House, 46 Eagle Wharf Road, London N1 7ED.

1.4 Textual and graphical conventions

The basic unit of cross-reference throughout the archive that supports this project is the context number. This is a unique number given to each archaeological 'event' on site (such as a layer, wall, grave cut, pit cut or fill, road surface and so forth). In the case of the two main excavations, each context is prefixed by a letter representing the site code under which it was recorded, thus: A[100] meaning context [100] from Site A (Tobacco Dock; TOC02), and B[100] meaning context [100] from Site B (Babe Ruth; HGA02). Context numbers are only cited in the publication text where a specific reference is required.

The analytical process involved forming the contexts into 'subgroups' and 'groups' but these are generally not referred to in this publication. Groups have been formed into land uses and these are assigned to Periods 1–7, as noted above.

Accessioned finds are individually identifed by unique numbers, thus: A <376> referring to Site A accessioned find 376, and so forth. Accessioning has been applied mainly to the small finds from the two sites.

Environmental samples were collected and analysed from Tobacco Dock (Site A) and form the basis for the specialist report in Chapter 3.10. Samples are shown thus: A{100}. A small number of samples taken at the Babe Ruth site (Site B) were the subject of separate analysis and the results are integrated with the chronological narrative where appropriate, referred to thus: B{100}.

Dating evidence is presented selectively by land use, referenced to key contexts, fabrics present (in the case of pottery and ceramic building materials) and the specialists' assigned date for the assemblage.

The period and phase plan illustrations are largely interpretative and show significant features as well as

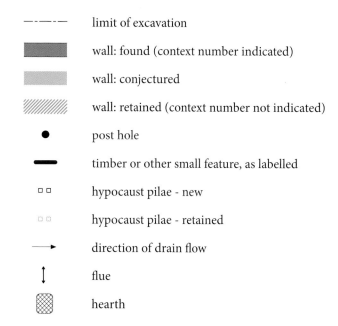

— · — · —	limit of excavation
▬	wall: found (context number indicated)
▬	wall: conjectured
▨	wall: retained (context number not indicated)
●	post hole
▬	timber or other small feature, as labelled
▫ ▫	hypocaust pilae - new
▫ ▫	hypocaust pilae - retained
→	direction of drain flow
↕	flue
▨	hearth

Fig. 7   Key to graphical conventions used in this volume

found and conjectured structural evidence. Generally speaking surfaces and layers are not illustrated, except where absolutely necessary, for example to show detail or the extents of buildings. A key to the graphical conventions used in the plans in this publication is provided (Fig. 7). Levels on plans are all expressed in metres above Ordnance Datum. Scales of reproduction are given in the figure captions.

Chapter 2 The archaeological sequence

2.1 Prehistoric evidence (Period 1)

Period 1 land uses

A palaeochannel and scattered evidence of occupation (Open Area 1)

No extant evidence of prehistoric activity was found on Site B, on the eastern side of the study area. To the west, on the south-east part of Site A, a roughly east–west aligned palaeochannel was recorded (not illustrated). The palaeochannel was up to 5.0m across and *c.* 2.50m deep, filled by a sequence of clayey and silty sands. The watercourse may have formed during a phase of downcutting that isolated the Taplow Terrace above the level of modern river activity, sometime during the late Quaternary period.

Column samples from the fills of the palaeochannel produced well-preserved taxa in the basal part of the sequence. The pollen record was dominated by Poaceae (grass), with *Chenopodium* type (goosefoot), Cyperaceae (sedge) and *Taraxacum* (dandelion). These indicate areas of open, possibly disturbed, ground dominated by grassland vegetation and open mixed deciduous woodland. The presence of warmth-loving vegetation, *Quercus (oak), Alnus (alder)* and *Corylus (hazel),* is surprising given the possible late Quaternary date of the sediments (Branch *et al.* 2004a, Table 8).

Part of the foreleg of a wild ox or auroch was also recovered from the palaeochannel (see Chapter 3.9) and these animals were probably extinct by the late Bronze Age/early Iron Age (Williams and Zeepvat 1994, 535).

Features truncating naturally deposited sand and gravel were recorded in the south-west part of Site A and included a posthole and a pit. The posthole measured 0.51m by 0.40m and was 0.13m deep, and its fill included a single sherd of pot that may date to the late Bronze Age/early Iron Age. Three pieces of a similar flint-tempered pottery were retrieved from Roman deposits.

The lithic assemblage collected from Site A, although mostly residual, provided more substantial evidence for prehistoric activity, including 22 struck flints and burnt flint fragments weighing just over 3.5 kg. The raw materials used varied considerably, the flint colour ranging from a cherty opaque brown to translucent black. Remnant cortex varied from weathered chalky with some heavily recorticated thermal scars, to fluvially battered and

rounded. No truly diagnostic implements were recovered, although considerations of the technology employed, especially in the manufacture of blades and blade-like flakes, would suggest that at least part of the assemblage was of Mesolithic/Early Neolithic date. Some of the more crudely produced pieces may be more characteristic of later industries such as those of the Bronze Age.

Burnt flint was recovered in small quantities from a variety of contexts, and probably represents residual 'background' waste. An exception was context A[845], which produced nearly 1.5kg of burnt flint, indicating the presence of a hearth or the deposition of refuse from a hearth.

Period 1 discussion

The evidence for prehistoric occupation at Shadwell remains slight and suggests that activity was sporadic and temporary, perhaps seasonal in nature, though sustained over a long period. The site joins a growing corpus of finds from the east London area that demonstrate the importance of the environment of the Thames floodplain to prehistoric people, with an abundance of exploitable resources that included fish, wild fowl, seasonal grazing and sedge.

2.2 Early Roman activity, *c.* AD 50–230 (Period 2)

Period 2 land uses

Fragmentary buildings and external activity

The earliest extant evidence for Roman occupation at Shadwell dates to the first and second centuries, consisting of fragmentary buildings and external activity, mostly confined to the southern part of Site A (Fig. 8).

A timber-framed building (Building 1)

Evidence for a timber-framed building (B1) with earth-fast foundations was unearthed on the south-western part of Site A. Two parallel, east–west aligned beam slots were set *c.* 2.30m apart (centre to centre). Both beam slots were truncated by modern intrusions to the east and extended beyond the limit of excavation to the west. The northern beam slot A[890] measured at least 3.76m in length and

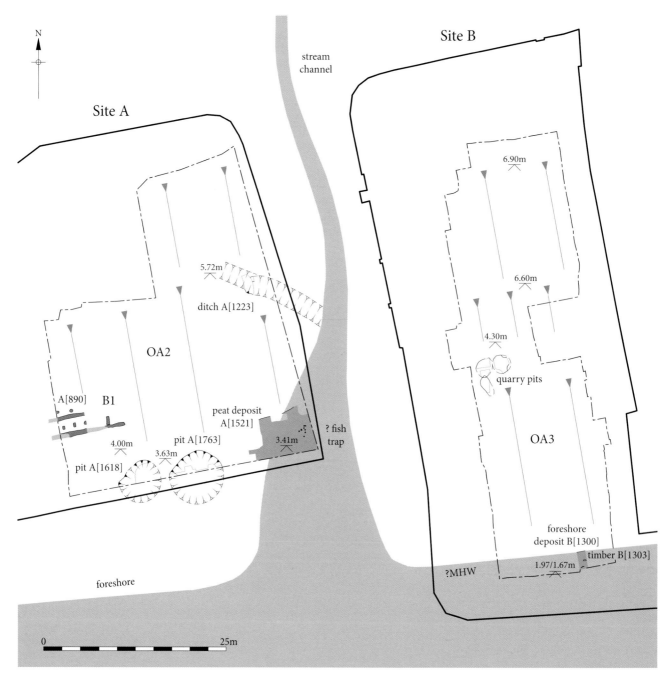

Fig. 8   Principal activity assigned to Period 2: Building 1 and Open Area 2 on Site A to the west and Open Area 3 to the east on Site B in relation to contemporary activity at LD74 and LD76 to the east; showing conjectured location of Thames foreshore and a stream channel between the two sites (scale 1:500)

was *c.* 0.50m wide and 0.20m deep. The southern beam slot was of similar width and depth but continued further to the east, giving it an overall length of at least 9.0m. A single rectangular posthole (not illustrated) measuring 0.15m x 0.12m x 0.05m deep was identified in the base of the southern beam slot near its easternmost extent. Adjacent to the eastern end of the southern beam slot, and extending north from it at right angles, was a short slot measuring 1.10m long, 0.40m wide and 0.18m deep. Both ends of the slot terminated where circular postholes (not illustrated) cut into its base. The northern posthole was 0.40m in diameter and 0.26m deep while the southern posthole was 0.30m in diameter and 0.26m deep. The slot

may have been a foundation trench for the two posts or a sill beam replaced by timber posts.

An east–west aligned row of three sub-rectangular postholes was located approximately mid way between the two east–west beam slots and spaced *c.* 1.50m apart. Two further postholes were located *c.* 1.90m to the north, about 0.30m north of the northern beam slot. All five postholes were between *c.* 0.40–0.50m across and 0.15–0.30m deep and may have been structurally related.

The southern beam slot could be the remains of an external wall of Building 1 but the northern limits of the structure are uncertain and probably lay further to the north of the recorded evidence where they may have been

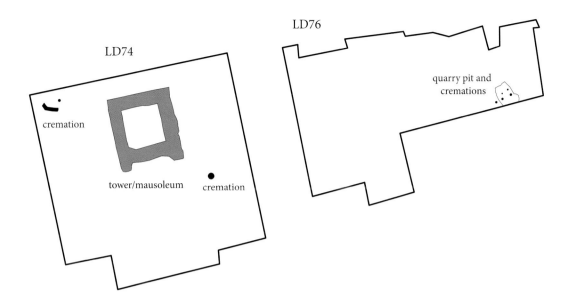

lost to modern truncation. The northern beam slot was probably the foundation for an internal dwarf wall, which along with the postholes to its north and south could have supported a raised floor. The north–south beam slot recorded to the east may indicate the location of an internal room division or entrance, perhaps from an east-facing veranda.

The only dating evidence associated with Building 1 consisted of a few pot sherds dating to AD 43–250, recovered from the northern beam slot A[890]. Sample A{333} from posthole fill A[1458] produced plant material dominated by *Sambucus nigra* (elder) and *Carex* sp. (sedges).

Pitting, drainage and other external activity south and east of Building 1 (Open Area 2)

In the southern part of Site A were two large sub-circular pits A[1618] and A[1763], which extended beyond the southern limits of excavation. Pit A[1618] had been heavily truncated but measured at least 4.50m east–west by 3.10m north–south and was 1.43m deep. Just to the east, pit A[1763] measured 7.50m east–west, at least 2.60m north–south and was in excess of 2.0m deep. Pottery from pit A[1618] was dated to AD 120–150. Mid third-century ceramics recovered from pit A[1763] are probably intrusive. Both pits may have functioned primarily as quarries used for gravel and sand extraction, though pit A[1763] could be the construction cut for a well. Both pits seem to have been filled in before the middle of the third century AD.

In the south-east corner of Site A a cluster of eight timber stakes were embedded into natural deposits at between 3.44–3.56m OD. The stakes were made from oak roundwood poles, either whole or cleft into quarters, but only the tips had survived. The V-shaped arrangement of the stakes may indicate that they were part of a wild fowl or fish trap. A 0.40m thick peaty deposit A[1521] covered the stakes, indicating that marshy conditions may have been prevalent in this low-lying area during the early

Roman period. Pottery recovered from the peat dated to the late third century and is interpreted as being intrusive, although it is possible that the area remained a water-logged external area until that time.

The peat deposit lay at a level just above the flood plain and only 15m to the north of the conjectured foreshore of the Thames at this time, based on the findings from Site B (see below). Wet conditions are confirmed by the presence of *Sphagnum* moss spores in column sample A{296}, recovered from the peat (Branch *et al.* 2004b, Table 13).

A diverse range of arboreal and non-arboreal taxa dominates the pollen assemblage from the peat. The former include *Quercus*, *Ulmus*, *Betula* and *Corylus*, indicating the presence of open woodland in close proximity to the site. The presence of *Alnus* is extremely important as it provides some indication of the type of vegetation growing on the nearby river floodplain during the late Holocene. The non-arboreal pollen record provides unequivocal evidence for the presence of grassland, disturbed or waste ground and cereal cultivation nearby.

The southeastern part of Site A may thus have been located on a minor stream channel which ran north–south, cutting into the hillside between Sites A and B, though this area could not be investigated.

A short length of an east–west aligned ditch A[1223] was recorded along the east side of Site A and about 20m to the north of the fish trap. The ditch was truncated to the west and extended beyond the eastern limit of excavation, but survived over a 1.20m length and was 2.70m wide and 0.64m deep. This ditch could have drained to the east, into the conjectured north–south aligned watercourse.

Pitting and foreshore deposits further to the east (Open Area 3)

The earliest surviving Roman features identified on Site B were three large but relatively shallow, sub-circular pits located in the central part of the excavation area. The pits ranged in size from 2.34–2.50m across and 0.23–0.36m

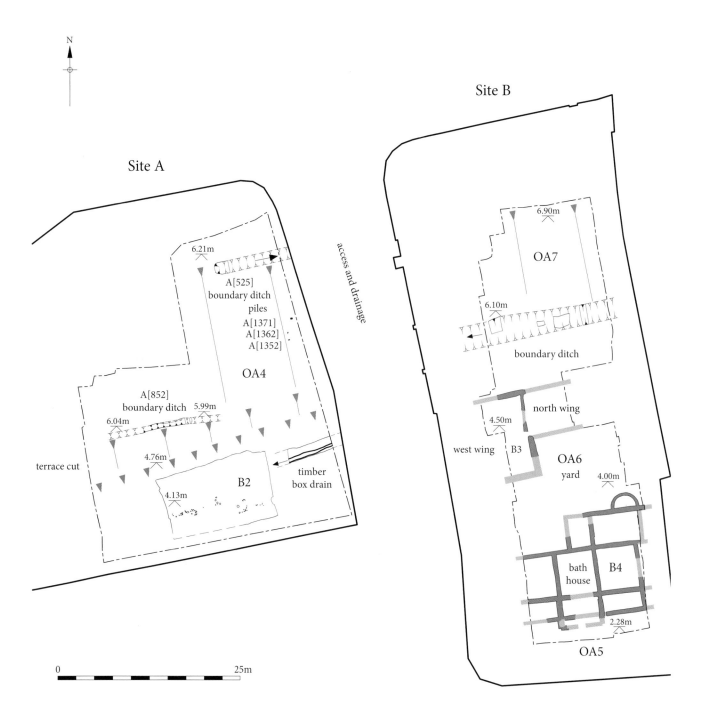

Fig. 9   Principal activity assigned to Period 3: Building 2 and Open Area 4 on Site A to the west, and on Site B the bath house B4, associated external areas (OA5, OA6), winged accommodation block (B3) and external area to the north (OA7) (scale 1:500)

deep, cutting into natural sand and gravel. They were all filled with a similar gravelly silty sand with occasional fragments of ceramic building material and flecks of charcoal. The pits may have been associated with sand and gravel quarrying but could not be dated.

A sondage at the south limit of excavation on Site B exposed a sandy silt layer B[1300] which was 0.10m thick and covered natural sandy gravel. The silt lay at 1.67–1.97m OD, just above the late first- and early-second century mean high water mark of the Thames, and may represent the foreshore. A single pot sherd dating to AD 150–200 was recovered from the deposit. Debris lying on the foreshore included a weathered fragment of an oak

plank B[1303] 0.43m long by 185mm wide and 45mm thick. The plank may have been driftwood or reused as a chock. It may originally have been a ship timber and it had two relatively unusual round holes at one end. These were *c.* 15mm in diameter, with a slight nail or bolt head impression around each. 'Romano-Celtic' boats such as the second-century Blackfriars 1 ship were pierced by similar shank nails (Marsden 1967), whereas smaller square shank nails are typically found in Roman land woodwork. The plank was tangentially faced, probably originally sawn from a moderately fast grown tree.

Parts of the left fore and right hind leg of a horse were also found on the foreshore (see Chapter 3.9).

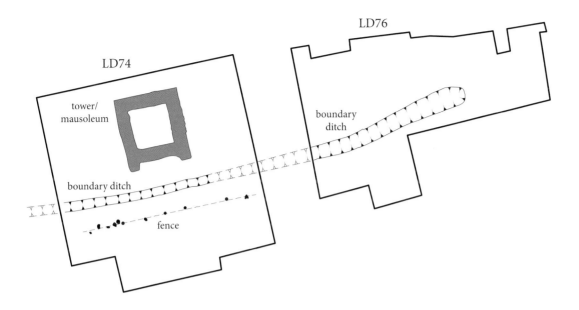

Period 2 discussion

The earliest surviving Roman features in the study area can be dated to the first and second centuries. The truncated remains of a clay-and-timber building with earth-fast foundations (B1) was located in the south-west part of Site A. The layout and size of the beam slots and postholes suggest that Building 1 was a single storey, rectangular structure at least 9.0m long and 3.5m wide, set on an east–west axis. It may have had an entrance porch to the east and a raised internal floor. A raised floor would have aided ventilation and help protect stored goods from vermin, and it is possible that Building 1 served as a granary.

Contemporary external activity in OA2 consisted of two large pits associated with sand and gravel quarrying. A low-lying area in the south-east part of the site may have been associated with a stream channel entering the Thames. The east–west ditch located along the east side of the area may have formed a boundary separating Building 1 from a roadside zone to the north. The marshy land on the south-east of the site was eventually reclaimed, with the peat deposits buried under dumps of sand and gravels, though this may not have happened until the third century.

To the east in OA3 the earliest activity consists of quarry pits, which predated third-century occupation but could not be closely dated. Sand and gravel quarried from the area may have been used in early Roman construction work in the immediate area. The northern edge of the Thames foreshore was recorded along the southern limit of excavation of Site B. As discussed further below (see Chapter 4.3) this evidence for foreshore may well represent a subsidiary channel of the Thames. Nevertheless, it is important to note here that the site at this period lay adjacent to water. The north–south running stream, possibly deriving in part from run-off from spring lines in the gravel terrace to

the north of the site, and the east–west flowing Thames, or subsidiary channel, appear to have been important factors in determining the overall layout and subsequent development of the site.

Although the Period 2 evidence is fragmentary, it indicates that there was a significant amount of activity, including some occupation, in the area in the late first and early second centuries. This accords with the findings at the sites excavated to the north-east, where the 'tower' or mausoleum structure and nearby cremations appear to also date from the late first or early second century (Lakin 2002).

Combined with the ceramic evidence, there certainly seems to have been some form of settlement in the Shadwell area during the early Roman period, though it may have been dispersed. A small, essentially rural, riverside community engaged in farming, fishing or boat-building immediately to the east of the main settlement of *Londinium* might be a possibility.

2.3 Construction of a bath house and other buildings, *c.* AD 230–275 (Period 3)

Period 3 land uses

The apparent intensity of development at Shadwell increased by the mid third century, when there is a dramatic rise in extant activity across the study area (Fig. 9). On Site A the escarpment slope was terraced along an east–west line, a property boundary set out and the lower-lying marshy area to the south reclaimed (all OA4), allowing construction of a clay-and-timber building (B2). Drainage ditches were cut and at least one timber drain installed. To the east on Site B an east–west boundary ditch was also established (OA7) and a complex of buildings constructed to the south. These buildings

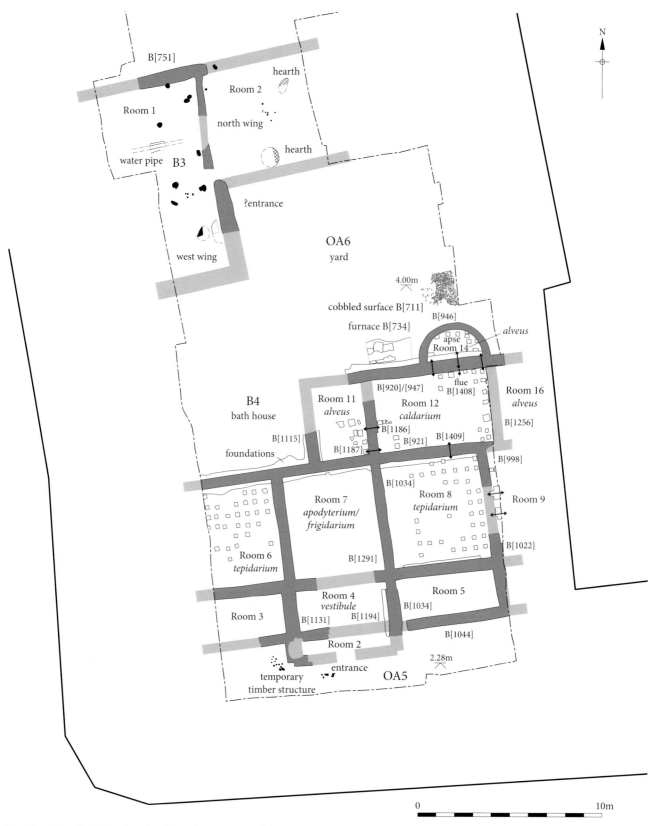

Fig. 10   Detailed plan showing Period 3 activity, Buildings 3 and 4 and Open Areas 5 and 6 (scale 1:200)

included a substantial bath house (B4) with a winged building (B3) to its north, the two buildings separated by a yard (OA6). These structures were similarly terraced into the slope (see Fig. 21). A separate external area (OA5) lay to the south of the bath house and close to the conjectured line of the Thames waterfront or an associated tidal creek.

Less structural evidence was recorded at Site A, to the west, than from the area of the baths on Site B, and there was generally less archaeological detail recovered from Site A. However, Site A does provide helpful general information about the topography and terracing of the overall area, and is therefore described below first.

External activity (Open Area 4)

On Site A the natural slope was terraced by a cut *c.* 0.75m deep that ran for at least 24.30m east–west but probably extended beyond the limits of excavation. The terrace cut created a level platform to the south at *c.* 4.10m OD, which was at least 9.50m wide. The highest surviving level of the terrace cut was 4.76m OD, though this may have been truncated by more recent terracing and extant features to the north appeared to have been cut from a horizon at *c.* 6.0m OD or higher.

In the southeast part of Site A a sequence of dumped sand and gravels covered the Period 2 peat deposits, indicating that this lower-lying and water-logged ground had been consolidated and reclaimed. The northern edge of these consolidation dumps was truncated by an east–west aligned ditch at least 6.20m long, 1.50m wide and 1.15m deep (not illustrated, recut by timber box drain, Fig. 9). The base sloped slightly downwards from 3.22m OD in the east to 3.17m OD in the west. A timber post measuring 0.15m x 0.12m and 1.34m long was driven into the base of the ditch. The post could have been part of the revetting of the ditch in order to stabilise the sides. The ditch extended beyond the eastern limit of excavation of Site A and was truncated to the west.

Earth-and-timber building (Building 2)

Layers of compacted sandy silts and gravel laid on the base of the OA4 lower terrace formed the floor make-up and surviving remnants of a beaten earth floor at 4.13m OD. The surface was truncated by a series of stakes and postholes on a rough east–west axis, which may have been associated with a structural alignment. The floor deposits may provide evidence for the footprint of Building 2, as the beaten earth floors would require a roof to protect the surfaces from weathering, whilst an external surface would be likely to have been metalled or mortared. No external wall lines survived but it is assumed that Building 2 lay to the south of the OA4 terrace line and shared the same alignment. The dimensions of the surviving floor surface indicate a building measuring 15m east–west by 10m north–south, with evidence for internal divisions. Pottery from associated deposits suggest a construction date in the second half of the third century.

External activity to the east and north of Building 2 (Open Area 4 retained)

The OA4 ditch recorded in the southeastern part of Site A was quickly superseded and truncated by an east–west construction cut that held a timber box drain. The construction cut followed the same alignment as the earlier ditch and was excavated to the same depth. Timber planks laid on edge formed the sides of the drain, which was *c.* 0.25m wide. It is likely that the box drain would originally have been covered by a timber lid, although no trace of a lid survived. The drain sloped slightly downwards to the west, suggesting that it may have been a conduit supplying water to Building 2.

An east–west aligned ditch A[852] lay *c.* 6m to the north of Building 2 and the terrace line. This ditch may represent a boundary, perhaps indicating the northern edge of the property associated with Building 2. The ditch was truncated to the east and west but was at least 7.30m long, up to 0.90m wide and 0.34m deep. Three timber piles, A[1352], A[1362] and A[1371] further north and close to the eastern limit of excavation, provided very precise tree-ring dates signifying their felling in the spring of AD 228 (see Chapter 3.8). These substantial timbers, roughly hewn to rectangular sections, measuring around 0.10m by 0.20m across and surviving to a maximum length of 0.9m, were thought on excavation to be part of a much later (Period 5.2) tank. Examination of these timbers revealed clear axe cut marks on their tips, surviving bark in places and little sign of drying 'shakes' (the cracks that typically appear when wood is allowed to dry out) indicating that they had not been reused within the later structure and indeed had been driven into the ground soon after felling. It is not possible to say with any certainty what type of structure these originally belonged to or for how long that survived. However it is tempting to suggest that they formed supports for the lining of a tank, a precursor to that seen in Period 5.2, possibly for provision of water to the newly established bath house (see below).

Approximately 19m further to the north, the rounded western terminus of another east–west aligned ditch was recorded. Ditch A[525] extended beyond the eastern limit of excavation of Site A and was *c.* 1.60m wide and 1.0m deep. Successive recutting of the ditch indicates that it may have been maintained in use for an extended period, with timber shoring used to support its sides. The primary purpose of the ditch was probably drainage, in this case from west to east, though it may also have marked a boundary.

Disuse of Building 2

Two large pits truncated the floors within Building 2. Sub-rectangular pit A[1602] measured *c.* 1.60m x 1.40m. At only 0.29m deep it was relatively shallow and respected the building alignment, following the line of internal stakeholes and parts of the southern and eastern edges of the floor, suggesting that it probably represents robbing of structural elements of the building. Roughly circular pit A[1611] measured 2.45m x 2.10m and was 0.20m deep. Pottery dating to AD 220–260 was recovered from both of the pits. Pit A[1611] also contained scraps of metal, fragments of ceramic building material and animal bone, including a horse skull.

Establishment of a bath house (Building 4)

The Roman topography at Site B dropped significantly from north to south, towards the river, whose northern edge is conjectured to lie approximately 150m to the south of the southern limit of excavation by the third century, when falling river levels would have reached around 0m OD (Brigham *et al.* 1995). The extant ground surface was *c.* 6.90m OD in the north and 1.54m OD in the south, a fall of more than 5m over a distance of *c.* 55m or 1:11 (Fig. 21).

The extensive remains of a multi-room heated building were revealed on the southern part of Site B (Fig. 9, Fig. 10). The initial construction of Building 4 is likely to date from about the mid third century. The layout of Building 4, which has been identified as a bath house, is described in detail below, though it should be noted that preservation *in situ* has meant that the structural remains were subject to limited excavation thus hindering a detailed understanding of the structural sequence.

The bath building extended beyond both the eastern and western limits of excavation of Site B. The exposed extent of the structure measured 17.75m east–west by 16.95m north–south and contained at least eleven rooms, of which at least six were heated. The original structure may have been 'L' shaped in plan, with a possible entrance to the south and at least one apse to the north.

The bath structure was preserved *in situ*, and as a consequence the underside of the sub-floor was only exposed and recorded at relatively restricted points, where it ranged in height from *c.* 2.50–2.70m OD, indicating the level of a horizontal construction terrace cut into the natural hillside in preparation for the construction of the building (see Fig. 21).

Most of Building 4 survived only to foundation level, although some wall superstructure survived to the north and northeast. The north wall and apse (Room 14) survived intact to a height of 3.96m OD, or *c.* 1.75m in total, just to the base of the suspended floors of the baths. Despite episodic robbing of the remains in antiquity the overall survival of the structural layout was very good.

The overall layout and room-size of this building is described below first, followed by more detailed description of constructional elements.

South-central Rooms 2–5 and 7

Rooms 3, 4 and 5 form an east–west range of rooms on the south side of Building 4. Room 3 extended beyond the western limit of excavation, whilst the full east–west extent of Rooms 4 and 5 were recorded as being between 4.90 and 5.35m. All three rooms were relatively narrow, measuring *c.* 2.20m north–south (Fig. 10). The overall layout of the primary phase of the baths suggests that another room may have lain to the east of Room 5, beyond the limit of excavation.

These rooms were relatively heavily truncated, with three courses of wall superstructure surviving at most, to a maximum height of 2.76m OD, though the foundation levels were largely intact. Later modification and truncation meant that little evidence survived to indicate the original function of Rooms 3–5. Any original surface associated with these rooms, particularly in Rooms 4 and 5, is likely to have been truncated by subsequent remodelling or in the case of all three rooms perhaps exist below the level of excavation. The policy of preservation

Fig. 11   View looking west across apsidal Room 14, located against the north wall of the bath house, and which may have held a plunge; this was the first part of the bath house to be revealed by the excavations on Site B

in situ adopted on site meant that these rooms were never fully excavated.

It is possible Rooms 3–5 may have originally been heated, with sub-floor levels similar to those that survive in Rooms 4 and 5 relating to a later phase of remodelling, but no evidence remains. There were no brick pillars or other substructures that would be indicative of a hypocaust system or heating flues linking the southern rooms to the heated rooms to the north associated with this phase, although it is possible that these were truncated in antiquity, destroyed, or reused during remodelling. Going on the limited evidence available it is perhaps more likely, particularly given that at least one and possibly two appear to have become heated at a later stage, that the rooms were originally unheated.

If unheated, however, it is not clear if they would have been filled in to the level of the suspended floor in the heated rooms to the north or if they represent sunken rooms or plunges with floor levels potentially surviving beneath the level of excavation. In either case no evidence is forthcoming; none surviving if the fill were dug out as part of later remodelling and none excavated if existing below the limit of excavation. It should be noted at this

Fig. 12   General view, looking southeast, showing archaeologists uncovering hypocausts beneath Room 7 in the foreground and Room 8 to the left; note the partially collapsed remnants of a suspended floor in the foreground and the left background

point that although unexcavated it was considered that Room 3 contained fill that unless redeposited, might suggest the presence of intact surfaces of structures below. This may therefore have functioned as a sunken plunge, but no evidence for steps was seen during excavation. Clearly a variety of interpretations remains possible and, despite being of a similar size and located in the same section of the building, it is not even certain that the rooms were all used for the same purpose.

The north–south walls of the central Room 4, B[1131] and B[1034], extended *c.* 1.3m beyond the main southern wall of the building, providing a narrow extension to the south which had an internal north–south width of 0.75m. The size and location of this space (Room 2) might be suggestive of a riverfront entranceway, which would be consistent with the overall arrangement of the heated and unheated rooms and with the Period 4.2 extension to this room to the south (Room 1), but again the evidence is scanty. The issue of layout and use is discussed in more detail below (see Chapter 4.2).

Room 7 lay directly to the north of Room 4 and was much larger, measuring *c.* 4.80m east–west by 5.60m north–south. Truncation meant that only the foundations survived to the west, north and south, but to the east the wall superstructure was present to a height of three courses or 2.79m OD. Rooms 4 and 7 were apparently amalgamated in a subsequent phase of use (see below) and the remodelling of the bath house makes interpretation of the primary phase difficult. The apparent absence of heating flues suggests that Room 7 was unheated in its primary phase of use, although it is important to note that it was subsequently modified to include a hypocaust extending over the truncated wall between Rooms 4 and 7 (see Period 4), the sub-floor level of which was similar to the adjacent heated Rooms 6 and 8.

Heated Rooms 6, 8–9, 11–12 and 14

Rooms 6, 8 and 9 lay to the west and east of Room 7. Only Room 8 lay entirely within the excavation area and measured *c.* 5.30m east–west by 5.55m north–south. All three rooms contained the remains of a hypocaust system.

Rooms 11 and 12 were located immediately to the north of Rooms 7 and 8 and were smaller. Room 11 measured 2.55m east–west by 3.80m north–south and Room 12 measured 6.50m east–west by 3.80m north–south. Room 14 was an apse located against the external north wall of Room 12 and measured *c.* 3.00m east–west and 1.25m north–south (Fig. 11). Although butted onto the north wall of Building 4, the apse is interpreted as part of the original build due to the presence of what is thought to be an original flue connecting the two. The maximum surviving height of the walls was 3.96m OD. Again all three rooms contained the remnants of a hypocaust system.

The hypocausts of Rooms 8, 9, 11, 12 and 14 were all linked by sub-floor flues to form a suite of heated rooms. Room 6 appears to have been separated from this suite of rooms but may have been connected to other heated rooms to the west, and possibly to the north, in a similar fashion.

Fig. 13   Part of the foundation level B[1305] for the main south wall of the bath house B[1044]; view looking north; note that the wider Kentish ragstone and chalk foundation supports a superstructure wall of tile facing courses and Kentish ragstone (*opus mixtum*) wall (scales 1m, 0.5m)

Hypocaust literally means 'a furnace that heats from below' (Yegül 1992, 356). Hypocaust systems are generally constructed of *pilae*, stacks of *bessales* bricks (*c.* 0.20m = 2/3 *pes*) built at the appropriate interval to enable *bipedales* bricks (*c.* 0.59m = 2 *pes*) to bridge the stacks and create a base for a 0.2–0.4m thick suspended floor (*suspensura*). The under-floor air space was heated by a furnace (*praefurnium*), usually housed in a structure adjoining the main building or in a room next to an outside wall. Hot air and combustion gases from the furnace circulated beneath the suspended floor and, in many cases, was drawn up the walls through hollow rectangular flue tiles (*tubuli*), attached beneath the interior render and wall finish. Sub-floor flues connected hypocausts in different rooms and when coupled with a slow-burning fire these systems provided a very effective method of heating (Yegül 1992, 368).

The *pilae* stacks in Building 4 were constructed on compacted sand and gravel sub-floors, identified in Rooms 6, 8, 11, and 12. The surface of the sub-floors varied slightly between rooms, being between 2.52 and 2.64m OD in the south and *c.* 0.35m higher in the northern rooms, up to a maximum of 2.87m OD in Room 11. The sub-floors which were investigated ranged from 0.05m to 0.16m thick and butted up to the adjacent walls.

In the northern rooms of the building the surviving evidence indicated that the underside of the base of the suspended floor or *suspensura* above the hypocaust started at *c.* 3.96m OD. The sub-floor surface B[1308] in this area was at *c.* 2.67m OD, indicating a hypocaust air-space *c.* 1.29m in height.

It was not possible to determine the original thickness and upper surface level of the suspended floors throughout the heated rooms as they were truncated, but they may have been *c.* 0.20 or 0.30m higher in the north, reflecting the difference in sub-floor levels. More likely, however, is that the *pilae* stacks in the southern rooms may have been taller, creating a single suspended floor surface level throughout the bath house. This would have required the *pilae* in Room 8 to be an estimated 1.44m tall. Commonly, *pilae* were between 0.65 and 1.00m in height, although examples up to 1.70m high have been recorded (Yegül 1992, 357) and examples of bath houses with floors at differing heights are not easily found.

The *pilae* in Room 6 and Room 8 are comprised entirely of *bessales* bricks and regularly spaced out in a grid aligned to the walls. The interval between the stacks, taken from centre to the centre, measures 0.55 to 0.60m suggesting they are likely to have been bridged by *bipedales* bricks, verified from fragments of collapsed floor (Fig. 12). The individual *pilae* had been truncated, surviving to a maximum height of 0.56m or 11 courses of tile. Comprised of *bessales* bricks, the stacks measured between 0.19m and 0.21m square (2/3 *pes*) with each individual brick being 30mm to 43mm thick.

Building 4 foundations and wall construction

The foundations of Building 4 were investigated in several localised areas, recorded in plan as contexts B[1115] and B[1194], and in section as contexts B[1256] and B[1305]. Where evident they were up to 1.0m wide, in excess of 3 Roman feet (1 *pes* = 0.296m). Beneath the south wall of the baths they had a base at 1.48m OD and top at 2.08m OD, whilst those recorded near the north side of the building had a base at 1.80m OD and top at 2.70m OD. This gives a depth of *c.* 0.60m or 2 Roman feet in the south and *c.* 0.90m or 3 Roman feet to the north. The difference in depth and overall height of the foundations, roughly equivalent to one Roman foot, is presumably related to the sloping topography of the site. It should be noted, however, that the values given for the northern foundations were derived from a later phase of remodelling and that consequently the values of the original build may in fact be different, possibly being even deeper. All of the foundations appeared to be sufficiently deep to rest on ground unaffected by freezing and thawing (Adam 2001, 125).

Foundation B[1305] was recorded beneath the southern external wall B[1044] and cut into the foreshore deposit B[1300], described in Period 2 OA3. Here, the foundation was set in a straight-sided, flat-bottomed construction trench B[1306]. The base of the foundation trench contained a layer of flinty gravel B[1369] which may have aided drainage. The foundation itself was made up of uncoursed and irregular fragments of chalk or Kentish ragstone in a matrix of mortar, and was presumably poured into an unshuttered trench (Fig. 13).

The walls of the original bath building were recorded under a number of individual contexts, including B[920] (Fig. 14), B[921], B[946], B[947], B[998], B[1022], B[1034], B[1036], B[1044], B[1131], B[1185], B[1291] and B[1404]. A 0.85m wide course of tile was set on top of the foundations, presumably to provide a level base for the construction of the superstructure. The walls were then built off this to a width of 0.60m, or approximately 2 *pes*, consisting of a rubble core of flint, chalk and tile fragments in a mortar matrix with *opus mixtum* facing. Wall B[920] was thicker at 0.66m, probably to provide support for the terracing.

The facing generally comprised two to four courses of stone alternating with a similar number of tile courses, the latter helping to level and strengthen the structure. The facing stone was commonly Kentish ragstone although chalk, flint, Reigate stone and Septaria were also evident. All of the stone was roughly hewn and measured between 50mm and 350mm. The lacing courses of brick and tile fragments were almost entirely in the local sandy London fabric group, although occasional examples from Kent were evident.

A range of Roman brick forms were identified, including *bipedales*, *sesquipedales*, *lydion*, *pedales* and *bessales*, although most were fragmented. Complete or near complete *lydion*, *pedales*, *bessales*, *tubuli* (box-flue tile) and *tegulae* (roof tile) were occasionally recorded but despite the width of the walls matching the size of the largest Roman brick, the *bipedalis* (0.60m), no complete examples of this type were identified. Indeed, the tile and brick fragments were generally used for facing the rubble core, although at least one complete horizontal tile course ran through the thickness of wall B[921]. Both techniques are a well-paralleled feature of *opus mixtum* (Adam 2001, 143).

The fragmented tile and brick from the lacing courses was irregular and could have arrived at Shadwell in a broken state or have been intentionally broken to maximise the material available for facing. In either case

Fig. 14   View looking west, showing the main north wall B[920] of the bath house, with apsidal Room 14 to the right (north); note the compacted yard surface (OA6) further to the right (scales 2m, 1m)

the majority of the tile and brick is early in date and must have been salvaged from another structure or location (see Chapter 4.2).

Two of the walls varied from the standard construction. The lacing courses in the apsidal wall B[946] of Room 14 were built entirely of *tegulae* placed with the flange side up. This wall was narrower than the others, at *c.* 0.40m, appropriately the average length of a *tegula*. The use of the *tegulae* flange side up is likely to have been intentional and would have held the mortar more effectively (Ken Sabel, pers. comm.). The bath building's southern wall B[1044] also exhibited a slight difference in having been faced with more regularly hewn blocks, all in Kentish ragstone, presenting a more orderly façade to the river (Fig. 13).

The bonding material used for all of the walls of the original structure was lime mortar. The colour and composition, in terms of the proportion of lime to aggregate, varied considerably as may be expected from batch production. Colours ranged from cream, yellow, beige and grey, to green, orange and brown. Sand was the most commonly occurring aggregate, although occasional to moderate tile, brick and siltstone, and occasional flint, charcoal and even copper-alloy grains were also incorporated into the mortar, the latter perhaps accidentally. The ratio of lime to sand varied from 1:2 to 1:5, with a mix of 1:4 or 1:5 occurring most frequently. The sand grains were up to 3mm in size, although most were below 1mm.

Several *pilae* were examined *in situ* to determine the fabric of the bricks used. Of eight stacks analysed from Room 8, seven were in fabric 3006 and one was identified as fabric 2459A. All eight are of the early and local sand-based 2815 group, common to the London region. The bricks were laid with their base, or sanded side, upwards, presumably a deliberate measure although it is not clear why.

The *pilae* bonding varied between individual stacks but was predominantly a green, brown or black silt or sandy silt. This may represent the remains of a degraded mortar from which the lime content had leached or, alternatively, a bedding layer to which lime was never added, perhaps due its unsuitability for use in areas that are continually exposed to high temperatures (Ken Sabel, pers. comm.). However, a few *pilae* were bonded with a light brownish yellow or pinkish lime mortar, occasionally containing crushed tile.

Only three *pilae* stacks were recorded in Room 9, located along the west wall of the room's hypocaust, just inside the eastern limit of excavation. The Room 9 *pilae* were of a similar construction to those in Rooms 6 and 8.

The Period 3 *pilae* in Rooms 11, 12 and 14 consist primarily of *bessalis* bricks but also include other forms of brick and tile, and in some cases are fairly irregular in composition and spacing. Two *pilae* in Room 11 are comprised entirely of *bessalis* bricks and square *tubuli*, the latter used on end to form a hollow, vertical tube *c.* 0.19m square. Three other *pilae* in Room 11 include *pedalis* bricks measuring up to 0.30m square and one *pila* consisted of a single *pedalis* forming the base for the smaller *bessalis*

bricks. The *pilae* in Rooms 12 and 14 also included a mixture of *pedales* and box-flue tiles as well as *bessalis* bricks.

It is possible that the differences in the construction of the *pilae* in different rooms is chronological, although this cannot be proven. The use of *tubuli* in the formation of *pilae* can be paralleled elsewhere (Brodribb 1987, 94). The presence of fragmented and reused building material may, however, indicate that the differences in construction simply reflect the changing availability of resources during construction.

At the east side of Room 12, just inside the eastern limit of excavation, the remains of four more substantial brick piers formed a north–south line. The piers were constructed of randomly coursed tile and brick set on a foundation of rough chalk blocks B[1256]. Piers B[1257], B[1258], B[1259] and B[1260] were between 0.42–0.48m apart and survived to a maximum height of 11 courses of tile or 3.38m OD. The two northern piers were up to 0.82m wide at the base, narrowing after three and five courses, to 0.60m or 2 *pes* (Fig. 15). The southern piers survived to a maximum of five courses and were only 0.50m wide.

The four piers were not excavated and their function remains uncertain, although it is likely that they represent the truncated base of an arcaded sub-floor wall, perhaps indicating a room division above, with a separate room area lying to the east, beyond the limit of excavation (conjectured Room 16). Evidence of scorching and vitrification on the pier bases indicates that the main source of heat for the hypocaust system may have lain nearby to the east, and the sole use of brick and tile in the construction of the piers would be consistent with their association with a *praefurnium* (Yegül 1992, 368–369).

Other aspects of the heating system

Flues, penetrating the sub-floor walls, allowed hot air to circulate through the hypocaust system. There appear to be two separate types present in Building 4. The main group comprise a simple opening in the sub-floor wall near the base of the hypocaust. Flues [B1186/7], [B1408] and [B1409] (see Fig. 10) had vertical abutments framing openings that ranged in width from 0.32m to 0.40m.

The abutments were usually faced with tile and brick, as evident in flues [B1408] and [B1409], although [B1186/7] simply consisted of a break in the normal stone and tile coursing. The use of tile and brick in the abutments was both to channel loads from above and to withstand high temperatures (as above). Depending on where the flues began in the sub-floor wall the base was either comprised of a course of tile, or less frequently stone.

Flue B[1408] in wall B[920] was the only one to remain intact (Fig. 16; Fig. 17) and was set on a base course of tile, with abutments of fragmented brick. The top of the flue was formed from two whole bricks, a complete *lydion* and complete *sesquipedalis*, placed on end and meeting to form a triangular apex. The wall directly above the flue was corbelled, with tile and brick butting onto the arch. The flue had a maximum height of 0.82m. The flue was later blocked, in Period 5.1, as can be seen in Fig. 17.

Fig. 15   View looking east and showing piers B[1257] and B[1258], representing the northern end of an arcaded sub-floor division at the eastern end of Room 12 (scale 1m)

Flues B[1015] and B[1016] (see Fig. 20) overlay the sub-floor of Room 9 but had been severely truncated. They were constructed of fragmented tile and brick, with the opening measuring between 0.32m to 0.54m by 0.64m to 0.70m. A *tegula*, placed flange up, projected from the west of flue B[1015], appearing to extend through wall B[998]. It is probable that B[1015] and B[1016] represent the bases of two separate flues which linked the hypocausts beneath Rooms 8 and 9 prior to the removal of dividing wall B[998].

The second type of flue recorded in Building 4 was much smaller and formed of *tubuli* running through the walls, located just beneath the *suspensura*. Three of these flues survived, B[1405], B[1406] and B[1407], all of them in wall B[920] on the north side of Room 12 (Fig. 16). It is not possible to determine how widespread the use of this flue type may have been as most of Building 4 was truncated below this level. Each flue measured *c.* 0.10–0.12m in width, 0.18–0.19m in depth and up to 0.54m in length. The three flues linked with others running horizontally around the inside of apsidal Room 14, presumably used for directly heating its walls.

The middle flue, B[1406], may have been inserted slightly after the outer two as it was been built into a section of wall above arched flue B[1408] which was somewhat different in build and may indicate a slightly later rebuild or modification. The space above flue [B1408] has been blocked in with a combination of *opus signinum*, chalk, *Septaria* and brick. The brick is almost entirely a fabric (2459b) that has a slightly later date range than much of local London sandy group (2815). The use of the *opus signinum*, however, may indicate that the construction of this section may simply have formed part of secondary element of the original build, during the process of fitting out and flooring (Ken Sabel, pers. comm.).

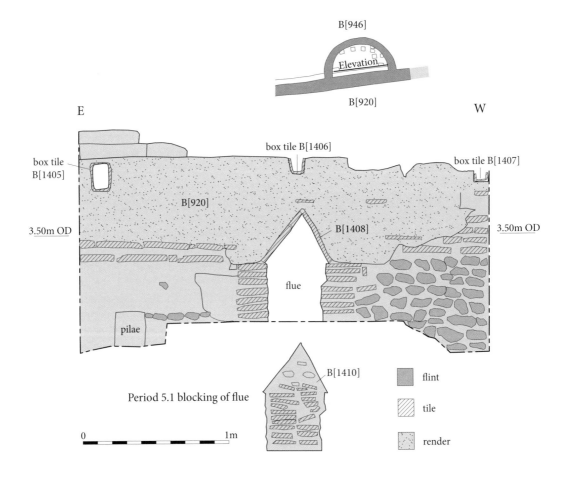

Fig. 16   North-facing elevation showing north wall B[920] of the bath house pierced by arched under-floor flue B[1408] and smaller box tile flues B[1405] set into the wall at a higher level (scale 1:25)

Truncation of the upper superstructure meant that there was no surviving *in-situ* wall jacketing associated with the primary Period 3 phase of Building 4. Demolition material associated with the building indicates that the cavity walling of the bath house was constructed of comb-keyed box-flue tiles (see Period 4). Two half-box-flue tiles were also identified, but these had been reused as general building material and may have come from elsewhere. The presence of two possible 'T' shaped iron cramps, small finds B<436> and B<437>, might imply that an early form of jacketing using wall tiles and spacer bobbins (Brodribb 1987, 67–69) may have been used to construct part of the cavity walling. Given the absence of spacer bobbins and limited number of wall tiles from the ceramic assemblage this seems unlikely, besides which 'T' cramps were sometimes used in association with box-flue tile (Brodribb 1987, 73).

External area to the south of the bath house (Open Area 5)

A small area lying immediately to the south of Building 4 contained a compacted clay deposit B[1082] and B[1233], which may represent a surface or floor make-up at 2.28m OD, perhaps associated with an approach to the bath house (OA5) (see Fig. 10). This surface level was *c.* 0.20m below the level of the bath house sub-floors, essential for the drainage of any water that got into the hypocaust areas. The external surface would have been nearly 1.5m lower than the conjectured floor levels within the bath building, indicating that a set of steps would have been necessary to access the building from the south.

A small group of oak stakes or small piles was recorded in the southwestern corner of OA5. The group lacked a coherent alignment and their function is uncertain. Timbers B[1280] and B[1281] were recovered and sampled.

Fig. 17　View looking south of flue B[1408] in the northern bath house wall B[920], connecting Room 12 with apsidal Room 14 (just visible in the foreground); note that the blocking of the flue was probably carried out during the final modification of the bath house in the late fourth century (Period 5.1)

Both were slow-grown, slightly crooked oak roundwood and had similar three-facet tips which had been cut with the same badly chipped axe blade. The axe would have been over 85mm wide and left a bold signature ridge 4mm wide. The structure originally associated with these timbers may have been a roughly-made temporary construction, such as scaffolding or supports for a riverside platform or walkway.

Yard to the north of the bath house (Open Area 6)

Immediately to the north of Building 4, truncated areas of make-up and a yard surface B[812] and B[796] were recorded and form OA6 (Fig. 10). Compacted layers of silty sand, gravel and crushed mortar and chalk formed a make-up layer overlain by a layer of cobble-sized chalk lumps. Part of the surviving chalk surface on the eastern side of the yard formed a level at 4.00m OD. The yard area measured at least 10.50m north–south and 11.0m east–west. To the south the yard surface make-up deposits abutted the north wall of the bath house (Fig. 14).

Small furnace abutting the north wall of the bath house (Open Area 6)

The OA6 yard surface was truncated by construction cut B[736] for a small external furnace B[734] etc, built against the external northern wall of Building 4 (Fig. 10; Fig. 18). The furnace was one of the few elements of Building 4 that could be investigated in detail. Construction cut B[736] measured 2.36m by 1.40m and was 0.73m deep, with steeply sloping sides falling to a flat base. A thin silty sand bedding layer lined the base of the cut and was overlain by a levelling deposit for the south wall B[735] of the furnace.

The north and south walls of the furnace were built using fragmented tile and brick bonded with a yellow brown sandy mortar. Between these walls, a tile and brick furnace base B[832] was recorded measuring 1.18m by 0.38m with a thickness of 0.04m. The base was made up of fragments of brick and tile laid flat and forming a surface at 3.29m OD. Four courses of tile and brick B[733] overlay the north wall and may represent the remains of a roof for the structure, forming a flat arch. The maximum surviving height of the structure was 3.84m OD.

The furnace was truncated, but is likely to have originally formed a small square or rectangular stoke hole parallel with the north wall of Building 4. It is unlikely to have served as the main furnace for the hypocaust system, which may have been located to the east of Room 12, beyond the eastern limit of excavation (see above). Minor furnaces were often added to bath houses to boost the supply of heat to certain rooms where the main furnace was insufficient, and these usually take the form of a simple arched structure in an external wall and in which a fire could be built in a stokehole accessible from the outside (Yegül 1992, 368–369). Normally the stokehole would be positioned at right angles to the wall, and not parallel to it, as in this case. The precise function of the

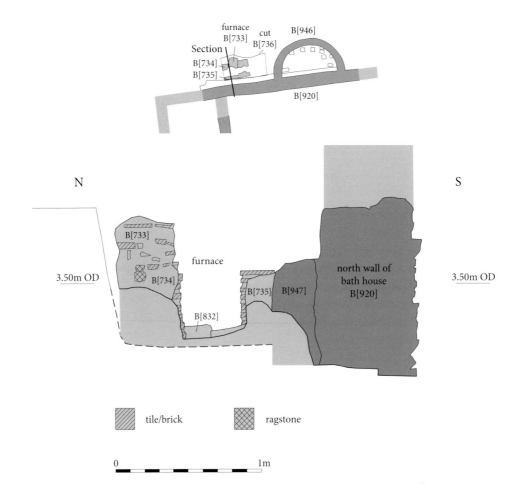

Fig. 18   West-facing elevation of furnace B[734] with conjectured construction cut and superstructure, built against the north side of the north wall of the bath house (scale 1:25)

furnace must therefore be open to question and it may have had a specialised function, such as heating a water tank directly overhead. (Yegül 1992, 369). Fittings found in the backfill of the furnace may support this interpretation, and it is possible that a hot water plunge was located nearby, perhaps in apsidal Room 14 or Room 11 (Fig. 11).

A winged building to the north of the bath house (Building 3)

To the north of the bath house and lying to the north and west of yard OA6, a brickearth foundation slab defined the limits of clay-and-timber Building 3 (Fig. 9; Fig. 10). Patches of a beaten earth floor survived at about 4.50m OD and defined an L-shaped structure. Areas of scorching on the floor indicate the position of hearths within the building. The west wing of the building (Room 1) measured at least 9.0m north–south and 3.0m east–west, whilst the northern range (Room 2) was at least 5.50m east–west and 6.0m north–south. Building 3 extended beyond the western and eastern limits of excavation.

In the west wing of the building, beam slot B[751] cut into the brickearth slab and was up to 1.0m wide and 0.20m deep. The beam slot continued west beyond the limit of excavation and formed the north side of Building 3, its unusual width perhaps relating to its later robbing.

A north–south return formed a division 0.38m wide, with Room 1 to the west and Room 2 to the east. Although the southern part of the north–south wall was truncated, it is estimated that it would originally have been *c.* 8.50m long. The beam slots were filled with silty sands including frequent fragments of daub, charcoal and *opus signinum*.

A small circular pit was found underneath beam slot B[751] on the north side of Room 1 and contained an amphora which may be a deliberately placed structured deposit of religious or ritual significance.

Several postholes cut into the floors of Building 3 and might represent scaffolding used during construction or indicate the line of a robbed sill beam. Four of the postholes were grouped in pairs and located in the north and south parts of Room 1 and still held the tips of wooden piles: B[892] and B[895] in the north and B[868] and B[869] to the south. The piles were very decayed but could be identified as oak hewn with neat, four facet, square section tips. Pile B[869] was hewn from a whole log and the others were radially cleft quartered logs, typical of timber piles found in Roman building. The best preserved of the piles measured *c.* 210mm x 180mm, which is relatively large for a timber building pile. Other postholes recorded in Rooms 1 and 2 may indicate the locations of internal subdivisions, fixtures such as shelving or supports for the ceiling.

A substantial north–south aligned foundation of compacted lumps of chalk in a matrix of silty sand was recorded at the north-west corner of the yard area. The foundation was set in a cut measuring at least 2.82m north–south, 0.94m east–west and 0.75m deep, and may have been associated with a portico or entranceway to Room 1 of the building.

An east–west orientated water pipe was found in the northern part of Room 1 and was at least 0.84m long, laid in a trench 0.44m wide and 0.16m deep, extending beyond the western limits of excavation. All that remained of the pipe itself were fragments of a junction collar B<458> and the ghost of a wooden pipe bound by iron hoops. The void left by the rotted pipe measured 0.17m wide by 0.14m deep.

Two pits located within the area of Room 1 were probably dug and backfilled when Building 3 fell out of use.

External area to the north of Building 3 (Open Area 7)

An east–west aligned boundary ditch A[165]/[154]/[177]/[141] crossed Site B *c.* 7.5m to the north of Building 3 (Fig. 9). The ditch, which cut into the truncated surface of natural sand and gravel between 6.1 and 6.6m OD, was investigated in four separate slots and was up to 2m wide and approximately 1m deep (Fig. 19). The base of the ditch sloped down to the west, from *c.* 5.20m to 5.01m OD over a distance of *c.* 17m. The ditch may demarcate the northern boundary of the bath house complex, as represented by Buildings 3 and 4, and may have carried surface water away from the property and into a north–south channel located between Sites A and B, running south to the Thames.

Period 3 discussion

Property layout

Activity assigned to Period 3 dates to AD 230–275 and may be contemporary with the reorganisation of the settlement at Shadwell and a substantial increase in the intensity of development.

Evidence relating to the organisation of property boundaries was found in OA7 on Site B, where a substantial east–west aligned boundary ditch lay 24.5m north of the bath building (Fig. 19). Only a few sherds of pottery were recovered from the ditch but these included very late East Gaulish Samian, Moselkeramik, and Lower Nene Valley Colour-coat fabrics, consistent with a deposition date of AD 230–260. On Site A, to the west, boundary ditch A[852] in OA4 also lay on a similar alignment and contained pottery of a similar date (AD 225–260). These boundary ditches shared the same alignment as a fence line and a later ditch identified further to the east on LD 74 (Lakin 2002, figs 7, 9). The overall evidence for a single boundary running at least 120m east–west, suggests a major planned reorganisation of property and land divisions in the mid third century.

The extension of this to the east on LD74 and LD76, gives a boundary extending for *c.* 800m, perhaps reflecting the presence of a parallel road to the north.

It is also noteworthy that a drainage ditch A[525] in the northern part of OA4 on Site A sloped downwards to the east, whilst the base of the ditch in OA7 on Site B sloped down to the west. The opposing slopes suggest that a natural north–south watercourse or channel may have lain beneath Wapping Lane (formerly Old Gravel Lane). This lower ground may have become the location of a north–south access road connecting the riverside development at Shadwell with the east–west road further to the north. There is no evidence for building continuity between Site A and Site B and it seems logical to presume that the north–south running channel would have been managed to some extent and that an access way existed. A metalled road with timber box drains channelling water to one or both sides might be envisaged.

The increased activity on Site A, represented by Building 2, is dated to AD 260 or later, broadly contemporary with the construction and use of the bath house Building 4 on Site B. Some of the ceramic building material recovered from Site A had the same signature mark as that recovered on Site B, which also suggests that the development of the bath house and the activity to the west were closely connected. Buildings B2 and B3 both appear to have been terraced into the hillside (see Fig. 21). There was also a marked increase in activity to the northeast after AD 260, at the LD74 and LD76 sites. The extent of this new but contemporary activity is in keeping with the development of a settlement at Shadwell more significant than hitherto realised.

The bath house complex

Layout and use

The bath house (Building 4) extended beyond the eastern and western limits of Site A, and the absence of a full ground plan for the building makes it difficult to assign functions to individual rooms with confidence, particularly given the general truncation of the remains above the sub-floor level. However, Roman bath houses are generally designed to one of a small number of patterns. Comparison with other bath houses therefore helps in tentatively ascribing functions to each of the rooms and understanding something of the way in which the building was used.

The organisation and layout of bath houses can only be very broadly categorised into groups. Some of the more common layouts include single axis row-types, more complicated intermediary types where the bather follows a cyclical route, and double symmetrical or asymmetrical baths that can be organised into either two distinct single routes or as a cycle (Yegül 1992, 57–91). In all cases the order of use of the various room areas follows the principle of warm to hot and then back to cold, whether in a cycle or by retracing the route of a single row of rooms (Adam 2001, 272; Yegül 1992, 38). So a bather would enter into a

Fig. 19   A third-century boundary ditch, located to the north of the bath house; view looking east during excavation

reception or changing room (vestibule and *apodyterium*), then move through the cold and tepid rooms (*frigidarium*, *tepidarium*) into the hot rooms (*caldarium*) and eventually back to the cold rooms.

Of the varying, loosely categorised types of bath, Building 4 appears to have begun its existence as an axial row or angular row bath, with two separate, heated suites to the east and west. These suites probably shared the same entranceway, changing area and cold room. The eastern suite has been most fully revealed by the excavations on Site B, but without the complete ground plan or any indication of original doorways it is not possible to determine if the route taken by a bather was retraceable or cyclical.

The evidence suggests that the primary Period 3 construction of Building 4 had its entranceway to the south (Room 2), leading into two unheated rooms (Rooms 4 and 7) which are likely to include the *apodyterium* and *frigidarium*. The bather may then have moved east or west into either of two possible *tepidaria* (Rooms 6 and 8). It is possible that Rooms 3 and 5 to the south held unheated plunge baths at the end of the *tepidaria*, but it is also quite possible that they were changing rooms accessed from Room 4. Alternatively they may have had differing functions, the fill in Room 3 suggests a lower floor level than recorded elsewhere, which may be indicative of a plunge, though no evidence for access steps remained.

It should be noted here, similarly to Rooms 3 and 5, that the interpretation of Rooms 4 and 7 as initially unheated has some problems associated with it given that the extant floor level of these rooms is similar to the level of the sub-floors in adjacent heated room areas, and that Rooms 4 and 7 contained hypocausts founded on this same level in later phases (see Period 4.1 and 4.2).

Essentially, if it is assumed that the finished floor was level throughout Building 4 and that Rooms 4 and 7 were unheated they would have had to have been filled to the level of the *suspensura* in the adjacent rooms (Rooms 6 & 8) (Fig. 22), or they may have had *suspensura*, but have been unheated. Another possibility, considered less likely, is that the floors were not level throughout the structure, incrementally rising from the cold rooms in the south to the hot rooms to the north. Unfortunately, there is no evidence to support any of these suggestions. If a fill existed in Rooms 4 and 7 it would have been removed during later remodelling for the addition of the hypocaust and the remains of any stairs linking the changing levels between rooms would not be expected to survive given the level of truncation.

While the effort of digging out the fill in Rooms 4 and 7 to later extend the hypocausts in adjacent rooms (see below) might seem excessive, the idea that the floor levels change throughout the building is not ideal either, potentially compromising the effective functioning of the hypocaust and with no apparent parallel in Roman construction. If the floors were level throughout Building 4 a staircase would have been necessary to access the building from the lower ground to the south, presuming the entrance does indeed lie in this direction. Fewer stairs would be required if the floor levels rose incrementally internally but with no evidence for any stairs surviving to the south of Building 4 little can be concluded with certainty, including whether or not the entranceway existed in this location at all. Given an external ground level to the south of the site at *c.* 2.50m OD (based on the level of the foundations) and an internal level at around 4.0m OD, 6 steps 0.25m high would be needed to access the building, assuming the entranceway was indeed in this location.

Conceivably stairs could have been accommodated within Room 4, but later modifications to the sub floor here make this seem unlikely, or stairs may have been to the south, but no traces survive later truncation.

A further option is that Rooms 4 and 7 were initially heated. This would still require a large staircase to the south or suggest that access to the building existed elsewhere. This would also give a large number of heated spaces in the initial phase of the bath house and mean that the mandatory cold rooms would need to exist beyond the limit of excavation, most likely to the west given the location of the surviving hot rooms, though space to accommodate the requisite rooms appears tight. A rather more fundamental problem is that the hypocaust that survives in Room 7 is considered to form part of a later phase of renovation as it extends over a tiled surface that in turn is laid over a truncated wall of the initial

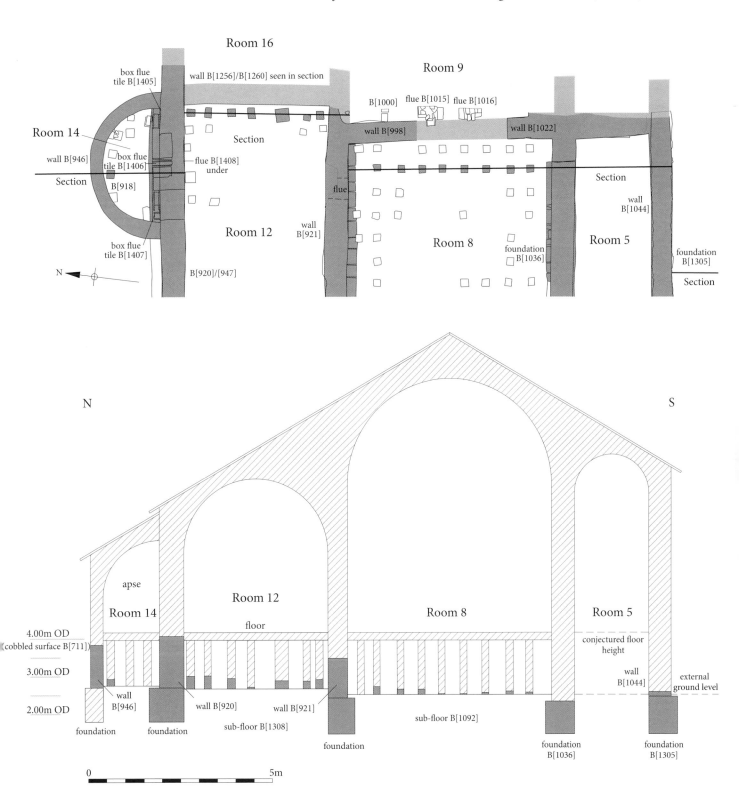

Fig. 20 A schematic north–south section through the bath house showing suggested floor and sub-floor levels (scale 1:100)

build. Of course the surviving hypocaust could represent the replacement of an earlier system but this seems an unnecessary and costly exercise for which no evidence exists. Indeed, the fact that a hypocaust was added during a phase of remodelling after the original build would perhaps suggest that the rooms were initially unheated, although as with Rooms 3 or 5, it is not possible to be certain of the level of the original floor.

A final possibility, that Rooms 7 and 4 originally held *suspensura*, but were unheated until later in the life of the bath house, should also be entertained. Such a floor is not without precedent, and as evidenced at Old Durham (Richmond *et al*. 1944) would be drier and warmer than one founded on solid fill. It would be free from chilling ground damp and would dry more rapidly after being soaked or splashed by bathers.

From the eastern *tepidarium* (Room 8) it is perhaps more certain that the bathers may then have moved to the north, or east and then north, into the hot rooms (Rooms 11 and 12). The presence of a scorched arcaded tile wall, flanking the east side of Room 12, is likely to indicate the proximity of the *praefurnium* to the east. A smaller furnace which butted onto the north wall of Building 4 is likely to have been used to boost the supply of heat or hot water. The arrangement and relative dimension of the *caldaria* and location of the ancillary furnace may indicate that Room 11 contained a hot plunge bath. The apse (Room 14) may also have contained a small plunge bath (Fig. 11).

A western suite may well have extended beyond the limit of excavation of Site B and have been similarly provided, although the layout may have been slightly different, as discussed in more detail below (see Chapter 4.2). It is clear, however, that this would include some form of furnace in order to provide heat for Room 6.

The yard area (OA6) to the north of the bath building and the winged building (Building 3), which enclosed it, were almost certainly a part of the same complex as the baths.

Date and possible status of the Shadwell bath house; comparison with other London baths

There was little in the way of dating evidence from the primary phase of the bath house itself but datable finds were recovered from the service yard to its north (OA6) and the adjacent clay-and-timber building (B3). Only a few sherds of pottery were recovered from the yard's make-up layers, though context B[752] produced 21 fragments. Although the assemblage was not particularly diagnostic the presence of an Oxfordshire Whiteware mortarium was considered significant and suggests that the layer was later than AD 240. A fragment of a glass cup (see Chapter 3.6, cat. no. 68) dated to the second or third century was also found in a yard surface make-up layer. It is likely that the first phase of the yard surface was contemporary with the primary phase of the bath house.

A Claudius II coin B<568> was also recovered from make-up deposits for the yard surface and dates to AD

268–270. However, the coin does not come from a secure context (see Chapter 3.2).

The bath house, which was clearly late in date, was built on a large enough scale to suggest more than domestic use. The topographical setting of the Shadwell bath house is similar to that of the large first-century baths at Huggin Hill, to the west of the Walbrook and set into a hillside terrace on a south-facing slope overlooking the Thames (Rowsome 1999). At Huggin Hill natural London clay was overlain by Thames terrace gravels and an active spring-line existed at the interface of the gravel and the impervious clay where it was exposed along the eroded south edge of the hill. The lower terrace of the Huggin Hill bath's primary phase was at *c.* 4.0m OD, just below the spring-line and above the tidal range of the river. The location of the Huggin Hill baths would have benefited from a constant supply of fresh spring water (Rowsome 1999). It is noteworthy that the bath house at Shadwell was built on the same contour as that at Huggin Hill, and within a similar geological and topographical setting, presumably for the same reasons (Fig. 21).

Courtyard Building 3 and its dating

Building 3, located to the north of the bath house and enclosing the service yard, was probably part of an accommodation block for guests and patrons of the bath. The western and northern wings of the building formed an L-shape but the full extent and layout remain unknown. It is possible that an east wing enclosed the eastern side of the yard, though this would have been located beyond the limits of the excavation.

Hearths identified in the north wing were probably used for heating or cooking. Standing braziers could also have been used for heating, although there was no archaeological evidence for such an arrangement.

The amphora used as a foundation deposit beneath the north wall of Building 3 dates to AD 200–400. Ceramics recovered from the floor layers and the structural features date to between AD 230–260.

Glass fragments from two Airlie cups (cat. nos. 80 and 81), dated to the late second or early third century, as well as fragments of a bowl or dish dated to the second to

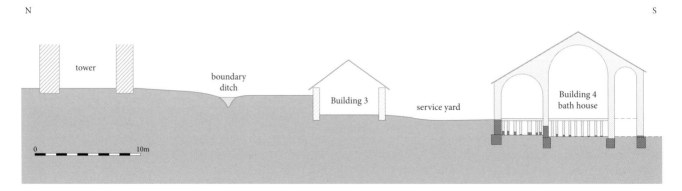

Fig. 21   Schematic north–south cross section through Site B, demonstrating the natural slope of the land and terracing of buildings. The LD74 'tower' is shown in relation to these features at the correct projected northing, however, the level of its foundation is unknown and therefore its projected construction level here is based on an extrapolation from levels on Site B.

fourth century, were recovered from the beam slot along the north and east sides of Room 1 in Building 3 (see Chapter 3.6).

Water supply or drainage and associated dating

On both Sites A and B it seems likely that other properties and structures lay to the north of the OA4 and OA7 boundary ditches, but modern truncation had removed all trace of such activity, with the exception of the drainage ditch near the northern edge of Site A. Pottery from the drainage ditch is consistent with it being open during the middle of the third century.

The drainage ditches and timber drains recorded on Sites A and B may have not only provided surface drainage but could include conduits supplying gravity-fed water to the bath house and neighbouring properties. Drainage ditches, gullies and sunken tanks recorded on the LD 74 and LD76 sites to the northeast may also be part of a water supply system. The dating of three timber piles to the east of Area A, to the spring of AD 228 provide a very precise date for activity in this area. These piles, in an area occupied by a later water tank, are arguably best interpreted as relating to the provision of water to the baths.

Public baths were large consumers of water, which may have been delivered by an open conduit, flowing between a series of collecting points and aerated by cascading from one tank to another. The water supply worked on a constant-flow principle, meaning that surplus had to be removed via drains or soakaways (Alcock 1996, 99), draining into the nearby Thames to the south possibly via the postulated north–south channel or drains to the west of the bath house beneath Wapping Lane.

A timber drain adjacent to Building 2 may also indicate a supply of running water. Pottery from this drain was dated to AD 180–250, consistent with use during the mid third century. Building 3 was probably also supplied with running water and the fragmentary remains of buried water pipes were found in Room 1.

Disuse of the Period 3 buildings

Pitting cut into the floors of Buildings 2 and 3 may mark the end of Period 3 activity. The pits may have been used for rubbish disposal as the buildings fell into disrepair and disuse or when the area was being cleared for rebuilding. A horse skull recovered from one of the pits in Site A could be related to a ritual or religious closure deposit. The use of animals or animal parts in Roman ritual deposits is not uncommon (Woodward 1992, 79).

A relatively small assemblage of ceramics was recovered from Period 3 contexts on Site A, suggesting that the most intensive occupation activity did not begin until after AD 260. During the latter half of the third century the tower or mausoleum structure to the northeast (site LD74) may still have been standing but could also have become a ruin. At site LD76 there was evidence for an intensification of activity at about this time.

2.4 Activity between *c.* AD 275–325 (Period 4)

Period 4 land uses

Intensive activity took place at Shadwell in the late third and early fourth centuries. Much of this was associated with the Site B bath house complex, which was renovated (B4, B3a, OA5 and OA6) at about the same time as new activity to the west at Site A (B5 and OA8), together interpreted as Period 4.1 (Fig. 22). The bath house was the subject of major remodelling (B4 and B3b) after a very short phase of use (Period 4.2; Fig. 25). Evidence for flooding of the bath house hypocausts and accumulated silt deposits indicate that the baths may have experienced a short period of disuse, perhaps during further renovation work, though the winged building to the north continued in use (B3c) (Period 4.3; Fig. 33). The evidence indicates that the winged building continued to see minor modifications (B3d), though it is unclear whether the bath house continued in use during this time (Period 4.4; Fig. 34). A final phase of modification and use of the winged building (B3e) may have been roughly contemporary with the last Period 4 activity on Site A to the west (OA9 and B6), though the dating evidence is uncertain in this regard (Period 4.5; Fig. 36).

Although five separate phases have been identified within Period 4 on the basis of the evidence for successive modifications within the bath house complex at Site B (Building 4 and, to a greater extent, Building 3), it is important to note that the relatively short overall time span of the period makes it difficult to claim these as true phases, let alone to accurately correlate them with activity on Site A to the west.

The most detailed and extensive archaeological evidence and changes in phase were identified in and around the bath house on Site B, and this information is therefore given precedence in the Period 4 narrative, below. The evidence from Site A is assumed to be roughly contemporary with the earliest (Period 4.1) and latest (Period 4.5) evidence at Site B but might in fact fall anywhere within the period.

Period 4.1 land uses

Renovation of the bath house (Building 4)

The bath house (Building 4) underwent extensive renovation, probably quite a short time after its initial construction and use, though preservation *in situ* of the remains has meant that it is difficult to fully interpret the changes made to the structure or their precise date. As a result it is not possible to work out the timescale of the renovations or the overall sequence of modifications, although the latter can be determined in some instances (Fig. 22). The main modifications to Building 4 consisted of the addition of a new room to the north-west (Room 10).

Addition of Room 10 on north-west side of the bath house

The original Period 3 footprint of the bath house was extended to the north-west by the addition of a new room area (Room 10), represented by wall B[1295], which extended the main north wall of the building westwards (Fig. 23). Wall B[1295] was 0.90m wide, 0.36m deep and survived over a truncated length of 4.35m and to a maximum height of 3.32m OD. Post-medieval truncation had isolated wall B[1295] from surrounding Roman stratigraphy. Although the wall could not be excavated, a modern intrusion revealed that the wall was of a different construction to the Period 3 foundations and wall lines, as it had a relatively shallow foundation (Fig. 24).

The foundation for wall B[1295] was constructed in a shallow trench with sloping sides and a curved base. It was made up of a conglomerate of flint, Kentish ragstone and mortar. Three courses of surviving wall superstructure consisted of a rubble core faced with chalk blocks, and it is noteworthy that there was no tile or brick in the surviving construction. Although the Room 10 northern wall cannot be precisely dated, it clearly post-dated the Period 3 build and is likely to have pre-dated the construction of Period 5 wall B[1251], which extended the bath house further northwards (see below). Although it is possible that wall B[1295] represents the rebuild of a Period 3 wall and foundation along the same line, this is felt to be unlikely, as no

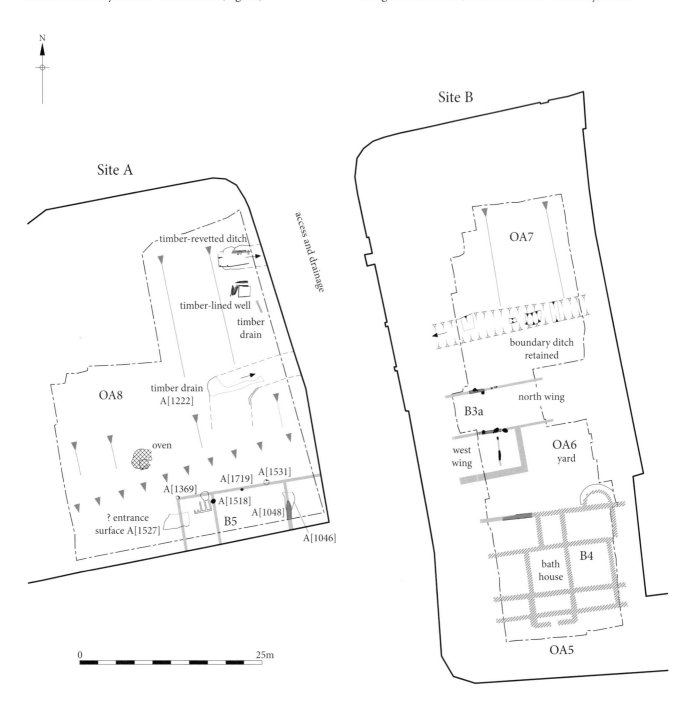

Fig. 22   Principal activity assigned to Period 4.1 on Sites A and B (scale 1:500)

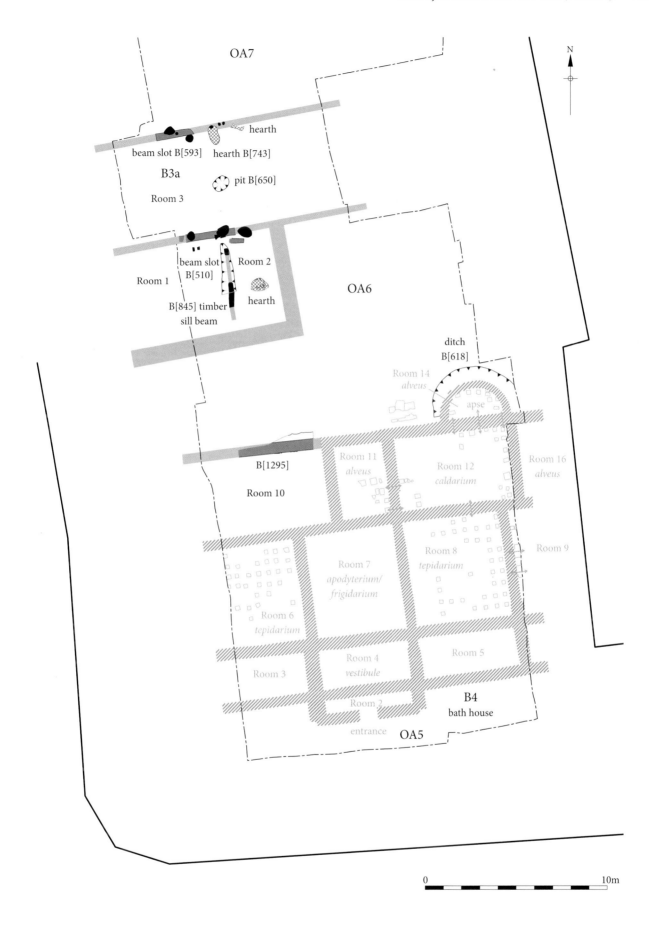

OA7

hearth

beam slot B[593]   hearth B[743]

B3a

pit B[650]

Room 3

beam slot
B[510]   Room 2

Room 1

hearth

B[845] timber
sill beam

OA6

ditch
B[618]

Room 14
alveus

apse

B[1295]

Room 11
alveus

Room 12
caldarium

Room 16
alveus

Room 10

Room 7
*apodyterium/
frigidarium*

Room 8
tepidarium

Room 9

Room 6
tepidarium

Room 5

Room 3

Room 4
vestibule

Room 2

B4
bath house

entrance   OA5

0   10m

Fig. 23   Detailed plan showing modifications to the bath house (Building 4) and associated areas (OA5 and OA6) and structures (Building 3a) (scale 1:200)

trace of underlying or truncated masonry was recorded beneath the shallow foundations.

Room 10 extended beyond the western limit of excavation and had the same north–south width as Rooms 11 and 12 to the east. The internal area of Room 10 was heavily truncated and there was no surviving evidence to indicate whether it had originally contained a hypocaust. A layer of redeposited sand and gravel may represent a truncated area of floor make-up.

Disuse of small furnace on north side of baths

The base of the small Period 3 furnace, located against the north wall of Room 12, was covered by a mixed disuse deposit B[809]. Pottery from the deposit dates to AD 270– 400. Environmental sample B{46} included bones of the black rat and the house mouse. To the east, and covering the opening or stokehole of the furnace, was a dumped deposit of sandy silt B[640] which contained pottery dating from AD 250–300. Deposit B[640] must post- date the disuse of the furnace, when it was in a partially collapsed state. Overall, the evidence indicates that the small furnace went out of use for a period early in the lifetime of the bath house, probably at the end of Period 3.

The apparent disuse of the small external furnace raises questions of whether new furnaces were constructed in Period 4 to boost the supply of heat or to provide hot water to Rooms 10 and 11, or whether they simply relied on the *praefurnium* to the east.

Fig. 24   View looking east, showing wall B[1295], the Period 4.1 extension of the bath house to the north-west to create Room 10 (scales 2m)

Retention of the service yard (Open Area 6) and provision of drainage adjacent to the Room 14 apse

The service yard to the north of the bath house was retained during Period 4 (OA6). Aside from the maintenance of the yard surface, a semi-circular ditch B[618] was established around the outside of the Room 14 apse wall B[946], truncating the disuse deposits that sealed the small furnace immediately to the west (see above). The ditch had vertical sides and a flat base, and measured 0.82m wide and 0.35m deep, cut from a maximum height of 3.98m OD. It was backfilled with chalk lumps B[613], and the sharpness of the cut and homogeneity of the fill suggest that it was backfilled deliberately shortly after construction.

Backfill B[613] contained pottery dating to AD 200– 300. The location of the ditch and nature of the fill suggest that it provided drainage, perhaps serving as a soakaway or eaves-drip for water from the eaves of the Room 14 apse and the yard surface to the north. It is likely to have been associated with the renovation and maintenance of the bath house.

Building 3a to the north and west of the service yard

The west wing of Building 3 was largely demolished and rebuilt as part of Building 3a, but without the possible portico entrance described in Period 3 (Fig. 22). Make-up dumps, floors and the remains of clay-and-timber walls and postholes were associated with the rebuilding. Parts of three new room areas (Rooms 1–3) were identified and the evidence is described in detail below (Fig. 23).

Dumped deposits of sand, silt and gravel with occasional lenses of clay mixed with fragments of brick and tile covered parts of the Period 3 structure of Building 3 and raised and levelled the ground surface.

The northern east–west aligned wall of Period 3 Building 3 had been rebuilt with a beam slot B[593] and associated postholes. To the south, a new internal east– west wall was constructed, also consisting of a beam slot and postholes. These new wall lines defined the north and south sides of Room 3. The location of the south wall of Room 3 was close to a possible earlier east–west partition line which crossed Period 3 Building 3 Room 1.

A beaten earth floor B[687] formed a surface between 4.47 and 4.66m OD in Room 3 of the new building. To the south, in new Room 1, a hard cream mortar and *opus signinum* floor had a surface between 4.02 and 4.20m OD.

The eastern side of Room 1 was defined by a north– south aligned beam slot B[510] that held a decayed oak beam B[845] which measured 166m x 210mm x 100mm thick. There was no evidence of mortice joints in the upper face of the sill beam, suggesting that it formed the base for a *pisé* or mudbrick wall, rather than a wall with an extensive timber frame. The north–south wall formed an internal partition, with evidence for a further internal area (Room 2) to the east.

Building 3a was badly truncated, with the extent of Rooms 1–3 uncertain. Rooms 2 and 3 contained hearths or scorched floor areas. Hearth B[743] in Room 3 produced an important assemblage of imported pottery from Central and Northern Gaul and from the Rhineland region (see Chapter 3.1).

Pitting within the footprint of Building 3a remains may mark the end of this phase of use. Pit B[650] cut into beaten earth floor B[687] in Room 3 and contained some unusual pottery, including a sherd of North African Red Slipped Ware and a fragment of unsourced amphora notable for post-firing perforations that suggested reuse for an unknown purpose (see Chapter 3.1).

External area to the north of Building 3a (Open Area 7 retained)

The northern part of Site B was heavily truncated but it is assumed that OA7 was retained, including the east–west boundary ditch described in Period 3 (Fig. 19).

Initial dumping and external activity on Site A (Open Area 8 south)

On Site A, to the west of the bath house complex, a layer of earth sealed Period 3 Building 2 on the southern part of the area. This earth may have been intentionally dumped or represent gradual hill-slip due to erosion or slumping down the hillside (Fig. 22). Coin A<492>, dated to AD 270–290, was recovered from deposit A[1154] on the west side of the area and provides some tentative dating evidence.

Building 5

A substantial clay-and-timber building (B5) was built overlying the OA8 dumping on the southern part of Site A. Three postholes A[1369], A[1719] and A[1531] formed an east–west alignment of over 12.50m representing the north wall of the building (Fig. 22). To the east, a short surviving length of a north–south beam slot A[1048] and robber trench A[1046] may indicate the position of the east wall of the building or an internal partition.

To the west, a fourth post-pit A[1518] may define the position of another north–south wall. Immediately to the west of the post-pit, decayed timbers may represent part of a collapsed stud wall A[1646] (Fig. 26; see Fig. 22). The evidence included an east–west timber 2.40m long and 0.20m wide and at right angles to it another five timbers set *c.* 0.50m apart and up to 1.65m long and 0.20m wide. A layer of fine sandy silt A[1648], containing charcoal, daub flecks, small patches of brickearth and occasional fragments of wall plaster, was present between the timbers.

Finds recovered from deposit A[1648] included coin A<593> dated to AD 268–270, bone hair pins, pottery and animal bone. Copper-alloy tweezers A<594> may be of particular interest (see Chapter 3.3) as such implements were used to remove unwanted body hair, a service offered to customers in Roman baths.

A roughly square pit measuring 1.18m by 1.10m and 0.13m deep, cut the north side of the possible stud wall, along the north wall of Building 5. The cut contained tightly packed lumps of chalk and broken tile A[1650] and may have been a stanchion base or structural feature associated with the building's north wall.

Immediately to the west of Building 5 a rammed gravel, metalled surface A[1527] at 3.56m OD may indicate the location of the entrance to Building 5.

External activity to the north of Building 5 (Open Area 8 north)

Scattered external activity and features were recorded on the northern part of Site A and formed part of OA8, though these may have been in use at the same time as Building 5 to the south (Fig. 22).

The remnants of a possible oven were found to the north-west of Building 5, represented by a rectangular pit measuring 1.20m square and 0.44m deep but truncated to the east. The pit contained a layer of bedding sand overlain by broken tile and brickearth A[714]. On disuse it was deliberately filled with fragments of burnt flint, charcoal and tile.

In the far north of the area, the Period 3 east–west drainage ditch was recut. The sides of the ditch were stabilised by timber planking laid on edge and secured in place by timber posts. Most of the timber was too degraded to survive lifting but pile tips A[1313] and A[1314] were both hewn, boxed heart style from relatively small logs with rectangular cross sections 130 x 100mm. The ditch was 5.0m long east–west, 3.0m wide and at least 1.0m deep, and continued beyond the eastern limit of the excavation. The timber shoring of the sides created a drainage channel 1.5m wide.

Approximately 4m to the south of the revetted ditch was a timber-lined well or cistern. Its construction cut was a large sub-circular pit measuring 4.35m north–south, 3.0m east–west, and 1.25m deep, but truncated to the east by modern intrusions. It was cut from a surface at 6.10m OD or above and was lined with timber planks laid on edge to form a structure 1.50m square. The space behind the timber lining was backfilled and timber planks were laid flat to create a platform surrounding the top of the lining. A jet bracelet A<485> was found in the primary fill of the well/cistern. Upon final disuse it was deliberately backfilled, and associated pottery dated to AD 200–270.

Part of a timber drain survived immediately to the southeast of the well/cistern, represented by a surviving timber base. The sides of the drain had decayed but there was some evidence for wooden stakes, which may have revetted side planking, which was backed by a clay backfill, indicating a deliberate attempt to make the drain watertight.

A further 10m to the south was a small dog-legged length of dugout drain formed from oak A[1222]. Three stakeholes truncated the bed of the construction cut, again providing evidence that stakes along the sides of the drain had held side planks in place.

Fig. 25   Detailed plan of principal activity assigned to Period 4.2: remodelling of bath house B4, adjacent external areas OA5 and OA6, and Building 3b to the north (scale 1:200)

Fig. 26 The remains of collapsed stud wall A[1646], associated with Building 5, located on the southern part of Site A; view looking north; note the chalk backfill A[1650] in a pit to the north (scale 1m)

It is possible that the well/cistern and both short stretches of truncated drain may have been part of a water supply system for Building 5, down the slope to the south, or alternatively that they were part of the water supply to the bath house.

Period 4.2 land uses

Remodelling of the bath house complex (Buildings 4 and 3b)

The bath house (B4), external areas to the south (OA5) and north (service yard OA6), and winged building further to the north (B3b) were the subject of a major remodelling, interpreted here as Period 4.2 (Fig. 25).

The structural changes made to Building 4 saw the number and size of the principal heated rooms increase. The alterations across the southern ranges of room areas involved the insertion of large openings through the lower parts of internal walls to link the sub-floors, and potentially the above floor spaces, of (i) Rooms 5, 8 and 9 in the southeastern part of the building, (ii) Rooms 4, 7 and 6 in the south-central and southwestern parts of the building, and (iii) Rooms 2 and 4 in the possible southern entranceway or portico. In the northern range of rooms a sub-floor partition was built perhaps to divide Room 12 in two, creating Rooms 12 and 13, or to strengthen the floor. Rooms 10 and 11 were apparently unmodified from their Period 4.1 layout.

There was no evidence for specifically contemporary activity on Site A to the west, where the use of Building 5 and OA8 may have continued (see Period 4.1).

Fig. 27 General overhead view of the Shadwell bath house, with west at the top; amalgamated Rooms 5, 8 and 9 in the centre-left foreground; newly divided Rooms 12 and 13 in the centre-right foreground; apsidal Room 14 in lower right, with service yard OA6 to its right

Remodelling of southeastern Rooms 5, 8 and 9: extension of hypocaust

The alterations across the southeastern rooms were represented by the insertion of large openings through the lower parts of internal walls between Room 8 and Room 5 to the south as well as Room 9 to the east (Fig. 27). The suspended floors above these wider sub-floor openings between the main rooms were supported by the addition of new *pilae* stacks.

The modifications made to the sub-floor areas may have been mirrored in the above floor spaces, although these did not survive and we can only speculate. The north–south wall B[1034], on the west side of Room 8, was strengthened by the addition of 0.26m of masonry, formed of Reigate stone blocks, along its east face B[1035]. This strengthening may have been needed to support the enlarged hypocaust structures, enlarged room areas above, or both. Abutments bordering the east and west sides of the new sub-floor opening between Room 8 and Room 5 to the south were also constructed, strengthening the ends of what had been a continuous east–west sub-floor wall in earlier phases.

The hypocaust in Room 8 was enlarged, extending over the truncated walls at sub-floor level into Room 5 to the south and Room 9 to the east. A gravel sub-floor was added where needed to raise and level the ground for the construction of new *pilae*. This was most apparent between Rooms 8 and 9, where gravel layer B[1253] overlay truncated wall B[998]/B[1022]. The *pilae* were built from a more diverse range of material than used during the original build, although again they are primarily comprised of complete *bessales* with less frequent *pedalis* bricks and *tubuli*.

Room 5 also contains the remains of a possible hypocaust flue B[1058] etc, apparently inserted through the eastern wall B[1022] during this phase of remodelling. The wall itself was completely truncated at this point but the base of the flue projected east–west onto the sub-floor of Room 5. The flue base was a layer of Kentish ragstone B[1064] covered with a surface of tile and brick B[1062] at 2.51m OD. On this base two parallel east–west aligned flue walls 0.58m thick (2 Roman feet) were constructed of fragmented brick, tile and Kentish ragstone with heat-resistant brick and tile lined internal faces.

The implication may be that a new furnace lay immediately to the east, just beyond the limit of excavation. Alternatively, the enlarged heated space formed by the amalgamation of Rooms 5, 8 and 9 may still have been heated by a *praefurnium* some distance away, perhaps to the north of Room 9, and the addition of the new flue in the east side of Room 5 may have been intended to help the through draught and thus the circulation of heated air.

The remains of a sub-floor vent were also recorded in the southern wall of Room 5. The top of the opening was truncated but appeared to be curving inwards towards a semi-circular arched top. This probably functioned as a vent, drawing combustion gases through the underfloor heating system and would have helped to create a through-draft. It is impossible to be certain when this was constructed, but it appeared to have been inserted through the original southern wall of Room 5 and therefore most logically fits with the extension of the hypocaust into the room.

The only surviving evidence of Period 4.2 flooring and cavity wall heating in Building 4 was also recorded in Room 5. Both would have been added with the extension of the hypocaust. The remains of three hollow rectangular box-flue tiles B[1043] were recorded *in situ*, mortared vertically to the western wall B[1034] of the room. The surviving flue tiles (*tubuli*) formed the lowest course of wall heating, which started at the base of the suspended floor and would originally have allowed the hot air from the hypocaust to rise up the walls to the chimney vents at roof level.

The *in-situ* box-flue tiles were unvented: however, a large proportion of the box-flue tiles recovered from demolition rubble associated with the bath house did have rectangular vents in their sides that might indicate that the wall cavity heating was laterally vented. These would have allowed hot air not only to move upwards but also horizontally through the walls in a more effective manner.

Butted up against the flue tiles in Room 5 and resting on the *pilae* stacks were the remains of a suspended floor B[1045], part of a partially collapsed area of the *suspensura* above the hypocaust (Fig. 27 and see Fig. 43). The extant suspended floor area measured 3.30m by 1.30m and was up to 0.37m thick. The suspended floor was constructed of *bipedales* at the base and covered with a thick layer of *opus signinum*.

Remodelling and amalgamation of south-central and southwestern rooms 4, 7 and 6 including extension of hypocaust

In the south-central and western parts of Building 4, a similar process of sub-floor hypocaust amalgamation took place to that in the southeastern part of the building.

The east–west wall B[1131] dividing Rooms 4 and 7 was partially demolished to allow construction of an enlarged opening, which was set off-centre to the east. A bedding layer and new tile surface was laid down in the new opening and extended slightly into Rooms 4 and further into Room 7 (Fig. 28). The surviving floor area measured 2.74m by 3.55m, butting up against the eastern wall of the combined room area B[1034]. The surface was a random construction of reused fragments of brick and tile, although some whole *bessales* had also been used and fragments of *tegulae* and *bipedales* were present. The floor surface lay at a maximum height of 2.70m OD, which is similar to the hypocaust sub-floor level in neighbouring rooms to the west, east and north. A 0.06m square notch B[1279] was cut into the surface on the line of the division between Rooms 4 and 7, but is of unknown function.

Consideration has been given to the possibility that the modification of Rooms 4 and 7 may relate to the sub-floor area of a hypocaust system, and the low surface level would be consistent with such an interpretation. The likelihood of having one section of tiled sub-floor, when throughout the rest of building compacted gravel has been used, is questionable. It is therefore possible that Rooms 4 and 7 were partly joined at this level as unheated rooms with a lower floor level than the adjacent heated rooms (though as discussed above changes of level within bath houses are without ready parallels). Alternatively these modifications may actually relate to the later hypocaust in the room with the tiles laid to stabilise a soft area unsuitable for the bedding of *pilae* or perhaps relating to the larger adjacent sub-floor masonry structures.

The eastern sub-floor wall of Room 6 was largely removed to amalgamate it with Room 7.

In the centre of the Room 7 hypocaust a new arrangement of piers or pillars were constructed from regular, mortared courses of reused brick and tile to form east–west and north–south aligned stub walls. Pillar B[1165] incorporated a reused oolitic limestone column base measuring 0.32m in diameter, which had been placed on top of a single *bessalis* tile (Fig. 29). Together these sub-floor structures measured 1.80m east–west and 2.82m north–south. They lay to the north and west of a large central pillar or pier B[1114], which measured

Fig. 28   Tile surface of a sub-floor level covering an earlier wall line and extending across amalgamated areas of Room 4 and Room 7 in the bath house, looking west; Period 4.1 (scale 1m)

Fig. 29   An oolitic limestone column base B[1165] reused as a *pilae* stack near the centre of heated Room 7 during Period 4.2 (scale 0.5m)

0.80m by 0.86m and was also constructed of fragmented brick and tile. The resulting shape in plan was presumably intentional and may have been related to the circulation of air within the hypocaust or, more likely, to supporting heavy partitions or other structures above the suspended floor in the centre of the room, perhaps even a large water basin or fountain.

The heat source for the extended hypocaust in this side of the building is likely to have existed beyond the limit of excavation to the west of Room 6.

Extension and remodelling of the southern entranceway Room 2

Room 2, which projected south from the main wall of the bath house, was amalgamated with Room 4/7 to the north by removing dividing wall B[1131]. Compacted mortar spreads B[1193] etc. formed a new surface across what had been the internal area of Rooms 2 and 4 at a maximum height of 2.40m OD. It is probable that these compacted spreads represent a sub-floor and that the new room area, which formed a continuous under-floor space with Room 7 etc. to the north, was heated, though no trace of a hypocaust survived.

An extension was also added onto the south side of the possible entranceway. The rebuilt south side of the original Room 2 wall B[1073] and a north–south extension B[1074] were built using the same technique and materials, suggesting that they were contemporary and related structures. Both of these walls had a chalk and mortar rubble core faced with Kentish ragstone and tile. In contrast to the original build, lacing courses were not evident and the tile used was all *tegulae* with the same notched flange profile (flange 40), suggesting a possible association or contemporaneity with the division of Room 12 (see below). The western side of Room 1 was not identified and may have been truncated, whilst the southern extent of the room would have lain beyond the southern limit of excavation (Fig. 25). The extension created has been ascribed a room number (Room 1) although too little survives or was investigated to determine if it represents the addition of more internal space, remodelling of the entranceway or an external structure built in an attempt to consolidate the ground in front of the entrance.

Sub-division of hot Room 12 to create Rooms 12 and 13

In contrast to the enlargement of the under-floor hypocaust systems, and possibly the above floor room areas, in the southern part of the bath house, the northeastern heated Room 12 was divided by the addition of a north–south under-floor partition (Fig. 27). The new wall had a substantial foundation B[1289] 0.60m wide and set in a construction cut 1.00m deep. This foundation was constructed differently from earlier Building 4 foundations, consisting of a primary course of chalk blocks overlain by a poured mixture of mortar, flint, tile and chalk. The top of the foundation lay at 2.71m OD, similar to the level of the Room 12 sub-floor.

The overlying partition consisted of a single primary course of tile topped by four piers B[1010]-B[1014] which may have formed an arcaded wall within the hypocaust (Fig. 30). The insertion of the partition wall dividing the hypocaust may have been mirrored by the creation of two smaller rooms above, although this cannot be known for certain, or may have simply been intended to strengthen the floor.

Fig. 31   View towards the northeast corner of Room 12, showing surviving *pilae* stacks, many constructed of *tegulae* placed flange down; visible in the background are two piers of a dividing wall inserted across Room 12 to form separate Room 13 to the east (scale 0.5m)

The sub-floor division necessitated the reconstruction of a small number of the original *pilae*, with the new stacks including *tegulae* placed flange downwards, in addition to *pedalis* and *bessalis* bricks (Fig. 31).

The Room 12 and 13 dividing piers were constructed of stone with tile lacing courses. The stone is mostly Reigate although both flint and Kentish ragstone were also used. In contrast to the majority of the original build, the lacing courses are primarily comprised of *tegulae* placed flange up, with the inclusion of some fragmented brick, all bonded in a less sandy mortar than that used in the original walls. Most of the *tegulae* have a distinctive notched flange (profile 40).

Truncation prevents an understanding of the way in which the piers were bridged.

Rebuild of the small external furnace on the north side of the baths

The ancillary furnace, to the north of Room 12 and west of apsidal Room 14, was rebuilt, although it cannot be certain whether this took place in Period 4.2, or immediately after its initial disuse, perhaps as a result of collapse or failure. Both the north and south walls of the furnace were rebuilt or repaired with reused, fragmented brick and tile bonded with a clayey sand. Spanning the walls were two fragmented but horizontally laid bricks B[641], representing the heavily truncated remains of the furnace or stokehole roof (Fig. 32).

Retention of service yard (Open Area 6)

The service yard area to the north of the bath house was retained in use, maintained and resurfaced as necessary. A drainage ditch B[433] was identified in the south part of the yard, next to the apsidal Room 14 and truncating a possible beaten earth yard surface B[456]. The drain was filled with a sandy silt which contained pottery dating to AD 250 to 280.

Fig. 30   Recording the divided northern heated Rooms 12–13, with two of the dividing sub-floor piers visible between the archaeologists in yellow coats; view looking west, with the apsidal Room 14 to the right

Building 3b

Parts of Building 3a to the north and west of the bath house service yard (OA6) were once again largely demolished and rebuilt. New dumping was used to level and raise the ground, with dump B[264] containing late third to early fourth-century pottery as well as a single sherd of intrusive later fourth-century imported Mayen ware.

Overlying floor make-ups, beaten earth and *opus signinum* floors define the rebuilding of the western and northern wings of the building to create up to five room areas and a possible internal corridor (Fig. 25). The rebuilt structure (Building 3b) extended beyond the eastern and western limits of excavation and was badly truncated, making a certain interpretation of the room layout difficult.

The south side of Building 3b was defined by an east–west aligned wall foundation B[725] constructed from broken tile and Kentish ragstone set in a sandy silt matrix. A posthole B[763] along the wall line may indicate the location of an entranceway. Another posthole B[610] may indicate the position of a second east–west wall, forming the northern wall of Room 1.

An internal corridor *c.* 1.50m wide appeared to run north from Room 1 and was represented by a line of postholes on its eastern side and beam slot B[282] on the west. To the west of the corridor were several more postholes and truncated patches of flooring. Posthole B[626] may indicate the position of a partition between two small rooms west of the corridor (Rooms 2 and 3).

To the east of the corridor, postholes B[661] and B[675] and beam slot B[562] may indicate the position of an east–west wall dividing another two small room areas, Room 4 to the south and Room 5 to the north. A new beaten earth floor lay to the north of beam slot B[562] in what may be

Fig. 32 View looking west, showing the small furnace B[641] built against the north wall B[920] of the bath house (to the left); part of the furnace's collapsed roof structure seals the remains; the furnace, which was established in Period 3 and modified in Period 4.2, may have heated a water-tank directly above (scale 0.5m)

Room 5. The northern wall of Building 3b, which would have defined the northern sides of Rooms 3 and 5, was completely truncated.

A rubbish pit B[560] (not illustrated) truncated the remains of the earth floor within Room 5 and may be related to the end of Building 3b's use. Pottery from the pit was dated to AD 270–400.

Period 4.3 land uses

Temporary disuse of the bath house (Building 4) and continued use of service yard (Open Area 6) and winged building (Building 3c)

The bath house sub-floor areas (Building 4) may have been subject to flooding and temporary disuse during Period 4.3, although the service yard (OA6) appears to have continued in use and the winged building further to the north was once again modified as Building 3c (Fig. 33). The external area to the north of Building 3c presumably continued in use at this time (OA7).

Once again, there was no evidence for definitely contemporary activity on Site A to the west, where the use of Building 5 and OA8 may have continued (see Period 4.1).

Flooding of the bath house (Building 4)

A dark brownish-black organic silt up to 0.20m thick was deposited around the *pilae* stacks and covering the sub-floor of the various room areas of the bath house. This fine silty sediment is thought to have been waterborne, indicating that ground or surface water penetrated and flooded the hypocaust system, presumably during a time of poor maintenance, possibly leading to a period of disuse. Sample B{44} from the silt layer contained numerous redeposited frog bones (see Chapter 3.9).

Retention of the service yard (Open Area 6)

The service yard to the north of the bath house seems to have been relaid with a compacted silty sand and gravel, which survived in truncated patches. The yard surface was truncated by an east–west orientated drainage gully B[653]. A probable refuse pit B[634] was identified immediately to the north of the gully. In the southern part of the service yard the surface was cut by several postholes and three pits B[436], B[397] and B[391].

Winged building north of service yard (Building 3c)

Further modifications were made to the building to the west and north of the service yard, and these are described here as Building 3c (Fig. 33). Truncation meant that the northern and southern external walls of the new building were not found, but these probably continued to occupy broadly the same positions as in Building 3b. The most prominent evidence for the existence of Building 3c is

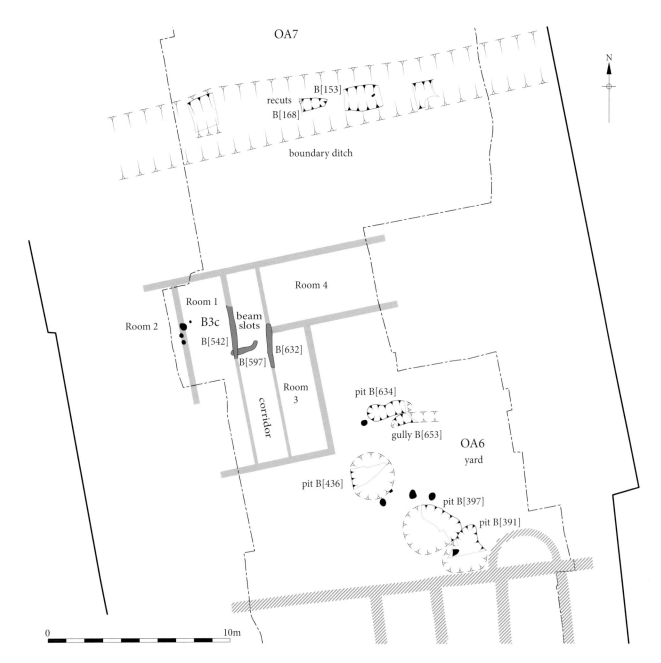

Fig. 33   Principal activity assigned to Period 4.3: flooding of the bath house B4, Building 3c, service yard OA6 and a boundary ditch further to the north in OA7 (scale 1:200)

a north–south aligned corridor. It was situated on the approximate line of the Period 4.2 corridor but was wider, as defined by beam slots B[542] to the west and B[632] to the east.

A north–south alignment of postholes identified to the west of the corridor may represent an internal partition between small Rooms 1 and 2. One small patch of beaten earth floor survived in this area, to the west of the corridor. Remnants of floor make-up capped by a beaten earth floor were identified to the southeast in a possible Room 3. A fragment of beaten earth floor in the northeast may represent part of Room 4 and appears to have been relaid before being sealed by a destruction layer rich in fragments of charcoal and broken roof tile, perhaps suggesting that the building had suffered a fire. A rubbish pit B[484] (not illustrated) truncated the demolition debris.

External area and boundary ditch to the north (Open Area 7)

The northern part of Site B was heavily truncated, but it is assumed that the external area to the north of Building 3c must have continued in use. The east–west boundary ditch which crossed the area was recut several times, so may have continued in use during this phase (see Fig. 33 and compare with Fig. 22).

An interesting find from a backfill of the OA7 boundary ditch recut B[153] in Period 4.3 was a fragment of a hipposandal B<570>, thought to have been used as a temporary horseshoe or as a protective covering for a horse's foot (Dixon and Southern 1992, 229). Iron punch B<15>, also found in the recut boundary ditch B[153], may have been a leather-working tool.

Period 4.4 land uses

Further modification of the winged building (Building 3d)

The Period 4.4 evidence is restricted to the further modification of the winged building to the north of the bath house, now renovated as Building 3d (Fig. 34). The service yard to the south (OA6) and external area to the north (OA7) presumably continued in use, although there was no surviving evidence that could be assigned to this phase.

Again, there was no evidence for contemporary activity on Site A to the west, where the use of Building 5 and OA8 may have continued (see Period 4.1).

Building 3d

Building 3c appeared to have undergone at least partial demolition and reconstruction as Building 3d (Fig. 34). Dumped layers of demolition material and silty sand levelled and raised the ground and were overlain by a sequence of floor make-ups and floors.

Building 3d included the continued existence of north–south internal corridor on much the same position as in the earlier phases. The corridor was represented by

parallel beam slots B[581] and B[587] set 1.20m apart (Fig. 35) The southern extent of the corridor was truncated, but to the north it intersected with an east–west wall line, represented by a series of postholes which were later replaced by a foundation trench filled with packed chalk fragments B[482]. A possible floor make-up deposit B[600] lay to the north of the east–west wall, suggesting that a 1.5m wide east–west passageway ran just inside the conjectured north wall of the building.

The two corridors defined two room areas, Room 1 to the west and Room 2 to the east, though truncation meant that the southern extent of these rooms remains unknown. Both rooms contained the remains of pink *opus signinum* floors 0.08m-0.10m thick. The floor surface in Room 1 lay at up to 4.37m OD and in Room 2 at up to 4.56m OD.

Room 2 also contained the remains of a hearth B[519], composed of a base of scorched, compacted silty clay overlain by horizontal fragments of tile. The Room 2 *opus signinum* floor was sealed by fragments of collapsed painted wall plaster, which may have been contemporary with the building (see Chapter 4.2).

A dump of wall plaster and trampled debris in the north–south corridor and a pit to the north may represent a short period of disuse or dilapidation of Building 3d.

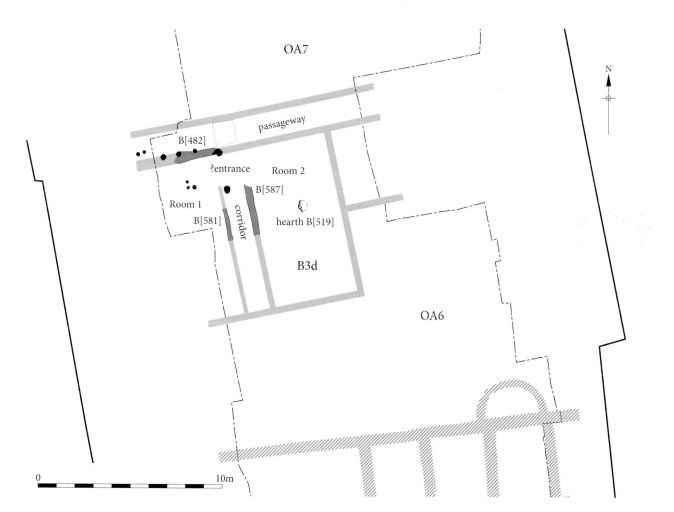

Fig. 34   Principal activity assigned to Period 4.4: Building 3d (scale 1:200)

Period 4.5 land uses

Further modification of the winged building (Building 3e)

The Period 4.5 evidence from Site B is once again restricted to the further modification of the winged building to the north of the bath house, now Building 3e (Fig. 36), though the service yard to the south (OA6) and external area to the north (OA7) presumably continued in use.

To the west, on Site A, there was some evidence for external erosion or hill slip (OA9) and fragmentary remains of a possible clay-and-timber building (B6, not illustrated), though this activity could be broadly contemporary with any of the Period 4.2–4.5.

Building 3e

A robber trench, pitting and dumps of demolition material (not illustrated) suggest that at least the west wing of Period 4.4 Building 3d was purposefully demolished. The ground was raised and levelled and a new building (B3e) erected on the footprint of the earlier structure (Fig. 36). The new building lacked the north–south corridor seen in several of the previous phases.

An east–west beam slot B[424] and associated postholes and stakeholes indicate the location of an east–west wall along the north side of the building. A north–south return wall is represented by beam slot B[493]. The north–south wall line partly defines two room areas.

In Room 1, to the west, there was a truncated beaten earth B[470] floor (not illustrated) and spreads of broken tile, chalk and *opus signinum* flooring forming a surface at 4.60m OD. To the east, in Room 2, a compacted silty sand *c.* 0.25m thick was the only remnant of the floor or floor make-up, at 4.70m OD. Some third-century pottery was recovered from contexts associated with Building 3e.

Fig. 35   View looking south across the fragmentary remains of Building 3d (Period 4.4); note the north–south corridor and *opus signinum* floors in rooms to either side (scales 2m, 1m)

External activity on Site A (Open Area 9)

External activity sealing the disuse of Building 5 (Period 4.1) consisted of gravelly silty sands up to *c.* 0.30m thick. These deposits may have been dumped or accumulations caused by erosion or hill slip of material from higher up the slope. The Period 4.1 east–west aligned drainage ditch, located in the far north of the area, may have been retained and continued in use (not illustrated).

Fragmentary evidence for a building (Building 6)

Overlying the slumped OA9 deposits were fragmentary and truncated traces of a series of possible brickearth walls for a building on the southern part of the site (B6, not illustrated) in the same location as earlier Building 5. The evidence included a wall line 0.30m wide and 1.50m long east–west, with a 1.0m long north–south return. A stretch of less substantial wall was recorded 1.50m to the southeast and was 0.16m wide surviving to 0.14m in height. Although these slight remains are clearly evidence for some kind of insubstantial building, further interpretation is difficult.

Period 4 discussion

Limitations to the evidence

Period 4 includes a total of five phases of activity taking place within a 50-year time span, from AD 275 to AD 325. Whilst it is clear that activity at Shadwell was particularly intense in the later third and early fourth centuries, it should be noted that the detailed phasing presented here might give an impression of a higher degree of precision in dating than the evidence can actually support. It is possible to identify up to five successive phases of building or modification in the winged building to the north of the bath house, at least two separate phases of activity within the baths themselves and two phases on Site A to the west. However, it is not feasible to identify with confidence how the various phases of activity on different parts of the site might relate chronologically, as the dating evidence is not precise enough to allow this. Five phases have been described, but as a mechanism to best present the evidence. It seems unlikely that there could have been five discrete phases across the entire area in such a short time period.

Period 4.1

Period 4 begins with a major renovation of the bath house complex on Site B (B4, B3a and associated external areas OA5, OA6 and OA7), whilst to the west on Site A there was evidence of external activity (OA8) and a clay-and-timber building (B5) (Fig. 22).

On the northern part of Site B the large east–west boundary ditch (OA7 retained) first identified in Period 3 was maintained and appeared to have been recut several times during Period 4 (Fig. 22). This indicates that the general property layout established earlier in the third century, when the bath complex was first built, was maintained for a considerable time. Pottery recovered from the ditch backfills included evidence for the importance of the Dorset (BB1) and Nene Valley pottery industries to the supply of ceramics to the London region during this period (see Chapter 3.1).

The bath house itself (Building 4) was extensively altered, at least at the sub-floor level. In terms of the overall footprint of the baths, at least one room was added, Room 10 to the north-west.

External areas to the south of the bath house close to the Thames (OA5) and in the service yard to the north (OA6) continued in use during Period 4.1. Pottery recovered from the external eaves-drip drains next to apsidal Room 14 on the north side of the bath house (OA6) is of particular importance as it is contemporary with the use of the baths and also appears to give some indication of the social activities associated with bathing. A significant number of vessels associated with the drinking of wine were present, which is perhaps not surprising given the activities that took place at the baths (see Chapter 3.1). It is notable that Site B produced a large number of glass vessels for drinking, though most of these were residual within later contexts.

A large clay-and-timber building (B3a) was established to the west and north of the service yard and, although largely truncated, occupied roughly the same footprint as Building 3 in Period 3. The use of *tegula/imbrex* roofing implies a shallow pitch of around 20–30°, allowing the tiles to be held in place by their own weight (Rook 1979, 295; Brodribb 1987, 10). The winged building may have served as accommodation for patrons of the bath house or have housed other associated functions. It may not be a coincidence that a stone mixing palette B<397>, possibly for mixing cosmetics, was recovered from the beaten earth floor B[687] in Room 3 of Building 3a (see Chapter 3.3).

On Site A, Building 5 extended beyond the south and east limits of excavation but presumably was restricted to any area lying to the west of a conjectured north–south access road and drainage corridor between the two sites (Fig. 22). The building measured at least 15m east–west and 6.50m north–south.

Evidence of what may be collapsed timber framing towards the western end of the building represents rare and important evidence for Roman timber building techniques. A simple line of posts represented the north wall of Building 5, providing evidence for walls built with earth-fast posts and covered by a woven wattle framework clad with daub and/or plaster, as seen at many other sites in *Londinium*. These walls may typically have stood to a height of 2m or more (Milne 1992, 78) and would have been strong enough to support a tile roof. No *tegula/imbrex* were recovered however, and the roofing material

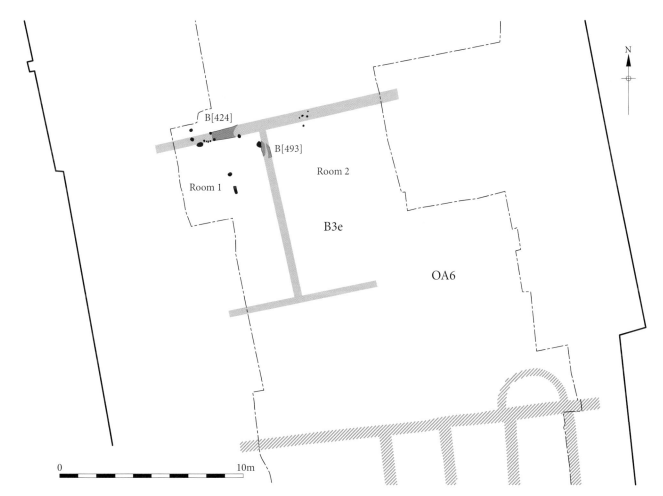

Fig. 36   Principal activity assigned to Period 4.5: Building 3e and external areas OA6 and OA7 on Site B (scale 1:200)

remains unknown, possibly thatch.

The evidence from Building 5 also suggests that at least some of the internal partitions were stud walls, that is, mortices were cut into the upper face of a beam to support timber uprights which held a framework of woven wattles subsequently packed with brickearth (Milne 1992, 78).

Overall, the excavated evidence from Shadwell indicates that the clay-and-timber buildings there were not of the highest standards but they do show signs of some refinement. The *opus signinum* floors recorded in some of the Building 3 phases would have provided a polished and waterproof surface and some rooms were decorated with painted wall-plaster (see below). Sherds of Roman window glass recovered from both sites suggest that at least some of the buildings were glazed, most likely the bath house.

The oven located just to the north-west of Building 5 may have been associated with it, as it is not uncommon to find ovens placed in adjoining yard areas to lessen the risk of fire (Ellis 2000, 159). The oven may indicate that at least part of Building 5 was used for food preparation, and a comparison of the pottery recovered from Site A with that from Site B seems to suggest that activities on Site A included more food preparation and consumption (see Chapter 3.1).

To the north of Building 5 several water supply or drainage features were recorded on the upper terrace (OA8). These included an east–west drainage ditch, in the far north of the site, which flowed to the east and may have carried surface water to a north–south drain and thence to the Thames. A well or cistern may have been associated with two physically separate sections of wooden drain to its south, and these may have supplied water to Building 5 or to a reservoir associated with the bath house to the east. Evidence from other sites in Roman London has shown that the largest wells incorporated continuous bucket and chain water-lifting systems and could extract large amounts of potable water (Blair *et al.* 2006). Although the wells and cisterns recorded at the Shadwell sites were much smaller, a few local wells connected to a network of timber drains could certainly have supplied sufficient water for the bath house and associated buildings, with water-lifting either done by hand or mechanically (see also discussion of *Castellum Aquae*, Chapter 4.2).

Pottery from the OA8 deposits spans a date range of AD 150–400 and is probably largely residual. The overall Site A dating evidence is inconclusive and suggests only that this activity could have taken place during the period AD 275–325.

Environmental information from Building 5 included a bulk soil sample A{295} taken from posthole A[1518] and sample A{334} from soil around the collapsed stud wall A[1648]. Both samples were relatively rich, with a range of well-preserved fruit seeds including *Rubus* sp. (brambles), *Ficus carica* (fig) and *Sambucus nigra* (elderberry), along with *Ranunculus* sp. (buttercup) and species from the *Apiaceae* (carrot) family. Although a relatively common find on Roman sites the presence of fig

seeds is of particular interest, as it is highly unlikely that they were indigenous and they are commonly believed to have been imported as a dried fruit (Willcox 1977; Tyers 1988). Some amphora types may have been suitable for the transportation of figs (see Chapter 3.1).

Elderberries and brambleberries are indigenous to Britain and their presence here and on other Roman sites is evidence that these fruits also supplemented the Roman diet. Soft fruits are considered too fragile to transport over long journeys (Alcock 2001, 66) so they are likely to have grown locally, though it is not known whether they were cultivated. It is certainly possible however, that there would have been vegetable and herb gardens in the vicinity of Shadwell, growing a wide variety of plants both for culinary and medicinal purposes.

The Shadwell bath house would have been a major consumer of materials, including foodstuffs, and both production and preparation might have taken place nearby (see Chapter 3.6). Food preparation for the bath house might even have taken place at Site A, in and around Building 5, though this cannot be proven.

The animal bone assemblages also indicate that the pattern of food preparation and evidence for diet differed between Sites A and B. Although meat consumption on both sites was apparently dominated by beef and supplemented by mutton and pork, the choicest cuts seem to have been reserved for use at Site B. The bones of newborn lambs and suckling pig are found on Site B but not Site A. The high percentage of domestic fowl bone recovered from Site B also suggests a high-status diet. Hunted game, represented by the remains of hare, was only found on Site B and there was also a greater variety of fish.

Period 4.2

Period 4 witnessed repeated modification of the bath house and associated buildings in the complex (Fig. 25). The bath house itself (B4) underwent extensive renovation and remodelling, most of which was only evident from changes to the sub-floor layout of the hypocausts, though these changes may also have been mirrored by a rearrangement of the actual room areas above. In the southeastern part of the bath house the Room 5, 8 and 9 sub-floor airspaces were amalgamated into a single hypocaust. The south-central and southwest parts of the baths saw Room 4 and 7 amalgamated with Room 6 to the west and the Room 2 porch or entranceway to the south, creating a single large heating system. It is important to note that the arrangement of actual room spaces is not known and may not have mirrored the layout and alteration of sub-floor hypocausts, though it might be presumed that they did in at least some instances.

These changes to the heating arrangements may have necessitated the addition of new furnaces and presumably indicate some changes to the use of the rooms above. In the northern range of rooms, heated Room 12 may have been subdivided into Rooms 12 and 13. Rooms 10 and 11 remained unchanged, as did apsidal space Room 14.

A new entrance or portico may have extended south from Room 2 into OA5, perhaps extending access to the building. To the north of the baths, the service yard (OA6) continued in use. The winged building to the north and west of the service yard was at least partially rebuilt (B3b).

The repeated alterations of room areas and apparent expansion of the Shadwell bath house may have been driven by attempts to improve the overall design. The changes might also represent an attempt to cope with growing use. The expansion of the baths at Huggin Hill was cited as a strong indicator for a public role in the bath house facility (Rowsome 1999, 267).

Periods 4.3 and 4.4

Disuse deposits within the bath's sub-floor spaces and hypocausts are probably indicative of a short period of failed maintenance and possible disuse of Building 4. This may have coincided with an uncontrolled event such as a flood, or with planned activity, such as maintenance or renovation work.

Neither the Period 4.2 remodelling of the bath building nor the subsequent flooding and disuse episode can be related directly to the chronological sequence recorded elsewhere on Sites A and B in Period 4, such as the repeated modifications to the winged building to the north, and could be contemporary with any of the later phases of Period 4.

Building 3b, situated to the north and west of the service yard OA6, underwent significant rebuilding three more times, with B3c and B3d nominally assigned to Period 4.3 and 4.4, whilst B3e is treated as representing the final phase of activity in Period 4 (see below).

The repeated rebuilding seen in the Building 3a–3e sequence suggests that individual phases lasted for only a decade on average. Compared to other Roman London clay-and-timber building sequences, the frequency of rebuilding associated with Buildings 3a–3e does seem to be relatively rapid. Evidence from many sites, both to the north of the Thames and in Southwark, suggest that the lifespans of clay-and-timber varied from 10 to 30 years on average. One might speculate that the hillside slope and terracing at Shadwell led to increased difficulties with subsidence or erosion. It seems that floors in the winged building required very frequent patching and resurfacing, and this may have been due to subsidence. The repeated renewal of the floors in Building 3 also led to differences in level between adjacent rooms and may have necessitated more extensive renovation from time to time. A similar pattern of rebuilding has been noted elsewhere in Roman Southwark and *Verulamium* (Douglas 2007; Frere 1972, 15).

In other aspects, the clay-and-timber buildings recorded at Shadwell were largely similar to those recorded elsewhere in *Londinium*. The buildings were usually founded on a levelled site, where a brickearth slab 0.15–0.30m thick provided a building platform (Perring *et al.* 1991, 69). Various construction techniques were employed for the structure, which might involve timber sill-beams, earth-fast timbers set in postholes, or sills of brickearth or mudbrick built without any timber support, such as the possible *pisé* or mudbrick wall recorded in Building 3a.

Two finds recovered from deposits associated with Building 3d suggest that some of the rooms were quite lavishly furnished. Dumping B[521] contained a broken piece of a bone plaque B<349> which may be part of a furniture inlay or some form of mount, and a miniature bronze foot for a small box or other item B<302> (see Chapter 3.3).

Period 4.5

The latest extant Period 4 activity on Site B was represented by a final structural phase of the winged building to the north of the bath house (Building 3e). All of the phases of the building were relatively badly truncated but probably had roughly the same overall footprint, though the internal layout of rooms and corridors varied over time.

The remodelled bath house (Building 4) had probably continued in use after Period 4.2 and the subsequent flooding of its sub-floor, though there was no extant and datable evidence to demonstrate this beyond doubt within this period.

Later Period 4 activity on Site A is also difficult to date precisely but can be identified with external deposits post-dating the disuse of Building 5 (see Period 4.1). The remains of Building 5 were buried beneath a layer of soil that may have been associated with dumping or a more gradual accumulation of material due to hillside erosion or 'hill slip' down the slope (OA9, not illustrated). These external deposits may have accumulated at any time during Period 4.2–4.5.

A brickearth structure, built over the deposits that covered Building 5, was probably a short-lived building (B6). Pottery associated with the brickearth walls dated to AD 250–70 whilst pottery from layer A[1219] overlying the walls dated to AD 250–300.

Items of personal adornment in and around the Shadwell baths

Some of the small finds recovered from Period 4 deposits may provide insight into the status and wealth of Shadwell residents and visitors, and their day-to-day life. Hair pins were a relatively common find and begin to appear in the archaeological record from Period 4 onwards. All are of late Roman type (Fig. 37; see Chapter 3.3). On Site A, fourteen hair pins or fragments of hair pins were recovered from Period 4 or later deposits. All were made of bone except for one jet example A<380>, recovered from context A[817] in Period 5. A total of 87 hair pins were recovered from Site B and the overwhelming majority were found within the footprint of the clay-and-timber Building 3. Of these, 83 were bone, three were made of jet and one was of copper-alloy B<228>.

Hair pins were used by Roman women to keep their elaborate hair styles in place. The jet and metal examples are considered to be the more expensive and desirable types. The much larger representation of bone hair pins in the assemblage may suggest that many of the women at Shadwell were of relatively low status. The concentration of hair pins in Buildings 3a–3e might indicate that some of the associated rooms were used for dressing or entertainment.

Other items of personal adornment from Period 4 or later contexts included bracelets of either shale or copper-alloy, with the former dominating the assemblage by 3:1 (see Chapter 3.3). These items tended to be worn by women; the majority were found on Site B. Rubbish pit B[397] in Period 4.3 contained two shale bracelets, B<256> and B<257> (see Chapter 3.3). A fragment of shale bracelet B<380> was found incorporated into the Building 3d floor make-up B[600] (Period 4.4, not illustrated) and a copper-alloy bracelet B<368> was recovered from beam slot B[581] in Building 3d (see Chapter 3.3). Another fragment of a shale bracelet B<316> was recovered from the floor make-up layer B[470] (not illustrated) in Room 1 of Building 3e (Period 4.5).

Copper-alloy rings were found in Period 4 deposits on both Sites A and B. Ring A<579> came from make-up deposit A[1525] in Period 4.1. On Site B a copper-alloy finger-ring B<18> was recovered from a recut to the boundary ditch B[168]. The ring is of a type that dates from the late second century until the end of the third century. A copper-alloy finger-ring B<335> was also recovered from the floor make-up B[470] in Room 1 in Building 3e (Period 4.5). Two further examples A<259> and B<39> and B<40> were residual finds from post-medieval deposits. Either men or women could have worn finger-rings and again these items attest that some of the inhabitants, if not of the highest levels of society, were aspiring to status.

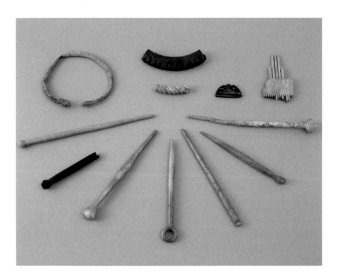

Fig. 37   A selection of items of personal adornment and grooming recovered from Site B contexts and perhaps associated with use of the bath house: copper-alloy bracelet, shale armlet fragment, ivory armlet fragment, jet armlet bead, fragment of bone comb and hair pins

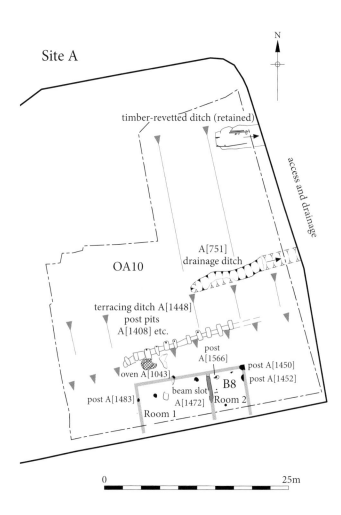

Fig. 38   Principal activity assigned to Period 5.1: alterations to the bath house (B4), adjacent external areas (OA5; OA6) and a small building to the north (B7; OA7), and to the west on Site A external activity (OA10) and a small building (B8) (scale 1:500)

2.5 Activity between *c.* AD 325–375 (Period 5)

Period 5 land uses

The Shadwell sites continued to be intensively occupied until the mid to late fourth century. Much of this activity was associated with the further alteration and use of the Site B bath house complex (B4) and adjacent external areas to the south (OA5) and north (OA6), along with a fragmentary building (B7) and external activity further north (OA7). Occupation to the west at Site A may have been contemporary and was made up of external activity (OA10), followed by the establishment of a building (B8) and a yard to its west. Together, the land uses from the two sites are interpreted as Period 5.1 (Fig. 38).

Period 5.2 is represented by further external activity on Site A (OA11) and the establishment of another building (B9) (see Fig. 47). To the east on Site B the bath house (B4) and adjacent external areas (OA5–7) may have been retained in use during this time.

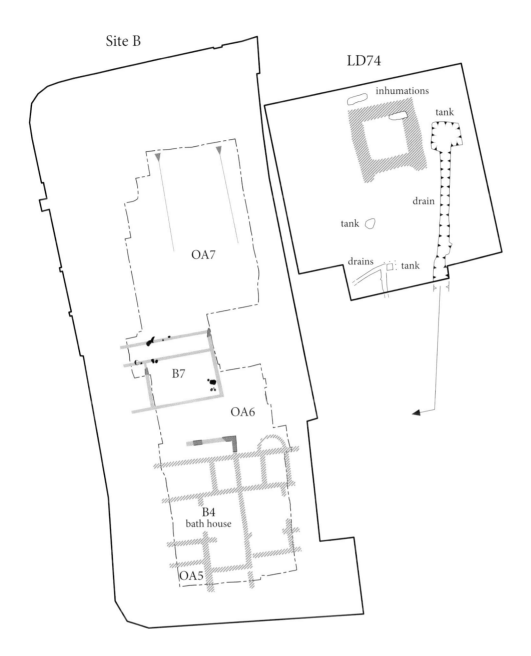

Site B

LD74

inhumations

tank

drain

tank

tank

drains

OA7

B7

OA6

B4
bath house

OA5

Period 5.1 land uses

Period 5 includes the final phase of alterations to the bath house (B4) on Site B, as well as the replacement of the Period 4 sequence of winged buildings to its north, Buildings 3a–3e, with Building 7 (Fig. 38; Fig. 39).

Alterations to the bath house (Building 4)

Construction of heated Room 15

Additional changes were made to the layout of the bath house (Building 4) during Period 5. The most major extant physical change was the addition of a new heated room area (Room 15) along part of the northern side of the building (Fig. 38; Fig. 39). This extension can be demonstrated stratigraphically to post-date the Period

4.3 sub-floor flooding, and represents the final major modification to the baths that was identified within the limits of excavation.

The construction of the new room required the digging of a vertically-sided construction trench B[905] for wall B[1251]. The wall formed the 2.10m long eastern end of the room and part of its north side, which was truncated to the west. The north–south aligned eastern part of wall B[1251] butted up to the north face of wall B[920]. The east–west aligned northern side of the room survived for a distance of 1.84m, though the construction trench and backfill could be traced for up to 8m and suggest the wall returned south to abut the earlier northern wall of the bath house. The wall B[1251] superstructure was 0.70m wide, the thickest identified in Building 4, and was faced with *opus mixtum*. The foundations of wall B[1251] were not excavated but it was observed that the foundation

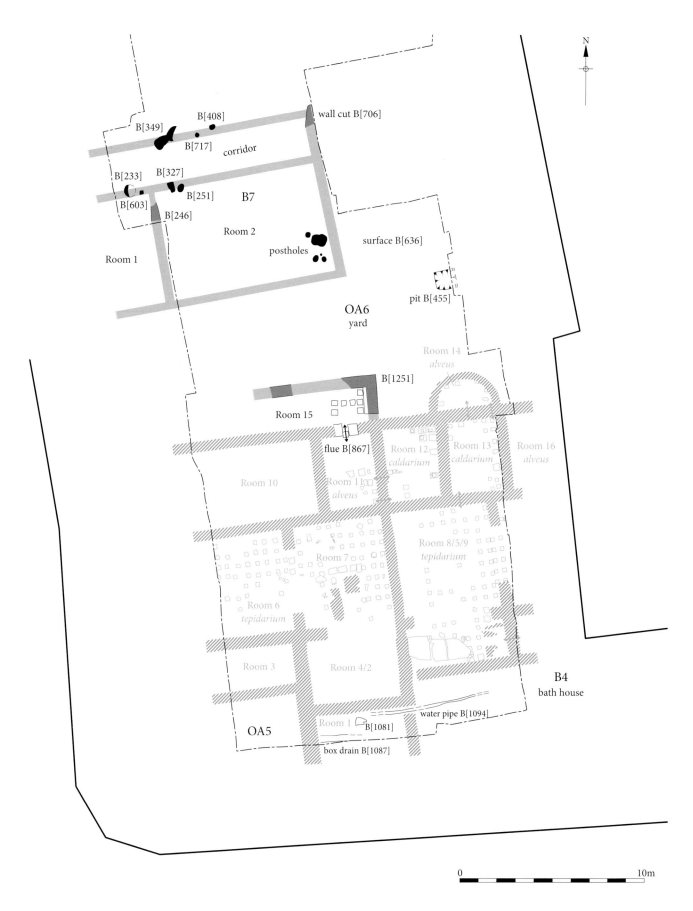

Fig. 39   Detailed plan of the final phase of the bath house (Building 4), adjacent external areas (OA5 and OA6) and Building 7 to the north (scale 1:200)

trench had been deliberately backfilled with a silty clay B[904]. The backfill was recorded at a maximum height of 3.47m OD, though it is not certain how this may have related to the contemporary ground surface in the service yard to the north of the baths. Clay B[904] was probably a deliberate lining intended to prevent surface or ground water from seeping through the wall and into the sub-floor areas of the bath house.

The Room 15 internal sub-floor space was connected to the main building via a new flue opening B[867] inserted through wall B[920] to allow heat through from the Room 11 hypocaust (Fig. 40). The construction cut for the flue measured 0.63m wide. Tile abutments backed by rubble and mortar packing created a flue opening 0.35m wide. The top of the flue was truncated but the base is formed of a single *pedalis* at 2.93m OD.

The hypocaust in Room 15 had a gravel sub-floor B[856] at 2.91m OD, which formed the base for *pilae* stacks, some of which survived at the eastern end of the internal sub-floor area (Fig. 41). The *pilae* are constructed primarily from *bessales*, stacked on top of single *pedalis* bricks. Two of the stacks include reused half-box-flue tiles (Fig. 42). Unusually both examples were complete, measuring 0.34m by 0.26m (see Chapter 3.4).

Other structural changes to the baths: Rooms 1 and 14

The heating flue which served the apsidal Room 14 to the east of Room 15 was deliberately blocked at some point during the later life of the baths, perhaps at the same time that Room 15 was added, though this cannot be proven. The flue was blocked with 13 courses of brick fragments and stone in a matrix of mortar (see Fig. 16). Room 14 may have remained in use, perhaps as an unheated space, as there is no evidence for demolition or robbing, although there is no evidence for the smaller, higher, flues formed of *tubuli* being blocked.

To the south of Building 4, a mortar bedding layer was overlain by horizontally laid tile fragments to form a floor surface B[1081] at 2.33m OD. The floor was badly truncated and only survived in a small, physically isolated patch, but may indicate the modifications to the room area on the south side of the building (Room 1). There are problems with this floor level and interpretation of Rooms 1, 2 and 4 and the possible access point to the building. Several possible alternative secenarios are presented below (see Chapter 4.2), though none is totally satisfactory.

Retained elements of the baths

Much of the Period 4.2 layout of the bath house was apparently retained in Period 5 (Fig. 39; Fig. 43). This included the amalgamated heated areas to the southeast and southwest. In the north-western part of the baths Room 10 was retained, and Room 11 continued in use, albeit with a flue which connected it to the new addition Room 15. The northeastern part of the bath house saw the continued use of heated Rooms 12 and 13, and an existing internal space can also be inferred to the east (Room 16).

External activity to the south of the bath house (Open Area 5)

To the south of the bath house an east–west aligned wooden water pipe B[1094] was laid in the bottom of a 0.40m-deep trench (Fig. 39). The pipe trench cut through wall B[1074] near the northeastern corner of Room 1 of the baths.

The drain pipe was partly decayed and compressed but intact in places and was lifted to allow more detailed examination, where it could be seen that timber components B[1283] and B[1284] were sections of a bored oak pipe with an original bore of around 75mm diameter. The oak pipe was made from two sections of radially and tangentially cleft oak log, taken from the inner and outer sections of a cleft one-eighth section of log. The rough cleft section of B[1284] had axe cut marks from very rough trimming. Better-preserved cleft log pipes have been found at several other sites in Roman London, where they were used to supply clean water, with the timber pipe sections clamped and joined by iron collars. Pipe section B[1283] was 1.45m long, which is rather longer than sections recorded elsewhere in the City of London.

The pipe B[1094] was recorded over a distance of approximately 5m and sloped from 2.12m OD in the east to 2.01m OD in the west, draining into Room 1. This suggests that it may have supplied clean water into this room.

To the southwest, within the conjectured area of Room 1, a truncated 1.50m stretch of an east–west aligned timber box drain B[1087] was also recorded (Fig. 44). The box drain had a plank base and oak plank sides supported by oak roundwood stakes, and may originally have had cross-bracing and a plank lid. The provision of the bored oak pipe entering the room and the timber box drain suggest that this part of the bath house was supplied with water. One of the stakes associated with the drain provided a tree-ring date of AD 235-262 (see Chapter 3.8).

Service yard to the north of the bath house (Open Area 6)

The service yard to the north of the bath house, first recorded in Period 3 and used throughout Period 4, was retained in use (OA6). The yard survived as a number of truncated patches of compacted silty clay and silty sandy gravel B[636] etc, creating a new surface between 4.39–4.58m OD (Fig. 39).

Surface make-up B[636] contained a shale bracelet B<475>, whilst another shale bracelet B<109> was recovered from make-up deposit B[617] (see Fig. 89.8, Chapter 3.3). Several small rubbish pits cut into the surface of the yard and might relate to a decline in maintenance. Pits B[388] and B[455] encroached on the eastern and western sides of the yard. Pit B[555] contained backfills which produced bone hair pins B<361> (see Fig. 90.9, Chapter 3.3), B<359> and B<360> (not illustrated).

A small building to the north of the service yard (Building 7)

Period 4.5 deposits associated with the disuse of Building 3e were overlain by dumped demolition debris up to 0.40m thick. The debris was composed of silty sand mixed with fragments of *opus signinum*, chalk, crushed mortar, broken tile, burnt daub, wall plaster and oyster shell. The dumping served to level and raise the ground surface for construction of a new building (B7).

Two parallel east–west aligned walls were set *c.* 2.50m apart and define a possible internal corridor in Building 7 (Fig. 39). The south wall of the corridor was represented by three post-pits B[233], B[327], B[251] and a posthole B[603]. Two of the post-pits contained chalk and sandstone post-packing. The north wall line was formed from post-pit B[349] and postholes B[717] and B[408].

The corridor extended beyond the western limit of excavation but may have extended eastwards to meet a north–south orientated wall foundation B[706], recorded just inside the eastern limit of excavation. Foundation B[706] was composed of compacted sandy silt and chalk rubble. The foundation was set in a cut 0.54m wide but only 0.08m deep. It was truncated to the south and east.

To the west, a north–south aligned beam slot B[246], set to the south of the east–west corridor described above, may represent a dividing wall between rooms to the west (Room 1) and east (Room 2). The surviving beam slot was 0.45m wide and 0.19m deep, continuing beyond the southern edge of the excavation. Small patches of truncated beaten earth floors survived within the room areas between 4.84m OD and 5.03m OD.

The overall extent of the building is not known and no external walls could be positively identified. A group of postholes, post-pits and stakeholes, cutting into the northern edge of the yard surface, were roughly aligned with a possible eastern side of the building that incorporated wall B[706] in the north.

Three rubbish pits cut into the floors of Building 7 and may mark its disuse.

Fig. 40   Flue B[867] inserted through wall B[920], connecting Room 11 to Room 15, Period 5.1; view looking north (scale 1m)

Fig. 41   View of Period 5.1 addition of Room 15, looking east; the hypocaust *pilae* stacks include use of rare half-box-flue tiles in stacks B[854] and B[855] in the lower foreground; a box-flue tile can be seen in situ in the northeast corner of the room, where it would have channelled hot air up the inside of walls B[1251] (scale 1m)

Fig. 42   Close-up of the half-box-flue tiles B[854] and B[855] used in the Room 15 hypocaust *pilae* stacks

External activity on the northern part of Site B (Open Area 7)

The northern part of Site B was heavily truncated but it is assumed that the area remained external during Period 5 and that OA7 was therefore retained in use.

External activity on Site A to the west (Open Area 10)

To the west of the bath house complex, extensive dumped deposits were recorded across the southern part of Site A, covering the remains of Building 6 (Fig. 38). This mix of silt, sand and gravel may have been colluvial action associated with erosion or 'hill slip', or intentional dumping to consolidate and raise the ground surface (OA10). On the western part of the site the ground surface sloped from 6.23m OD in the central part of the site down to 3.61m OD in the south, a slope of *c.* 1:6.

Fig. 43   General overhead view of the Shadwell bath house (Building 4) uncovered within the Site B area; note the surviving large fragments of a suspended floor above the hypocaust in Room 5 in the lower foreground; view looking north-west; compare with the Period 5.1 plan, Fig. 39 (scale 2m)

Pottery and coins recovered from the dumping indicates that it took place after AD 325. A total of eleven third or fourth-century coins were recovered from layers A[856], A[654] and A[800] (not illustrated), with the latest coin A<362> dating to AD 364–378.

The OA10 slope was stabilised by construction of an east–west aligned terrace revetment. This involved the digging of a ditch A[1448] at least 15m long, 0.75m wide and 0.30m deep. The sides of the ditch sloped to a concave base at 4.27m in the west and 4.21m OD to the east. Compacted silty sand filled the ditch, which had a genuine western terminus but extended beyond the eastern limit of excavation.

East–west ditch A[1448] may represent a boundary ditch or property division as well as enabling works for a land revetment (Fig. 45). The revetment was represented by eleven post-pits set 1.5m–2m apart. The post-pits were all rectangular in shape with rounded corners and vertical sides. All of the post-pits were orientated north–south and measured *c.* 0.88–1.5m north–south, 0.5–0.8m wide and 0.80 to 1.38m deep. The bases of the post-pits lay between 3.25–3.62m OD. Post pipes were recorded in some of the pits and suggest that they had held timber posts, at least some of which were held in

position by chalk packing.

Approximately 5m to the north of this land revetment, and aligned parallel with it, was an east–west drainage ditch A[751]. The ditch had a butt-end to the west and was truncated to the east, but was at least 10.2m long. It was 0.66m wide at its western terminus, widening to 1.56m in the east, and was 0.86m deep. The cut had steeply sloping sides and an even base that sloped from 5.17m OD in the west to 5.09m OD in the east. Stakes and postholes lined the sides of the ditch but there was no trace of horizontal timbers and these uprights may have held wattle hurdles in place to support the sides of the drain. The fill of the ditch was a dark grey clay A[942] overlain by a silty sand gravel A[750], the latter containing a copper-alloy penannular bracelet A<378>. Two postholes might indicate a second phase of revetting of the ditch, followed by a final fill of dark green brown silty clay A[862]. This uppermost fill contained two bone hair pins A<381> and A<382>, coin A<401> dated AD 270–290 and coin A<402> dating to the third or fourth century, as well as some fragments of copper-alloy A<383> and iron nails A<400>.

Further to the north, the Period 4.1 east–west aligned drainage ditch may have continued in use.

Fig. 44   Plank-lined box drain B[1087] Period 5.1; view looking west (scale 0.5m)

A building on the south of Site A (Building 8)

A new building (B8) was erected to the south of the land revetment, on the southern part of Site A (Fig. 38), with a layer of compacted brickearth forming a base for construction. The east–west aligned, northern side of Building 8 may be represented by a line of five surviving postholes. Post-pit A[1607] lay further to the west and may also have been associated with the same wall line. More substantial postholes may continue the line of the north wall of Building 8 at least as far west as posthole A[1485], with several of the postholes packed with stone and broken brick and tile. The eastern side of Building 8 was defined by post-pits A[1450] and A[1452].

A north–south aligned beam slot A[1472] formed an internal partition 0.50m wide and 0.29m deep, defining Room 1 to the west and Room 2 to the east. A sequence of floor make-ups and beaten earth floors were recorded in both room areas, with the highest floor surface at *c.* 3.81m OD. A trample layer of sandy silt and charcoal A[1341] represented occupation in Room 2.

Yard to the north-west of Building 8 (Open Area 10)

Remnants of brickearth stub walls A[1164] and A[1165] might indicate the position of an external oven or other small ancillary structure, located to the north of Building 8 and immediately south of the east–west timber land revetment (Fig. 45).

The brickearth-built structure was superseded by a sunken masonry feature which may also have been an oven and measured up to *c.* 2.0m east–west, 1.38m north–south and 0.28m deep. The feature's primary construction cut was obscured by a sequence of fills and recuts which indicated repeated use. The upper part of the oven sequence included a burnt brickearth slab sealed by a burnt daub bedding layer for a tile base A[1043]. Tile wall A[704] survived on the north side of the oven to a height of 8 courses. A rubble backfill of cobble-sized chunks of Kentish ragstone, sandstone and flint nodules lay behind the wall to the north (Fig. 46).

Fig. 45   View north across Site A, with a line of post-pits visible in the lower foreground related to an east–west revetment that stabilised the sloping ground

Fig. 46   The substantial remains of a large oven A[1043]/A[704] on Site A, Period 5.1; view looking east

Other activity adjacent to Building 8 and possibly associated with the same property, included rubbish pits A[1366] and A[1508] to the west.

The end of Period 5.1 activity on Site A is marked by the apparent demolition of Building 8 and destruction of the oven to its north, which was covered by debris and a spread of broken tile A[1044] that may have derived from the oven structure. A layer of broken brick/tile and chalk fragments A[1053] sealed the remains of Building 8. Pottery from this demolition layer dates to the fourth century.

Period 5.2 land uses

Continued use of the bath house (Building 4)

It is likely that the bath house (B4), adjacent external area to the south (OA5) and the service yard to the north (OA6) continued in use in Period 5.2, but the archaeological evidence for the bath house use could not be separated from Period 5.1 and is not separately illustrated.

Disuse of Building 8 and renewed external activity (Open Area 11)

External activity on Site A in Period 5.2 included dumping and the establishment of east–west and north–south aligned drains and water supply conduits (Fig. 47). The disuse of Building 8 may have been contemporary with the collapse of the Period 5.1 timber land revetment to its north, which would have allowed significant downslope erosion or hill slip. Building 8 demolition debris was sealed by a layer of sandy silt A[1307] which contained frequent fragments of tile, chalk and burnt timber.

The destruction layer A[1307] was particularly rich in small finds and included 23 coins (see Appendix 2). Although many of these were illegible, the latest, a coin of *Carausius*, <515>, provides a date of AD 286–293. There were also three bone hair pins A<508>, A<529> and A<532>, a glass gaming counter A<509> (see Fig. 84.1; Chapter 3.3), the handle of a ?key A<501>, some

unidentifiable scraps of copper-alloy A<524> and A<542>, part of an iron handle A<525> and a number of iron nails.

In the far north of Site A, a timber-lined east–west aligned ditch A[665] represents a recut of a long-lived drainage ditch first established here in Period 3 (Fig. 48). Pottery recovered from ditch A[665] suggests that it was filled in some time after AD 350. The ditch had a western butt-end and continued beyond the eastern limits of the excavation. It was 2.30m wide and 1.55m deep and survived to a maximum level of 6.31m OD. The sides of the ditch sloped steeply to a concave base that sloped from 5.18m OD in the west to 5.09m OD in the east. The sides of the ditch were revetted with horizontal planks held in place by stakes and posts to create a channel *c.* 1.0m wide. Eight of the postholes contained surviving tips of wooden posts. All the stake tips were hewn to square section points and came from small oak logs, the largest *c.* 100mm square.

Approximately 7.0m to the south of ditch A[665], part of the western side and possible north and south sides of a timber-lined cistern A[971] was recorded. The western side of the feature was 3.85m long and it was at least 1.80m wide and 0.75m deep. The feature was truncated to the east and south. Decayed timber planks set on edge lined the sides and were held in place by stakes and posts. A parallel

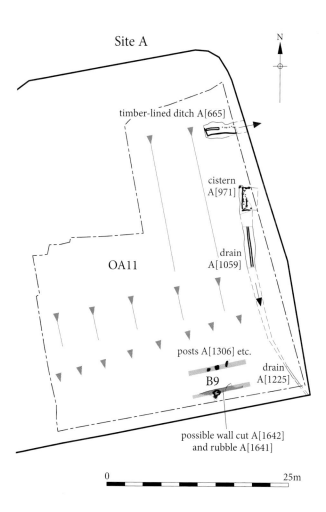

Fig. 47   Principal activities in Period 5.2, including an east–west ditch and north–south drain in OA11 and Building 9 (scale 1:500)

north–south plank lay 0.60m to the east of the western side of the cistern, though its purpose was uncertain. An east–west aligned plank across the southern end of the feature may have been part of a sluice which regulated the flow of water into a north–south drain running southwards.

Many of the post positions associated with the cistern contained the surviving tips of oak posts. Some of these piles were clearly reused, as shown by their weathered faces and redundant features, such as a blind mortice in pile A[1340], but others were freshly hewn. Three timbers originally thought to be part of this structure provided tree-ring dates of AD 228 indicating that they derived from an earlier structure in this location (see Period 3). The timbers were clearly not reused (see Chapter 3.7) and therefore must have survived *in situ*, being truncated by the construction of the tank. However, other driven timber piles, such as A[1340], bore clear evidence of reuse and yet examination of the axe signature marks on the tips of piles revealed that reused timber A[1340] and pile A[1352] were hewn with the same axe. Other piles had been hewn with different axes, and pile A[1360] had been cut with a blade over 85mm wide. It appears that in constructing tank A[971] an attempt was made to salvage and reuse as many piles as possible from an original surviving structure, or structures, though some timbers remained in the ground. It is tempting to suggest that the construction of tank A[971] marked the replacement of a similar earlier structure in the same location which had fallen in disrepair or decay, or become heavily silted.

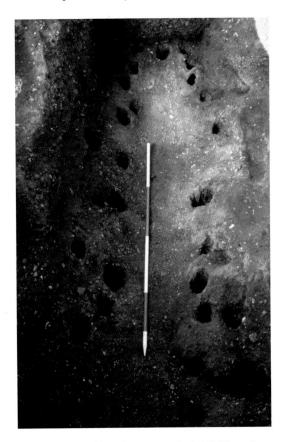

Fig. 48   The base of fourth-century ditch A[665] on the northern part of Site A (Period 5.2); view looking west towards the ditch's butt-end (scale 2m)

Fig. 49   Floor make-up layers associated with Building 9 on the southern part of Site A; view looking west (scales 2m)

About 2.0m south of the southern end of A[971] part of a north–south timber drain A[1057] was recorded. The construction cut for the drain was 1.40m wide and 0.90m deep. It contained a timber box drain which had a flat base and vertical sides, being 0.20m wide and at least 0.20m deep. A 5m length of the drain was recorded, truncated to both the north and the south.

In the southeast corner of the site another section of drain was found, consisting of a timber dugout drain A[1225] 0.17m wide and 0.07m deep, which extended beyond the southern limit of excavation. This drain had first been hewn into a rectangular section and then hollowed down the centre. It was probably originally covered by a plank lid. The proportions of this drain are closer to that of guttering than a typical dugout drain.

The three separate sections of cistern A[971], timber box drain A[1057] and dugout drain A[1225] may all be elements of a single gravity-fed conduit, channelling water southwards towards the Thames or into the bath house. The base of the proposed conduit slopes downwards from 4.60m OD in the north to 3.66m OD in the south, a fall of 0.93m over a distance of 28m or *c.* 1:30. However, it seems odd that the width of the water channel should decrease as the conduit progresses down the slope, and this, as well as the differences in construction, may indicate that they represent separate phases of repair along a single drain line. It may be worth noting that the narrowing of a water channel could be intended to increase the water pressure.

A small structure on the south of the site (Building 9)

At the extreme south end of Site A a new clay-and-timber building (B9) was built directly above the footprint of the Period 5.1 Building 8 (Fig. 47). Building 9 was badly truncated, but enough survived to say something of its layout. An east–west line of three substantial post-pits A[1306], A[1312] and A[1309], *c.* 0.45m deep and regularly spaced at 1.20m apart, may have formed part of the north wall of the new building. To its south was a truncated remnant of a beaten earth floor A[1243] at 3.86m OD (Fig. 49).

Fig. 50   Gold ear-ring B<240> B[383]

Approximately 4m south of the possible north wall of the building was a linear, east–west orientated cut A[1652] which might indicate the position of an internal wall, with the area to the south being cut to a lower floor level and extending beyond the southern limit of excavation. Rubble A[1641], located along this linear edge, may be the remnants of a collapsed wall.

A circular cut 1.0m in diameter and 0.28m deep, recorded further to the west at 4.36m OD, may have been a rubbish pit or a post-pit associated with a westward continuation of the north wall of Building 9. Overall Building 9 measured at least 7.50m east–west and 4.70m north–south, extending beyond the southern limit of excavation, and was probably divided into at least two rooms.

The possible collapsed internal east–west wall within Building 9 was covered by demolition debris A[1610]. Finds recovered from the debris included a pair of hobnail boots A<583> and A<584>, coin A<588> dated AD 270–290, jet bead A<589>, glass bead A<590> and nail fragments A<591>.

Period 5 discussion

Period 5 includes the final phase of alterations and use of the bath house (Building 4) and the associated external area to its south (OA5), service yard to the north (OA6) and the rebuilt possible accommodation block Building 7 to the north (Period 5.1).

The main extant evidence of physical alterations to the bath house is the addition of a new heated room area to the north-west (Room 15). The internal arrangements of the other room areas, represented mostly by the under-floor hypocausts, were apparently unchanged from Period 4. To the south of the baths in OA5 an east–west water pipe B[1094] may have supplied water to Room 1. To the north of the resurfaced service yard, the surviving evidence for

Building 7 included two room areas to the south of an east–west corridor. The pottery evidence from Period 5.1 is consistent with a mid fourth-century date and the coin evidence largely supports this dating.

A particularly rare coin B<200>, dating to AD 341–348, was recovered from a Building 7 post-pit B[251]. It is one of several unusual coins from the Shadwell sites, suggesting that the settlement was out of the ordinary (see Chapter 3.2). Dump B[386], covering Period 4 Building 3e, contained a notable but residual group of three silvered radiates B<268> dating to AD 270–285. It has been suggested that, because the coins had retained their silver wash, they were not in circulation for long before loss (see Chapter 3.2). Two groups of three coins each were found fused together in the fill of Period 5.2 timber drain A[1225]. The first group was identified after cleaning as three Tetrarchic *folles* and the second group, though it could not be separated, was of a similar size (see Chapter 3.2). This suggests that the drain fill contained a probably 'purse group' of six *folles,* dated to *c.* AD 296–306; these coins were quickly driven out of circulation and thus must be considered residual in this context. An iron leather-working awl B<272> was also recovered from B[386] (see Fig. 94.2; Chapter 3.3).

Some of the small finds are indicative of wealth and status, such as a residual first-century bow brooch B<231> from Building 7 posthole B[327] (see Fig. 87.4; Chapter 3.3), whose early date may suggest that the piece was an heirloom. A copper-alloy hair pin B<228> was also retrieved from the same posthole and silver finger-ring (B<204>) (see Fig. 87.1; Chapter 3.3) was found in pit B[294], which cut into the floors of Period 5.1, Building 7. A gold ear-ring B<240> came from Building 7 posthole B[717] (Fig. 50) (also see: Fig. 85; Chapter 3.3), whilst part of a gold and bead necklace B<33> (see Fig. 51; Chapter 3.3) came from a Site B post-medieval context.

Fig. 51   Six links and clasp from a gold and bead necklace B<33> B[180]

Although the evidence from excavations at LD74, to the northeast, suggested that a complete change in the use of the area had taken place by the mid fourth century, with earlier land uses replaced by industrial activity and possibly tanning (Lakin 2002, 22), there was no sign of such a drastic change at Sites A or B, where the use of the bath house and an associated residential building to its north continued into the later fourth century.

The identification of an industrial phase at site LD74 rests on the interpretation of three sunken timber structures as 'tanks' used in tanning hides. However, a review of the overall evidence may now indicate that their position and the location of associated drains suggests that these structures may in fact have been cisterns and associated features supplying water to the bath house (Fig. 38).

To the west of the bath house, on Site A, external dumping or erosion of the hillside slope (OA10) sealed Period 4 occupation levels before a terrace revetment was built to stabilise the ground and a new building was established on the southern part of the area (Building 8).

Colluvial deposition remained a problem at Site A in Period 5.2, as the disused Building 8 was also covered by debris (OA11). Drainage and water supply systems were established on the eastern side of the external area and a new building (B9) was established on the same footprint as Building 8. The pottery and coin evidence is consistent with this activity taking place in the middle decades of the fourth century.

Small finds from Site A included a copper-alloy needle A<365> recovered from OA10 dumping A[800]. Another uncommon find was a gaming counter A<509> from OA11 debris A[1307] (see Fig. 84.3; Chapter 3.3; neither layer illustrated).

Environmental column sample A{107} (Chapter 3.10, Fig. 111; Fig. 112) included Period 5.1 occupation deposit A[1427], which was overlain by Period 7 colluvial deposition and anthropogenic 'dumping' A[722] and A[721]. Column A{107} contained well-preserved pollen grains and spores, and the sequence is dominated by herbaceous pollen taxa, including Poaceae, Cyperaceae, *Taraxacum* type, *Polygonum aviculare*, *Ranunculus* type, *Trifolium* type and *Artemisia*. These indicate vegetation communities consisting of tall and short grassland, waste or disturbed ground and damp ground plant species. These communities are entirely consistent with areas in close proximity to human occupation. This interpretation is supported by the presence of cereal pollen and taxa strongly associated with cultivated fields (eg cornflower).

Further environmental evidence for the local vegetation cover in the middle of the fourth century was provided by column sample A{106} (Chapter 3.10, Fig. 113; Fig. 114) which was taken from the fill of the Period 5.2 ditch A[665] in the northern part of OA11 (see Fig. 110). It contained well-preserved pollen taxa throughout most of the sequence and provides a valuable insight into fourth century local vegetation cover and land use. The pollen assemblage contains a diverse range of taxa and is dominated by Poaceae (grass). They indicate an open vegetation cover with tall grassland (eg *Centaurea nigra*) and disturbed or waste ground (eg *Taraxacum* type). The evidence for cereal cultivation is compelling, but it is unclear whether the crops were cultivated locally or if the pollen was transported to the site within the bracts of hulled grains.

Further bulk samples were taken from selected deposits on Site A and originating in Period 5.1 and 5.2 (Branch *et al.* 2004b, 359). Period 5.1 samples included A{257}, A{259} and A{282}, all from layers. These assemblages contained a range of species, including charred *Hordeum* sp. (barley) grains, waterlogged *Rubus* sp. (brambles), *Sambucus nigra* (elderberry), and Chenopodiaceae (goosefoot) species. Charcoal was also frequent. Samples A{273}, A{304}, A{264}, A{325} and A{335} were from cut features, including postholes, ditches and pits, with fruit seeds the most prevalent species and both charcoal and waterlogged wood occurring in several samples (a fuller description of the samples can be found in Chapter 3.10).

Period 5.2 samples include A{38}, taken from the fill A[467] behind an area of timber planking in ditch A[665], contained a rich and relatively diverse assemblage including species from the Lamiaceae (dead-nettle) family, and other grassland species along with occasional charcoal and frequent wood. Sample A{101} from a fill of ditch A[751] provided a varied assemblage that included charred grain, *Sambucus nigra*, *Carex* sp. and other fruit seeds. Sample A{235} was predominantly *Sambucus nigra* and *Carex* sp., whilst sample A{307} contained purely *Sambucus nigra*.

The presence of seeds from the Lamiaceae family, which includes herbs like rosemary, thyme and dead nettle, highlights the importance of herbs to the Romans, both as flavouring in food and for their medicinal qualities. Herbs native to Britain could have been collected in the wild or cultivated in a kitchen garden (Alcock 2001, 69).

Cereals grown locally would probably included barley and wheat, as charred grains of both were found on Site A. Wheat was baked as bread and barley could also have been used in bread-making but may also have been used for brewing and as fodder for animals (Alcock 2001, 29).

2.6 Activity between *c.* AD 375–410 (Period 6)

Period 6 land uses

Occupation continued at both of the Shadwell sites until the end of the fourth century. On Site B, to the east, the bath house was abandoned and deposits of debris and dumping sealed the structure of the baths (OA13) but the fragmentary remains of a new timber structure (B10) were recorded to the north. To the west, on Site A, a relatively large building, including some masonry walls, was constructed in the south (B11) and external activity (OA12) was recorded on other parts of the site (Fig. 52).

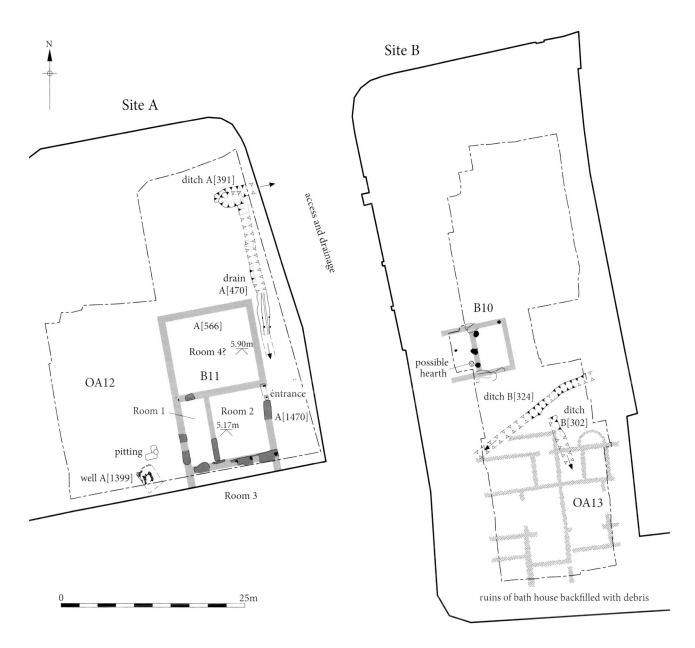

Fig. 52   Principal activity assigned to Period 6: debris associated with the disuse of the baths and other external activity (OA13) and a fragmentary timber structure (B10) on Site B and, to the west, a new building (B11) and external activity (OA12) on Site A (scale 1:500)

Abandonment of the bath complex and external activity (Open Area 13)

By far the most significant development in Period 6 was the abandonment of the bath house and its associated yards and structures. The bath house structure itself may have been the subject of a campaign of partial demolition and salvaging of valuable materials before the remaining ruins were dismantled or levelled. The general robbing and demolition of the bath structure is thought to have occurred in the sub-Roman or post-Roman period (see Period 7).

The service yard to the north of the bath house fell out of use and clayey-sandy silt was allowed to accumulate

over its surface. The area may have become susceptible to flooding and two substantial ditches were cut into the former yard, dissecting it. Ditch B[324]/B[330] ran northeast-southwest, whilst a second ditch B[302] lay slightly to the south and was aligned north–south. The ditches, which were up to 1.10m wide and 0.55m deep, would have drained surface water southwest and south towards the Thames.

Ditch B[324]/B[330] was deliberately backfilled with oyster shell, chalk and crushed mortar in a soil matrix. A fragment of an iron water pipe junction collar A<580> and bone hair pin B<223> were found in the ditch (see Fig. 90.5; Chapter 3.3). Pottery recovered from fill B[379] of the ditch was dated to AD 375–400.

Fragmentary evidence for a timber structure (Building 10)

To the north of the former service yard area, a trample layer of clayey silt B[250] and demolition debris B[476] covered much of the footprint of the Period 5.1 Building 7. A large sub-rectangular pit B[249] (not illustrated) may have been associated with the building's demolition.

A series of post-pits and postholes provide evidence for a new timber-framed structure (Building 10) erected at the same location. A 4.0m long, north–south line of post-pits may indicate the position of a wall line, whilst a single posthole offset 2.50m to the west may be part of the same structure. A possible hearth was located immediately to the west of the north–south line of post-pits.

Immediately to the north of the post-pits was a curvilinear east–west aligned cut B[289]/B[319] and a later post-pit B[223], which may represent an east–west return wall, although the cut could also represent a drainage ditch intended to channel surface water away from the structure.

Scattered rubbish pits of various sizes indicate the disuse of structure B10. The pit fills were characterised by mixed fills that contained fragments of wall plaster, *opus signinum*, chalk, tile, oyster shell, charcoal, animal bone and sherds of pottery. A fill of pit B[197] contained a fragment of an ivory armlet B<77> (see Fig. 88; Fig. 89.1; Chapter 3.3). The same pit contained a small group of late fourth-century pottery, several residual coins and coin B<65>, which is dated AD 365–380.

Building 11

On Site A, to the west, the Period 5.2 Building 9 was demolished and a new and relatively substantial building (B11) was erected, constructed at least in part with masonry foundations (Fig. 52). The extant remains include the foundation of what may be the building's west wall, which was 0.60m wide and 0.40m deep, composed of ragstone and tile in a matrix of mortar. Foundation A[1470] formed the building's east wall and was 0.66m wide and 0.59m deep, made up of sandy gravel, and fragments of chalk, ragstone and tile. Two large post-pits, one containing a decayed timber post, were set *c.* 1.50m apart and were located on the eastern wall line. The posts may indicate the position of a doorway to Building 11.

A group of three post-pits might define the north-west corner of the building, though it should be noted that they were cut from *c.* 5.47m OD, significantly higher than the foundations recorded to the south, suggesting that the building may have had a split floor level that stepped up the terraced slope.

A layer of gravelly sand A[799] formed a surface at 5.17m OD within the postulated southern area of Building 11, as defined by the eastern and western wall lines described above. Further to the north there were other surfaces, including a beaten earth floor A[556], at 5.98m OD and possibly associated with an upper terrace room area in the same building or a separate structure.

Although the full extent of Building 11 could not be determined, it measured at least 12.50m east–west and 10.0m north–south, extending beyond the southern limit of excavation.

Internal wall lines and features provide some idea of the layout of Building 11. Four metres to the east of what may have been the western wall of the building, was a north–south beam slot. To its south was east–west aligned brickearth wall. A horizontal timber A[1138] 2.85m long, 0.28m wide and 0.16m thick was found near the east–west partition line and appeared to have eroded joints on its underside, suggesting that it was a reused base plate or had been discarded when the partition was removed.

It seems probable that Building 11 was partitioned into at least three separate rooms. A large room, Room 2, measuring 9.0m north–south by 6.75m east–west, may have been present on the eastern side of the building, with an external doorway to its east. On the west side of the building the wall alignments suggest a narrower room, Room 1, *c.* 3.20m wide. The evidence suggests at least one other room, Room 3, to the south of the east–west partition and lying beyond the limit of the excavation.

The building remains were covered by a layer of debris A[1139]. This disuse deposit produced thirteen coins. The coins predominantly date to the third/fourth century, but three are Constantinian and date to the mid fourth century. A bone needle A<456> and a gaming counter A<446> were also recovered from A[1139] (see Chapter 3.3, Fig. 81; Fig. 84.2). Rubbish pit A[1643] also cut into the remains of Building 11 and may post-date its disuse. Pottery from the pit fills dates to AD 370+.

External activity (Open Area 12)

Scattered external activity was recorded across Site A (OA12). Sandy silt layers in the west-central part of the site may have been the product either of colluvial erosion or deliberate dumping. Elsewhere, stone backfill in the Period 5.2 north–south drain A[971] seems to indicate that it was deliberately filled in. The Period 5 drains were replaced by a new north–south drain along the east side of the site A[470]. This heavily decayed timber box drain was 0.20m wide and lay on the base of a wider ditch A[469]. The ditch was revetted by timber planking at least 0.37m high, held in place by driven posts.

Further to the north the Period 5.2 east–west aligned drainage ditch A[665] was also recut, suggesting that it remained an important weapon in the battle to prevent surface run-off and erosion. Ditch recut A[391], fill A[369] contained the rim of a copper-alloy vessel A<179>, whilst a piece of pottery reused as a gaming piece A<188> came from fill A[378] (see Chapter 3.3).

In the southwestern part of the site, just to the west of Building 11, two successive construction cuts contained timber-lined well A[1399] (Fig. 53). Pottery from the construction cut backfill A[1373] provides a *terminus post quem* for the construction of the well of *c.* AD 350 (see Chapter 3.1, key group 4). The well was lined with interlocking timbers that formed a structure 1.0m square at the top and *c.* 1.0m deep. The base of the well was only 0.47m².

The well-lining was very crudely constructed from a mixture of materials, some of which were clearly reused. There appeared to be two phases of construction and repair. The principal elements were a lining of small assorted, sawn oak planks wedged in place by small oak piles that were either round or minimally hewn to sub-rectangular sections. A group of narrow but thick planks in the well-lining appear to have come from the same or similar sawn baulks. Plank A[1717] was *c.* 230mm wide and 60mm thick, hewn on one side and sawn on the other. The axe marks show that an axe blade *c.* 70mm wide was used to hew a square baulk by swinging it along the grain. The baulk was then marked out and sawn into four thick but relatively narrow planks with sapwood left in places. The parent tree(s) were relatively young at *c.* 55 years old and relatively fast grown, and the parent log would have been *c.* 0.4m diameter at the mid length. These relatively small planks are in general most typical of later Roman woodwork.

At the top of the well, roughly cleft logs were used to form a sort of kerb and included a small halved beech log A[1637], one of several beech items from the well. There was tentative evidence for one or more wattle fences around the well head, represented by a scatter of small stake tips and fragments of roundwood.

Upon disuse, the well was deliberately backfilled with clayey silts capped by dumped flint nodules, tile and sandstone.

Also lying to the west of Building 11, and to the north of the well, was a series of three intercutting pits which may have been associated with votive offerings. The earliest pit A[967] was rectangular with vertical sides and a flat base, its north side consolidated with tile/brick A[1166]. The pit was truncated by an east–west aligned pit A[860] of a similar shape and size. The basal fill of the second pit produced pottery dating to AD 350–400 and two coins A<408> dated AD 321–4 , and A<409> dated AD 364–375. Circular pit A[937] truncated both of the rectangular pits and contained complete pot A<406>, dated to AD 350+, which had been placed on a bed of sandy clayey silt and covered with sandy clayey silt A[903].

Period 6 discussion

Roman occupation continued into the late fourth century and probably into the early fifth century. Although the bath house on Site B had fallen out of use, other structural activity continued and included a fragmentary timber structure (B10) on Site B and a larger building (B11) on Site A to the west.

The abandonment of the bath house may have been accompanied by the disuse of the service yard to its north (OA6) and the possible accommodation block represented by Building 7, which also seems to have been demolished

at the beginning of Period 6. The service yard itself was neglected and dissected by ditches (OA13). Post-pits overlying the location of Building 7 provide very tentative evidence for a crude new stucture (B10), which is unlikely to have been in the same tradition as the clay-and-timber buildings recorded in Periods 3–5.

It is not possible to identify the precise date that the bath building fell out of use, although the evidence from the destruction or abandonment of associated structures and features suggest that it is likely to have occurred before AD 375. The absence of fixtures and fittings, including lead pipes, metal water tanks and brackets, either *in situ* or amongst the demolition rubble, suggests that these are likely to have been stripped prior to the dismantling or demolition of the building (see Period 7). Given the relative value of some of the piping and other materials likely to be found in the bath house, it seems probable that salvage stripping took place quite soon after abandonment, although general robbing may have been much later.

The animal bone assemblage from Period 6 contexts at Site B indicates an increase in the exploitation of local wildfowl such as geese and ducks, and the keeping of pigs and hens, perhaps in individual 'backyards'.

A large pit B[204] on Site B contained roughly squared blocks of greensand, Kentish ragstone and chalk as well as a large block of weathered oolitic limestone. The stone probably originated from the destruction of nearby buildings. It may be noteworthy that the final phases of the 'tower' sites, LD74 and LD76 to the northeast, were marked by an extensive spread of masonry rubble and other debris thought to have derived from a domestic building beyond the limits of those sites (Lakin 2002, 23). The coin evidence suggested that the demolition debris was deposited in or after AD 365 and the large quantity, mixed nature and wide scatter of the demolition material was thought to be an indication of deliberate demolition rather than gradual decay (Lakin 2002, 24).

A new north–south drain was established along the east side of Site A, running south towards the Thames. An east–west timber drain on the far northern part of Site A was recut and maintained as ditch A[391], continuing a long-lived drainage feature. Environmental samples A{17} from context A[369] and A{18} from context A[378] are both from ditch recut A[391]. Both contain charred wheat grains, along with waterlogged *Sambucus nigra* and seeds from the Lamiaceae family. Sample A{24} from context A[414] in ditch A[415] also contains frequent *Sambucus nigra*, along with other wild fruit seeds and grassland species.

A crudely built timber-lined well cut A[1399] (timbers A[1760]) was recorded on the southwestern part of the site (Fig. 53). A pottery assemblage from the lowest well fill A[1615] confirmed the very late date of the well and indicated that Shadwell continued to maintain long distance trade contacts, importing exotic produce until the end of the Roman occupation (see Chapter 3.1, key group 5). The final backfilling of the well may represent 'ritual closure' of a feature that marked a liminal location and

Fig. 53   View south towards a Period 6 timber-lined well A[1399] in the southwest corner of Site A

could have had a supernatural significance between this world and the 'underworld'. The large number of complete or semi-complete vessels recovered from the lower well fill may be an indication of ritual, and the preponderance of Oxfordshire fine wares in the upper fill A[1281] may be evidence for 'feasting' (see key group 6, Chapter 3.1). A copper bowl A<596> retrieved from the lower fill A[1615] may also be significant. Nearby pits may also have contained structured deposits.

Of the coins recovered from Period 6, most were residual. Some 19 coins were found on Site A but only a Valentinianic coin A<409>, dated AD 364–378 and recovered from the basal fill of a possible ritual pit, is likely to have been in circulation at the time. Similarly, the 16 coins recovered from Site B included only three that dated to the second half of the fourth-century.

2.7 Sub-Roman activity after AD 410 (Period 7)

Period 7 land uses (not illustrated)

External activity on Site A (Open Area 12 continued)

On Site A, to the west, post-Roman deposits of dark grey sandy and clayey silts A[721] and A[722] up to 0.30m thick accumulated in the southern part of the area. These deposits contained fragments of Roman brick and tile, *opus signinum*, mortar, charcoal and oyster shell, as well as late third- or fourth-century pottery and twelve coins, which also date to the third and fourth centuries.

The post-occupation deposits that sealed the area formerly occupied by Building 11 produced the largest group of late Roman pottery recovered from Site A. The assemblage reflects the dominant position of the Alice Holt pottery industry in the supply of ceramics to Shadwell during the late Roman period.

External activity on Site B, including demolition and robbing of Building 4 (Open Area 13 continued)

Careful examination of the condition of the building material recovered from bath house demolition deposits, as well as the evidence of collapsed *pilae* in robber trenches, indicates that at least some elements of Building 4 were deliberately demolished in order to salvage particular types of building material, such as Kentish ragstone, but perhaps not others. The absence of more valuable materials from the demolition debris, such as metal, indicates that the building was probably stripped and robbed of any plumbing, flooring, glass, fittings and other bathing implements prior to demolition and robbing.

The floor in the small apsidal Room 14, on the north side of the bath house, was completely removed upon final disuse and the space filled with building rubble B[467] which included broken tile, lumps of chalk and *opus signinum* mortar mixed with a silty sand. Pottery recovered from B[467] dated to the late fourth century.

The more complete survival of the *pilae* around the periphery of the Building 4 room areas, close to the walls, suggests that the centres of the floors may have been broken through in order to salvage many of the bricks used to construct the hypocaust. The damaged under-floor spaces were filled with demolition rubble up to 0.65m in depth, consisting of clayey or sandy silt mixed with large quantities of ceramic building material, mortar, stone, gravel and charcoal. The quantity of *tegula* and *imbrex* recovered from the debris suggests that much of the material may have been derived from roof collapse, although there was also a substantial amount of brick and stone from the walls.

Robber cuts truncated several of the Building 4 walls and foundations. The robbing followed the course of the walls and was therefore linear in plan, with vertical sides and flat bases. Complete sections of some walls, and in many cases the associated foundations, were robbed out (Fig. 54). Interestingly, demolition deposit B[646] contained an iron socketed chisel B<426> of the type that may well have been used for dismantling masonry (see Fig. 94.3; Chapter 3.3).

Unfortunately, no dating evidence was recovered from the fills of any of the robber cuts. Although not exhaustively robbed, a large quantity of building material had clearly been salvaged from Building 4 sometime in antiquity. Pottery recovered from the demolition deposits is dated to the late fourth century but this can only provide a *terminus post quem*. It is possible that some of the building material was salvaged for reuse in other late fourth-century structures such as Building 11 on Site A, but there can have been very little large scale building in masonry in or around *Londinium* at this time. It may therefore be more likely that the majority of robbing and salvage took place at a much later date, perhaps with the revival of masonry construction in Britain from the seventh century.

Fig. 54   View looking east across the heated room areas of the bath house, with Rooms 10–13 on the left (north) and Rooms 6–8 on the right of the east–west wall line B[921]; note the robbing cut B[1060] in the foreground and how some *pilae* stacks have collapsed into the robber trench (scale 2m)

Period 7 discussion

Study of the make-up of the demolition material associated with the bath house, along with evidence of collapsed *pilae* within the robber trenches, indicates that the baths were deliberately demolished or dismantled, probably in the Middle Ages. Very little late Roman pottery was recovered from deposits associated with the demolition and robbing. In any case, the Roman pottery can only confirm to us that demolition happened at the very end of the Roman occupation or sometime afterwards.

If the demolition of the bath house took place at the end of the Roman period then the scale of the robbing might suggest that it was carried out under the direction of a central authority and destined for use on another official project. It may be noteworthy that there is evidence from the Tower of London for a partial rebuilding of the riverside wall during the 390s AD. But

post-Roman masonry structures may have been a more likely destination for the robbed material from Shadwell, and these are unlikely to have been built before the seventh century. An example of reuse of Roman building material in the area can be found in the Saxon church of All-Hallows-by-the-Tower (Taylor and Taylor 1980, 399), founded by the Abbey of Barking in *c.* AD 675. Roman building material was also reused at Barking Abbey (Taylor and Taylor 1980).

To the northeast of the present site, both of the 1970s excavations at LD74 and LD76 recorded the end of the Roman period as being marked by the formation of a dark silty soil 200–300mm thick (Lakin 2002, 24). This soil horizon was broadly similar to that recorded in OA12 on Site A. The evidence from Sites A and B, as well as the 'tower' sites, suggests that the late Roman settlement at Shadwell was abandoned in the final decade of the fourth century or the first decade of the fifth century.

Chapter 3 Specialist reports

3.1 Roman pottery

James Gerrard with contributions by Joanna Bird, Kay Hartley, Malcolm Lyne and David Williams

The supply of pottery to London during the late Roman period was summarised by Symonds and Tomber (1991) almost twenty years ago. Considerable work since the early 1990s has further advanced our knowledge of Late Roman London, its pottery and economics (for instance Seeley and Drummond-Murray 2005; Bluer *et al.* 2006, 58–62, Rayner and Seeley 1998). However, there still remains something of a discrepancy between how the ceramics of the early and late period are treated (Rayner and Seeley 1998). In part this is due to the nature of the archaeological record. Within the City and Southwark the Late Roman period has been more heavily disturbed by medieval and later activity than first and second-century deposits. Where third and fourth-century layers do survive, the interpretation of Late Roman pottery assemblages is complicated by residual material and the nature of the assemblages' depositional context: pottery recovered from the still enigmatic 'dark earth' deposits has traditionally be seen as unpromising and unrewarding (*passim* Symonds and Tomber 1991, 84–85).

This is not the place to embark on a detailed reappraisal of the significance of late Roman pottery to the study of London. What is important though is to understand that the nature of ceramic supply and use in London and its hinterland during the third and fourth centuries is of direct relevance to how we interpret the settlement's function. Was *Londinium* little more than a fortified wasteland studded with decaying public buildings and the occasional grandiose elite residence, as Reece (1980), Faulkner (2001) and others would have us believe? Or do the ceramics show that, despite the fundamental changes visible in London's archaeological record that mark the shift from the Classical world to late Antiquity, the settlement and its environs continued to be a populous and economically vibrant centre between AD 250 and AD 400 (Dark 1996)? The Shadwell sites do shed some light on this vexed question and the virtual absence of pre-third-century activity means that there is little early Roman material to complicate the study of the later periods' ceramics.

Pathway to the archive

The two sites produced 6396 sherds of Romano-British pottery weighing 170.071kg from 444 individual contexts. A total of 4061 sherds (112.342kg) were recovered from Site A with a smaller assemblage (2335 sherds, 57.729kg) derived from deposits at the Site B site. The assemblage was catalogued and quantified by Dr Malcolm Lyne using standard terminology as advocated by MoLSS (Symonds 2000). The unpublished assessment reports contain a complete catalogue of the pottery assemblage. These catalogues were converted into a database for ease of data manipulation during the final stages of post-excavation analysis by the author. This database, the assessment reports, along with further discussion of the pottery by Dr Lyne are available for consultation in the archive at the LAARC.

The following report is divided into five main sections. The first section discusses the supply of pottery to the site by phase. This is followed by the presentation of quantified data for a number of key groups of pottery that aid in the interpretation of the two sites' chronology and function. The imported pottery or so-called 'specialist' wares are presented as four individual reports. The samian, mortaria, amphorae and other imports are examined individually. The presentation of the data is then followed by two more discursive sections, which deal with the possibility of identifying specialised activities on site and broader issues of site interpretation.

Ceramic supply by phase

The total assemblage from the two sites amounts to a considerable quantity of pottery. Over 6000 sherds were recovered, weighing more than 170kg. However, the size of the overall assemblage is misleading and the pottery is not evenly distributed between the two sites. Only one third of the pottery was recovered from features and deposits associated with the bath house on Site B and almost twenty percent of the Site B pottery was found redeposited in post-Roman contexts. Site A yielded almost twice as much pottery. Once the material recovered from post-Roman deposits has been removed from consideration and the pottery assemblage is divided by site and period it becomes obvious that the quantities of stratified pottery by

Period	Date	Site A		Site B	
		Sherd Count	Weight (g)	Sherd Count	Weight (g)
1-3	AD 50-275	85	2257	227	6278
4	AD 275-325	295	8695	991	22324
5	AD 325-375	1146	25968	286	7660
6	AD 375-410	1338	39291	365	9091
7	AD 410+	794	25735	67	2624
Residual		403	10402	399	9752
Total		4061	112342	2335	57729

Table 1 The quantity of Romano-British pottery recovered by period.

period are actually fairly small. Even the amalgamation of periods producing very small quantities of pottery, or the combination of those periods that occur in close temporal succession, does little to ease this situation (Table 1). Furthermore, with such small quantities of pottery the validity of any conclusions drawn from the data must remain tentative. One fragile vessel fragmenting into a hundred sherds might lead to an erroneous conclusion about ceramic supply in a particular period. Nevertheless, and bearing these caveats in mind, the significance of the pottery and sites is such that a discussion of pottery by period remains a useful exercise.

The main Romano-British activity at both sites began in the late third century and continued until the end of the Roman period in the early fifth century. This time span equates to the excavator's Periods 3–7. Period 3 represents the decades between AD 230 and 275, Period 4 the 50 years from AD 275 to AD 325 and Period 5 the middle decades of the fourth century from AD 325 until AD 375. Period 6 represents the latter years of the fourth century until the formal end of Roman imperial administration in Britain in AD 410. The final period, Period 7, is termed 'sub-Roman'. Given that the quantities of stratified pottery by period are quite small, there are some interpretive difficulties in analysing the data. These difficulties are particularly acute in Period 3 at Site A and Period 7 at Site B where the total assemblage numbers less than a hundred sherds.

Late Roman ceramic supply in London has been discussed by Symonds and Tomber (1991) and its general outlines are relatively well understood. Unlike the early Roman period where pottery supply to *Londinium* and its hinterland was characterised by a diverse range of imports and locally produced wares, the supply in the Late Roman period was dominated by larger regional producers situated many miles away. The material from Tobacco Dock and Babe Ruth restaurant conforms well to this general pattern. However, it is worth exploring the detail of the sites' conformity, as the virtual absence of earlier Roman activity provides a useful opportunity to study a late assemblage without the problems associated with residual early Roman material (Fig. 55).

In common with the pattern identified by Symonds and Tomber (1991, figs 2 and 3) the most obvious feature of pottery supply to both sites is the increasing importance of kilns in the Alice Holt/Farnham (AHFA) and Oxfordshire (ALL OX) regions through time. Southeast Dorset Black Burnished ware (BB1) offers a parallel but inverse trend, which is present at both sites, though most pronounced at Site A. The importance of BB1 in Periods 3 and 4 is reflected by the City sites where broadly contemporary assemblages from Leadenhall Court Group 53 and Dowgate Hill contained thirteen percent and seven percent BB1 by Estimated Vessel Equivalent (EVE) (Symonds and Tomber 1991, 71–73). The supply of BB1 would appear to peter off during the mid to late fourth century (Periods 5–7), although the presence of what may be a very late BB1 sherd (see below) might indicate that the sites continued to receive some diminished supplies from the Dorset kilns until the end of the Roman period. Late products of the Thames estuary BB2 producers barely figure, which is in keeping with the apparent decline of the kilns during the mid third century (Monaghan 1987) and the pattern from the City of London sites (Symonds and Tomber 1991, fig 2).

The Hadham kilns (ALL HAD) are also worth considering. They produced some vessels that were broadly analogous to Oxfordshire Red Colour Coated pottery (OXRC) and were connected to Shadwell, the Thames and London by the navigable River Lea (Pomel 1984, 80). However, the Hadham kilns supplied only a minor part of the two sites' pottery (Fig. 55).

The remaining fabrics that are worth discussing are all relatively minor components of the overall assemblage. The most significant fabric is the colour-coated ware from the Nene Valley (NVCC). At Site A NVCC fluctuates between about seven and eleven percent of the assemblage by sherd count and two and a half and four and a half percent by weight. In general terms this is reflected in the City groups, although its absence in Leadenhall Court Group 53 (dated AD 230–260) is noticeable (Symonds and Tomber 1991, fig 2) given the quantities present in roughly contemporary Period 3 deposits at Site B (and to a lesser extent in the statistically unreliable Period 3 assemblage from Site A). One aspect that should also be noted is the higher percentage of NVCC at Site B when compared with Site A. This is a point that will be returned to below.

The NVCC wares could be considered to be broadly analogous in functional terms to colour-coated wares from Colchester (COLCC). COLCC is considered to be a pre-AD

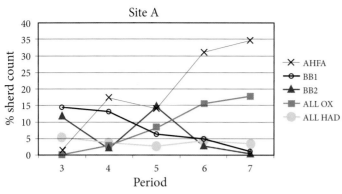

Figure 55.1 Major fabrics from Site A quantified by sherd count

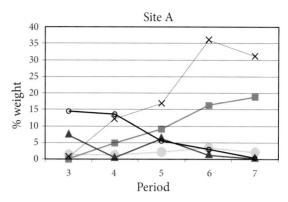

Figure 55.2 Major fabrics from Site A quantified by weight

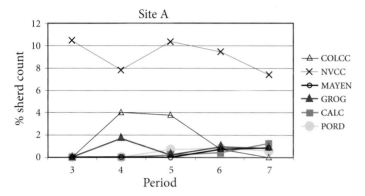

Figure 55.3 Minor fabrics from Site A quantified by sherd count

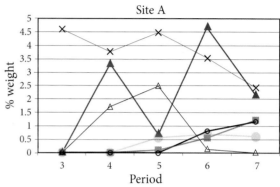

Figure 55.4 Minor fabrics from Site A quantified by weight

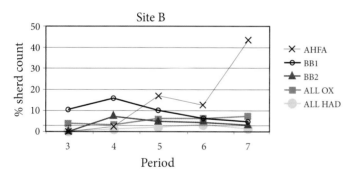

Figure 55.5 Major fabrics from Site B quantified by sherd count

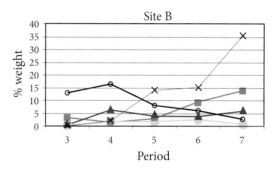

Figure 55.6 Major fabrics from Site B quantified by weight

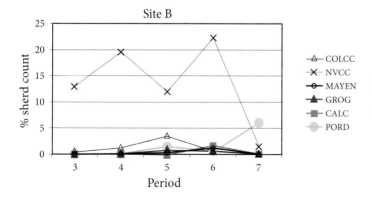

Figure 55.7 Minor fabrics from Site B quantified by sherd count

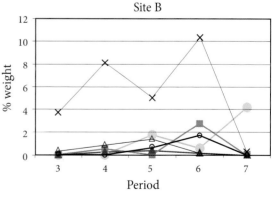

Figure 55.8 Minor fabrics from Site B quantified by weight

Fig. 55   Pottery quantification by fabric: (1) major fabrics from Site A quantified by sherd count; (2) major fabrics from Site A quantified by weight; (3) minor fabrics from Site A quantified by sherd count; (4) minor fabrics from Site A quantified by weight; (5) major fabrics from Site B quantified by sherd count; (6) major fabrics from Site B quantified by weight; (7) minor fabrics from Site B quantified by sherd count; (8) minor fabrics from Site B quantified by weight

250 fabric in London (Symonds 2000) and the majority of the sherds are probably of a similar date. There is, for instance, one example of a CAM392 beaker (AD 150–250) from Site B. However, some sherds, including a pentice beaker from Site A (AD 270–350), ought to indicate the sites were receiving beakers from Colchester into the fourth century, albeit in very small quantities. Given the relatively small numbers of sherds involved (93 sherds from the two sites) the presence of COLCC throughout the sequence may reflect residuality and redeposition, alongside the careful curation of drinking vessels, rather than true ceramic supply.

The remaining fabrics include grog tempered wares (GROG), Portchester D/Overwey ware (PORD), Late Roman shell tempered wares (CALC) and German Mayen ware (MAYEN). All four fabrics represent very minor components of the overall assemblage but are of interest as they can be seen as important indicators of Late Roman activity.

The GROG sherds first appear in Period 4 at both sites, but in slightly greater quantities at Site A. The Period 4 and 5 material is dominated by sherds from Essex storage jars, whereas the Period 6 and 7 sherds are largely derived from vessels manufactured in Kent, including flanged dishes thought to be made in the east of that county (Lyne 1994, Industry 7A). This suggests that the Kentish GROG vessels could be taken as an indicator of mid to late fourth-century activity and the presence of such vessels in the late Billingsgate group (Symonds and Tomber 1991, 77) might reinforce this view.

The other late fabrics present include PORD, often seen as indicative of a date after AD 350 (Drummond-Murray *et al.* 2002, 145; Bluer *et al.* 2006, 58–62), and CALC. Both fabrics are uncommon and first appear in Period 5. Hook rimmed jars (Symonds 2000, 2W) dominate in both fabrics but convex dishes (5J) and flanged bowls also occur (Symonds 2000, 4M). The other 'late' fabric is MAYEN ware from the Eifel region of Germany. Again, it is present in very small quantities but the assemblage contains a variety of types of dish, bowl and jar (Gose 1950, Types 474, 480, 488, 545 and 546). Mayen ware is distributed thinly but widely around the south-eastern coast and Thames estuary (Fulford and Bird 1975) and on typological grounds some of the London finds must

have been imported 'early' in the late Roman period (Drummond-Murray *et al.* 2002, 144). Nevertheless MAYEN ware only occurs in Periods 6 and 7 at Site A and its presence in Period 4 at Site B is surely due to intrusion, as it is derived from a layer B[264] cut by Period 6 pit B[244]. This suggests that Mayen ware, at Shadwell at least, is indicative of the mid to late fourth century and this conclusion has been reached in other regions (Pollard 1988, 148–149).

Key Groups

A number of key groups have been published below and illustrated. The rationale for the selection of these groups has been based on two criteria: firstly, that the group demonstrates some aspect of ceramic supply to the site discussed in period terms above; secondly, that the group contains pottery of significance to dating buildings or other important structures on the site. Given the small size of the groups the pottery has been quantified by sherd count and weight. In the following discussions figures are always given as percentages by sherd count and weight unless otherwise stated.

Key Group 1 (Site B, Period 4.1)

Key Group 1 is a very small 'group' of pottery included here for its intrinsic interest (Fig. 56). Recovered from the fill of pit B[650] in Building 3 at Site B and the fill of hearth B[743] were seventeen sherds of fresh pottery (442g).

The pit contained two sherds that are worthy of comment. The first is a fragment of unsourced amphora with a post-firing hole drilled through it (Fig. 56.1). The second sherd is North African in origin and part of a Hayes (1972) Type 50A red-slipped ware dish dated *c.* AD 230/240–325 (Fig. 56.2). Other fragments of this vessel were recovered from later phases of Building 3 and possibly even from the Shadwell 'tower' site (Bird below) and this highlights the level of residuality and redeposition at these sites. Other sherds from this context included an abraded fragment of East Gaulish samian and three unsourced, sand tempered jar sherds.

The hearth produced four fragments of a Central Gaulish Black Colour-Coated (CGBL) ware beaker, a fragment of an Eifelkeramik jar (EIFL), two sherds of

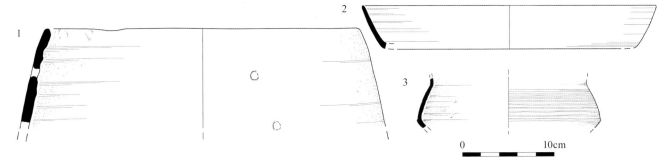

Fig. 56   Selected pottery from Key Group 1: (1) unsourced amphora (AMPH) with its rim removed and neck ground down with holes drilled in its sides from B[649]; (2) dish of Hayes Type 50A (1972) in North African Red Slipped (NARS) ware dated AD 230/240–325 from B[649]; (3) *'Bol carenée'* in hard off-white North Gaulish (NGGW) fabric fired pale blue-grey with *bandes lustrées* decoration (Tuffreau-Libre 1980, fig 11–6) dated AD 200–270 from B[738] (scale 1:4)

a North Gaulish Grey Ware (NGGW) jar (Fig. 56.3), a piece of a North Gaulish White Ware (NGWH) vessel of uncertain form and three sherds of amphorae (GAUL and NAFR).

There are two important points to make regarding this tiny assemblage. Firstly, it is contemporary with the use of the building. Brickearth structures by their very nature tend to incorporate much redeposited material. Thus this assemblage offers a tiny glimpse at the pottery being used within the building. Secondly, with the exception of the unsourced sand tempered sherds, all of the pottery from these features, derived from at least ten different vessels, is imported. There are no Romano-British products. The significance of this is discussed below.

Key Group 2 (Site B Period 4.3)

Key Group 2 is comprised of pottery from the fills of the Period 4.3 (recut) boundary ditch at Site B (Fig. 57). Quantification of the pottery from these fills (Table 2) demonstrates the importance of Dorset BB1 (25.64/33.13)

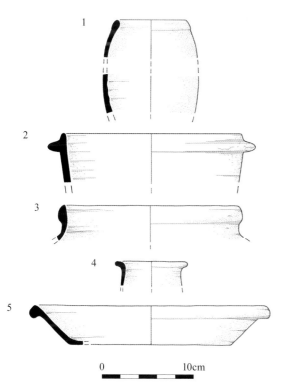

Fig. 57   Selected pottery from Key Group 2: (1) small hole-mouthed vessel in very-fine-sanded rough white fabric with blackened patches (SAND); AD 220–300 from B[140]; (2) undecorated BB1 beaded-and-flanged bowl of Bestwall Type 6–8; *c.* AD 300–370 from B[137]; (3) storage-vessel with attenuated beaded rim in Essex BB2 fabric. The rim form is characteristic of central Essex (Going 1987, G42 3.1) and is paralleled at the Inworth kiln, dated *c.* AD 270–37, (Going 1987, fig 41.23) but in a different fabric; from B[137]; (4) beaker rim with out-turned bead in Essex BB2 fabric. Paralleled in the AD 300–400 dated Kiln III at Mucking (Jones and Rodwell 1973, fig 11–130) from B[137]; (5) beaded-rim pie-dish with chamfered base in Essex BB2 fabric. Paralleled in Kiln II at Mucking (Going 1987, fig 4.9, AD 200–270) and at Colchester (Symonds and Wade 1999, fig 6.42–70, AD 170–275) from B[135] (scale 1:4)

(Allen and Fulford 1996) and also the Nene Valley industry (19.78/9.38) during Period 4. A variety of BB1 forms were present including cooking pots (Symonds 2000, 2F13), straight sided dishes (Symonds 2000, 5J) and beaded and flanged bowls (Symonds 2000, 4M) of mid to late third-century date. The Nene Valley wares included sherds from folded 'scale' beakers (AD 230–300), hunt cups (AD 160–270) and a funnel-neck example with beaded rim (AD 250–350). It is also noticeable that the Alice Holt/Farnham and Oxfordshire kilns provided only very small quantities of pottery (3.30/2.27 and 1.46/4.01 respectively). The latter includes an OXWW M17 mortarium dated AD 240–300 (Young 1977). This suggests that most of the pottery in this ditch was deposited before *c.* AD 300. A similar group of pottery was recovered from the boundary ditch excavated in 1976 (Lakin 2002, Tables 7 and 8).

Key Group 3 (Site B, Period 4.1)

Key Group 3 is a small group of pottery (Table 2) derived from a number of features associated with the remodelling of the bath house at Site B (Fig. 58). These features include two drainage gullies B[432] and B[618] and a small pit B[591]. The importance of this material lies in the fact that it can almost certainly be considered as contemporary with the use of the bath house, a building which by its very nature produced little pottery.

In spite of the small size of this group a late third or early fourth-century date can be advanced for it. The eighteen fragments of Nene Valley beakers include

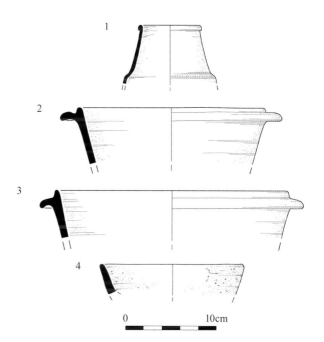

Fig. 58   Selected pottery from Key Group 3: (1) funnel-neck beaker in NVCC with bead-rim; AD 270–350 from B[432]; (2) beaded-and-flanged bowl of Bestwall Type 6–4 in BB1 fabric with external burnished arcading; AD 240–300 from B[432]; (3) beaded-and-flanged bowl of Bestwall Type 6–8 in BB1; AD 300–370 from B[432]; (4) straight-sided dish in Hadham Black Surfaced ware (HAD BS); AD 250–400 from B[432] (scale 1:4)

Key Group/context	2				3		well A[1339] lower		well A[1339] upper			7		
Fabric	sherd count	% sherd count	weight (g)	% weight	sherd count	weight (g)	sherd count	weight (g)	sherd count	weight (g)	EVE	sherd count	weight (g)	EVE
AHFA	9	3.30	110	2.27	1	64	66	3780	36	1538	1.16	258	7544	10.98
AMPH	3	1.10	106	2.19	1	8								
BAET	5	1.84	234	4.84										
BB1	70	25.64	1604	33.13	9	306	24	390	3	118	0.15	4	84	0.21
BB2	13	4.76	214	4.42	1	2	1	14	1	130	0.31	3	48	0.98
CALC									2	66	0.16	9	306	0.47
COLCC					1	16								
COLWW	1	0.37	90	1.86					1	6	0			
FINE	3	1.10	22	0.45								3	64	0.07
GAUL	18	6.59	408	8.43	9	564			1	12	0			
GROG							1	8				7	554	0.12
NVCC	54	19.78	454	9.38					3	94	0.21	46	545	1.37
NVWW												6	328	0.22
MARB									1	14	0			
MAYEN									1	80	0.08	5	290	0.44
MHAD	4	1.47	28	0.58	1	22	1	26	11	238	0.08	25	506	0.59
MICA	1	0.37	8	0.17										
MISC	18	6.59	196	4.05								8	162	0.05
MOSL	2	0.73	6	0.12										
NACA/NAFR							3	1218						
NVCC					18	108	9	238						
OXID	3	1.10	8	0.17	3	22	1	4				7	186	0.23
OXMO							3	390	3	284	0.31			
OXWW	2	0.73	186	3.84								37	2504	1.66
OXPA							2	106	4	78	0.33	7	260	0.16
OXRC	2	0.73	8	0.17			7	434	45	1018	2.06	83	1912	1.96
OXWS												1	38	0.08
PORD									1	56	0.08	5	156	0.12
SAMEG	7	2.56	250	5.16			1	72				109	4152	4.3
SAMLZ	10	3.66	80	1.65	1	52								
SAND	45	16.49	804	16.61	32	1306	9	558	3	92	0.14			
VRW	3	1.10	26	0.54										
VRWL					1	50								
TOTAL	273	100	4842	100	88	2520	128	7238	116	3924	5.07	623	19639	24.01

Table 2 Quantification of pottery from key Groups 2, 3 and 7 and the upper and lower fills of well A[1339].

examples of 'slit-folded' Type 53 and also Type 39 dated to AD 270–350 and AD 230–300 respectively (Howe *et al.* 1980) as well as a funnel-neck beaker with bead-rim (AD 270–350). There are also examples of BB1 beaded-and-flanged bowls dated AD 240–300 and AD 300–370. A large lid-seated jar is probably an Essex product and is similar to Jones and Rodwell's (1973) rare Type M dated AD 200–300.

The presence of nineteen beaker sherds derived from a number of different vessels may be significant. Socialising and drinking might be expected as activities in and around a bath house and these sherds, the presence of wine amphora sherds (GAUL and AMPH) and the relatively poor showing of utilitarian vessels and kitchen wares could be interpreted as supporting evidence for these activities. However, caution must be exercised given the extremely small assemblage size.

Key Group 4 (Site A, Period 6)

Key Group 4 is derived from the fill of pit A[1373], a Period 6 feature at Site A (Fig. 59). The quantity of pottery is extremely small but the assemblage size is not as important as its significance for dating purposes. This pit was truncated by the construction of well A[1399] and thus provides a *terminus post quem* for the construction of the well.

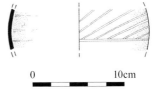

Fig. 59   Selected pottery from Key Group 4: Jar or bowl in BB1 with diagonal burnished line decoration on its girth, dated AD 350–450? (Gerrard 2004) from A[1372] (scale 1:4)

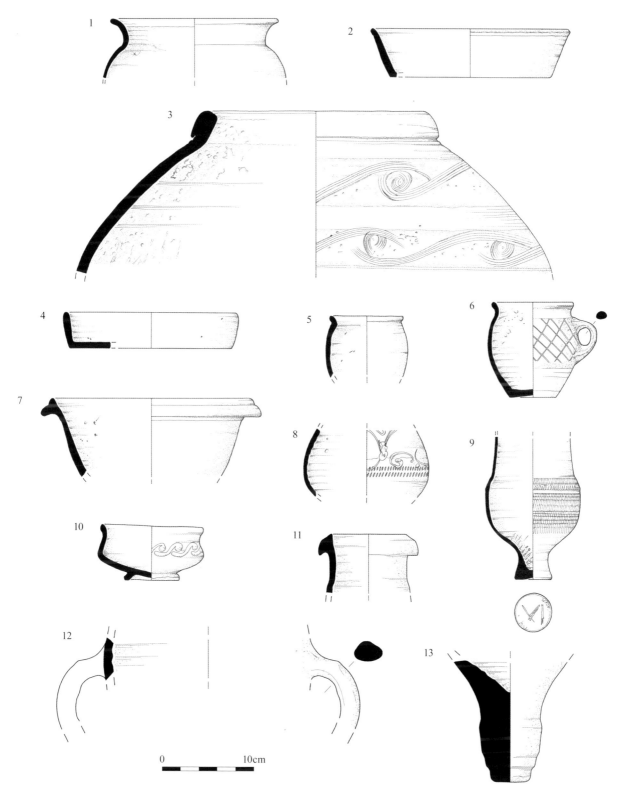

Fig. 60 Selected pottery from Key Group 5: (1) everted rim cooking-pot in grey AHFA with black slip on rim. AD 270–400+ A[1615]; (2) deep straight-sided dish with very straight sides and slightly turned over rim in AHFA with internal black slip. AD 370–400+ A[1615]; (3) large lid-seated storage jar of Lyne and Jefferies (1979) Type 1C-6 in grey AHFA with black slip. AD 350–400+ A[1615]; (4) straight-sided dish of Bestwall Type 8–14 in BB1. AD 350–400+ A[1615]; (5) bead-rim beaker in BB1. A[1615]; (6) greater part of everted-rim beaker in very-fine-sanded grey-black fabric (SAND) with external acute-latticing and rod handle. A[1615]; (7) beaded and flanged bowl in very fine grey-black fabric with profuse white and colourless quartz (SAND) up to 0.30mm and concave internal band just below the rim. Observations elsewhere suggest that this feature is a characteristic of some of the latest bowls of this type from sites in the London area. AD 370–400+ A[1615]; (8) large beaker or bottle in white NVCC with white-painted decoration over black colour-coat. AD 250–370 A[1615]; (9) rouletted pentice beaker in NVCC with brown/black colour-coat with graffito 'VI' scratched on base post firing (see Chapter 3.5). AD 250–370 A[1615]; (10) complete bowl of Young Type C77 in OXRC with white paint scrolling. AD 340–400 A[1615]; (11) top of spatheion type 1 amphora in NAFR AD 300–450 A[1615]; (12) handle from another such NAFR amphora. A[1615]; (13) ground-down amphora spike in NAFR A[1615] (scale 1:4)

The pit contained 48 sherds of pottery (1352g) of which almost half originated at the Alice Holt/Farnham kilns. Fragments from Lyne and Jefferies (1979) bowl and dish types 5B-8, 5B-9 (AD 270–400+) and 6A-8 and 6C-1 (AD 330–400+) were present, alongside a large and fresh fragment of the very late dish Type 6C-2 (AD 370/390–400+). Also present were sherds of a Portchester D/Overwey jar usually dated to after AD 350 in London and sherds of Oxfordshire red colour-coated vessels, including a Young (1977) C13 jug of mid fourth-century or later date.

The most unusual find though was a fragment of a BB1 vessel decorated with just diagonal lines instead of the more usual lattice. This type of decoration is characteristic of a late globular necked bowl form identified at Dorchester (Dorset) and other sites in south-western Britain. The most recent discussion of this type of vessel has drawn attention to its appearance in the latest Roman deposits (AD 388+) at many sites in Somerset and Dorset and suggested that it did not appear until *c.* AD 350 at the earliest. Indeed, it might have appeared slightly later and continued to be produced during the first half of the fifth century (Gerrard 2004). If this sherd is from such a vessel it would be the first occurrence of this form in eastern England (the nearest examples being from Basingstoke and the Isle of Wight: Malcolm Lyne, pers. comm.). However, the sherd is too small to confidently assign it to the bowl form and is hence not illustrated (see Gerrard 2004, 68 for the difficulties in identifying these vessels). Nevertheless, it is an important find and potential addition to the late distribution of this class of vessel (Gerrard 2004, fig 8.4).

Key Group 5 (Site A, Period 6)

Key Group 5 comes from the fills of well A[1399] at Site A, which produced large quantities of pottery that are potentially of significance in understanding the end of Roman pottery supply to the London area in the fifth century (Table 2) (Fig. 60). Certainly the material from pit A[1373] provides a very late *terminus post quem* for the construction of this feature and it seems difficult to believe that the inhabitants of Late Roman Shadwell would have required a well during the life of the piped water system (Alistair Douglas, pers. comm.). The latest sherd from a small and probably residual assemblage from the construction backfill of the well A[1537] was an OXRC C75 bowl dated AD 325–400+. This helps to confirm the late date for this well indicated by the material in pit A[1373].

The assemblage from the lower fill A[1615] amounted to a reasonably sized group but statistical analysis of the material is hampered by the presence of a number of complete and semi-complete vessels (Table 2). Alice Holt/Farnham wares are the main fabric and a variety of Oxfordshire fabrics are also present including an intact OXRC C77 bowl with white paint scrolling dated AD 340–400+. A beaded and flanged bowl in SAND fabric with an internal concave band just below the rim is another late type, characteristic of the latest Roman deposits in London and dated AD 370+ (Malcolm Lyne, pers. comm.). A similar AHFA vessel from Old Ford was recovered from

a deposit containing coins of the House of Theodosius (AD 388+) (Gerrard and Lyne forthcoming). In keeping with the late date of this group BB2 is almost absent and the apparent importance of BB1 is actually a product of a single fragmented jar base, although some other sherds are present. Perhaps of most importance are the three sherds of amphora. The most significant is a complete everted rim from a North African amphora, probably of spatheion type 1, which can be dated AD 300–450. The two other sherds are also North African products and include a small handle and a spike, possibly from an Africana II vessel (Williams this report). These sherds may indicate that the importation of exotic foodstuffs continued until the very end of the Roman period.

Key Group 6 (Site A, Period 6)

Key Group 6 pottery is from the upper well fill A[1281], which has slightly less pottery by sherd count (116 sherds, 3924g) but was more broken up and thus just suitable for quantification by EVE (Table 2) (Fig. 61). Alice Holt/Farnham and Oxfordshire wares again dominated the assemblage with all Oxfordshire products accounting for more than fifty percent of the pottery from this fill by EVE. Vessel forms present included a Lyne and Jefferies (1979) 1C-6 storage jar of post-AD 350 date and a Type 6C-2 dish, which is also a late fourth-century form possibly introduced *c.* AD 390 (Malcolm Lyne, pers. comm.). The Oxfordshire vessels included exclusively fourth-century forms C56, C68, C72 and M22 alongside late fourth-century forms C77 (AD 340–400+) and C52 (350–400+).

Other indicators of the very late Roman date of this group are provided by the minor fabrics. Overwey/Portchester D ware hook rimmed jar sherds were present in small quantities and these are usually taken as an indicator of a date in the second half of the fourth century (Drummond-Murray *et al.* 2002, 145). Similarly the presence of calcite-gritted jar sherds is also viewed as a late phenomenon and Mayen ware appears to become more common in the latter half of the fourth century. The form represented here, a Gose 545 lid-seated cooking pot dated AD 350–400 (Gose 1950), would not contradict this dating. Finally, a black slipped beaded and flanged bowl from the Much Hadham kilns with internal groove (see Key Group 5 above) may also be a very late Roman vessel form (AD 370–400+).

As was noted above, the most striking aspect of this group of pottery was the quantity of material originating in the Oxfordshire region (Fig. 62). Oxfordshire products are common in late Roman London but rarely in such high percentages (for instance Drummond-Murray 2002, 145). A number of explanations for this phenomenon can be presented. First, that this material represents the residue from some type of specialised activity. The presence of a large number of intact or semi-complete vessels in the lower fill might suggest ritual deposition (see below) and the discard of 'finewares' like the Oxfordshire red-colour coats could also be seen as structured deposition.

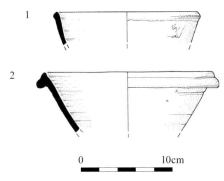

Fig. 61   Selected pottery from Key Group 6: (1) dish of Type 6C-2 in AHFA with internal white slip extending over the beaded rim. AD 350–400+; this is a very late dish form and its starting date could be as late as AD 390 (Malcolm Lyne, pers. comm.); from A[1281]; (2) beaded-and-flanged bowl in HAD BS with internal groove just below the rim; AD 370–400+ from A[1281] (scale 1:4)

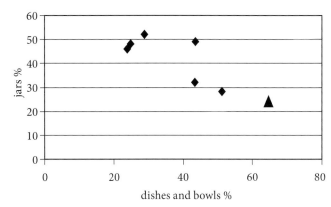

Fig. 63   Proportions of jars vs dishes/bowls quantified by EVE in a number of very late fourth- or early fifth-century assemblages from London (Symonds and Tomber 1991, table 5: Bluer *et al.* 2006, table 2), Shadwell (this report), Old Ford (Gerrard and Lyne forthcoming) and Essex (Going 1987, table 9; Wickenden 1988, table 2). Note the unusually high percentage of dishes and bowls in the material from the upper fill of well A[1399], which is indicated by a triangle

Alternatively, analysis of the forms by EVE shows a preponderance of bowl and dish forms that might suggest that this material was waste from the serving of food. Feasting and ritual may go together so these interpretations are not mutually exclusive. Second, this material can be seen as a product of chronology. We could speculate that it represents the very latest Roman phase on the site when carefully curated finewares were finally broken and discarded after all supplies of new pottery had ceased and the more utilitarian wares had already been broken. A similar explanation has been invoked for a comparable phenomenon in the latest pottery assemblage from deposits in the *Verulamium* theatre (Lyne 1994) and in the early post-Roman groups from the temple at Uley (Woodward and Leach 1993, 241). Finally, it is worth considering an unpublished study on late Roman ceramic supply in Essex (Martin 2004) that suggested the appearance of Oxfordshire wares in that county occurred after *c.* AD 380. A group of material from the upper fill of a well at Elms Farm (Essex) had Oxfordshire wares forming forty percent of the assemblage and Martin tentatively suggested that this quantity of Oxfordshire pottery could indicate a date in the period AD 400–450.

Key Group 7 (Period 7, Site A)

Key Group 7 was the largest group of late Roman pottery from the site, recovered from a number of dumped deposits overlying Building 11 at Site A (A[1060], A[722], A[660], A[720], A[718] and A[940]). This assemblage amounted to some 623 sherds (19639g) and equated to 24.01 EVEs (Table 2).

The quantification of the group demonstrates the importance of AHFA at almost fifty per cent of the assemblage. This material, however, is not exclusively of late fourth-century date. Lyne and Jefferies (1979) forms 1–33, 5B-4 and 4–44 should all pre-date AD 350. Later vessels are represented by 6A-10, and 6C-1 should post-date AD 330 and the presence of a type 4–45 storage jar and a 6C-2 dish ought to indicate dates after AD 350 and AD 370 respectively. Other generic 'late Roman' types include 3B-10, 6A-4 and 1A-17 (AD 270–400+). The mixture of early and late fourth-century types suggests that there is a strong residual or heirloom component in this assemblage.

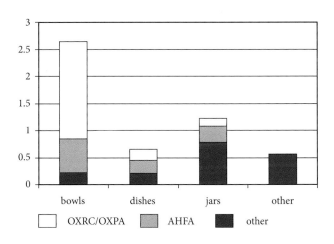

Fig. 62   Quantification of the Oxfordshire wares, Alice Holt wares and other pottery from well A[1399]

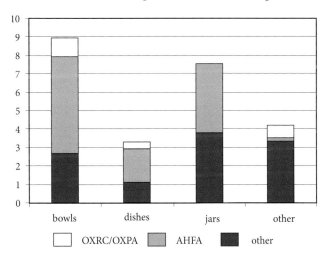

Fig. 64   Quantification of pottery from layers overlying Building 11 (Site A) by EVE (compare with Fig. 55.8)

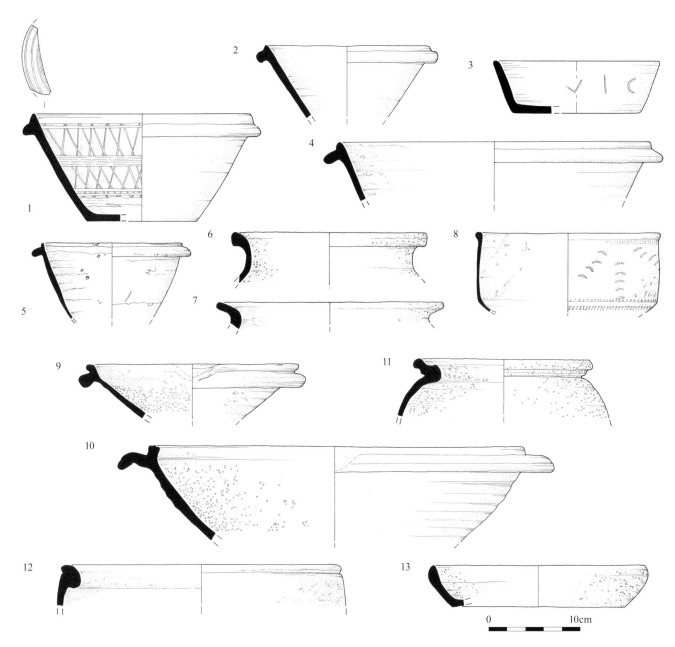

Fig. 65 Selected pottery from Key Group 7: (1) beaded and flanged bowl of Lyne and Jefferies Type 5B-10 in AHFA greyware with internal burnished lattice decoration. AD 350–400+. A[1060]; (2) beaded-and-flanged bowl in AHFA with streaky internal grey/black slip. AD 370–400+. A[660]; (3) deep straight-sided dish in AHFA with internal black slip and 'VIC' graffito on its exterior surface (see Chapter 3.5). AD 350–400+. A[1060]; (4) large beaded-and-flanged bowl in very-fine-sanded Essex greyware (SAND) fired rough black. AD 270–400+. A[940]; (5) beaded-and-flanged bowl with an internal horizontal groove below the bead, in smooth silt-tempered leaden-grey fabric with orange margins and occasional up to 3.00mm rounded vesicles. AD 370–400+. This fragment is particularly fresh. A[660]; (6) hook-rim jar in CALC AD 350–400. A[722]; (7) handmade everted-rim jar with very-fine-sand and siltstone grog filler fired grey with darker surfaces (GROG). Probably from a source in the Dartford area of West Kent (Lyne 1994, Industry 8A, Fabric 8A.3). AD 360–400+. A[722]; (8) bowl of Young (1977) Type C83/85 in OXRC AD 350–400+. A[660]; (9) mortarium of Young Type M22 in OXWW AD 240–400+. A[722]; (10) large mortarium of Type M23 in OXWW AD 350–400+. A[660]; (11) lid-seated MAYEN cooking-pot of Gose (1950) Type 545 fired pimply brown-grey. A[722]; (12) bowl of Gose (1950) Type 488 in MAYEN fired patchy black/cream. A[722]; (13) bowl of Gose (1950) Type 474 in MAYEN. AD 350–400+. A[1060] (scale 1:4)

Other late fourth-century indicators in the group include PORD, CALC and MAYEN vessels (mainly jars) and OXRC forms C52, C61, C83/85, all of which are post-AD 350 in date (Young 1977). Other less chronologically diagnostic Oxfordshire vessels also occur in this group as do 'early' mortarium forms (OXWW) like M18 (AD 240–300).

Quantification of this assemblage by form demonstrates that in functional terms bowls and jars are the most important elements of the assemblage. The overall impression is of a fairly even division between eating vessels (dishes and bowls) and kitchen or storage vessels (jars). The 'other' category includes specialist kitchen wares (mortaria) at a relatively high 2.24EVEs and beakers and flagons (1.44 and 0.52EVEs) being poorly represented. One striking aspect of this analysis is the difference between this material from dumped deposits and layers and the quantified group from well A[1399] (Fig. 64).

One final question remains regarding this group of pottery: what is its origin? We have seen that it contains both early and late fourth-century material and some of the latter could have been current in the early decades of the fifth century (Fig. 65). The presence of chronologically distinct types within the group might suggest that it is redeposited rubbish from different sources (middens?). However, the average sherd weight (15.47g) is relatively high and the brokenness figure (29.95 sherds per EVE) is low suggesting that the material has not travelled far or been heavily reworked (Orton *et al.* 1993, 178–181). Thus it may be that the pottery is derived from the use of Building 11 and incorporated into later layers during robbing activities. There is really no way of telling and thus no way of establishing anything more than a broad hypothesis about the formation of the assemblage and its significance.

Key Group 8 (Site B, Period 7)

Key Group 8 is a small group of pottery recovered from deposits B[467], B[595], B[607], B[795], B[801], B[1020], B[1029], B[1033] and B[1262], associated with the demolition and robbing of the bath house on Site B (61 sherds, 2400g) (Fig. 66). This group is too small for valid quantification and the large average sherd size (*c.* 40g) is inexplicable. However, suitably Late Roman fabrics (for instance PORD and BIV) and forms (for instance AHFA: 6C-2 and OXWS: WC6) indicate a very late Roman *terminus post quem* for the demolition and robbing of the structure, assuming that the three sherds of post-medieval pottery from B[595] are intrusive.

One important point that should be made here and applies equally to Key Group 7 is that the presence of Late Roman pottery in robbing deposits cannot be held to date the robbing and demolition of the structure (Gerrard 2008). Stone robbers need not drop material culture in

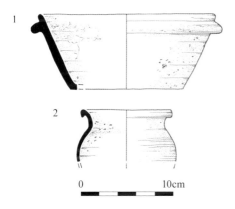

Fig. 66   Selected pottery from Key Group 8: (1) developed beaded-and-flanged bowl in grey, sand and grog tempered fabric (GROG) fired pimply black with poor internal polish. B[607]; (2) horizontally-rilled jar in heavily-blackened PORD AD 350–420; B[1029] (scale 1:4)

the process of robbing and the example of Wroxeter is enlightening. A major robbing episode of the baths basilica could only be dated to the ninth or tenth century because a single Anglo-Saxon strap end of that date was recovered from a robber trench (Barker and White 1998, 138 and Pl. 24; see also P. Ellis 2000, 345). Indeed, it is unlikely that the site was robbed out in the fifth or sixth century as there was little stone construction during those centuries. Thus, the robbing occurred after the currency of the latest Roman material culture and probably after the seventh century when the construction of stone churches reusing Roman building materials began (Eaton 2000).

The imported pottery

The samian

Joanna Bird

The samian ware from the excavations at Site A and Site B consists of a maximum of 150 vessels, of which 43 have surviving elements of moulded decoration and three are stamped, one of them in the mould. A full catalogue of the samian ware is presented in Appendix 1, along with rubbings of seventeen of the fragments with moulded decoration (Fig. 123). Although there is only a third the amount of samian, the assemblage of late East Gaulish ware is comparable with the extraordinary group recovered from the 1974 and 1976 excavations immediately to the east (Bird 2002), and a similar date of *c.* AD 235–250 is indicated. The sources of the samian and the forms present are summarised in Table 3; in addition to the Gaulish wares there is an African Red Slip Ware platter of third- or early fourth-century date, which may be part of the vessel found in 1974 (Bird 2002, 31–32), and a wall-sided bowl, probably from the Argonne, of later third- to fourth-century date.

The first notable feature is that there is no samian at all from the first-century potteries at La Graufesenque; this fits with the evidence from the earlier excavations, where only a small amount was recovered, and indicates that there was probably little or no activity on the site at that period. Here the only South Gaulish piece is a stamped Drag 33 from the workshop at Montans, dated *c.* AD 120–145, comparable to the single piece of Montans decorated ware found in 1976 (Bird 2002, fig 17, 6). There is much less Central Gaulish ware than from the earlier excavations: one probable piece of Trajanic–Hadrianic samian from Les Martres-de-Veyre, and only fourteen vessels from Lezoux. These include three decorated bowls, one by a Hadrianic–early Antonine potter, perhaps Quintilianus, the others both of Antonine date but not attributable (cf. Bird 2002, 32–3 and fig 17, 8–20, where decorated bowls by several Lezoux potters were identified). The Lezoux plain forms consist of Drag 18/31 and an unidentified dish, of Hadrianic–Antonine date, and Drag 31 or 31R, Drag 31R, Curle 15 and Drag 45, all of mid to later Antonine date.

The remaining 134 vessels, 89% of the total, come

from the East Gaulish potteries at Trier (83) and Rheinzabern (51). The decorated Trier ware includes a small sherd which is probably from Werkstatt I and six or seven bowls from Werkstatt II; while these anonymous potters were active in the Hadrianic–Antonine period, there is evidence from Trier for the reuse of their moulds by potters working around the middle of the third century (Huld-Zetsche 1972, 81–88), and the quality of the moulding and finishing, the fabrics and the slips of these bowls are characteristic of such late work. The bowls by the mid to later Antonine mould-makers Dexter (two) and Comitialis are probably also later, while the other potters, Afer (two bowls, plus one possibly by Afer or Marinus), Atillus (possibly one or two), the Dubitatus-Dubitus group (three or four) and the Primanus group (one) all date within the third century. A further bowl has motifs used by Criciro, Amator and Atillus-Pussosus. The latest are the Dubitatus-Dubitus group, *c.* AD 225–245, and the Primanus group, *c.* AD 235–250. With the exception of Comitialis and the Criciro/Amator/Atillus-Pussosus bowl, and the definite presence of Werkstatt II, these potters were all represented at the earlier sites (Table 4; Bird 2002, fig 18, 23–35).

Apart from the decoration, there are other features of the Drag 37 bowls which support a date towards the middle of the third century for this samian. A thick heavy footring of late type probably comes from the Afer bowl found in the same context, and a base fragment which probably comes from one of the Werkstatt II bowls has the scar of a similar footring (*cf.* Bird 1993, 4). Drag 37 rim bands of high late type are on the Primanus bowl (at least 60mm high), on two of the Werkstatt II bowls (55 and 67mm) and on a bowl without surviving decoration (at least 60mm). The Criciro/Amator/Atillus-Pussosus piece is in an unusual fabric (see catalogue). Certain of the Trier plain wares also show late features. The Drag 45 mortarium which still has its lion-head spout is dated to the first half of the third century, and there are at least ten other examples of the form; where the rims are present, they lack the incised rim grooves of earlier versions. There are five examples of form Drag 33, two of them certainly unstamped; this is a late feature, as is the heavy base with small conical space within the footring noted on the same pots (Bird 1993, 2–3, 8). There are also two shallow, almost lid-like examples of Drag 38, and again this is a late version of the form (Bird 1993, 10).

Form	SAMMT	SAMLZ	SAMEG (Trier)	SAMEG (Rheinzabern)
Dr 18/31		2		
Dr 30				1
Dr 30 or 37		2*		1
Dr 31/Lud Sa			1	
Dr 31 or 31R		1		
Dr 31R		2		
Dr 31R/Lud Sb			9	5
Dr 31/Lud Sa or Dr 31R/Lud Sb			1	1
Dr 33	1		5	6
Dr 36			1	
Dr 37		3	36	23
Dr 38			9	4
Dr 41				1
Dr 45		2	11	
Mortaria		1	7	1
Curle 15		1		
Walters 79/Lud Tg			1	
Dish		1	1	3
Bowl/dish				1
Bowl			1	
Dr 53				1
Jar/beaker				2
Jar				1
Total	**1**	**15**	**83**	**51**

*Table 3 The identified samian forms from each production site, based on a sherd count, showing the maximum possible number of vessels. * = bowl which probably originates at Les Martres-de-Veyre rather than Lezoux.*

The decorated Rheinzabern series begins with two bowls that are probably by Cerialis I and Cerialis IV, active at the end of the second century and beginning of the third, but there is evidence at Rheinzabern too for reuse of earlier moulds in the mid third century (Bird 2002, 33). The other attributable bowls are all by potters dating well within the third century: three or four by the Julius I-Lupus group, one probably by Primitivus I (a Drag 30), one by Primitivus IV and two or three by the Julius II-Julianus I group, including the mould-stamped bowl of Victorinus II. The latest are the Julius II-Julianus I group, dated *c.* AD 225–245. These later potters are all well represented from the previous excavations (Table 5; Bird 2002, figs 19–22). As with the Trier wares, high rims of late type, some with a slightly flared profile, are on the probable Cerialis I bowl (45mm), on one of the bowls of the Julius I-Lupus group (67mm), on a Julius II-Julianus I bowl (50mm) and on an unattributed fragment (51mm).

Apart from the mould-decorated ware there is an example of the third-century handled crater form Drag 53 with barbotine decoration, and a sherd from a second barbotine-decorated jar or beaker. A foot from a third jar or beaker has a small conical space beneath. The base of a small cup of form Drag 41 has no surviving decoration; three examples of the form with incised ornament were found during the earlier excavations (Bird 2002, fig 21, 75–76, and Table 13). The most significant plain-ware vessel is the dish base stamped by Severianus ii; he was one of the latest potters exporting to Britain (Bird 1993, 3), active *c.* AD 235–250, and his presence, together with the mould-makers Victor I, Perpetuus and Pervincus I whose bowls were found at the earlier excavations (Bird 2002, 34), indicates a closing date of *c.* AD 250 for this group. There is only one mortarium sherd, but four more unstamped examples of Drag 33, three of them with the heavy base and small conical space beneath. A foot, probably of form Drag 38, has a similar base, and the other Drag 38 has the characteristic late shallow profile.

It is assumed above that these late East Gaulish wares probably reached the site at approximately the same time. The reasons for this were given in the report on the samian from the earlier excavations (Bird 2002, 34–35), and they remain valid here. With the exception of the assemblage from the Roman quay at St Magnus House, London, which apparently belonged to a single shipment of *c.* AD 235–245 and was presumably intended for sale and dispersal (Bird 1986, 142–145), the quantity and proportion of both Trier and Rheinzabern wares, and particularly of decorated bowls, remain unique for a British site, suggesting that they arrived in response to a specific demand. Unfortunately, the 2002–2003 excavations go no further towards explaining the circumstances of that demand. Most of the pieces are relatively small, and a high proportion of them were recovered from later features such as pits, ditches, dumped deposits and the structural slots and postholes of buildings. There are also a number of cross-joins between bowls from different features, with some pots showing a marked variation in the quality of the slip on joining sherds.

Potter/Workshop	LD74/76	Sites A and B
Werkstatt I, A	1	
Werkstatt I		1
Werkstatt I or II	1	
Werkstatt II, A		1
Werkstatt II, B		2
Werkstatt II, B, or Atillus		1
Werkstatt II, E or F		1
Werkstatt II, F		1
Werkstatt II		1
Dexter	1	2
Criciro	2	
Criciro, Amator or Atillus-Pussosus		1
Comitialis		1
Afer	2	2
Possibly Afer-Marinus		1
Dexter, Atillus or Dubitatus-Dubitus	1	
Atillus or Dubitus		1
Afer, Paternianus or Dubitatus	1	
Dubitus		2
Dubitatus		1
Dubitatus-Dubitus	2	
Primanus	2	1
Total	**13**	**20**

Table 4 Trier mould-makers identified at Shadwell, ordered chronologically.

There is no evidence from the samian itself to suggest that it comes from a warehouse or similar structure: the vessels are much more fragmentary than the St Magnus House material and some pieces also show signs of heavy wear, distinct from the abrasion which can be seen on many of the surfaces and broken edges. Apart from worn footrings, the wear is particularly marked on the interiors of mortaria, where slip and grits are heavily eroded, and on several of the Drag 38 bowls which have had the interior slip almost completely worn away, clearly by use.

Shadwell is not part of a major town, where some late East Gaulish wares might be expected. Those towns with the highest proportions are London (Bird 2002, fig 16), Colchester (Bird 1999, 75–76; Bird 2002, 34), York (Dickinson 1997, 944; Monaghan 1997) and perhaps Lincoln (Bird forthcoming). On the other hand, a number of military sites with mid third-century occupation have late stamped or decorated wares in common with Shadwell, which might indicate a trade aimed at a military or official market, though none of them has anything approaching the same quantity. The samian from Piercebridge includes bowls by Primanus, Julius I-Lupus and Julius II-Julianus I, with a plain-ware stamp of Severianus ii (Ward 2008). Caister-on-Sea has bowls of Dubitatus-Dubitus and Severianus (Dickinson 1993). Brancaster has bowls of Julius I-Lupus and Julius

II-Julianus I, with a plain-ware stamp of Severianus ii (Dickinson and Bird 1985). While at South Shields the Trier wares end somewhat earlier but the Rheinzabern products again include Julius I and the Julius II-Julianus I-Victorinus II group, and a plain-ware stamp of Severianus ii (Dore *et al.* 1979; Hartley and Dickinson 1979). Much of the late samian from Richborough remains unpublished and unstudied; it includes bowls of Paternianus, probably Dubitatus-Dubitus and Julius II-Julianus I (Peter Webster, pers. comm.). Reculver, like Shadwell, had a number of mortaria in Trier ware, though too fragmentary to estimate at all accurately, as well as bowls of Julius II-Julianus I (Bird 2005). Some form of military or official use of the site would therefore seem to be the most likely explanation for the presence of this late samian at Shadwell.

Potter/Workshop	LD74/LD76	Sites A and B
Cobnertus III	1	
Probably Cerialis I		1
Cerialis IV		1
Probably Cerialis	1	
Arvernicus-Lutaevus	1	
'Kreis des Cerialis Ware B'	1	
Secundinus-Avitus/Comitialis I	1*	
Comitialis V	1*	
Comitialis VI	1	
Lupus	1	
Julius I-Lupus		3
Reginus II-Julius I-Lupus		1
Verschiedene Waren . Reginus II-Julius I-Lupus	1	
Julius I-Lupus or Perpetuus	1	
Victorinus I	1	
Verecundus II	2	
Helenius	1	
Attillus	1	
Attillus or Primitivus (III)	1	
Primitivus I	3	1
Primitivus IV	3	2
Julius II-Julianus I	5*	3
Victorinus II		1*
Respectinus II	1	
Victor I	1	
Perpetuus	1	
Pervincus I	1	
Regulinus	1	1
Total	**32**	**14**

Table 5 Rheinzabern mould-makers identified at Shadwell, ordered chronologically (cf Ricken and Thomas 2005). * = mould-stamped bowl

The mortaria

The excavations produced an interesting and significant assemblage of imported and locally produced mortaria, including evidence for the migration of a potter from Oxfordshire to the Nene Valley. Further details are provided below and in the archive.

Kay Hartley

Fabrics

Fabric 1: Soller, Kr. Düren in Lower Germany (Tomber and Dore 1998, 79–80)
Fabric: fine-textured cream with pale grey core; cream to dark cream slip.
Inclusions: packed with small to medium, sub-rounded, transparent quartz, but not evenly distributed, there are very occasional small pockets of fabric with few if any inclusions; very rare orange-brown material. The addition of the abundant inclusions produces a very hard fabric although the cream matrix would probably have been only moderately hard at best.
Trituration grit: very little survives, all of it quartz.
The example from context B[507] is a variant of Fabric 1 with smaller sized inclusions; giving a rather finer textured finish.

Fabric 2: Soller, Kr. Düren in Lower Germany (Tomber and Dore 1998, 79–80)
Fabric: fine-textured cream; cream slip.
Inclusions: packed with mostly small to medium, sub-rounded, but with some large fragments of orange-brown sandstone and quartz with occasional quartz sandstone and red-brown and black material.
Trituration grit: too little of inside surface survives.
As with fabric 1, the inclusions show in the surface.

Fabric 3: Soller, Kr. Düren in Lower Germany
Fabric: fine-textured cream; self-coloured.
Inclusions: moderate or more, extremely tiny inclusions which are barely indicated at x20 magnification; red-brown material with some quartz and probably rare black rock; very rare larger grains.
Trituration grit: (broken just below the bead) only four grits survive, three quartz and one black rock.
(Tomber and Dore 1998, 79–80 does not specifically mention this fine-textured version of the fabric, but it was produced occasionally by Verecundus (Verulamium, unpublished); both coarse and fine fabric versions were used at Soller for form Gillam 272 (Gilliam 1970) (see Haupt 1981, p389, taf 3, no.8 for examples of this form)

Fabric 4: Import, Taverny in the Val-D'Oise could be the source (Vermeesch 1993)
Black throughout except for the surface skin only, which is cream with patches of pink in places. This effect can almost certainly be attributed to post-firing oxidation (see Hartley 2007, 344–5, Fabric 4 for a discussion of this phenomenon).
Inclusions: moderate, mostly tiny quartz with occasional

orange-brown material and rare, medium-sized quartz. No trituration grit survives on the example for context B[316].

It should be mentioned that Vermeesch does not claim Taverny as a centre of pottery production, but the presence of such a large quantity of mortaria (also 'amphores' and 'cruches') at Taverny demands explanation. The only obvious explanation lies in either local pottery production or the presence of a store. Vermeesch does believe that some of the pottery present was probably made locally and the suggestion that all of the relevant light wares were being produced locally, at least in the second and third centuries, has to be considered as a serious possibility. The forms present differ from those made in the fairly extensive pottery production in the Oise and Somme areas (Hartley 1998, 203–206), and the main groups of mortaria at Taverny are mostly slightly later in date. It can also be said that the mortaria in figs 16 and 17 (Vermeesch 1993) follow a tradition that predominated in the Rhineland. Only careful examination of the pottery and further research can resolve the problems.

Fabric 5: Lower Nene valley, probably in the Castor-Stibbington area.
Fabric: self-coloured, drab cream with some pink near the surface; slightly sandy to the touch and tending to laminate in fracture.
Inclusions: frequent, minute (barely visible at x20); probably mostly quartz, but with some tiny red-brown and rare larger red-brown fragments.
Trituration grit: frequent, small to largish black slag with hackly fracture.

Fabric 6: Unknown source, probably fairly local
Fabric: fine-textured, orange-brown (up to 1.5mm thick) with thick dark grey core; probably self-coloured.
Inclusions: moderate, mostly very tiny red-brown material with occasional medium-sized red-brown and rare quartz.
Trituration grit: well-mixed, white and pinkish quartz, red-brown sandstone, quartz sandstone and rare black rock.

Fabric 7: Unknown source.
Fabric: Hard, off-white fabric, but pale brownish-pink near the surface, with an excellent, samian-like red-brown slip.
Inclusions: frequent, minute, transparent, quartz and very rare orange-brown material.
Trituration grit: small neatly fragmented, angular, white quartz, with few grey quartz and very rare red-brown material.

Catalogue

Context B[394], Period 4.5, Building 3e (Fig. 67.1)
(1705g, diam. above 800mm, 11%)
Fabric 1, Soller, Kr. Düren, Lower Germany. A mortarium with decorated band, 11mm wide, on top of the flange and adjacent to the bead, which gives a plaiting or basketwork effect. The best-recorded examples of this treatment are on mortaria found at Silchester (Haupt 1981, 385) and Soller (Haupt 1984, tafel 177). It was probably done with a wheeled tool and would have continued all round the circumference and along each side of the spout. This decoration is probably identical to that used on some of their jars (Haupt 1984, tafel 195); their jars have never been identified in Britain, but it is unlikely that only the mortaria were imported.

The fabric, form, size and decoration are entirely typical for the workshop, known to have existed close to Soller, Kr. Düren, in Lower Germany (Haupt 1984). Only a part of this pottery has been excavated, but the evidence suggests that it began at some point in the Antonine period and continued in the third century. The only potter there who stamped with a name, was Verecundus 2 and his mortaria are indistinguishable in form from those with decoration similar to the Shadwell example. The latter could well be products of Verecundus, but there is no known example where this type of decoration is associated with a stamp of Verecundus though he did sometimes impress his mortaria with 'eyes' to each side of the spout and with dents in the ends of the spout. There is, however, no doubt that the stamped and the heavily decorated mortaria are of generally similar date.

Such evidence as there is points to this production being within the period AD 170–230 (for discussion of the date and of Verecundus see Frere 1984, 289, no. 100); the unstamped and undecorated mortaria, both flanged and wall-sided, may be largely later in date but the flanged mortaria, at least, are unlikely to be later than AD 230–240. There is some indication in the rim-profiles to suggest that the decorated mortaria could have continued in production marginally longer than those stamped with the name Verecundus, but this example is strictly contemporary with those stamped with the name Verecundus.

There is no doubt that this pottery was serving markets in the Rhineland and in Britain and to date most of the decorated mortaria as well as those stamped by Verecundus have been recorded in Britain. Although the pottery did produce some more normal sized mortaria (still large with diameter *c.* 400–420mm) it is clear that there was a specialization in these huge flanged vessels which no doubt had a specific use. At Silchester the large number recorded were believed to indicate a kitchen.

Context B[507], Period 5.1, fill of pit B[508] within Building 7
(190g, diam. *c.* 560mm, 6.5%)
Fabric 1 with smaller inclusions giving a finer textured finish. Soller, Kr. Düren, Lower Germany. There is an excellent parallel in a decorated mortarium from Silchester, with an incised plain panel in place of a stamp (unpublished, now in Brighton Museum). Optimum date, AD 190–230. The smaller ones like 507 seem rarely to be stamped and it is possible that these are slightly later than the larger ones which, so far, are invariably stamped in some way or have decoration reminiscent of no. 394.

Context B[127], Period 4.3, boundary ditch recut
(90g, diam. 420mm, 7%)
Fabric 3. Soller, Kr. Düren in Lower Germany. This is the

finest version of Fabrics 1–2, the sole difference lying in the size and quantity of inclusions used. The rim-profile of this example is typical for the Soller workshop and can be matched at Silchester and Soller (Haupt 1984, tafel 176, no. 6). It could be contemporary with the potter who decorated his mortaria. Although Verecundus mostly used Fabrics 1–2 there are examples of his mortaria with stamps, in Fabric 3 (Verulamium, unpublished (Ver 63 A X 1)). The use of this fabric is always associated with the mortaria of smaller dimension, though with diameters of 400–420mm they are still fairly large. Optimum date AD 180–230.

Context B[511], Period 5.1, fill of pit B[508] within Building 7

Body sherd. Soller, Kr. Düren in Lower Germany.

Context B[316], Period 5.1, Building 7
(128g, diam. *c.* 760mm, 3%)

Fabric 4. This flange fragment is from a mortarium with a very distinctive profile. It is an import and on present evidence Taverny in the Val-d'Oise is perhaps the most likely source (see Vermeesch 1993, 132, fig 23, no. 831 for a good example). Mortaria of this type were normally in white to cream fabrics and this example is unique in being reduced except for the surface which has presumably become oxidised after firing (see Fabrics). Other examples of the type are known from Amiens (Stephane Dubois, pers. comm.); Caister-on-Sea (Darling and Gurney 1993, fig 158, no. 716), Carlisle (McCarthy 1990, fig 194, Period 9u), Wroxeter (Ellis 2000, 238, fig 4.73, M6.61) and elsewhere. There appears to be no good dating evidence, but it is not earlier than the third century and its import would fit within the period of import from Soller, and with that from other workshops in the Rhineland and ?Taverny, of type Gillam 272 (Gilliam 1970) (see Vermeesch 1993, figs 16–17) which probably continued into the second half of the third century.

Context B[465], Period 4.3, make-up for yard surface OA6
Oxford potteries (Cream fabric with deep pink core). Burnt. (Young 1977. M17) AD 240–300.

Context B[323], Period 6, fill of ditch B[324]
Oxford potteries (Cream fabric with brownish core) (Young 1977. M22) AD 240–400.

Context B[1300], Period 2, foreshore deposit
(135g, diam. 290mm, 10%)

VRW fabric, but greyish-brown in colour with grey core. There is no evidence to suggest that it would have been made other than in that region. Some mortaria were made in Verulamium region clay which had been transported down to a production area in the Walbrook valley in London in the period *c.* AD 110–140 (Seeley and Drummond-Murray 2005), but the later mortaria made there, including this general type were being made in oxidised fabrics and it seems unlikely that they continued to use VRW fabric there after *c.* AD 140. Worn.

The practice of stamping fell out of use in the Verulamium region potteries in the mid second century and this example is the type which took the place of the earlier flanged mortaria which were always stamped; these,

on the contrary, were not stamped. A good parallel for this example comes from *Verulamium* (Frere 1972, fig 130, no. 1038) and was in a deposit dated to AD 150–160, but this type could be attributed to the period AD 140–180.

Context A[51], Period 5.2 colluvium (Fig. 67.2)
(400g, diam. 260mm, 29%)

Fabric 6, unknown source, probably fairly local.

A mortarium with four-reeded, near vertical collar, which would best fit a third-century date. The vast majority of mortaria of the third and fourth centuries were produced in large potteries, which are now well-known. Small productions with local distributions continued to be active in parts of East Anglia, but there is little evidence of such activity elsewhere. The absence of flint in the trituration grit suggests that it is not from there or from Kent, and the likelihood is that it was made not far from Shadwell. Because small-scale production was limited and, in general, being eclipsed by the large potteries, one would expect it to belong to the first half of the third century rather than later and a date in the last decade of the second century is not impossible.

Context A[719], Period 4.3, clay layer in OA6
(160g, diam. *c.* 490mm, 6%)

Fabric 2, Soller, Kr. Düren, Lower Germany.

The slightly rounded, flange with thick distal end (Haupt 1984, tafel 176, no. 6) is more downward pointing than that on B[394]; this suggests a later date, probably later than the work of Verecundus. It could, however, just date within the period when the decorated mortaria were made or be only slightly later. Its optimum date is within the first decades of the third century; it unlikely to be later than AD 240.

Context A[722], Period 7, accumulation/colluvial deposit (Fig. 67.3) (300g, diam. 330mm, 25%)
Fabric 5, Lower Nene valley, west of Peterborough (Hartley 1960).

The form and spout (with thumb depression) are a perfect example of the form M18 made in the Oxford potteries (Atkinson 1941, fig 5, no. 68), but the fabric and especially the trituration grit are typical for potteries active in the Nene valley in the third and fourth centuries. It is perhaps just possible as an unusual product of the lower Nene valley potters, but it seems much more likely to be the product of an Oxford potter who had moved to the lower Nene valley. There are many compelling examples of migration from one pottery to another including several for the movement of Oxford potters: pottery and a kiln at Hartshill, Warks (Hartley 1973, fig 2, G); pottery at Cantley (unpublished); pottery in York attributed to Crambeck (Hartley 1995, fig 127, no. 74); see also Bird and Young 1981, 302–311. Young dates M18 to AD 240–300 (Young 1977).

Context A[1613], Period 5.1, dumped deposit (25g)
Fabric 5, Lower Nene valley, west of Peterborough (Hartley 1960).

Rim fragment with incomplete rim-section from a, reeded, wall-sided mortarium probably made in the late third or fourth centuries (Hartley 1960, fig 3, no. 11).

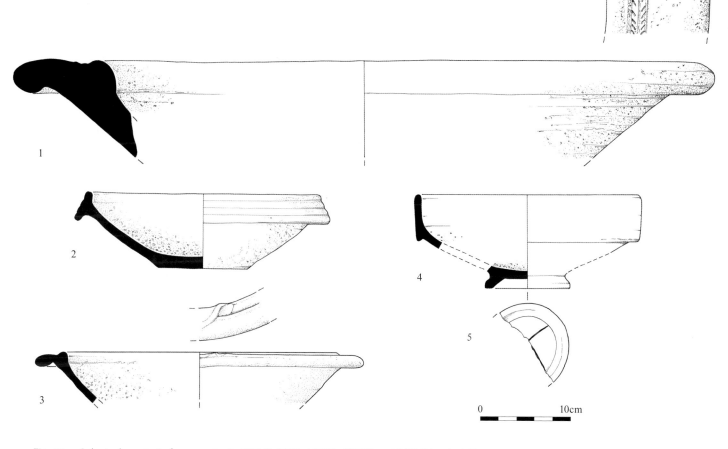

Fig. 67   Selected mortaria from contexts B[394], A[51], A[722], A[862] and A[916] (scale 1:4)

Context A[529], Period 6, dumped deposit
Painted wall-side missing.

Context A[935], Period 5.2, accumulated colluvial deposits covering revetment
Body sherd. Colchester.

Context A[668], Period 6, pit fill
Incomplete rim-section of a Young type M17/18 (Young 1977). AD 240–300.

Context A[904], Period 6, pitting adjacent to well A[1339]
Fabric 5, Lower Nene valley, west of Peterborough (Hartley 1960). In fabric this mortarium appears to be identical with Fabric 5 and it has the reeded form commonly used in the lower Nene valley, but it, nevertheless, has the basic attributes of the Oxford form M18. Young's dating for the M18, AD 240–300 (Young 1977) seems appropriate for it and it may well be from the same workshop as Context A[722] (see this for further comment). Burnt.

Context A[862], Period 5.1, fill of drainage ditch A[751] (Fig. 67.4)
Fabric 7. Two sherds, not joining, from a wall-sided mortarium of the samian form Drag. 45 or in the Oxford potteries, Young C97. The fabric and source are unknown. Young's dating for this form at Oxford is AD 240–400 and this example is either the product of a potter who had

moved from the Oxford potteries. It was suggested that a similar mortarium found at Lympne (Cunliffe 1980, 277, Other Fine wares) might have been made at Trier, but, if so, it would be very exceptional, because there is no evidence of regular import of colour-coated mortaria from the Continent. A potter working in Britain is more likely.

Context A[916], Period 3, construction make up for Building 2 (Fig. 67.5)
A base sherd from the same or a similar mortarium to A[862]. Fabric 7; source as A[862]. Presumably within the period AD 240–400. No slip survives on the inside probably due to wear.

Discussion

The most notable, single feature in this sample of mortaria is the number of mortaria imported from Soller, Kr. Düren in Lower Germany (1 from Site A and 3 from Site B). Soller mortaria are found at sites throughout England, but in small numbers, so that four in a sample as small as that from the stratified contexts on these two sites is large enough to be noteworthy. Three, at least, are strictly contemporary though B[394] might be somewhat earlier. It is also surprising that all four are flanged mortaria and that none of the collared mortaria of form Gilliam 272 (Gilliam 1970) are present, either from Soller or from other workshops in the Rhineland (Holbrook and Bidwell 1991, fig 56, C56 and fig 85, nos. C57–58); the reason for their absence is unclear.

It is assumed that the vast amount of East Gaulish samian, dated AD 235–250, reached the sites at approximately the same time (Bird above) and it would make good sense for the Soller mortaria to have come at the same time. This is a late date for the Soller mortaria (AD 170–240), which I would expect to have come earlier, rather than later in this period. In general imports from the Rhineland, including Gillam 272, might have been expected to supply a need before the Oxford potteries reached their peak of production in the mid third century.

Apart from the two, perhaps three mortaria, from unknown sources, the workshops involved are entirely normal for sites in London in the third and fourth centuries, with the Oxford potteries in the clear ascendant AD 240–400. The two Oxford M18 type mortaria apparently made in the lower Nene valley are worthy of note, implying as they do the migration of an Oxford potter.

The presence of three mortaria from unknown sources is perhaps unexpected since mortaria in this period came increasingly from large potteries producing pottery on what might be considered an industrial scale.

The amphorae

David Williams

General discussion

There are a relatively small number of amphorae types represented in the Shadwell assemblage, with only three general forms present in any appreciable numbers: Gauloise 4, Dressel 20/23 and North African cylindricals. Nevertheless, the assemblage is important not only because of the chronological range of the forms of imported late Roman amphorae which reached the site, where the vast majority of pottery recovered is of a mid third to late fourth-century date (Gerrard above), but also the insight which can be obtained from the consumption of imported foodstuffs and commercial contacts available.

The amphorae assemblage from Shadwell comprises 308 sherds (19.841kg), mostly bodysherds but with some featured sherds as well. The majority of these are Gallic in origin, comprising well over half of the total by count. No Gallic rims are present but a consideration of the fabrics present suggest it is likely that most of this material belongs to the flat-bottomed Gauloise 4 type, the commonest Gauloise amphorae form found in Roman Britain (Peacock and Williams 1986, Class 27; Laubenheimer 1985; and in Williams and Keay 2006). This form predominantly carried wine and the period of importation to Roman Britain is from the second half of the first century AD to the end of the third century AD. Any of this material found in later contexts on the site should be regarded as residual.

At Shadwell, Gauloise 4 is by far and away the main visible carrier of imported wine. However, during the fourth century, after Gauloise 4 ceased production, imported wine was almost certainly still reaching the site, though probably in smaller quantities. The single bodysherd displaying the unmistakable 'black sand' fabric of the Bay of Naples region from Period 5 must, at this date, surely represent the almond-rimmed type and have carried wine from the region. Although the contents of LR3 are unknown, wine is a strong possibility. LR3, and its predecessors, cover a very long period of production (Williams 2006). At Shadwell, small bodysherds typical of this type occur in Period 4 and Period 7. In addition, wine may also have been possibly carried in the Africana IIa and IIIa or *spatheion* recovered from Shadwell, for these vessels are suspected of carrying a range of goods. It is also quite possible that some of the undesignated amphorae sherds may represent amphorae that transported wine. Of course, there is no reason why imported wine should not have reached the site in other forms of containers such as barrels, or that locally produced wine was still available at this time. There is certainly evidence for Romano-British amphorae during the first two centuries AD though at present nothing later (Grew and Seeley in Williams and Keay 2006).

The Baetican olive-oil container Dressel 20, which on a wide range of sites in Roman Britain commonly reaches between 50–80% by weight of the total amphora assemblage (Williams and Peacock 1983), only represents some 27% at Shadwell. However, these figures should be put into some kind of perspective since Dressel 20 were large, thick walled vessels and many other amphorae forms, the Gauloise series for instance, were much smaller-sized and thinner-walled. Nevertheless, the smaller sherd count and weight totals at Shadwell may suggest that lesser amounts of Dressel 20 were actually reaching the site. These vessels were made specifically to transport by sea the large surplus of olive-oil produced by the many estates situated in the valley of the River Guadalquivir and its tributaries between Seville and Cordoba in the southern Spanish Roman province of *Baetica,* and some 150 kiln sites are presently known (Ponsich 1974, 1979, 1991; Remesal 1986; Peacock and Williams 1986, Class 25). This region of Spain was famous in antiquity for its fertility (Columella *De Re Rustica,* 5, 85; Pliny *Naturalis Historia,* 17.93) and especially for the intensive cultivation of the olive, which produced an abundance of good quality olive-oil for exportation (Pliny *Naturalis Historia,* 15.3.8; Strabo iii.2.6). Most of this appears to have been used to supply the city of Rome and the army, with a lesser amount earmarked for the civilian market (Haley 2003).

Dressel 20 amphora were occasionally stamped on the handle and sometimes still bear a complex arrangement of *tituli picti* which are variously interpreted as fiscal controls or information to enable traders and shippers to claim benefits for supplying the state with Baetican olive-oil (Rodriguez-Almeida 1989; Haley 2003). The Dressel 20 form was made over a long period, from the reign of Claudius until shortly after the middle of the third century AD. The latest *titulus pictus* found on a Dressel

	AMPH	BAET	CAMP	GAUL4	NACA	BIV	Total
Site A Sherd Count	16	33	1	31	38	0	119
Site B Sherd Count	12	22	0	140	12	3	189
Site A Weight (g)	1461	3814	68	1620	3348	0	10311
Site B Weight (g)	1050	1842	0	5086	1520	32	9530

Table 6 Quantification of the amphorae from Sites A and B.

20 vessel is from Rome and dated to AD 255, during the reign of Gallienus (Rodriguez-Almeida 1989). The end of production of Dressel 20 was due to a number of reasons, including strong competition from North African olive-oil (Williams and Carreras 1995). However, Baetican olive-oil was still exported after this date, though on a much reduced scale and in a smaller, thinner-walled version of Dressel 20 known as Dressel 23, which was made until the late fifth century/early sixth century AD (Carreras and Williams 2003; Carreras in Williams and Keay 2006). Unfortunately for identification, the fabrics for Dressel 23 are the same as for the earlier Dressel 20, so it is extremely difficult, if not impossible, to attribute and therefore give some general date to individual bodysherds such as those from the Shadwell site. If they belong to the Dressel 20 form the latest production date is just after the middle of the third century AD, if there are any Dressel 23 sherds amongst the assemblage, and Dressel 23 is present in Roman Britain (Carreras and Williams 2003), then they can be dated much later.

As a general group, North African cylindrical amphorae are known in Roman Britain from contexts as early as the Hadrianic–early Antonine period, though they are becoming increasingly more common in third and fourth century AD contexts (see Williams and Carerras 1995). However, compared with the Baetican olive-oil amphora Dressel 20, their numbers so far appear comparatively few. Moreover, the amount of North African olive-oil entering Roman Britain, even when Dressel 20 supplies were diminishing, could have been quite small in total, since these North African cylindrical types which once were automatically thought to have transported olive-oil, now seem to have carried a wider range of contents, including wine and fish products (see Bonifay in Williams and Keay 2006). In London, Africana I is known from Bishopsgate (Tyers 1984) and Billingsgate (Green 1980), both dated to the middle years of the second century AD. While African IIB occurs towards the end of the second century at West Tenter Street (Williams and Carreras 1995) and Africana IIC and D to the early to mid third century AD at New Fresh Wharf (Miller *et al.* 1986).

The earliest North African type at Shadwell is probably the Africana IIA form, found in Period 3, which was produced from the second half of the second century AD until the end of the third century AD. Although there are chronological differences between the remaining identifiable North African forms at Shadwell, they do centre around the fourth century AD. The Africana I rim from Shadwell, which comes from Period 5 is a variant on the IC form, with production extending into the fourth century AD. Africana IIIA found in Period 5 was also produced in the fourth century. While the *spatheion* type 1 from Period 7, was produced from the fourth to the middle of the fifth century AD. As for contents carried, as has been previously mentioned, apart from African I, which probably seems to have been restricted to olive-oil, the remainder of the North African types identified may well have carried a variety of goods, including wine, fish products and olives.

Catalogue

Gauloise 4 (GAUL)

Some one hundred and seventy-one sherds (6706) almost certainly belong to a series of flat-bottomed, thin-walled, wine amphorae produced in southern France, of which Gauloise 4 is by far the most common and it is likely that most, or indeed all, of the material below belongs to this form (Laubenheimer 1985; Laubenheimer in Williams and Keay 2006). Importation into Roman Britain of Gauloise 4 started sometime soon after the Boudiccan revolt (Peacock 1978) and by the early second century AD the type had became the most common wine amphora imported into the province (Peacock and Williams 1986, Class 27). The majority of the production was localised in the Narbonne region, while smaller centres were also situated in Languedoc and Provence (Laubenheimer 1985; Laubenheimer and Schmitt forthcoming). Local imitations are often found in other parts of France with different fabrics and in reduced quantities. *Tituli picti* mention that several different types of local wine were carried in Gauloise 4 (Laubenheimer 1985; Laubenheimer and Schmitt forthcoming). Production ceased towards the end of the third century AD.

North African Cylindricals (NACA/NAFR)

North African amphorae sherds (50, 4868g) were recovered in small quantities. Unfortunately, the assemblage was highly fragmented and few vessel forms could be distinguished. Africana I and II and IIIA were present along with a few sherds in the distinctive lime rich fabric from the Salakta region in Tunisia.

Africana I variant

Two joining parts of rim, probably from a variant of the Africana 1C form (Bonifay 2004, fig 56) from A[1533]. Production of Africana 1, which is thought to have carried olive-oil, occurred widely in Tunisia, at Carthage and especially at a number of sites along or near the eastern coast, at Hadrumetum, Leptiminus, Hr Ben Hassine, Sullecthum, Acholla, Thaenae, Nabeul and Oued el Akarit (Bonifay 2003; and in Williams and Keay 2006). It was widely distributed in the western Mediterranean during the second half of the second to the end of the third century AD but the later variants continue into the fourth century AD.

Africana IIA

Half of a rim and a bodysherd from an Africana IIA amphora from B[750]. There is a small corner of a stamp just under the rim but unfortunately too little remains to identify any characters. Strictly speaking, the rim-type is a variant of the Africana IIA form (Bonifay 2004, fig 58 no. 11 from the production site of Pupput, Tunisia). This is a fairly large cylindrical amphora type and is dated to the second half of the second century AD until the end of the third century AD. It was produced mainly at Zeugitana at Nabeul, in the Sahel region at Leptiminus and Hadrumetum, in the Sullecthum region (Salakta), at El-Assa near Cap Bon, at Ariana near Carthage, and at Thaenae in Byzacena (Bonifay 2004; 2005). It perhaps carried wine or fish-sauce (Bonifay 2004; 2005).

Africana IIIA

Two rim sherds and a bodysherd, almost certainly all from the same vessel, an Africana IIIA type (Bonifay 2004; 2005) from B[1473]. This is one of the most widely distributed African amphora forms that are found in the western Mediterranean, typologically falling between the amphorae of the Africana Grande series and the larger cylindrical African amphorae of the later fifth/sixth centuries AD. It is dated mainly to the fourth century AD, although early variants may occur during the third century AD. The form was produced at various centres in Tunisia and, as some of these vessels have been pitched internally, were presumably used for transporting ?wine or even fish sauce (Bonifay 2003; 2004; 2005).

Site A, A[1615] produced a complete everted rim, probably from a *spatheion* type 1, with long narrow body and tapering spike; it is not possible to say whether the rim belongs to the long or short varieties, though given the size probably the former (Bonifay 2004, fig 67) (see Fig. 60.11). The form was produced at several different centres from the fourth to the middle of the fifth century AD. Workshops are known at Carthage (Panella 1982) and Sidi Zahruni in the Nabeul region (Ghalia *et al.* 2005) and also Cartagena in Spain (Keay 1984). The fabric of the Shadwell rim suggests a North African origin. At times this form of amphora probably carried a variety of goods. Preserved olives can be deduced from the Dramont E wreck, as olive stones were found inside these vessels, but wine or even fish sauce may also have been carried (Bonifay 2003; 2004; 2005). It was fairly widely distributed, especially in the western Mediterranean (Bonifay in Williams and Keay 2006). Other North African amphorae sherds from this context include a small, curved, oval-shaped handle and a spike, possibly one of the Africana II series (*cf.* Bonifay 2004) (see Fig. 60.12, Fig. 60.13).

Salakta fabric

Two small bodysherds from the North African amphorae series in a very distinctive, noticeably calcareous, fabric from contexts on Site A (A[935] and A[1060]). These were almost certainly made at the production site of Sullechtum (Salakta), on the eastern coast of Tunisia, which produced a wide range of amphorae types, including Africana I, II and III (Bonifay 2004; 2005; and in Williams and Keay 2006).

Dressel 20/23 (BAET)

Fifty-five sherds (5656g) belong either to the globular-shaped Dressel 20 amphora form or its successor the smaller Dressel 23 (Peacock and Williams 1986, Classes 25 and 26; Carreras in Williams and Keay 2006). These two types carried olive-oil from the valley of the River Guadalquivir and its tributaries between Seville and Cordoba in the Roman southern Spanish province of Baetica and both appear in a similar fabric, so differentiation of undistinguished sherds can be difficult (Peacock and Williams 1986, Classes 25 and 26; Carreras in Williams and Keay 2006). The dating of production and supply of Dressel 20 and 23 forms are presented in the general discussion above.

Black Sand Fabric (CAMP)

A small plain bodysherd in the distinctive 'black sand' fabric commonly associated with amphora production (and other coarse ceramics) around the Bay of Naples region of Italy (Peacock 1977) was found on Site A, A[1327]. This amphora fabric is normally representative of the late republican and early imperial Dressel 1 and 2–4 forms (Peacock and Williams 1986, Classes 3, 4, 5 and 10). However, in recent years a later amphora form has been recognized which was also produced in Campania, including the Bay of Naples region, which due to the shape of its rim, is generally known as the 'almond-rimmed' type (Arthur and Williams 1992; Williams and Keay 2006). This was one of the regional products that superseded the Dressel 2–4 amphora form when Italy began to lose its trade dominance in amphorae shipments during the second/third centuries AD. This new form has a broadly similar shape to Dressel 2–4, although there are some noticeable typological changes. The handles are oval or round in section instead of bifid and the rim is almond-shaped, although with the same long cylindrical body and slightly flaring spike (*cf.* Williams in Williams and Keay 2006). As the form is similar to the wine-carrying Dressel 2–4, wine is a very strong possibility for the contents. A *titulus pictus* on a vessel of this type from San Clemente in Rome, gives an absolute consular date of AD 216 (Arthur 1987). It has also been found in contexts at Ostia dating to between AD 230 and 283 and at South Shields dated to the period AD 250–350 (Arthur and Williams 1992). It is not possible to identify which type of amphora the Shadwell bodysherd belongs to from the bodysherd alone, but the context of the find point to the later almond-rimmed type.

Late Roman 3 (BIV)

There are three small, deep reddish-brown, micaceous bodysherds with broad shallow ribbing from Site B. These sherds belong to the Late Roman Amphora 3 form or, perhaps more likely, to one of the earlier forms in the series. This general type of amphora has a long tradition in the eastern Mediterranean, from the first century BC to the fifth century AD , beginning with one short strap-handle and a small flat base and ending up with two handles and a more elongated form with hollow pointed spike (Lang 1955; Peacock and Williams 1986, Class 45; Sciallano and Sibella 1991; Williams in Williams and Keay 2006). There were probably several production sites in western Asia Minor, including Ephesus, the Meander Valley, Kusadasi, Miletos and possibly Pergamon (Reutman 1995; Ladstatter 2000). At present the exact contents carried are unknown. The one-handled form of LR 3 is known from several sites in Roman Britain (Thomas 1981a). Micaceous bodysherds, in all probability of this amphora form, are known from New Fresh Wharf in London dated to early to mid third-century AD levels (Miller *et al.* 1986), third century AD from Billingsgate Buildings (Green 1980) and AD 270–350/60 for a foot at Dowgate Hill (Symonds and Tomber 1991). The later form of this type has a particularly widespread distribution, including many post-Roman sites in western Britain and Ireland, where it has commonly been referred to as Biv (Thomas 1981a). Unfortunately, the three bodysherds from Shadwell are too small to identify the exact type they represent.

Other imports

James Gerrard

One explanation for the presence of the unusual amphora and samian assemblages is that the Shadwell sites lay near a point of importation for pottery and other goods into Britain. No formal dock installations of fourth-century date have yet been identified in London; in fact, no port facilities later than those of early third-century date excavated at New Fresh Wharf have been shown to exist (Brigham 1990a). Furthermore, dropping river levels and the construction of London's riverside wall may also have had an influence on the location of port facilities. Therefore the suggestion that the fourth-century maritime focus of London shifted downstream to Shadwell is an interesting hypothesis and one worthy of some further investigation.

The samian and amphora assemblages have been considered elsewhere and here the discussion is limited to the presence of other types of ceramic imports. These are summarised in Table 7 by fabric code and quantified by sherd count for both of the sites. Thirteen types of pottery imported into Britain and found in varying quantities in London during the third and fourth century are listed. As can be seen from the table the majority of the imports are derived from various sources in Gaul with the only

Code	Date	Source	Site A	Site B	Total	Old Ford
ARGO	250-400	E. Gaul	0	0	0	P
CGBL	150-250	C. Gaul	0	9	9	P
EIFL	250-400	E. Gaul	1	9	10	-
EPON	200-400	Gaul	0	0	0	P
LRMA	200-400	Gaul	1	1	2	-
MARB	50-400	Unknown	7	1	8	-
MAYEN	200-400	E. Gaul	22	6	28	P
MOSL	200-275	E. Gaul	8	43	51	P
NARS	70-400	N. Africa	0	5	5	P
NGGW	50-300	N. Gaul	2	14	16	P
NGWH	50-300	N. Gaul	12	2	14	-
SPEC	200-400	E. Gaul	0	0	0	-
SOLL	150-200	E. Gaul	0	7	7	-
Total			53	97	150	

Table 7 Imported pottery fabrics found in London (excluding samian and amphora) post-AD 150, with quantification for Site A and Site B by sherd count. The presence (P) or absence (-) of fabrics from Old Ford (Sheldon 1972, LFR69, LEK95, PRB95 and PNL98) is also indicated.

material sourced from further away the fragments of North African Red Slipped Ware (NARS). However, the imported material amounts to a mere two percent of the total assemblage, which is somewhat low for a site in direct contact with a point of importation (Symonds 2001). This point is further reinforced by a consideration of how many vessels this material might represent. No quantification by Minimum Number of Vessels was undertaken but what is immediately obvious is that if every sherd was derived from a different pot then we would still be talking of a very small number of vessels. Indeed, as all of the NARS sherds are likely to come from the same dish then we might, by extension, be talking of a much smaller population of imported vessels than that represented by the sherd count figures.

The pottery may not demonstrate that Shadwell was located in close proximity to a port. However, this material, the amphorae and samian were still imported into Britain and must have reached the mouth of the Thames by some maritime route. A comparison of the imported pottery at Shadwell with that recovered from a variety of sites at Old Ford is included in Table 7 and provides some comparable and contrasting data. While it is noticeable that there are many similarities there are also significant differences. In particular the absence of *Céramique à la Eponge* and Argonne ware, both of which are present at Old Ford and widely if thinly distributed around the Thames estuary, is noteworthy. Their absence may mean nothing or alternatively might suggest that there were slightly different exchange mechanisms supplying different points on the coast.

Specialised activities

The Shadwell site potentially offers an almost unique insight into the nature of an exclusively late Roman assemblage associated with bathing and other related activities. However, in practice ascertaining whether specialised activities took place that required specific ceramic assemblages is difficult and the problems inherent in 'reading' room or building function from associated finds have been well rehearsed over the last two decades (for instance Schiffer 1985). At Shadwell the usual problems are exacerbated by a lack of good groups. There are few substantial pit assemblages, no frozen moments of buildings and their contents destroyed by fire and an impression that most of the site's waste was disposed of off-site. Given this, it is difficult to provide more than an impressionistic view of site or building function from the pottery assemblage.

Two elements emerged from the analysis of the pottery by phase that might be interpretable in terms of site function. It was noted above that Site A produced a substantially greater proportion of AHFA than Site B and that conversely NVCC appeared to be more common on Site B. The Alice Holt/Farnham industries mainly produced fairly utilitarian kitchen and table wares and the Nene Valley products at Shadwell are mainly represented by drinking vessels. This *may* suggest that there is a broad functional distinction between Sites A and B with the former engaged in more cooking and eating orientated activities and Site B associated to a greater degree with consumption, especially of liquids. Unfortunately, this point cannot be demonstrated conclusively (or with statistical validity) in the absence of EVEs data for the two sites. However, such a study could be supported by the pottery archive.

The apparent emphasis on drinking vessels at Site B may be paralleled in the legionary baths at Caerleon (Wales), where the main drain produced a relatively high proportion of beakers (Greep 1986, 50). The pottery from the bath building on Site B amounted to a very small collection of 106 sherds (3156g). Such small assemblages are not unusual for baths, which by their very nature tend not to produce large groups of pottery (for instance Timby 2000, 281). It is noticeable, however, that almost twenty-three percent of the sherds from the baths are in fabrics usually used for drinking vessels (NVCC and COLCC, see also Key Group 3).

An attempt was made to ascertain whether other buildings on the two sites were associated with drinking (Table 8). Fabrics particularly associated with beakers and other drinking vessels (NVCC, COLCC, MOSL) were quantified by weight and sherd count for all of the structures (with the exception of Building 11) on Site A and the various phases of the baths and Building 3 on Site B. As was noted above, in the absence of EVEs quantification any conclusion drawn from such a study can only be impressionistic. Furthermore, it should be noted that taphonomic issues may be at work. A fine beaker will shatter into a greater number of sherds than a coarse jar, and a tiny thin beaker sherd is more likely to become incorporated into a brickearth floor than a large chunk of amphora, which someone could stub their toe on (Schiffer 1972).

Bearing the caveats outlined above in mind, the analysis reveals that the total assemblage associated with the various structures on Site A contains almost twice as many sherds in the beaker fabric as the overall Site A pottery assemblage. Similarly, at Site B the baths and the various phases of Building 3 reveal elevated percentages in the 'beaker' fabrics. This may suggest a concentration of vessels associated with drinking in these structures in contrast to other deposits at the two sites. A similar phenomenon was noted in the glass assemblage (see Chapter 3.5).

In the analysis of the pottery recovered from the urban baths at *Viroconium* (Wroxeter) Timby (2000, 308) suggested that a typical bathing assemblage might be expected to contain unguent flasks (Timby 2000, fig 4.94.40; Symonds 2000, 2J/9N), glass bath flasks and perhaps narrow-necked large jars alongside drinking vessels. All of these vessels would be associated with the pouring of liquids and the unguent flasks and glass bath flasks with oils for use in ablutions. No unguent flasks and surprisingly only one distinctive *aryballos*, were identified during these excavations, nor was there any apparent emphasis on narrow-necked large jars. That said, the presence of amphorae, which includes vessels from southern Spain and North Africa (Williams above) associated with olive-oil transportation, may be of significance here.

The amphorae assemblage is small but is divided in a seemingly significant fashion between Sites A and B (Fig. 68). Site A produced higher quantities of Spanish and North African amphorae than Site B. Three explanations

Site	Sherd Count	% Sherd Count	Weight (g)	% Weight
A Buildings (not 11)	234	20.94	6486	6.88
A Total	4061	10.10	112342	4.05
B Baths	106	22.64	3156	5.26
B Building 3	574	18.64	14538	4.73
B Total	2335	17.56	57729	6.86

Table 8   The proportions of sherds in fabrics associated with drinking vessels (NVCC, COLCC, MOSL) from various structures at Sites A and B compared with the proportions of such fabrics in the overall site assemblages.

for this phenomenon present themselves. Firstly, Baetican amphorae and probably North African amphorae were used for transporting olive-oil (Williams above; Williams and Carreras 1995). Thus their concentration at Site A may be connected to the higher percentage of 'cooking wares' discussed above. Secondly, given the proximity of the bath house the olive-oil amphorae may have been stored on Site A and the oil decanted into smaller vessels for use in bathing. Finally, we should note that it is impossible to tell whether our Baetican sherds were derived from the Dressel 20 or Dressel 23 form. As the Dressel 20 amphorae went out of production in the mid third century it is tempting to assume that the Baetican sherds indicate the continued importation of olive-oil in the smaller Dressel 23. However, Dressel 20 amphorae were useful containers once emptied and could have long and complex secondary uses (van der Werff 2003). Thus the importation of old Dressel 20 vessels onto the site as empty containers should be entertained as a possibility. This would favour a kitchen or storage function for aspects of Site A.

The other notable feature of the amphorae assemblage is the presence of substantially more Gauloise wine amphorae at Site B. This might lend support to the notion that drinking was an important activity at the baths. The end of Gauloise amphorae production *c*. AD 300 presents similar problems to that of the Baetican oil amphorae. However, it remains possible that all of the Gauloise amphorae reached the site toward the end of the production period, during the site's early phases (AD 250–300).

The only other evidence for specialised activities comes in the form of a number of complete vessels recovered from a well or placed in pits. The material from well

A[1399] has been discussed above and the possibility that the pottery and other finds from the fills of this feature may represent a structured deposit has been raised. Another very late Roman (Period 6) pit, A[937], also produced a complete pot, an AHFA jar of Lyne and Jefferies (1979) type 3B.14, dated AD 350+. There is a growing recognition that pits, shafts and wells formed important ritual foci, perhaps with chthonic undertones in the late Roman period (for instance Pearce 2004, 92–96). In London parallels for such deposits occur in Southwark, where a late third-century well contained in its backfill a variety of religious and funerary sculptures as well as the skeletons of a cat and a dog (Hammerson 1978) and also from Union Street where a pit contained a late Roman curse tablet (Heard 1989). In the City the recent discovery of a hoard of copper-alloy vessels deposited in or after the late fourth century at Drapers' Gardens may be an analogous, if higher status, deposit (Hawkins *et al.* 2008; Gerrard 2009; Ridgeway 2009).

It is difficult to demonstrate conclusively that any of these pots or groups of pottery is evidence of ritual activity and the Shadwell sites do not at first glance appear to be the type of site to attract such activity. Nevertheless, low level ritual acts appear to be a consistent thread from the Iron Age through the Roman period and even beyond in to the early middle ages. It is also worth remembering that bath houses are intimately connected with water and fresh water supplies (usually springs) that might form obvious ritual *foci* (the most famous example being Bath) and that ablutions and cleanliness can form an important part of ritual life.

Discussion

James Gerrard

In this final section an attempt has been made to bring the various elements of the pottery analysis together in a more general and discursive fashion. The aim of this is to explore some of the broader interpretive themes that run through the site narrative.

The nature and function of the late Roman settlement at Shadwell has been under discussion for some time and elsewhere in this volume (see Chapter 5) those issues are discussed at length. The contribution of the pottery assemblage to that debate essentially lies in what information it can provide regarding the function and status of the site: was it a military installation, an importation point or something else?

Given the difficulties over the interpretation of the structural remains (signal station or mausoleum) found at LD74/76 and the absence of any explicitly military items from either phase of excavation the 'military hypothesis' becomes extremely reliant on the interpretation of the East Gaulish samian assemblage. As Bird (above) has noted "some form of military or official occupation of the site [is] the most likely explanation" for the presence of this material. However, this explanation does lead to

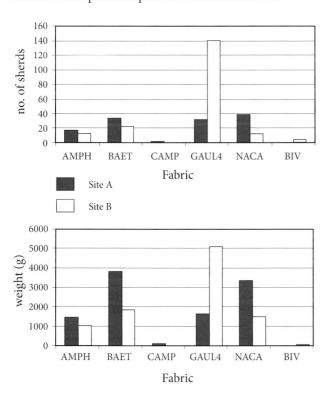

Fig. 68   Quantification of amphorae from Sites A and B by (a) sherd count, and (b) weight

a certain circularity of reasoning: East Gaulish samian assemblages are 'military' because they occur on 'military' sites and therefore the presence of East Gaulish samian (in the absence of all other military indicators) makes a site 'military' in function.

It is true that East Gaulish samian occurs on what appear to be military sites in the east of Britain. Substantial collections of East Gaulish samian from sites such as the 'Saxon Shore' forts at Brancaster and Caister-on-Sea and from the northern frontier zone seem to imply that the army was a primary consumer of these goods (Willis 2004, 6.7). This statement does, however, need to be qualified at a number of levels. After the cessation of samian supply from Central Gaul *c*. AD 200 (see King 1984; 1985 for a contentious alternative) samian supplies from Eastern Gaul were only a fraction of the level of previous imports from Lezoux. If there was demand for red-slipped tableware in the period AD 200–250/260 and, given that there were no insular producers of such wares until the rise of Oxfordshire red-slipped pottery in the mid third century (Young 1977), then one might expect those closest to the points of importation to be the recipients of all the pottery and to retain it (Willis 2004, 6.7.3). Under this model the concentration of East Gaulish samian in the east and on 'military' sites may be nothing more than the product of the simple geography: the east of Britain is closer to the mouth of the Rhine and thus the shipping carrying the pottery from Eastern Gaul (*passim* Plouviez 2004, 119). In this context it is worth noting that some of our explicitly military sites (such Saxon Shore forts) are also now seen as serving a multiplicity of functions: defence, safe storage of taxes and import/export nodes (Pearson 2005).

The second point that should be made concerns the 'high percentage' of East Gaulish samian that some of the eastern, military sites produce. The key issue here is the use of a percentage as a measure of comparability. If like is compared with like then percentages may indicate substantial differences. However, the high percentages of East Gaulish samian are only so striking because there is virtually no second century activity and thus very little Central Gaulish material (Willis 2004, 6.7.3). If there was a samian-using second century phase then the percentage of East Gaulish samian would be depressed. This in turn raises the spectre that when we discuss sites with high percentages of East Gaulish samian we are actually discussing sites founded in the late second or third century. Saxon Shore forts would largely fall into this category.

To summarise, the presence of East Gaulish samian *may* indicate an official or military connection *but should not be used to conclusively demonstrate such a function.* Other explanations can be advanced to explain the presence of this material. These include the simple fact that the site is a third-century foundation in eastern Britain or that it is close to an entry point for goods being imported into Britain from the continent. These arguments can also be levelled against Swan's (2009) recent and unconvincing interpretation of North Gaulish pottery (NGGW and NGWH) as indicators of contact with the *Classis Britanica*.

There is some evidence (other than the samian) for

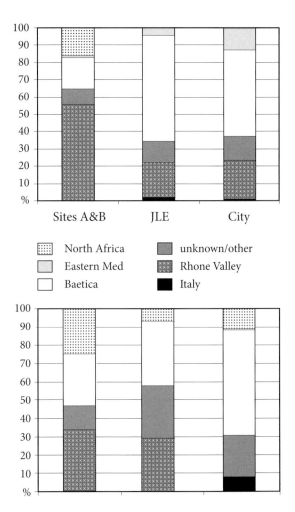

Fig. 69   The percentage of amphorae from various geographic regions (a) quantified by sherd count from Sites A and B, City of London sites and Jubilee Line sites; (b) quantified by weight from Sites A and B, the 'tower' site LD74/LD76, and New Fresh Wharf

long-distance trade at Shadwell. The most obvious element within the pottery assemblage is, of course, the amphorae (Williams above). The assemblage is small but distinctive as the following analysis demonstrates. The most striking aspect is the relatively high percentage of amphorae sherds from North Africa and the Rhone Valley. This makes the site stand out from the London background of the Jubilee Line Extension Project and the City (Fig. 69a). It also offers a substantial point of difference when comparison is made with New Fresh Wharf and LD74/76 (Fig. 69b). There is a danger here of falling into the same trap we have just explored with the samian. Substantial deposition of pottery on the site during the early Roman period would increase the percentages for Baetican and Gaulish amphorae and depress the North African total. Nevertheless, the total assemblage size for North African amphorae from Sites A and B (50 sherds, 4868g) still remains significant. The published statistics for the Jubilee Line Extension and the City indicate that only 23 and 9 North African sherds were present in those larger assemblages (Drummond-Murray *et al.* 2002, table 99).

Unfortunately, the amphorae present severe interpretive difficulties, which have been touched on above. Firstly, it is difficult to discriminate between the importation of the cargo-carrying amphorae and their sometimes complex and long-lasting secondary reuse (van der Werff 2003). Secondly, even if every one of the 308 amphorae sherds came from a different amphora then the assemblage is still smaller than a single ship's cargo. Thirdly, if that hypothetical population of 308 amphorae were consumed over the one hundred and fifty years from AD 250–400 then the inhabitants of the site were only consuming one amphora every six months – hardly conspicuous consumption. Alternatively, if all of the Spanish and Gaulish amphorae were imported before AD 300 then over two thirds of the hypothetical amphorae's contents were consumed in the first fifty years of the site's intensive occupation. Of course, site taphonomy is an issue. It is impossible to demonstrate how much rubbish was disposed of beyond the limit of excavation but this hypothetical exercise does bring the analysis face-to-face with some difficult issues. We can say that the inhabitants of the site probably consumed olive-oil, wine and other commodities such as figs, imported from the Mediterranean, but we cannot conclusively prove this or demonstrate the scale of consumption.

Similar problems confront the interpretation of other types of pottery import. They must have reached the site through long-distance maritime trade and exchange but they are not direct evidence of a 'port'. They could, for instance, have been traded to another point on the Thames and been traded on to Shadwell. Equally, it ought to be noted that the import-rich riverside 'dump' assemblages (so familiar to London archaeologists from sites such as New Fresh Wharf) may not exist at Shadwell even if the site did function as major importation point. If there were no formal wharves and dockside installations (which would require channel-side land reclamation and thus dumping) and the ships were beached and offloaded then any waste generated by such activities would probably have been rapidly washed away by the Thames. In short, the idea that goods moved along the Thames and reached Shadwell by water is clearly demonstrated by the ceramics. However, the case for Shadwell being a major importation site must, on present evidence, remain unproven.

The interpretation of the pottery assemblage offers few straightforward or hard and fast conclusions. Indeed, for much of the two sites' history there is little to distinguish Shadwell from any other fourth-century settlement in or around London. Dorset Black Burnished ware, Oxfordshire wares, pottery from the Alice Holt region all occur in ways that are more or less within the London norms (Symonds and Tomber 1991) and a picture of a 'normal' site with largely 'domestic' activities appears. However, there is one final issue that is worth exploring.

As has been discussed, the samian assemblage is dominated by East Gaulish products of third-century date and there is very little earlier Central Gaulish samian. It has been argued that this is largely due to the absence of second-century activity. However, as Wallace (2006) and others have observed the *production* of Central Gaulish samian may have ceased *c.* AD 200 but its *use*

did not. If the Shadwell settlement - which it seems clear was founded on an almost virgin site in the mid third century – had been established by a migrant population from nearby (for instance within *Londinium's* walls) it is surprising that there is not more Central Gaulish samian, which would have made it to the site as either treasured heirlooms or tableware, in use. Thus it might be speculatively suggested that the very low quantities of Central Gaulish samian on the site reflect an incoming population that did not bring its good and chattels (or at least Central Gaulish samian) with it.

If this interpretation is accepted then the next question to ask is where did such a population originate? Here it is noticeable that features associated with the occupation of Building 3 on Site B (Key Group 1) produced small assemblages of pottery that were almost exclusively composed of continental imports. When the pottery from Building 3 and its successive phases is considered (Fig. 70) it is noticeable that Buildings 3 and 3a, phased to Periods 3 and 4.1, appear to produce a higher percentage of imported pottery than the later incarnations of Building 3. This is based on small numbers of sherds but, when compared with Key Group 1, is suggestive that the earliest users of this building were using more pottery that originated on the continent than might otherwise be expected. This might in turn indicate that some of the people who established the Shadwell site originated on the far side of the English Channel and we are seeing the use of vessels imported as personal possessions during the earliest phases of the settlement.

Admittedly, an interpretation such as the one advanced above is highly speculative and probably beyond direct proof. However, other categories of finds from the site both oppose and lend support to this hypothesis. There are, for instance, no small finds which need have originated outside of Britain (see Chapter 3.3) but there are a number of unusual coins that might be best explained as direct imports (see Chapter 3.2, also Bird 2008, Lakin 2002). Why a population was moved or migrated to Shadwell remains a point for further speculation. The troubles of the third-century crisis probably caused population movement within Gaul and the Rhine frontier and it has been suggested before that Gallic refugees may have fled

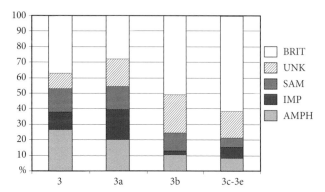

Fig. 70   The percentages of British, unknown, samian, imported and amphorae sherds from Building 3, Site B (3, N=140-; 3a, N=118; 3b, N=127; 3c-3e, N=147). Note the decline in imported wares from Building 3b onwards

to Britain with their wealth (Branigan 1976, 125–127). Equally, what we may be seeing is a manifestation of the growing power of members of the elite and their increasing control over the lives of their clients/tenants (Cameron 1993, 117–122).

Perhaps the Shadwell settlement, which was conveniently located close to the centre of political power but far enough away from it to avoid being under the direct gaze of the late Roman administration, offered an opportunity to develop a vibrant economic settlement populated and controlled by a *dominus* (patron/lord). Here the bath house would be a symbol of patronage and status while yielding income and many types of economic activity may have gone on in the surrounding settlement. Later medieval planned settlements created by the lord of the manor offer parallels that may not be too far wide of the mark (for instance Dixon 2007).

Conclusion

At the beginning of this report the significance of pottery in understanding the status of *Londinium* and its hinterland in the late Roman period was highlighted. The Shadwell pottery offers an unrivalled glimpse into a late assemblage of pottery largely uncontaminated by earlier, residual first- and second-century material. The assemblage has also raised more questions than it has answered. A satisfactory explanation for the presence of the East Gaulish samian and amphorae remains elusive and many of the other conclusions advanced above remain tentative. However, those conclusions do point at avenues that need to be explored and perhaps future developer-funded excavations will shed more light on whether the patterns identified here are typical of the Shadwell settlement as a whole.

3.2 Roman coins

James Gerrard

As is common with many Late Roman sites Site A and Site B both yielded large numbers of Roman coins. Two hundred and twenty-four coins were recovered from the former site with a further 210 from the latter (this high total is probably due in part to on-site metal detecting). When the collection is combined with the 474 coins found in earlier excavations at the 'tower' site (Hammerson 2002) it is clear that Shadwell has generated a substantial assemblage of Roman coinage. Unfortunately, many of the coins from Tobacco Dock and Babe Ruth were very poorly preserved with x-rays of the coins showing that no traces of any surfaces survived. This has meant that only two thirds of the Babe Ruth coins and fifty percent of the Tobacco Dock coins could be identified. A summary list of all coins is provided in Appendix 2. James Gerrard undertook the identifications of the Tobacco Dock coins and Mike Hammerson provided identifications for the Babe Ruth group. More detailed archive lists will be deposited along with the coins at the LAARC in due course.

Unusual or noteworthy coins

A small number of coins are worthy of detailed discussion as they are rare or otherwise unusual finds in a British context. Given the poor state of preservation of the assemblage the occurrence of these 'oddities' is worthy of some note as mintmarks and so forth were only rarely legible. Thus the actual number of examples with exotic origins and other unusual aspects may be greater than the few examples listed here.

A[1139], A<448>
OBV: [CON]STA[N-TINVS]AVG
REV: PROVIDEN-[TIAE] AVGG//SMANTE, Camp gate.
Ref: *RIC* VII (Antioch), 63, AD 325–326

B[210], B<80>
OBV: […]AVG
REV: VOT/XX/S, wreath
Ref: *RIC* VI (Ticinum), 36–38, AD 299

B[252], B<200>
OBV: Illegible, Constantinian
REV: [VICTORIA AVGVSTORVM] Victory advancing l. with wreath
Ref: *LRBCI*, 254–255 AD 341–348

Coins A<488> and B<80> are unusual in that they were both struck at mints under-represented in British assemblages (Fulford 1978). The mint at Ticinum in northern Italy was closed in AD 327 and its coins are uncommon finds in Britain. Coins from eastern Mediterranean mints are generally considered to be modern imports if found unstratified. However, our example, from Antioch in Syria, is noteworthy as a rare coin that has travelled an extremely long distance from mint to point of deposition. The other coin, B<200>, is also a rarity and a very unusual British find (Hammerson 2004). It is difficult to advance firm conclusions regarding these exotic or unusual coins. However, they and an issue of Aurelian B<572> (also rare as a site find in Britain) confirm the suggestion that the Shadwell coins have an unusual aspect (Bird 2008).

Group of silvered radiates

A group of three radiates of Postumus (B[386], B<268>were recovered fused together in a small stack and may be considered a small 'hoard'. Cleaning of these coins showed them to be in good condition and they still retain a silver wash, this suggests that they were not in circulation for long before loss.

B<268.1>
OBV: IMP C POSTVMVS PF AVG
REV: HERC DEVSONIENSI. Hercules stg. R., leaning on club, holding bow and lion's skin
Ref: *RIC* V(II), Postumus, 64

B<268.2>
OBV: IMP C POSTVMVS PF AVG

Fig. 71   Obverse of silvered radiate, coin B<268.2>

REV: HERC DEVSONIENSI. Hercules stg. R., leaning on club, holding bow and lion's skin
Ref: *RIC* V(II), Postumus, 64

B<268.3>
OBV: IMP C POSTVMVS PF AVG
REV: [SAR]API COMITI AVG. Serapis stg. l., raising r. hand and holding sceptre; in background, vessel.
Ref: *RIC* V(II), Postumus, 329

Group of Tetrarchic folles

Two groups of three coins each were found fused together in the fill (A[1050]) of Period 5.2 drain A[1225]. The first group A<429> was separated and partially cleaned to reveal three Tetrarchic *folles* of GENIO POVLI ROMANI type. The second group A<430> of three coins could not be separated by the conservator but are of a similar size and module. This suggests that the drain fill contained six *folles* of the period *c.* AD 296–306+. As these coins were soon driven from circulation it is likely that they represent a small 'purse group' but their presence in a drain of AD 325–375 indicates that they are 'residual' in the context in which they were found.

Fig. 72   Reverse of the three silvered radiates, B<268.1>, B<268.2>, B<268.3>

The distribution of coins by phase

The primary archaeological role of coins is as an aid to dating relative stratigraphic sequences. However, coins are small objects, easily disturbed and displaced from their original stratigraphic location by a variety of means. The Shadwell sites were excavated under difficult circumstances in the winter and it seemed appropriate to examine the distribution of legible coins by phase (Table 9). This enables the level of disturbance on site to be gauged and this information is potentially of use in the interpretation of other classes of artefact.

Site A produced no legible coins from Periods 1–3 and Period 4 produced only seven legible coins. Only one of these was later than AD 294 and the date of the exception, AD 364–378, indicates that it is intrusive. Period 5 covers the middle decades of the fourth century and ten coins of AD 330–378 confirm this date. However, there is a strong residual element in this phase with twenty-three coins of the late third or early fourth century present. The latest fourth-century phase (Period 6) produced fewer coins of the late third and early fourth centuries than in the preceding period. The only stratified coin minted near AD 375 in this phase is a single Valentinianic (AD 364–378) issue. Period 7, the 'sub-Roman phase' (perhaps of early fifth-century date) presents a similar pattern. This, combined with the fact that only a single Theodosian coin (AD 388–402) has been recovered from any Shadwell site, suggests that in the last decades of the fourth century the only coinage in circulation were Valentinianic issues and older coins. If Casey and Hoffman's (1999, 103) suggestion that virtually all pre-Valentinianic coinage was driven from circulation in the AD 360s is correct, then most of the coins from Periods 6 and 7 are residual and not just old currency continuing to circulate.

The picture presented by the coin finds from Site B is somewhat different. Periods 1–3 produce a few late third-century coins, which is not unreasonable but Period 4 yielded twelve coins of post-AD 330 date, including late fourth-century issues. This must surely be a product of intrusion and the complexities of excavating brickearth structures and their associated deposits in difficult conditions. Periods 5–7 show some chronological progression. Late third-century coins are present in smaller numbers and mid fourth-century finds are relatively common. The coins from Site B appear to indicate that there is a greater degree of disturbance or contamination than was present at Site A.

Analysis of coin loss

Various methods have been proposed to analyse the loss of coins on Roman sites. They are all based around dividing the Roman period into 'coin periods'. During the first and second centuries these 'coin periods' are imperial reigns, but by the fourth century changes in coin design are used. Various classification systems have been advocated by a number of different numismatists (Brickstock 2004;

Site A		41–259	259–275	275–294	294–317	317–330	330–348	348–364	364–378	378–388	388–402
Period 1–3	AD 50–275										
Period 4	AD 275–325	1		5				1			1
Period 5	AD 325–375		3	18	2		6	3	1		
Period 6	AD 375–410		2	7	1	1	4	3	1		
Period 7	'Sub-Roman'		1	4	3	3	5	2	1		
Site B											
Period 1–3	AD 50–275			1			1				
Period 4	AD 275–325	7	12	22	1		6		1	3	2
Period 5	AD 325–375	1	8	8			4	2			
Period 6	AD 375–410		3	9	1		3				
Period 7	'Sub-Roman'			1		1					

Table 9 The occurrence of legible stratified coins by site period at Sites A and B.

Lockyear 2007). However, the majority of coins from excavations in and around London have been published with reference to Hammerson's (1996) system and finds from southern England are usually discussed using the methodology suggested by Reece (1991; 1995). Both of these systems are used in this report to facilitate the comparison of Shadwell with London sites and those situated further afield.

A histogram of coin loss at the Shadwell sites can be presented using Hammerson's (2002) coin periods (Fig. 73). In crude terms coin loss begins in a significant fashion in the post-AD 253 period and continues with various fluctuations until the end of the Roman period. There are relatively few differences between the four groups of coins. It is, however, noticeable that the period AD 296–310, which is not represented in the LD74/76 finds, produced coins from Sites A and B. It may also be significant that the peak of Carausian coinage at LD76 in the period AD 287–296 is not followed by the coins from the other three sites. This may suggest that the Carausian peak at LD76 is the product of some special circumstance, such as a dispersed hoard. Finally, the presence of a single coin of Honorius in the last period (AD 388–402) is the first indication of the loss of coins minted after AD 388 at Shadwell.

Comparison of the Shadwell coins with those from the nearby settlement of Old Ford (Fig. 74) is also enlightening. Given the geographical proximity of these two sites, one might expect them to share similar patterns of coin loss. In broad terms this is true. Both sites appear to be late third-century foundations. Nevertheless, there are significant differences. The final period at Shadwell contrasts sharply with that at Old Ford. At Shadwell the period AD 388–402 is barely represented but a smaller overall number of coins from Old Ford contains a far higher number of coins of this period. Given the pottery evidence for late fourth-century activity at Shadwell it seems difficult to interpret this pattern in terms of a lessening in activity and an economic difference between the two sites should be entertained.

Shadwell coin loss and its deviation from the British mean

The analysis of the coin finds using Hammerson's coin periods represents a clear cut and straightforward method of interpreting the Shadwell sites against a local London background (Hammerson 1996, fig 19.4). However, Reece has pioneered a more sophisticated approach based on a sample of coins from one hundred and forty sites of all types from across Britain (1991; 1993; 1995). There is no need to explain this methodology in detail here as a full exposition has been published (Reece 1995). Nevertheless, a short summary of the approach is needed.

Essentially Reece (1995) took the numbers of coins per period per site and converted them into 'per mills' figures, which are basically percentages. These figures can then be viewed cumulatively and from the one hundred and forty sites a notional British mean figure can be established for each coin period. Any individual site can then be viewed as a deviation from this mean figure. This can be displayed as a line diagram with the horizontal axis representing the British mean and time and the vertical axis the deviation of the site in per mills (Fig. 75). It is important to note that these diagrams say nothing about the absolute numbers of coins lost in any period. What is significant is the direction of the line. If the line is parallel for two sites then coin loss is consistent, if the line moves down then less coins were being lost compared to the 'average' and vice versa (Reece 1995, 188).

The coins from the various phases of excavation at Shadwell reveal a remarkably consistent pattern of loss (Fig. 75). The only exception to this is Tobacco Dock, which broadly follows the same pattern but with some minor differences. However, this can be explained as a function of the smaller assemblage size at that site and when the coins from Tobacco Dock and Babe Ruth

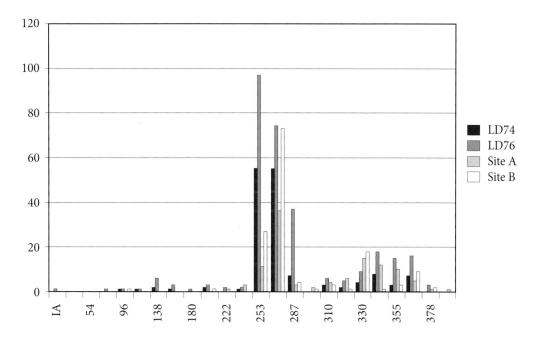

Fig. 73   Histogram of coins from Shadwell (coin periods after Hammerson 2002)

are combined or indeed amalgamated with the coins from the 'tower' site a consistent pattern emerges. This strongly suggests that the four sites (LD74, LD76, TOC02 and HGA02) represent excavations of different areas of a settlement with a homogenous history that began in the late third century. There is, for instance, no evidence from the coins for considerable early Roman activity in one area and not another.

Given the subtle but significant differences between Hammerson's and Reece's coin periods it is difficult to compare Shadwell to other London sites using this methodology. An attempt has been made though using data from finds in Southwark and a collection of coins from London in the Guildhall Museum (now the Museum of London) (Reece 1991). Coins from the satellite settlement of Old Ford (Gerrard *et al.* forthcoming), but a few kilometres from Shadwell, have also been included (Fig. 76). The pattern of loss is at first sight remarkably different. Both Southwark and the Guildhall Museum collection show rapid and extensive

loss in the early Roman period while Shadwell and Old Ford both lack early Roman occupation. Shadwell displays a dramatic rise in coin loss between periods 12 and 14 (AD 238–294), which is echoed by a far less spectacular rise at Old Ford. For the remainder of the Roman period Shadwell's coin loss appears similar to that expressed by the Southwark and Guildhall Museum coins.

The coins also enable us to come to grips with some of the grand interpretive issues that surround the interpretation of the Shadwell settlement and its status and function in the late Roman period. The 'tower' was originally interpreted as a signal station connecting the City of London to installations on the so-called Saxon Shore. This interpretation has been questioned recently and the tower reinterpreted as a mausoleum (Lakin 2002) with the surrounding buildings as part of a small but economically vibrant settlement. Comparison of Shadwell with Lympne, Portchester, Richborough and Reculver (all 'Saxon Shore' forts), Maryport (a coastal

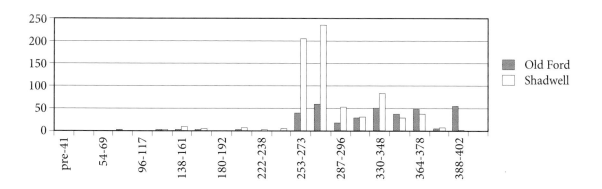

Fig. 74   Histogram of coins loss at Shadwell compared with Old Ford data

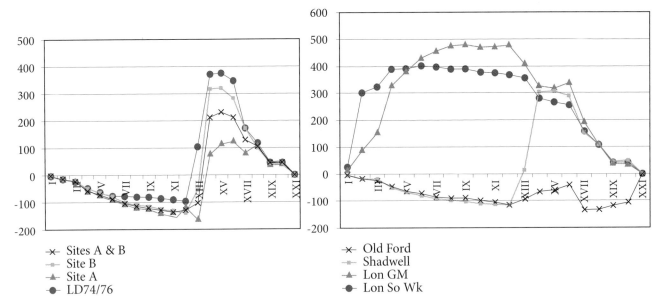

Fig. 75   The Shadwell sites and their coin loss deviation from the British mean (I – XXI = Reece's coin periods, see Appendix 2)

Fig. 76   Shadwell's coin loss deviation from the British mean compared to that for Southwark (Lon So Wk), coins in the Guildhall Museum (Lon GM) and Old Ford (Gerrard *et al.* forthcoming) (I – XXI = Reece's coin periods, see Appendix 2)

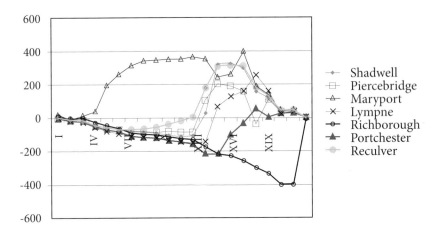

Fig. 77   Shadwell coin loss deviation from British mean compared to selected military sites (Reece 1991)

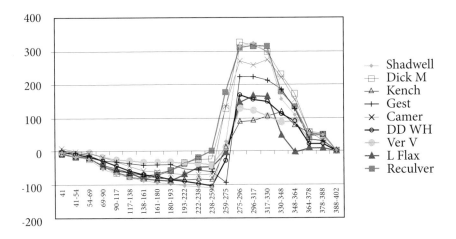

Fig. 78   Shadwell coin loss deviation from British mean compared to selected, mainly urban, sites showing similar deviations (Reece 1995, fig 16). Dicket Mead (Dick M), Kenchester (Kench), Gestingthorpe (Gest), Camerton (Camer), Dorchester, Wollaston House (DD WH), Verulamium, Lord Verulam (Ver V), Lincoln Flaxengate (L Flax) and Reculver (Reece 2005)

fort in Cumbria) and Piercebridge (a fort in Co. Durham that received East Gaulish Samian) reveals that Shadwell has very little in common in terms of coin loss with any of those sites, with the exception of Reculver (Fig. 77).

Reculver is the closest analogue among the military sites for Shadwell in terms of coin loss. However, coin loss at Reculver began during the second century - substantially earlier than at Shadwell. From Period XIV (AD 275–294) the pattern of loss at the two sites is almost exactly parallel but this cannot be held to suggest that Shadwell is a military site. As we have seen, the Saxon Shore forts do not display a consistent pattern of coin loss. It could be suggested that Shadwell was an installation manned by troops from Reculver. However, this would require those troops stationed at Shadwell to have existed in an economic bubble isolated from other coins users. A more likely explanation is that the similarity in the late third- and fourth-century patterns of loss at these two sites is the product of a similar economic history. Here we might look toward the two sites' coastal location for a possible explanation.

In contrast to the military sites, Shadwell's coin loss can be seen to be closely comparable with a group of mainly urban sites (Reece 1995, 197 and fig 16) (Fig. 78). These include major urban sites like Lincoln Flaxengate, Lord Verulam's collection of coins from St Albans (*Verulamium*) and Wollaston House, Dorchester (Dorset). There are also two 'small towns': Kenchester (Herefordshire) and the roadside settlement of Camerton (Somerset). Other non-urban sites include villas at Gestingthorpe (East Anglia) and Dicket Mead (Herts). Interestingly, it is these two villa sites that the Shadwell (and Reculver) pattern most closely follows.

Clearly, the group of sites that Shadwell sits most comfortably among includes a number of urban and semi-urban centres as well as sites that one might think are closely connected to urban economic systems. This strongly suggests that Shadwell should be seen in this light. It is also worth noting that the Wollaston House coins, Dorchester, come from the excavation of an unfortunately unpublished public bath house in a *civitas* capital. This may be significant given the structures excavated at Site B although it should be noted that statistical analysis of coin loss is not yet advanced enough (and may never be) to discriminate between different types of building and their functions.

A number of key points can be drawn from this discussion. Firstly, the Shadwell site is a late Roman settlement whose coin loss in the fourth century looks similar to that exhibited by London sites. Secondly, Shadwell's coin loss has little in common with military sites either located on the 'Saxon Shore' or further afield. Finally, Shadwell's coin loss shares many points in common with a number of urban sites. This combination of factors suggests that an interpretation of Shadwell as a semi-urban type of settlement appears more likely than that of the settlement as a military installation.

3.3 Romano-British small finds

James Gerrard

The Romano-British small finds from Sites A and B were originally assessed and catalogued by Lynne Keys and Märit Gaimster (2004) and Hilary Major (2004) and their work laid the foundations for this report. Site A produced 57 small finds and Site B 140 small finds (these totals exclude nails and objects of uncertain identification). The small finds are catalogued by site and by functional category following Crummy (1983) (Table 10). These functional categories are not unproblematic (Cool and Baxter 2002, 366; Crummy 2007, 64). Category 1 (personal adornments) is a very wide category encompassing many different types of object, Category 10 (tools) also encompasses a wide range of objects and activities, while Category 13 (military equipment) is very narrow in scope. Nevertheless, the categories are widely accepted and have been used elsewhere in London (for instance Keily 2007) and thus they provide a convenient way of summarising the assemblage and enabling comparison with other sites (Table 10).

The report is divided into two main sections. The first section is an illustrated and descriptive catalogue of selected small finds from Site A and Site B. This is followed by a more general discussion that focuses on what the small finds can reveal about the social and economic status of the Shadwell settlement.

Catalogue for Site A

Site A produced far fewer small finds than Site B and the majority of items are in a poorer state of preservation. For this reason only a summary discussion of these objects is provided here and the very similar classes of objects are well-illustrated in the finds catalogue provided for Site B. The exceptions to this rule are a small group of objects not represented in the Site B finds. These items are illustrated and discussed below.

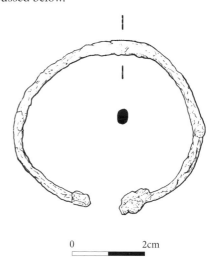

Fig. 79   Copper-alloy penannular bracelet, A<378> (scale 1:1)

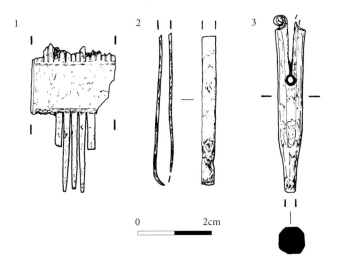

Fig. 80   Toilet, surgical and pharmaceutical instruments (1) double-sided bone comb, A<479>; (2) copper-alloy tweezers, A<594>; (3) copper-alloy scalpel handle (Milne 1907), A<398> (scale 1:1)

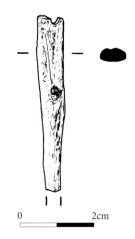

Fig. 81   Bone needle, A<456> (scale 1:1)

Personal adornments

Fourteen hair pins were recovered and with the single exception of a jet example were all manufactured in bone (see Fig. 37). They are all well-known late Roman types of Crummy's (1983) Types 3–6. There were also eight bracelets or bracelet fragments. Again they were all of late Roman types and mainly manufactured in copper-alloy (eg Fig. 79, A<378> from Period 5.1 fill A[750] of ditch A[751]). The exceptions to this were three Kimmeridge Shale examples. Other objects include two beads in jet and glass, as well as a jet bead spacer and poorly preserved fragments of what may be two brooches.

Toilet, surgical and pharmaceutical instruments

Three objects from Site A could be assigned to this category (Fig. 80). A pair of tweezers and a bone comb (A<594>, from Period 4.1, [1648], B5, A<479> Period 7, A[1060], dumping over B11, respectively) represent fairly common types of toilet instrument and an interest in controlling body hair. A less common find is a scalpel handle (A<398>, from Period 6, A[618]). Bathing establishments were often presumed to have curative properties in the Roman world (Jackson 1999). Wealthy visitors to the baths often brought their own personal doctors with them and 'general practitioners' might be found nearby, catering for the passing trade (Jackson 1999, 110).

Objects associated with textile working

Textile working was poorly represented in the finds assemblage, being represented by a mere two needles. The absence of spindle whorls and other textile working equipment suggests that any textile working was practised at a low-scale, domestic level. A single bone needle of Crummy's (1983) Type 2 (Fig. 81, A<456>, from Period

Category Number	Description	Site A	Site B
1	Objects of personal adornment or dress	34	112
2	Toilet, surgical or pharmaceutical instruments	3	1
3	Objects used in the manufacture or working of textiles	2	2
4	Household utensils and furniture	3	4
5	Objects used for recreational purposes	4	0
6	Objects employed in weighing and measuring	0	0
7	Objects used for or associated with written communications	0	1
8	Objects associated with transport	0	1
9	Buildings and services	0	2
10	Tools	0	5
11	Fasteners and Fittings	9	12
12	Objects associated with agriculture, horticulture and animal husbandry	0	0
13	Military equipment	0	0
14	Objects associated with religious beliefs and practices	0	0

Table 10 The Site A and Site B small finds assemblage summarised by Crummy's (1983, v) functional categories for the analysis of small finds.

6, A[1139], B11) was recovered alongside an incomplete copper-alloy needle (not illustrated).

Household utensils and furniture

Four items fall into the category of household utensils and furniture (Fig. 82). Pride of place among these items must go to the copper-alloy vessel from Period 7, well A[1399], perhaps a class of item that was more common than archaeological finds suggest. A copper-alloy drop handle

was found associated with this vessel but is not part of the bowl. A small fragment of copper-alloy vessel rim, A<179>, was retrieved from Period 6, A[369], fill of ditch A[391]. There is also a fragment of Kimmeridge Shale tabletop (A<698>, from Period 7, A[722], OA12) and a quern stone.

The quern stone A<696>, from the backfill A[1537] of the construction cut for well A[1399] (Fig. 83) was examined by Dr K. Hayward, who described it as 'Basal Quartz Conglomerate (Upper Devonian) of The Forest of Dean/South Wales region. Dark grey–brown matrix

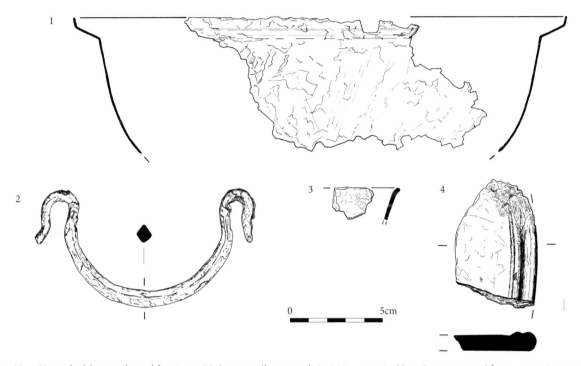

Fig. 82   Household utensils and furniture (1) Copper-alloy vessel, A<596>, a typical late Roman vessel form sometimes termed a '*bassin uni*' (Kennett 1969, fig 4.4–7); (2) copper-alloy drop handle; (3) copper-alloy vessel rim, A<179>; (4) Kimmeridge Shale tabletop fragment, A<698> (scale 1:2)

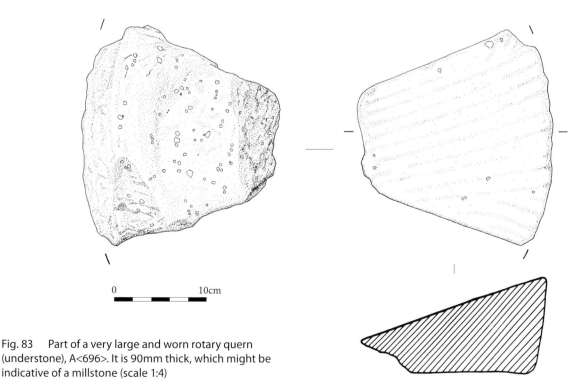

Fig. 83   Part of a very large and worn rotary quern (understone), A<696>. It is 90mm thick, which might be indicative of a millstone (scale 1:4)

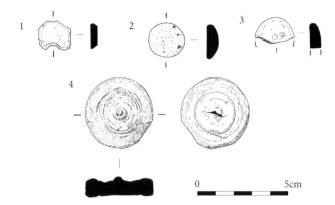

Fig. 84   Recreational objects (1) dark blue glass gaming counter, A<417>; (2) yellow glass gaming counter, A<446>, associated with coins of AD 268–364; (3) dark blue-green gaming counter, A<509>; (4) pottery beaker base in OXRC reused as a gaming piece, A<188> (scale 1:2)

supporting relatively small 1–2cm angular fractured quartz fragments and rusty brown lithic fragments (Old Red Sandstone). These materials were used in large quantities at Roman rural sites throughout central southern England (Shaffrey 2006). Its use in London is, however, unusual. The preferred material is nearly always German Lavastone or less frequently, Millstone Grit. However, the site's proximity to the River Thames (and therefore outcrops in Western England) no doubt would have been a factor in its use here' (Kevin Hayward, pers. comm.).

These objects sit at either end of the social spectrum: an exotic and presumably high status item of furniture, the tabletop fragment, and the labour in the kitchen that went into grinding flour.

Objects used for recreational purposes

The only recreational objects recovered in the excavations were four gaming counters (Fig. 84). Three were manufactured from glass and one from pottery. Gaming is an activity associated with baths and the presence of these objects at Site A may reflect the proximity of the baths at Site B. However, it should be noted that no gaming pieces were recovered from Site B (below) although a gaming board was found at the 'tower site' (Lakin 2002, fig 25 <S23>).

Catalogue for Site B

Personal adornments

Gold ear-ring B<240> (see Fig. 50; Fig. 85) made from a rectangular plate with filigree decoration. A hexagonal-sectioned green glass bead, now slightly damaged, is affixed to the centre by a length of wire. Four strips formed into a cruciform are soldered to the back, and the hook apparently soldered onto the centre of the cross rather than inserted. This was retrieved from Period 5, B<240>, B[383], pitting over Building 7. This object is paralleled by a less elaborate fourth-century ear-ring from Wincle, Cheshire. However, the Wincle ear-ring lacked the glass bead and had a less complex fixture for the hook (Allason-Jones 1989, 61, no. 73; variant on type 11). There is also an ear-ring with a round plate and similar cross on the back from Silchester (Allason-Jones 1989, 57, no. 59).

Six links, alternately short and long, from a fine gold and bead necklace B<33> came from a residual context B[180] (Fig. 51; Fig. 86). The links are formed from straight lengths of wire twisted at the ends to form loops. The fifth link from the hook has a small, opaque greyish-white glass bead with a pearl like sheen. The hook has a leaf-shaped plate soldered on, decorated with small nicks along the edges.

Several finger-rings and brooches were recovered from Site B, four of which are illustrated below (Fig. 87).

Silver or white-metal finger-ring with a plain circular section (B<204>, from Period 5 B[283], Fig. 87.1) was recovered from Period 5 pitting. A copper-alloy finger-ring, broken and in poor condition, with a hoop with humped shoulders and a line down each edge (B<18>, B[166], Fig. 87.2) came from Period 4.3 recut of the ditch in OA7. The raised oval bezel is missing its stone. Broadly identifiable as a Guiraud (1989, 185) Type 4 dated late second to the end of the third century.

A copper-alloy finger-ring comprising the bezel and a part of the hoop was recovered in two pieces and in a very poor condition, was residual in its context (B<39> B<40>, B[180], Fig. 87.3)

A one-piece copper-alloy brooch was recovered with the foot missing (B<231>, B[326], Fig. 87.4), from Period

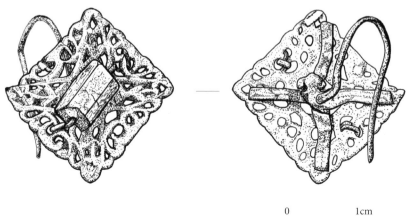

Fig. 85   Gold ear-ring, B<240>; front and back (scale 2:1)

5 pitting. The bow is round in section with transverse grooves along the top. This brooch belongs to a group of brooches with wire bows that are probably an indigenous development of continental wire bow brooches (Olivier 1996, 237). A first-century type. Given that there is very limited early Roman activity at Shadwell, it seems reasonable to suppose that this item either survived in use as an heirloom or found its way to the site in the late Roman period.

Sixteen fragments of bracelets were recovered from Site B. Of these fourteen examples were manufactured from Kimmeridge Shale, one bracelet was made from ivory and there was a single copper-alloy example. A representative selection is illustrated and described below.

Ivory armlet fragment (Period 6, B<77>, B[196]; Fig. 88; Fig. 89.1). A curved rod carved in imitation of cabling. Bone and ivory bracelets are relatively rare. Slender ivory examples with D-shaped cross sections are known from Late Roman burials at Lankhills (Clarke 1979, 312) and the Eastern Cemetery, where a complete example with a sub-rectangular section is also known (Barber and Bowsher 2000, 147). Outside of funerary contexts bone and ivory bracelets appear to be rarer finds and Hilary Cool (pers. comm.) suggests that they are a late fourth- and fifth-century phenomenon. The Late Roman fort at Portchester produced six bone bracelets and one (Cunliffe 1975, fig 117.100) appears to be a parallel; the inner precinct of the temple at Bath produced nine, including ivory examples (Henig 1985, 139 and fig 79.32). The latter site merely reinforces the unusual nature of this find and it is worth noting that the bracelet was found in a Period 6 pit fill with a coin of AD 364–375 and a small late fourth-century pottery assemblage.

Other bracelet fragments include the following:

A copper-alloy strip bracelet with edge decoration (B<368>, from Period 4.4, B[560], pit cutting B3b; Fig. 89.2).

A jet, segmented armlet bead, semi-circular and decorated with notches (B<17>, B[140], from Period 4.3, recut of boundary ditch OA7; Fig. 89.3). Such bracelets are known from the Eastern Cemetery (for instance Barber and Bowsher 2000, 224, B687.2) but direct parallels are provided by a burial from York (Allason-Jones 1996, no. 28) and finds from Colchester (Crummy 1983, 35). Late third or fourth century. The shale bracelets have been classified according to the scheme proposed by Mills and Woodward (1993) and all are well paralleled in late Roman assemblages from London (Barber and Bowsher 2000, table 111) and Dorset, where these items originated (Woodward 1987).

A shale bracelet with rectangular section (Type 65). Decorated with bands of notching on either side, alternating with plain bands (Mills and Woodward 1993, fig 78.3). (B<475>, Period 5, B[636]; Fig. 89.4)
Two shale bracelet fragments recovered from Period 4.3 pitting in OA6. A shale bracelet with sub-rectangular section (Type 52) was decorated with opposed nicks on

0   1cm

Fig. 86   Gold and bead necklace; six links, B<33> (scale 2:1)

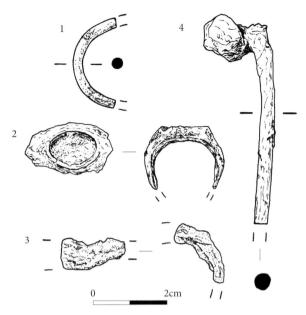

Fig. 87   Finger-rings and brooches: (1) silver or white-metal finger-ring, B<204>; (2) copper-alloy finger-ring, B<18>; (3) copper-alloy finger-ring, B<39>, B<40>; (4) one-piece copper-alloy brooch, B<231> (scale 1:1)

Fig. 88   Ivory armlet fragment, B<77>, B[196]

the outer edge of the broad faces (Mills and Woodward 1993, fig 78.6) (B<256>, B[396], Fig. 89.5). A shale bracelet with circular section (Type 2) and undecorated (B<257>, B[396], from Period 4.3, OA6 pitting; Fig. 89.6).

A shale bracelet fragment: the outer face has a central crest with two circumferential ridges either side, all decorated with notches. The inner face, unusually is also decorated, with a row of shallow oblique scoops, creating a cable effect, set down a central panel. The section would have been D-shaped (Type 57), but one edge has spalled off along the bedding plane, leaving the ridge along one edge incomplete. This must have occurred during manufacture or use, as the flat face has been carefully smoothed off (B<316>, B[470], from Period 4.5, B3e; Fig. 89.7).

A shale bracelet: rounded section (Type 2), the outer face of which is decorated with cabling (Woodward and Mills 1993, fig 78.4) (B<109>, B[617], from Period 5.1, OA6; Fig. 89.8).

Eighty-seven hair pins or fragments of hair pins were recovered from Site B with eighteen hair pins found in association with the various phases of Building 3. The vast majority of hair pins were manufactured in bone (83) with smaller numbers in jet (3) and copper-alloy (1). Where identifiable, the types present are late Roman and many of the hair pin shafts are 'swollen' in the manner considered by Greep (1995, 1117) to have begun in the mid second century and become more common during the third century. Twelve complete bone pins are illustrated along with one of the best preserved jet pins

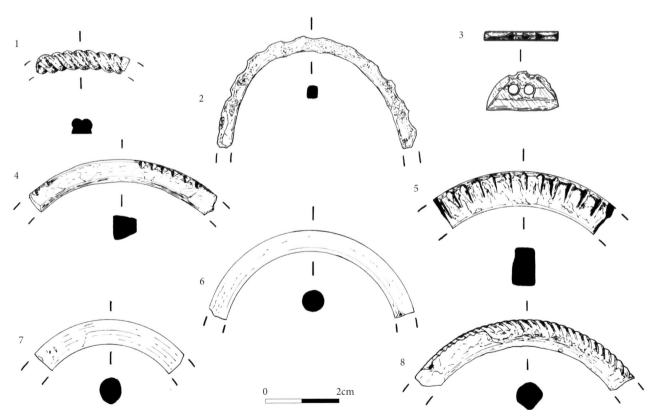

Fig. 89   Armlet and bracelets (1) Ivory armlet fragment, Period 6, B<77>, B[196]; (2) copper-alloy strip bracelet, Period 4.4, B<368>, B[560], pitting cutting B3b; (3) jet, segmented armlet bead, Period 4.3, B<17>, B[140], recut of boundary ditch OA7; (4) shale bracelet, Period 5 B<475>, B[636], OA6; (5) shale bracelet, Period 4.3, B<256>, B[396], OA6 pitting; (6) shale bracelet, Period 3.4, B<257>, B[396], OA6 pitting; (7) shale bracelet fragment, Period 4.5, B<316>, B[470], B3e; (8) shale bracelet, Period 5.1, B<109>, B[617], OA6 (scale 1:1)

and the lone copper-alloy example. Of the illustrated examples, six were recovered from Period 4 deposits, two from Period 5, one from Period 6 with the remaining five being residual or unstratified. These fourteen hair pins are a good representative sample of the types present in the assemblage and full details of the remaining pins can be found in the archive.

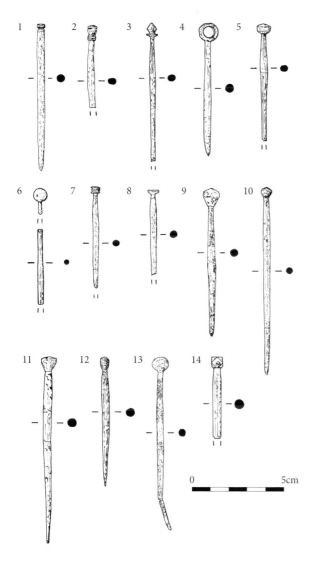

Fig. 90   Hair pins (1) bone hair pin with disc head and tapered shaft, B<21>; (2) bone hair pin with irregular faceted head, slightly domed on top, above two collars, B<22>; (3) bone hair pin with biconical head above a single collar, B<434>; (4) bone hair pin with ring head in the same plane as the shaft, B<202>; (5) bone hair pin with sub-globular head with a distinct facetted band around the middle, B<223>; (6) bone hair pin with spherical head, B<298>; (7) bone hair pin with three reels, B<362>; (8) bone hair pin with flat topped cylindrical head and facetted sides, B<379>; (9) bone hair pin with inverted conical head and low conical top, shaft is swollen, B<263>; (10) bone hair pin with sub-spherical head and an almost straight shaft, B<264>; (11) bone hair pin with an inverted conical head, slightly domed top and a swollen shaft, B<277>; (12) bone hair pin with elongated oval head, B<185>; (13) copper-alloy hair pin with knob head of Cool's (1990) Group 1, slight swelling of the shaft places it in sub-group E, tip is missing, B<228>; (14) jet hair pin with a small facetted cuboid head, B<279> (scale 1:2)

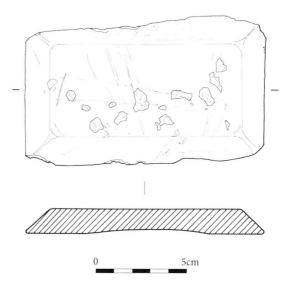

Fig. 91   Mixing palette, B<397>, probably Kimmeridge Shale/mudstone (Kevin Hayward, pers. comm). One face has bevelled edges and the other is dished. Both the face and edges have numerous fine cut marks (scale 1:2)

Fig. 92   Mixing palette and scalpel handle (scale 0.1m)

Toilet, surgical and pharmaceutical instruments

The only object assignable to this category was a stone mixing palette (B<397>, from Period 4.1, B[687], B3a). Such objects were used for mixing cosmetics and medicines and are often scored with marks made by either using or sharpening a scalpel (Crummy 1983, 57). The present example exhibits such marks, which is of interest given the recovery of a scalpel handle from Site A.

Household utensils and furniture

There were few objects that can be considered household utensils or furniture. Of the four objects that were found three were poorly stratified and of uncertain date, although the balance of probability is in favour of the Roman period. Two objects are illustrated here and it should also be noted that there is some overlap between this category and others, particularly fasteners and fittings. The everted rim of a copper-alloy sheet vessel (B<547>; Fig. 93.1) was unstratified. The form is not closely datable but may be Roman. A copper-alloy miniature human foot wearing a broad-toed sandal and possibly a sock (B<302>; Fig. 93.2) was recovered from Period 4.4, Building 3d. It is broken at the ankle. A similar foot from Alcester (Lloyd-Morgan 1994, 181 no. 125) retains a socket at the top, which would have formed the foot for a stand or small piece of furniture. The sandal's style suggests a third-century date (Major 2004).

Literacy and written communications

No styli or seal boxes were recovered from the site and the evidence for literacy is thus limited. The only possible object that might be associated with written communications is an unstratified lead sealing B<131>. Late Roman lead sealings are known from a number of sites, with Richborough and Ickham (Kent) producing examples of Constantius II and Julian as well as sealings of cities in the eastern half of the Empire (Hassall and

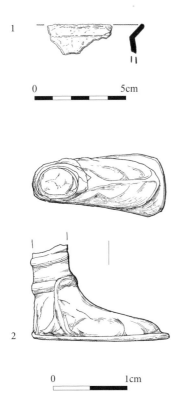

Fig. 93   Household utensils and furniture (1) The everted rim of a copper-alloy sheet vessel, B<547>; (2) miniature human foot wearing a broad-toed sandal and possibly a sock, broken at the ankle, B<302> (scales 1:2; 2:1)

Tomlin 1979, 350–353). If the sealing from Site B is of Roman date, then it may say more about the site's trading connections than literate communication.

Transportation

A fragment of a hipposandal was recovered from a Period 4.3 ditch (B<570>, B[135], not illustrated). The function of such temporary horseshoes is debatable. Some see them as horseshoes in the normal sense and others (Dixon and Southern 1992, 229) as veterinary aids (perhaps for holding poultices in place). Manning (1985, 63) argues that they are more common in towns and may be a response to riding horses on metalled streets.

Buildings and Services

Water pipe collars were recovered from Periods 3 (B<458>, B[835], B3) and 6 (B<580>, B[323], B4). These, along with the wooden finds, attest to a piped water supply, which would have been a necessity for the bath house.

Tools

The small collection of tools may be indicative of domestic or small-scale craft activity or even the maintenance of buildings. The absence of knives is noteworthy, although a whetstone attests to blades in need of sharpening.

An iron punch with a slightly rounded head, slightly swollen shaft and a blunt point was recovered from Period 4.5 dumping (B<290>, B[448]; Fig. 94.1). The slenderness of this example may suggest use in leather-working rather than metal-working (Manning 1985, pls. 5 and 16). Another punch was recovered from the fill of a Period 4.3 ditch (B<15>, (B137]). An iron leather-working awl of Manning's (1985, 41) Type 4b was recovered from Period 5 dumping over Building 3e, (B<272>, B[386]; Fig. 94.2). A damaged iron socketed chisel was recovered from a Period 7 layer associated with demolition of the bath house. The blade is broad and tapers towards the handle with sloping shoulders. The edge is bevelled. The socket is faceted with a hexagonal section (B<426>, B[646], Fig. 94.3). A broken greensand whetstone came from demolition deposits overlying Building 7. One side is worn, the other has a pronounced medial ridge. (Period 6, B<170>, B[250]; Fig. 94.4).

Fastenings and fittings

In common with many Roman sites the excavations produced large quantities of iron nails, copper-alloy studs, joiner's dogs, angle brackets and other types of fixtures and fittings. Full details of these are retained in the archive. From Building 3d a broken bone plaque fragment was recovered. One face is smooth and slightly curved, the other face has knife marks where it has been trimmed flat. The edges are well finished indicating that this is a broken object rather than waste; possible furniture inlay or some kind of mount (B<349>, B[521], from Period 4.4, B3d; Fig. 95).

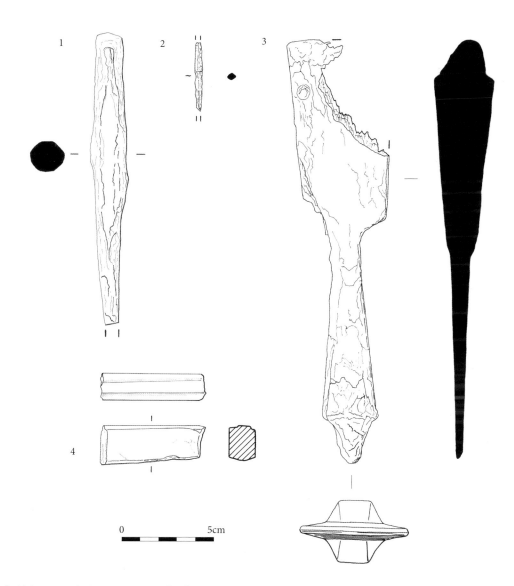

Fig. 94   Tools (1) Iron punch, B<290>; (2) iron leather-working awl, B<272>; (3) iron socketed chisel, damaged, B<426>; (4) greensand whetstone, broken, B<170> (scale 1:2)

Discussion

Elsewhere in this report (Chapter 1.4) major questions have been raised regarding the nature of the late Roman settlement at Shadwell. The excavations of the 1970s suggested that the site was essentially military in character and associated with a late Roman signal tower. More recent analysis has questioned this interpretation, which nonetheless remains well-embedded in archaeological literature. The current excavations have further complicated the situation by uncovering the structural remains of what appears to be the largest bath house constructed *de novo* during the late Roman period in Britain. Furthermore, a late Roman port or 'beachmarket' has been suggested as an alternative to the military context for the Shadwell settlement. The small finds from Sites A and B have much to add to this discussion.

Identifying 'military' small finds assemblages is rarely clear-cut (Gardner 2007) and Allason-Jones (1999) has reminded us that even seemingly 'civilian' and 'female'

Fig. 95   Bone plaque fragment, broken, B<349> (scale 1:2)

artefacts might be expected in a military installation. That said, one of the most striking aspects of the 1970s excavations of the 'tower' was the absence of any diagnostic military artefacts. The only object suggested as having possible military connections was a horse pendant recovered from an uncertain context and only known from an archive drawing (Lakin 2002, 26 and fig 25.26). This was described as of late second or third-century date and found "frequently in military contexts" (Lakin 2002, 53). Chance loss, either by a soldier or someone using 'army surplus' items, might explain its occurrence at the site. Furthermore, we should note that Sites A and B produced no military items. When this pattern is compared with small finds assemblages from less controversial military sites of third- and fourth-century date the contrast could not be more stark (Table 11).

As Table 11 demonstrates the Saxon Shore forts (Portchester, Reculver, Brancaster and Caister) produce a significant number of military items. The assemblages from those sites are, admittedly, larger. However, they are not so large as to invalidate direct comparison with the assemblage from Site B. The drain groups present a less clear-cut pattern. The number of military items from the Caerleon baths is small and there were no distinctively military objects from the York drain. Here two issues come into play. Firstly, both of the drain groups are from legionary sites and not directly comparable in date to

	Military items	Other objects
Site A	0	57
Site B	0	140
Portchester	18	220
Reculver	14	171
Brancaster *Vicus*	13	85
Caister on Sea	49	1028
Caerleon drain	5	310
York drain	0	67

Table 11 Comparison of the number of objects from Sites A and B with 'military' assemblages from the Saxon Shore forts of Portchester (Cunliffe 1975), Reculver (Philp 2005), Brancaster Vicus (Hinchliffe and Sparey Green 1985) and Caister-on-Sea (Darling and Gurney 1993). 'Military' groups from drains associated with two legionary bathhouses at Caerleon (Zienkiewicz 1986) and York (MacGregor 1976) are also included.

	Toilet, pharmaceutical and medical	Recreation	Other objects
Site A	3	6	48
Site B	1	0	139
York drain	0	25	42
Caerleon drain	4	42	269
Bath: inner precinct	1	3	41
Wroxeter	7	3	140

Table 12 Comparison of toilet and medical items and recreational objects with 'bath' assemblages from the drains associated with the legionary baths at Caerleon (Zienkiewicz 1986) and York (MacGregor 1976), the urban baths at Wroxeter (Ellis 2000) and the inner precinct of the temple attached to the bathing complex at Bath (Henig 1985).

Shadwell. Secondly, they are derived from the fills of drains and the drain fills at Site B remain unexcavated. Nevertheless, if one is looking for a military site then the absence of military objects or even quasi-military items (such as Hawkes and Dunning 1961) belt fittings and crossbow brooches) at Shadwell strongly indicates that this was not a military installation during the third and fourth centuries.

The military drain groups neatly bring this discussion to the question of the bath house at Site B. Many bath houses (civilian and military) have been dug in Roman Britain and elsewhere but there have been few modern publications of small finds assemblages associated with such structures. Out of the urban bath houses (both public and private) identified in London none has yet been fully published and the majority of such structures in London and elsewhere are of early Roman date. Even large urban baths with late Roman phases, like those dug at Wroxeter (Shropshire), cannot provide a straightforward comparison with Shadwell. Their small finds assemblages are often extremely large and only partially published and usually contaminated with large numbers of residual objects. Thus in attempting to identify a 'bath house' small-finds assemblage one is left reliant on impressions rather than clearly identifiable patterning.

The most obvious items that might be expected of a bath house assemblage are the accoutrements of bathing and its ancillary activities: strigils, oil flasks, toilet instruments, medical instruments and recreational items. Strigils are rare finds (for instance Zienkiewicz 1986, 157) and the search for oil flasks is probably better directed toward the pottery and glass assemblages than the small finds. There are certainly no copper-alloy vessels that would have suited such a purpose in the assemblages from Sites A and B. Such valuable vessels would be unlikely to escape reuse and recycling and their absence from the assemblage need not indicate that they were not used on the site (Nenova-Merdjanova 1999). The remaining toilet instruments are few in number: a comb A<479>, tweezers A<594> and a cosmetic or mixing palette B<397>. There are no toilet spoons, spoon-probes or nail cleaners (Crummy 1983, 59–61), which may be significant given that such items are not uncommon in late Roman deposits (for instance Keily 2007, 148).

The only medical instrument is the scalpel handle A<398> from Site A. The practising of medicine and surgery at baths is well attested in Classical literary sources and supported by archaeological finds from some sites (Jackson 1999). The stone palette B<397> discussed above could conceivably have been used in the preparation of medicines rather than cosmetics (Crummy 1983, 57). Recreational items are also in short supply with only four gaming pieces recovered from Site A.

Comparison of the numbers of toilet and medical objects and recreational items with a small number of other bath assemblages is enlightening (Table 12). The drain groups from Caerleon and York both have high numbers of recreational objects, mainly gaming pieces. However, as was noted above directly comparable features were not excavated at Shadwell so it remains to be seen whether the poor representation of gaming pieces is a real phenomenon (a fragment of gaming board from LD76 should be noted: Lakin 2002, 53). Two other sites have also been included for comparison purposes. The first of these is the late Roman phases in the inner precinct of the temple at Bath. Strictly speaking this should be seen as a religious assemblage associated with a bathing complex. The second site is the late Roman phases of the urban baths at Wroxeter. Here caution is needed because the small finds were published selectively. Neither site produced many recreational objects and it may also be significant that there were few toilet and medical items recovered from any of the four sites used in this comparison.

The small finds assemblage does not on its own suggest that Sites A and B were a bathing establishment. However, it is difficult to identify a suite of objects that can be used to 'demonstrate' bathing. A number of objects, such as the scalpel handle and palette, are suitable in a baths context and, when combined with the structural analysis (see Chapter 2.3) support the interpretation of the Site B structure as a bath house and the Site A buildings as ancillary to that structure.

So far this discussion has concentrated primarily on establishing whether the Shadwell site had a military and/or bathing complex. No evidence has been found for a military component to the site but some evidence has been forthcoming relating to bathing. In this final section the remainder of the small finds assemblage is examined in order to shed light on the two sites' status and function.

A number of objects suggest that some who lived at or visited the Shadwell settlement were of relatively high status. There are two gold objects — an ear-ring B<240> (Fig. 50; Fig. 85) and a part of a necklace B<33> (Fig. 51; Fig. 86) – that should indicate the presence of wealthy women. The evidence for a practising doctor, discussed above, would also indicate either the presence of such a professional in a wealthy individual's entourage or the ability of people locally to pay for a doctor's services (Jackson 1999, 110). Indeed, the use of oily hot baths to ease labour is attested in the ancient world (Jackson 1999, 112) and specialist gynaecological surgeons seem to have operated in late Roman Britain (Farwell and Molleson 1993, 152, pls 51 and 52). This would provide one possible link between the wealthy female artefacts and the evidence for a doctor's presence.

Other high status personal objects include a silver or white-metal finger-ring B<204> and four copper-alloy examples (A<259>, A<575>, B<39 & 40>, B<18>), which suggest some pretension to status. They recall Ammianus Marcellinus' contemporary (if geographically distant) moralizing account of the wealthy bathing in late fourth-century Italy:

When they leave the bath of Silvanus or the spa of Mamae, each of them as he emerges from the water dries himself with a fine linen towel. Then he has his presses opened up and makes a thorough inspection of his shimmering robes, of which he has brought enough to dress eleven people. Finally, he makes his choice and puts them on, takes back from his valet the rings which he has left with him to avoid damage from the water, and goes his way. Ammianus Marcellinus 28.4.18–19, (Hamilton 1986, 361).

The presence of fragments from three copper-alloy vessels (A<179>, A<596>, B<547>) suggests that the tables of some were well set. Some may also have had access to richly furnished rooms, if the miniature bronze foot B<302> and Kimmeridge Shale tabletop fragment A<698> are any guide. Investment in maintaining the internal decor of the building is further demonstrated by the surviving wall plaster (see 3.4 below).

One other element of the small finds assemblage is also of note when considering the sites' status. Only a single fragment of quern was recovered A<696>. Given that broken querns tend to become incorporated into levelling dumps or cobbled surfaces the virtual absence of this type of object is intriguing. It may suggest that grain grinding took place in a different part of the site. Alternatively, it might indicate that the inhabitants were supplied with or bought flour ground off-site by water or animal power.

Despite the evidence for some relatively high status objects, the majority of personal adornments are more run-of-the-mill. Bone hair pins were extremely common with almost one hundred identified. This total includes fragments of shafts and points that might conceivably be derived from needles. This seems unlikely though as very few needles were identified in the assemblage. Five other hair pins were manufactured from jet (4 pins) and copper-alloy (1 pin). The ratio of bone to copper-alloy pins seems somewhat high at 96:1 and comparison with other London sites appears to confirm this with the

Hair pins	Bone	Shale/jet	Cu	Reference
Site A	13	1	0	
Site B	83	3	1	
Tabard Square, Southwark	37	2	9	Gerrard 2007
15-23 Southwark Street	68	4	4	Cowan 1993
71 Fenchurch St	18	0	1	Keily 2007, 148
E. Cemetery	11	3	0	Barber and Bowsher 2000, Table 115

Table 13 A comparison of hair pin finds from a number of London sites. Note the relatively low number of copper-alloy hair pins at Shadwell.

understandable exception of the eastern cemetery (Table 13). It is reasonable to assume, following Crummy (1983, 20), that copper-alloy and jet hair pins were more valuable or desirable than their bone counterparts, which could be produced in the home. This may, therefore, be an indicator of the relatively low status of a major part of the site's population.

The bracelet assemblage also has some unusual elements (Table 14). The most obvious of these is the ivory example B<77>. Bone armlets are relatively rare, though this may be due, at least in part, to their fragility. Ivory examples are even harder to find but fragments of three have been published from fifth century and later contexts in the temple precinct at Bath (Henig 1985, 139). If the exotic nature of the material was appreciated by the wearer then the bracelet could be seen as a high status object.

The remainder of the bracelet assemblage is dominated by Kimmeridge Shale and, to a lesser extent, jet objects. These materials may have been seen as the same in the Roman period and it has been argued that jet/shale were exclusively female materials (Allason-Jones 1996). The ratio of shale/jet to copper-alloy bracelets stands at approximately 3:1. This appears unusually high and from a broad range of sites can only be paralleled in Dorchester (Dorset) (Table 14).

Comparison of the diameters of the shale bracelets from Shadwell with those from Greyhound Yard, Dorchester reveals a close similarity in size, perhaps suggesting some uniformity in production between bracelets manufactured for the 'Durotrigian home market' and those produced for 'export'. The relatively small diameters exhibited by these bracelets would also seem to confirm that they predominantly worn by women.

Women surely performed a variety of roles at the baths and in the adjacent settlement. Some were no doubt users of the bathing establishment and others may have worked, either for wages or as slaves, in nearby buildings. Historical analogy would also suggest that a bath house would serve as a focus for prostitution (both male and female) and the contemporary Ammianus Marcellinus was moved to comment cuttingly that:

Some dressed in gleaming silk, go about preceded by a crowd of people… and are followed by a throng of noisy slaves in formation. When such people, each attended by a train of some fifty, enter the public baths they shout in a pre-emptory voice: 'What has become of our girls?' If they hear of the sudden appearance of some obscure strumpet, some old street-walker who has earned her living by selling herself to the townsfolk, they vie in courting and caressing the newcomer… Ammianus Marcellinus 28.4.8–9 (Hamilton 1986, 359).

The Emperor Julian's description of what an ideal city should be also makes clear the link between bath house and brothel; such a city was:

…full of many shrines and many secret rites, with countless holy priests within its walls dwelling in holy enclosures. For the sake of this, I mean keeping everything in the city pure, they have expelled what is superfluous, sordid, and vicious from the city—public baths, brothels, shops and everything of that sort without exception. Julian, Orat. 6, 186d (Barnes 1998).

Bracelets	Bone	Shale/jet	Cu	Reference
Site A	0	3	5	
Site B	1	14	1	
Tabard Square, Southwark	0	8	5	Gerrard and Major 2007
15-23 Southwark Street	1	5	7	Cowan 1993
71 Fenchurch St	0	2	0	Keily 2007, 148
E. Cemetery	2	17	20	Barber and Bowsher 2000, Table 111
Gillingham, Kent	0	0	14	Gerrard and Gaimster 2007
Ilchester	0	6	25	Leach 1982
Portchester	6	6	20	Cunliffe 1975
Bath	9	0	2	Henig 1985
Chichester	0	0	2	Gerrard 2007
Dorchester	0	70	28	Woodward *et al.* 1993
Exeter	0	20	12	Holbrook and Bidwell 1991
Shepton Mallet	0	3	16	Leach and Evans 2001
Reculver	1	4	9	Philp 2005, 164 and 176
Brancaster *Vicus*	0	8	4	Hinchliffe and Sparey Green 1985, 41-62
Caister-on-Sea	1	28	34	Darling and Gurney 1993, 81-85

Table 14 A comparison of bracelet finds from a number of London sites, a late Roman site in Kent, West Country sites and 'Saxon shore' sites. Note the relatively high number of shale bracelets at Shadwell compared to other types. A ratio of approximately three shale bracelets to one copper-alloy bracelet is only encountered at Dorchester, which is close to the region where these objects were produced.

A recovered pair of women's leather underpants from the tower site (Lakin 2002, 57–60) might be related to this type of activity. Wilmott (1982, 52–55) associated this type of garment with semi-nude acrobats and dancing girls, although van Driel Murray (Lakin 2002, 58–59) has preferred a less lascivious interpretation.

Other activities have left more obvious traces in the small finds assemblage. The discovery of a chisel, whetstone, an awl and two punches suggest that the bathing complex and adjacent structures may have had some sort of craft working function. The awl B<272> and punches B<15>, B<290> may all have been used in leatherworking and a small cobbler's shop would be a suitable adjunct to the baths. The chisel B<426> points to wood or stone working and may be associated with the upkeep of the buildings and the whetstone B<170> merely indicates the sharpening of tools. Interestingly, and in contrast to many sites, there are no knives or cleavers. This suggests that domestic areas, where food might be prepared, lie outside of the excavated area. Similarly, the lack of objects associated with textile working strongly suggests that this domestic activity also took place elsewhere within the settlement.

Conclusion

The value of the Shadwell finds lies in their almost exclusively late Roman nature. Unlike many City sites the assemblage can be studied without any serious complications imposed by residual material from early Roman phases of activity. They also enable something of the site's social and economic nature to be characterised. There is no evidence for any military activity at or near the site. The overwhelmingly civilian assemblage indicates that high status individuals did visit the establishment and lost items of jewellery, some made from precious metals. Those visitors may also have stayed in well-appointed rooms decorated with expensive furniture and eaten from tables set with metal vessels. Yet, that high status element in the population was served by a much greater population of more limited means. However, it is difficult to clearly identify what that population's role was. We can identify a doctor, perhaps a cobbler and contemporary literary accounts would suggest that prostitutes, hawkers, vendors, slaves and lackeys would also have been active around the baths.

3.4 Building materials

Berni Sudds

A large assemblage of Roman ceramic and stone building material was collected from Sites A and B amounting to over 1500kg. The majority was recovered from Site B where remains of a large bath house were revealed. Although preserved *in situ*, and subject only to limited excavation, the material sampled from the bath house remains and

recovered from associated demolition deposits accounts for nearly half of the combined site assemblages by weight. The condition of the material from both sites is generally good, but particularly so with the material from the bath house demonstrating low fragmentation and a high average fragment weight of 878g. From Site A 332 fragments, weighing 84.182kg were recovered, while totals from Site B amount to 3096 fragments, weighing 1418.955kg.

Methodology

The building materials were examined using the London system of classification. A fabric number has been allocated to each object, specifying composition, form, method of manufacture and approximate date range. Examples of the fabrics can be found in the archives of PCA and/or the Museum of London. The material was examined under magnification (x20) and quantified by dimension, number and weight. Following analysis the majority of the assemblage was discarded with type samples of each fabric retained for the archive. Unusual or marked fragments were also kept. The assemblage retained is available for consultation at the LAARC (see Chapter 1.3), along with a digital copy of the full building material database.

This report focuses upon the sampled and loose building material directly related to the individual buildings on site, highlighting any unparalleled or intrinsically interesting fragments. The marked and stamped tile is then discussed collectively from Sites A and B, including many as yet unparalleled types.

Characterisation of the Roman buildings

Building 4: the bath house (Site B)

A total of 678,604g of building material was recovered from the bath house, the majority from deposits associated with the final robbing and collapse of the building. A limited number of masonry samples were also collected and the *in-situ* recording of fabrics and forms in selected elements of the structure undertaken on site. The materials associated with the structure and the various phases of remodelling are presented below in Table 16. As derived from a single dated structure the large assemblage not only represents a good group for quantification but also an opportunity to observe the range and utilisation of materials during the third century. An outline of the techniques used in construction appears in the archaeological sequence and a more general discussion of the appearance of the bath house and supply of materials for construction in Chapter 4.

Ceramic building material fabrics

Ceramic building material was used in the construction of the bath house to form lacing courses, to frame

Fabric group	Number	%	Weight	%
2815 *(2452; 2459a; 3004; 3006)*	553	76.5	512995	79
Kent *(2454; 3022)*	13	2	6225	1
Hertfordshire *(3023; 3060; 3023b; 3060b)*	54	7.5	51937	8
North-east London/ Essex? *(2459b and 2459c)*	70	10	57606	9
Late calcareous tile *(2453; 2457; 3026)*	24	3	14584	2
Other	9	1	4806	1

Table 15 Quantification of building material fabrics for Building 4.

openings and for more specialised structures including the *pilae* stacks and cavity walling of the hypocaust. Where analysed *in situ* the lacing courses and flue abutments include fragments of brick and tile, almost entirely in the local 2815 fabric group made predominantly at tileries located along Watling Street into Hertfordshire. Occasional examples of fabric 2454 and 3022 are evident, manufactured in Kent, but fabrics 2452, 2459a, 3004 and 3006 of the 2815 group represent the most frequently occurring types. Smaller quantities of tile in fabrics 2459b and 2459c were also identified, originally included under the 2815 group but now thought to be of a different origin, potentially somewhere to the north-east of London or in Essex. Other elements of the building demonstrate the more selective use of a single main fabric. Of the eight *pilae* stacks of the original build analysed *in situ* (B[958] to B[965]) the vast majority were constructed of bricks in fabric 3006. Similarly, a section of masonry located above the arched flue linking the apse with the main building (wall B[920]), thought to represent a secondary phase of fitting out and flooring of the original build, was found to be built almost exclusively of bricks in fabric 2459b.

A more complete and reliable representation of the fabrics used in the construction of the bath house is revealed, however, when the sampled and loose demolition is also considered. A breakdown of the main fabric groups recorded for Building 4 appears in Table 15 and Table 16. The local 2815 group indeed represents the dominant type with 2459b and 2459c and Kentish examples (2454 and 3022) evident in smaller quantities but use of Hertfordshire iron oxide fabrics (3023/b and 3060/b) and late calcareous tile (2453, 2457 and 3026) is also apparent. The remaining types include 3024, an uncommon fabric with distinctive calcareous moulding sand, and a small number of unsourced examples (fabric 3500). A provenance for 3024 is not yet known but it always occurs as roofing tile and may represent a late fabric (Ian Betts, pers. comm.).

If, as proposed, Building 4 is likely to have been constructed sometime between AD 230 and 260, a minimum of 85% of the ceramic building material must have been reused. The Kent fabrics, 2454 and 3022, were manufactured during the second half of the first century (*c.* AD 50 to 80) and the local 2815 group and early Hertfordshire fabrics (3023 and 3060) from the mid first to early or mid second century. Production of

Period	Fabrics	Forms	Marks*
3	2452; 2459a; 3006; 3006nr2452; 2454; 3022; 3023; 2459b; 2453; 3023b; mortar; Kentish ragstone; chalk; flint; Reigate stone; Septaria	Box-flue (combed); half box-flue; hollow voussoir; brick (*bessalis; pedalis; lydion*); *imbrex*; *tegula*; tile	3006nr2452 (SX26); 2452 (SX14); graffiti
4.1	2452; 2459a; 3004; 3006; 3006nr2452; 2454; 3023; 3060; 3024; 2459b; 2453; 3026; 3060b; Kentish ragstone; chalk; flint	Box-flue (combed); brick; *imbrex*; *tegula*; tile; unfaced stone	3006 (S1); 3006nr2452 (SX21); 3023 (SX7); semi-circular type signature
4.2	2452; 2459a; 3006; 2454; 3023; 3060; 2459b; 2459c; 3026; 3023b; mortar; Kentish ragstone; chalk; flint; oolitic limestone; Reigate stone	Brick (comb keyed; *bessalis; pedalis; lydion*); *imbrex*; *tegula*; tile; moulded stone column base (reused)	2452 (S26); 3006 (SX17); 3023 (SX19=S6); 2452 (SX20); 2459c (S3); curvilinear signature
4.3	Carrara marble; Forest marble	Paving stone	-
5.1	2459a; 3023; 2453; *opus signinum*; Kentish ragstone; chalk; flint; Reigate stone; Septeria	Box-flue (combed); half box-flue; *tegula*; tile	3023 (SX16) & numerals
7	2452; 2452nr3006; 2459a; 3004; 3006; 2454; 3022; 3023; 3060; 2459b; 2459c; 2453; 2457; 3026; 3060b; 3500; mortar; *opus signinum*; Kentish ragstone; calcareous tufa/limestone	Box-flue (combed); hollow voussoir; brick (*bessalis; pedalis; lydion; sesquipedalis; bipedalis*); *opus spicatum*; *imbrex*; *tegula*; tile; unfaced stone; faced stone; architectural moulding	2452nr3006 (SX22); 2452, 2452nr3006, 3006 (SX23); 3006 (SX6); 3006 (SX2; SX3; SX24); 2459a (SX5); 3023 (SX7); 3023; 3060 (SX4); 2459b (S2; SX1; SX25); semi-circular type signature; double circle type signature: graffiti

Table 16 Summary of building materials by period for Building 4. *Excludes accidental marks. S = signature followed by number in corpus. SX = unparalleled signature type.

the later Hertfordshire examples (3023b and 3060b), beginning in the second half of the second century had also ceased by *c.* AD 230. The late Roman fabrics identified would, however, have still been in production during construction represented by the late calcareous tile fabrics (2453, 2457 and 3026), dated from *c.* AD 140 to 300, and just possibly the north-east London or Essex 2459b and 2459c types, manufactured from *c.* AD 120 or 140 until *c.* AD 250.

Table 16 depicts a breakdown of the different fabrics, forms and tile marks encountered in each period of the bath house. When viewed overall there is no apparent chronological pattern to the use of materials in successive phases of remodelling with each of the main fabric groups present from the original build throughout. As largely reused, where one fabric predominates, as evident with 3006 in the *pilae* stacks and also with the box-flue tile, this is not representative of batch ordering direct from the tilery but more likely reflects the materials utilised at the source of salvage or perhaps that specific fabrics were used in the manufacture of certain forms. From the sampled assemblage it is also evident that other fabrics, namely from Hertfordshire (3023, 3023b and 3060b), were also used in the construction of the *pilae* of the original build and later modifications and might suggest materials were sourced from more than one structure from the outset.

Some of the later Roman brick and tile (2459b, 2459c, 2453, 2457 and 3026) associated with Building 4 is fragmented and apparently also reused as general building rubble (Table 16). Indeed, although potentially just still in production at the time of construction the 2459b used in a secondary fitting out of the original build noted above is mostly fragmented and probably reused. This could mean that initial construction of the building is more likely to have post dated *c.* AD 250 when the production of 2459b ceased although it could equally be argued that the structure pre-dates 250 and that even though new examples were still available sourcing material from disused buildings was deemed preferable for economic reasons. It is likely, however, that at least some of late Roman calcareous roof tiles (fabrics 2453, 2457 and 3026) recovered from the demolition deposits were acquired new. None demonstrate any obvious sign of reuse and whilst it is possible to reuse fragmented brick and tile to build walls and foundations it is not likely to have been so easy to find or salvage sufficient complete roof tiles from derelict buildings that would be essential for the construction of a new roof.

A source for the late calcareous tiles has not yet been identified although it was likely to have been at some distance from London, possibly along the south coast or perhaps even on the continent (Betts and Foot 1994, 32–33). Due to the frequency with which these fabrics occur in third and fourth century deposits in London it has been suggested that production was taking place until at least *c.* AD 300. It is also clear from the forms recovered that the tilery predominantly manufactured roof tile, most likely for the reason suggested above.

Ceramic building material forms

Walls

The reuse of material is particularly evident in the walls of Building 4. Examples of each of the main Roman brick types have been identified from the smallest to largest, including *bessales*, *pedales*, *lydion*, *sesquipedales* and *bipedales*. The use of *tegulae* and box-flue tiles has also been recorded. Despite the walls being two Roman feet thick (*c.* 0.60m), however, equating exactly to the dimensions of a *bipedales* no complete examples of the latter were recorded. Similarly to the roof tile, if for different reasons, these are likely to have been more difficult to salvage whole. Where complete these were probably set aside to bridge the *pilae* stacks of the hypocaust, representing one of the functions for which they were designed and as recorded in a surviving collapsed section of the *suspensura*. Complete or near complete *bessales*, *pedales* and *lydion* were identified in the walls but the majority of the lacing courses were constructed of fragmented brick and tile, generally restricted to facing the rubble core rather than forming a continuous course throughout. Exceptions to this were recorded, most notably with the use of complete *tegulae* running perpendicular through the apsidal wall (B[946]) flange upwards as a continuous lacing course. Instead of measuring two feet wide the wall thus measured 0.40m, matching the average length of *tegula*.

A single triangular brick was recovered from the loose building material assemblage on site that, if not coincidental, may have been made by sawing a brick in half. This technique is common on the continent in the construction of brick facing but occurs far less frequently in Britain (Adam 2001, 145–148; Brodribb 1987, 49).

Cavity walling and hollow voussoir tile

From the *in-situ* remains, masonry samples and demolition material it is evident that the cavity walling of the bath house was probably constructed exclusively of comb-keyed box-flue tile. Over 90% is of the local 2815 fabric group with 3006 representing just over half of this and fabrics 2452, 2459a, and 3004 accounting for the remainder. The other 8% is mainly from Radlett in Hertfordshire (3023 and 3060) with just two examples identified in fabric 2459b. The majority was produced from the late first to early or mid second century but the two fragments of 2459b post date *c.* AD 120 by which time the production of the Hertfordshire box-flue had ceased. As with much of the rest of the assemblage the box-flue tile is reused in Building 4 but the presence of material of mixed date may provide further evidence that the material was derived from more than one structure. The majority, however, is likely to have originally derived from a hypocausted building or buildings constructed at the end of first century or early second century.

The Hertfordshire examples have complex combing typical to the industry comprised primarily of combinations of vertical, horizontal and diagonal combing, often crossed. The 2815 group is also combed

Fig. 96   A selection of the box-flue tiles from the site

with a variety of patterns, most equally elaborate, including vertical, horizontal and diagonal patterns, often crossed, but also wavy and curvilinear designs. The combed-keying usually occurs on the two opposing faces of the box-flue. The sides are predominantly plain, often pierced by a lateral vent. The majority of vents identified are rectangular although a handful of circular examples were also recorded. A small number of box-flue tiles demonstrate combing to the sides as well as the face. With small fragments this can cause some confusion in identification as hollow voussoir tiles are often keyed on all four faces.

Two half-box-flue tiles manufactured at Radlett (fabric 3023) were also recorded from the bath house, both reused as general building material (see Fig. 42). Half-box-flue tiles represent rare finds in London but the examples from Shadwell are particularly unusual in that they derive from a tilery that is thought to have produced only combed box-flues (Betts 2003, 114) and they have unscored bases. Prior to this half-box-flue tiles have been recorded in London only in fabrics 2454 and 2815 and with diamond-lattice scoring (Pringle 2007, 207; 2002, 154; Crowley 2005, 96). Both are also complete, representing the first whole examples recovered from London, albeit in a new fabric (Pringle 2002, 154). They are considerably smaller than the average recorded elsewhere across Britain being 336mm in length, 260mm in width and with a flange depth of 67mm (Brodribb 1987, 67). One has a batch mark and what appears to be a complex combed signature (see Fig. 100).

The marked half-box-flue was sampled from the final phase of remodelling of the bath house where it, and the second complete example left *in situ*, were reused in a *pilae* stack. Half-box-flue tiles are early, dating to the second half of the first century and were probably superseded by standard box-flue and wall tiles during the late first or early second century (Betts 2003, 114; Pringle 2002, 154–155). No other early forms of wall jacketing were identified but the presence of these tiles in the assemblage alongside later cavity walling emphasizes the likelihood that sources of salvage varied, particularly between phases of remodelling.

Hollow voussoir tiles are similar to box-flue tiles except they taper to one end forming a wedge shape. They were used in the construction of hollow vaulted ceilings allowing for the circulation of heat to continue up from the top of the walls through to the roof. A fairly small group were identified but due to fragmentation the number is likely to be under-represented with a proportion quantified as standard box-flue. Hollow voussoirs are normally comb-keyed on all four faces (Crowley 2005, 96; Betts 2003, 116) but the form could not be positively identified when a fragment displayed two adjacent keyed faces as some of the standard box-flue tile recovered was also keyed on all four sides. A more reliable indicator, apparently exclusive to the hollow voussoir, is the presence of a small hole penetrating the wall (Ian Betts, pers. comm.). These were recorded in the Shadwell assemblage, all circular in shape, located towards the centre of the face and ranging in diameter from 20mm to 33mm (Fig. 100.1). The hollow voussoirs occur primarily in fabric group 2815 (fabrics 3006 and 2459a) although a single possible example was also recorded from Radlett (fabric 3023).

Pilae

The hypocaust *pilae* of the original build were constructed primarily of complete *bessales* and *pedales* bricks. Both of these bricks were manufactured for use in the construction of hypocaust *pilae* with the smaller *bessales* forming the actual stack standing on, or capped by, the one-foot square *pedales* (Brodribb 1987, 34–37). The top of the hypocaust of Building 4 was missing or had collapsed but the majority of the *pilae* were constructed of *bessales* standing directly on the gravel sub-floor although a few *pedales* were noted at the base. These specialised bricks are relatively small and were probably fairly easy to

Fig. 97   *Bessales* and *pedales* showing how these tile forms would have been used to form the base of *pilae* stacks

salvage whole and transport. A smaller number of non-specialised brick and tile forms were also made use of in the original build to form *pilae* including the use of box-flue standing on end on top of *bessales*. A chronological explanation for the use of differing forms has been considered but as with the variability in fabric, is likely to result from the changing availability of salvage resources during construction.

The reuse of an even wider range of forms is apparent in the construction of *pilae* associated with subsequent phases of remodelling. In addition to *bessales* and *pedales*, half-box-flue tile and *tegulae* placed flange down have been used in place of *pedales*. Two *pilae*, B[932] and B[936], have been built entirely of *tegulae*, all in fabric 2459a and with Type 1 or 2 flanges. Indeed, all of the brick and tile associated with the remodelling of the hypocaust in Room 12 (Period 4.2) is of fabric 2459a. Even more unusual is the use of a stone column base (see stone section below) in the sub-floor masonry of Room 7. This variation again reflects that more than one source of salvage was probably exploited and that, particularly with the later phases of remodelling, use was made of whatever material was available whether designed for the purpose or not.

Suspensura

The floor (*suspensura*) of the bath house survives only as a small collapsed section, forming part of the Period 4.2 remodelling, and was recorded *in situ*. The floor is composed of *bipedales* 0.07m thick, which bridged the *pilae* stacks, covered with a 0.30m thick layer of *opus signinum*. It is not clear if the *opus signinum* represents the actual finished surface or a bedding layer for floor tiles or *tesserae*. Given the smooth finished surface of the *opus signinum* and absence of impressions or any remaining fragments of tile or *tesserae*, however, this seems unlikely.

Ceramic flooring

Very little evidence for ceramic flooring was recorded either *in situ* or from the demolition horizons directly associated with Building 4. Just a single *opus spicatum* brick was retrieved from the Period 7 demolition layers within the bath house. The example, in fabric 2459a, was heavily worn to one edge indicating that it was likely to have been used as intended in a herringbone patterned *opus spicatum* floor. A second *opus spicatum* brick in fabric 3006, also worn to one edge, and a small group of cut-tile *tesserae* were identified in other deposits across the site. It is possible that some of these may have originated from the bath house, particularly where recovered from the adjacent service yard, but at least some of the *tesserae* were found within deposits directly associated with Building 3 to the north.

Stone building material

Building stone

The building stone used in the construction of the foundations and walls of the bath house is comprised predominantly of types well paralleled in Roman London. Both chalk and Kentish ragstone were used in the foundations and the walls were built of a rubble core of mortared flint, chalk and tile faced primarily with Kentish ragstone. Chalk, flint, Septaria and Reigate-type stone were also used less frequently as facing stone. Both chalk and flint represent materials widely available in southern Britain and Septaria is a form of calcareous clay common to the London clay geology. The Kentish ragstone is likely to have originated from the Lower Greensand in the Maidstone area, representing the closest source of suitable heavy duty general building stone, and as such was transported into London and exploited extensively in masonry construction, shipped by boat down the Medway and up the Thames (Marsden 1967, 39–41; Blagg 1990, 39; Rowsome 2000, 20; Crowley 2005, 90).

The use of Reigate-type stone in Roman construction, however, is less well paralleled although an increasing number of identifications are being made that would appear to suggest it was being used from the first to at least the third century, although evidently some could be recycled (Drummond-Murray *et al.* 2002, 25–26; Sudds 2008, 38–39; Coombe *et al.* in prep.). Three large ashlar blocks of calcareous tufa were also retrieved from the demolition horizons associated with the bath house. These may have been used in the construction of the quoins although no examples survive *in situ*. Calcareous tufa is a carbonate deposit that forms by the precipitation of calcite around springs in chalk and limestone. Tufa was exploited from a very early date in Roman London as it could be sourced fairly locally where the chalk outcrops (Kevin Hayward, pers. comm.). The closest potential source for the Shadwell tufa is likely to have been the Thames estuary to the east or the Medway (Kevin Hayward, pers. comm.). As a lightweight stone tufa was often used in bath houses, specifically in the construction of vaulted roofs (Crowley 2005, 91), although in this instance the large blocks appear to have been fashioned specifically for use in a wall.

As largely recorded *in situ* it is difficult to see how much of the building stone is reused. The majority of the facing stone is roughly hewn with one flat face and is of varying size, measuring between 50mm and 350mm. It is perhaps unsurprising to note that more regular blocks of Kentish ragstone were selected for use in the southern façade of the bath house, facing onto the river.

A stone column base was also recorded, forming part of a *pilae* (B[1165]) in Room 7, associated with the Period 4.2 remodelling of the hypocaust. The column base is carved from a South Cotswolds Middle Jurassic oolitic limestone, quarried near Cirencester or more probably from the hills around Bath (Kevin Hayward, pers. comm.). The Combe Down Oolite, from the Bath region, was being exploited from the middle first century onwards, used in the construction of the Temple of Sulis Minerva, but was also used in London from a similarly early date until at least the third century (Kevin Hayward, pers. comm.). It was used extensively for statuary, architectural elements and in funerary monuments but the column base is likely to have originated from a well-appointed masonry structure, perhaps in the City.

Stone flooring

A single group of stone paving was recovered from the flooding horizon in the bath house (Period 4.3), represented equally by imported white Carrara marble and indigenous dark greenish-grey Forest marble, and may be demolition material which had sunk into the deposit. Carrara marble, originating from Tuscany in Italy, was exploited in Roman London from an early date and continued to be used and reused throughout much of the occupation (Pritchard 1986; Crowley 2005, 92). The fragments recovered from the bath house may have derived from one large slab but although the breakage appears to have taken place in antiquity no traces of mortar could be detected over the broken edges to indicate reuse. In contrast, the fragments of Forest marble, although originally part of a larger slab, have *opus signinum* mortar adhering to the broken edges suggesting they were reused in a fragmented state. The use of Forest marble from Northamptonshire can be predominantly dated to the third and fourth century in Roman London, during a period of increased trade with the Midlands, although it has also been recorded in a tombstone from Bishopsgate dated stylistically to late first or second century (Pritchard 1986, 187). More recently, Forest marble paving slabs, probably quarried from the Cirencester region, have been identified at the Roman amphitheatre, dated to the second or third century (Hayward 2008). The slabs from site were probably quarried from Oxfordshire or east Gloucestershire (Kevin Hayward, pers. comm.) but it is not evident where or even when they may have been used originally.

Architectural moulding

A single large fragment of moulded Carrara marble (Fig. 99) was retrieved from one of the bath house demolition deposits B[1059]. It is not clear if the fragment was reused in Building 4, or indeed what it may have been originally used for. Given that the moulded face demonstrates evidence of weathering it could be argued that the fragment was used externally, perhaps forming part of a door surround to the entranceway. However, the weathering may equally indicate that the fragment had been used previously in another building and was simply reused in the bath house, possibly as veneer or for paving.

Building material from other buildings

The building material directly related to other structures on Sites A and B is presented below (Table 17 and Table 18). The majority is attributed to Building 3, from Site B, which underwent a number of phases of remodelling and refurbishment (Table 18). Material from structural contexts is listed in addition to that retrieved from the make-up deposits and demolition horizons attributed to each of the buildings.

Much of the material is evidently early in date and reused although late Roman tile (fabrics 2453; 2457) is present from Period 3 in certain structures (Buildings 2 and 3). Building 3, in particular, demonstrated a similar range of fabrics to Building 4, down to occurrence of the more uncommon and possibly late roof tile fabric 3024. A few other types that were not recorded in the bath house were, however, also evident.

Early fabrics include 2458, a rare quartz and

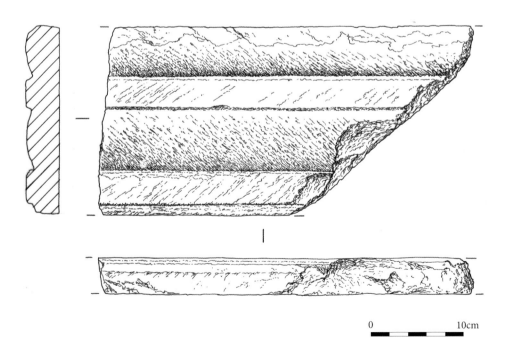

Fig. 98   Fragment of moulded Carrara marble, possibly derived from the bath house (scale 1:4)

Fig. 99   Fragment of moulded Carrara marble

limestone tempered tile of uncertain origin and the more common silty fabric 3011. The source of the latter is also unknown and the dating poorly defined, possibly occurring as early as *c*. 70/100 AD and continuing until *c*. 200 AD or later. Late tile fabrics include 3013, part of the late calcareous group, and the rarer 3012, both post-dating *c*. 180 AD. Less well dated, but also uncommon fabrics include 3056 and 3089. A source for these fabrics is again unknown and 3056, a distinctive fabric with rounded clay pellets and silty bands, is a particularly rare find. Finally, two unmatched fabrics were recorded, assigned the codes 3500A and 3500B. The examples included under the code 3500A contain clay pellets and are often vesiculated, possibly from burnt out organic material. Some examples are close to the 2815 group in character and may represent the products of a distinct phase of production, or of a different kiln, relating to this industry (Ian Betts, pers. comm.). The second fabric, 3500B, is sandy with abundant fine calcareous inclusions and coarse moulding sand with no readily identifiable

parallel. It is not clear why a broader range of fabrics was noted within Building 3 than in the bath house. It could reflect varying sources of salvage, or be the misleading result of differing collection policy for each of the structures.

Given the difficulties associated with reuse the presence of certain fabrics and forms is not necessarily informative of date or of the original appearance or function of the structures. The presence of fragments of box-flue in Buildings 3, 5, 8, and 11 does not, for example, indicate that these structures were heated, but rather that fragments of box-flue were utilised as general building rubble. In the same way much of the tile and brick from Buildings 2, 5, 7, 8, 9 and 11 is likely to have been used for a similar purpose and given the small quantities this was probably limited to hearth areas or perhaps bedding layers for surfaces in what are essentially clay-and-timber structures.

Whether or not these structures were roofed with tile is more difficult to ascertain. The small numbers of *imbrex* and *tegula* recovered from demolition deposits associated with the majority is not necessarily reliable if the buildings were subject to robbing in antiquity. Building 3 on Site B, however, provides the exception with over 500 fragments of roof tile with roughly equal proportions of *imbrex* to *tegula*. Although of timber and clay construction this building probably had a tiled roof. *Opus signinum* floor surfaces were also identified *in situ* in Building 3, one of which produced a hard chalk *tesserae*. A cut tile *tessera* was also recovered from elsewhere in the structure but the presence of a tessellated surface cannot be suggested on the basis of such scant evidence.

Very little daub was recovered from deposits related to any of the buildings on Site A or B. It is possible given the wet conditions associated with both sites that much of this, if unaffected by heat or fire, was reabsorbed. Indeed, the general dearth of other unfired building mediums,

Period	Building	Fabrics		Forms	Wall plaster	Marks*
		Make-up	Structural/demolition			
3	B2	2459a; 2457		*Imbrex*; tile	-	-
4.1	B5	-	2815	Box-flue (scored); *imbrex*; *tegula*	-	Tally
4.1	Oven	-	2815	Brick	-	Linear signature
5	B8	-	2452; 2459a; 3006; 2455; 3022; Ferrug sandstone; Kentish ragstone; Hassock sandstone; Septaria	Box-flue (combed); brick; *imbrex*; tile; unfaced stone; paving stone?	-	Curvilinear signature; crossed signature
5.2	B9	-	2459a; 2453	*Imbrex*; tile	-	2452nr3006 (SX22)
6	B11	2459a; 2453	2452; 2459a; 2815; 2455; 2459b; Kentish ragstone	Box-flue (combed; roller-stamped); brick; *imbrex*; *tegula*; tile; unfaced stone	-	Curvilinear signatures; tally
5.1	B8 Oven	-	2459a; 2815	Brick	-	Curvilinear signature; linear signature

Table 17 Summary of building materials by building for Site A. *Excludes accidental marks. S = signature followed by number in corpus. SX = unparalleled signature type.

including plaster, render and mortar, is a notable feature of the majority of demolition deposits and potentially the result of depositional conditions rather than any genuine absence (see Chapter 4.1, appearance of the bath house). Building 3, however, again proves something of an exception producing the largest assemblage of plaster recovered from site. This material is discussed below.

The range of building stone identified mirrors that observed in Building 4, an exception being the green tufaceous mudstone recovered from the earliest phase of Building 3. The fragment is partially cut and partially split and may have been used for paving but is an unusual find in the region, originating from the Lake District (Borrowdale Volcanic Group; Kevin Hayward, pers. comm.).

Painted wall plaster

The only significant assemblage of wall plaster recovered from site can be attributed to Building 3, derived almost entirely from Room 2 and the corridor (B[557]; B[588]; B[594]). Unfortunately, the material is very fragmented and it is impossible to reconstruct the decorative scheme in any detail but it does indicate that by Period 4.4 the building had undergone at least one phase of replastering and painting.

The original scheme is partly obscured by the subsequent phase of replastering but it is still possible to build a general impression of appearance. The base coat or *arriccio* is comprised of a lime-rich matrix containing sand and some crushed tile. In some fragments the

Period	Building	Fabrics		Forms	Wall plaster	Marks*
		Make-up	Structural/demolition			
3	B3	2459a; 3006; wall plaster	2452; 2459a; 3004; 3006; 2454; 3060; 3024; 2459b; 2453; 3060b; Kentish ragstone; medium laminated sandstone; tufaceous mudstone	Box-flue (combed); brick; *imbrex*; *tegula*; tile; unfaced stone; paving stone	-	Semi-circular type signature
4.1	B3a	-	2452; 2459a; 3004; 3006; 3500A; 3023; 3060; 3089; 2458; 2459b; 2453; 2457; 3026; mortar; wall plaster	Box-flue (combed); brick (*pedalis/lydion*; *sesquipedalis/bipedalis*; voussoir); *imbrex*; *tegula*; ridge; tile; *tessera*	-	2452 (SX23); 3006 (S1)
4.2	B3b	2452; 2459a; 3500A	2452; 2459a; 3004; 3006; 3006nr2453; 3500A; 2454; 3023; 3060; 3056; 3011; 3024; 2459b; 2453; 3013; 3026; 3012; 3500; daub; flint; Upper greensand	Box-flue (combed); hollow voussoir; brick (*bipedalis*); *imbrex*; *tegula*; tile; unfaced stone; worked stone (reused)	-	2459a (S5); 3006 (S2); 3006nr2452 (SX21); 3500A (double semi-circular type); semi-circular type; 3060 (S4)
4.3	B3c	-	2452; 2459a; 3004; 3006; 3500A; 2454; 3022; 3023; 3060; 2459b; 2459bnr2452; 3026	Box-flue (combed); brick; *imbrex*; *tegula*; tile	-	2459a (S5); 3023 (S1; SX7); 2459bnr2452 (SX15)
4.4	B3d	2459a; 3006; 3500A; 3023; 3024; 2459b; 2459c; mortar	2452; 2459a; 3004; 3006; 3500A; 3023; 3060; 3024; 2459b; 2459c; 2453; 3026; 3060b; 3500B; wall plaster; Kentish ragstone; medium laminated sandstone; indurated chalk	Box-flue (combed); brick; *imbrex*; *tegula*; tile; *tessera*; unfaced stone; faced stone	-	2459c (SX12); 3500A (double semi-circular type); 3006nr2452 'v' stamp; 3023 (SX4); 3060 (S2);
4.5	B3e	-	2452; 2459a; 3004; 3006; 3500A; 2454; 3023; 2459b; 2453; 3026; daub	Box-flue (combed); brick; *imbrex*; *tegula*; tile	-	3023 (SX7)
5.1	B7	-	2459a; 3004; 3006; 3060; 3089; 2453	Brick; *imbrex*; *tegula*; tile	-	-

Table 18 Summary of building materials by building for Site B. *Excludes accidental marks. S = signature followed by number in corpus. SX = unparalleled signature type.

base coat was simply smoothed to a finish but in others a distinct fine lime and sand layer or *intonaco* was identified. Where the *arriccio* was simply smoothed it was also always painted red, probably when the plaster was still wet as the pigment had soaked in. The *intonaco* retained a plain white ground and was painted with blue/grey, green and red panels or panel borders and black stripe borders. The combination of a vertical or horizontal and a diagonal line in grey/black on one fragment may also indicate the presence of a more decorative or complex panel border design. The red paint was again applied *buon fresco*, whilst the lime was wet, in order to fix the pigment but the other colours appear to have been added once the plaster was dry.

Decoration on walls was normally divided into three zones, the lower dado, the main or middle zone and the upper zone or frieze (Davey and Ling 1981, 31). If both finishing techniques are contemporary within the same scheme, as they appear to be, these could be specific to different sections of the wall. The smoothed and red painted base coat may have used where a plainer finish was acceptable, namely the dado section. The finer *intonaco* is likely to have been added where a white ground was required for the addition of decoration, specifically in the middle zone. Taken together the various elements are suggestive of a two dimensional panel scheme, representing the most commonly occurring type (Davey and Ling 1981, 31; Ling 1985, 21). Panel schemes are evident throughout the Roman period but it is during the third century that simple linear and striped patterns on a white ground reach their zenith (Davey and Ling 1981, 36). Roughly contemporary parallels include the panel-system delineated by lines and stripes of red, yellow and green applied in the villa at Iwerne Minster in Dorset and the simple trellis patterns of the Gadebridge villa in Hertfordshire (Davey and Ling, 1981, 37).

Wall plaster of the third and fourth centuries is often coarser and more roughly finished in contrast to the evenly applied pigments and highly burnished surfaces typical of first and second century (Davey and Ling 1981, 30). The plaster from Building 3 is not highly burnished but is well finished with smooth surfaces and crisp, evenly painted strong pigments that have for the most part retained their colour. This would suggest investment of both time and money with an obvious intention to impress.

The second scheme, directly overlying the first, is also a two-dimensional panel scheme. In Room 2 this comprises a white ground with black, grey and yellow panels or panel borders and stripes. Both pink and red fragments were also recovered but these could have formed part of the dado or main zone of decoration. The smaller quantity of plaster from the corridor is all red painted. Like the original scheme, the second phase of plastering is also quite technically accomplished and well painted. The maintenance of Building 3 was evidently a priority with resources continuing to be expended upon updating and refreshing the internal décor.

The very little plaster recovered from elsewhere on site includes a small fragment with a dark reddish purple ground with pink flecks in imitation of 'imperial' red porphyry. The fragment has a sandy base coat and is smooth and well painted. It was retrieved from make-up deposits (B[754]) associated with the initial construction of Building 3 and thus must derive from another earlier structure, possibly somewhere in the vicinity.

Marked and stamped tile

Signature marks

A total of 125 signature marks were identified on the brick and tile from Site A and Site B. Of these 84 can be paralleled to known types or are too incomplete to identify but 41, representing 20 different marks, are new examples as yet unparalleled in the London corpus (see catalogue below and Fig. 100).

The marks are made predominantly with the fingertip, although more unusually two appear to have been made with a tool or comb (fabric 3023). The majority occur on brick and *tegulae*, as seen elsewhere, although one of the combed marks occurs on half-box-flue tile alongside a possible batch number (Fig. 100.24). Single or concentric semi-circular designs occur most frequently, a feature noted throughout London (Betts 2002, 76; 2003, 117). Variants of the semi-circular mark also occur amongst the unrecorded types but alongside a few more unusual and complex marks.

The previously unrecorded marks occur primarily in the local 2815 group, principally in fabric 3006, 2452nr3006 and 3006nr2452. Simple marks include a large semi-circle (Fig 100.12 and 100.13) and crossed straight lines, either with single or multiple fingers (Fig. 100.16 and Fig. 100.17). Wavy lines also occur, near to type 81 (fabric 3006) in the corpus, but neither offer an exact match (Fig. 100.6 and Fig. 100.14). These may represent incompletely executed examples, variations or even unique signatures given the infinite number of variations possible with handmade marks. More complex marks include a double semi-circle with a cross in the centre (Fig. 100.3 and 4), a single semi-circle with an 's' shaped mark within (Figs. 100.8-11), and an elaborate double finger mark (Fig. 100.15).

Other examples in the 2815 group include two in fabric 2452. The first has a double semi-circle with a 'kick' (Fig. 100.7), similar to type 33 in the corpus, and the second has crossed straight lines (Fig. 100.31), near to types 30/62. Finally, a line and semi-circle mark was recorded, executed at an oblique angle on a brick in fabric 2459a (Fig. 100.27).

A smaller number of unrecorded marks were noted in fabrics 2459b and 2459c. Both of these were formerly included within the early 2815 group but are now thought to have derived from a distinct production centre. This may have been located in north-west London or Essex but appears to have operated at a later date, and as somewhat of a successor, to the London kilns (Betts 2002, 74). In fabric 2459b a simple diagonal straight line (Fig. 100.30), a circle (Fig. 100.28), and a double circle (Fig. 100.26) have been recorded, although the latter is close to type 15 in the corpus. In fabric 2459c just one mark, representing three vertical straight lines on a fragment of brick, was noted (Fig. 100.5). The presence of shell, however, means that the fabric identification of the latter must remain tentative (Ian Betts, pers. comm.). An unusual curvilinear mark was also noted on a brick in fabric 2459bnr2452 (Fig. 100.29). This fabric represents a less silty version of 2459b with a possible source in Kent as opposed to north-west London or Essex (Ian Betts, pers. comm.).

Lastly, four unparalleled marks were recorded on tiles from Radlett in Hertfordshire, predominantly in fabric 3023 but also in 3060 and the later 3023b. A straight line and single semi-circle mark occurs most frequently in both fabric 3023 and 3060 (Figs. 100.19-22). A wavy line was also noted in fabric 3023 (Fig. 100.23). Two tiles appear to have been marked with a comb or a tool as opposed to a finger (Fig. 100.24 and Fig. 100.25). Both have a semi-circle to the bottom edge comprised of four separate lines but the half-box-flue tile also has a vertical wavy mark down the centre, again made with a comb-type tool. The two semi-circles are similar in execution on both tiles but the half-box is in fabric 3023 and the *tegula* in the later dated 3023b variant. A double semi-circle on a *tegula* in fabric 3023 is also illustrated but is near to type 6 in the corpus (Fig. 100.18).

The purpose of signature marks remains somewhat ambiguous but the diversity of types has led to the suggestion that they represent tilemaker marks (Betts 2002, 76). Other possibilities have been put forward but their multiplicity, and the correlation of marks to production centres (although these do overlap with some of the more common types), may indeed suggest they were intended to denote the work of individual tilemakers or of different production centres (Warry 2006, 90–91). More than one type of mark often occurs on tiles of contemporary date from the same production centre which would imply that tilemakers, who were presumably paid piecemeal, needed to mark their own output. The same mark, however, crops up at Shadwell on two tiles from Radlett of different date. The two tiles cannot have been made by the same maker but the mark could have been adopted by another maker or represent an umbrella mark of the tilery.

In terms of distribution the bath house in particular, probably as the only masonry structure, produced the greatest number and variety of signature types (Table 15). It is also evident that the bath house shares examples in common with both Building 3 to the north of Site B (S1 fabric 3006, SX4, X7, SX21 and SX23; Table 18) and to Building 9 on Site A (SX22; Table 17). These shared marks, particularly with regard to the more unusual examples including SX22 and SX23, may indicate a degree of contemporaneity between these structures, or as reused that a common source of salvage was being exploited.

Civilian stamp

Despite the fact that many of the tiles in London are likely to have been made at civilian-run tile works it has been observed that very few of these appear to have been marked with tile stamps (Betts 2002, 76). Just a handful of civilian stamps have been recorded on tiles from London and these all differ from procuratorial stamped tiles by being impressed as opposed to in relief (Ian Betts, pers. comm.). A fragment of *tegula* from a floor attributed to Building 3d (B[466]; B<477>) has a clear and deeply stamped 'V' aligned with the bottom of the tile (Fig. 100.2). This is likely to represent a civilian stamp and one currently unparalleled in London (Ian Betts, pers. comm.). A civilian tile stamp was recorded at Baltic House in the city but with more characters (Betts 2002, 76). The example from Shadwell has only one letter, although more could be missing. The tile from Baltic House occurred in fabric 3006 and the *tegula* from Shadwell in fabric 3006nr2452.

Tally marks, batch marks and graffiti

Tally marks, mostly representing the knife-cut marks on the edges of tile and brick, are less frequently identified than signature marks. One *tegula* with a least four straight cut marks on the outer edge of the flange was recovered from Site B (fabric 3060; B[379]; Fig. 100.32). These have been suggested to represent a numbering or 'stock control' system operated at the tilery (Betts 2002, 76; 2003, 117). The numerals may have been recorded when a batch of tiles were made so it would be known when, or what sequence to fire them in, although some doubt has been thrown on this (Warry 2006, 92). Equally, the numbers could have been specific to an individual order or perhaps even a tilemaker (Pringle 2002, 156; Brodribb 1987, 135). Tally marks appear to have been made later in the tile-making process than signature marks, cut into the leather-hard clay. The numerals 'CXXII' scored into a half-box tile from Radlett (Fig. 100.24), however, are perhaps more likely to denote the output of a tiler (Brodribb 1987, 130; Warry 2006, 119). Given that around 220 *tegulae* could be made in a day, a total of 126 may represent half a days work, or perhaps have been the total required to fulfil a specific order (Warry 2006). Graffiti has been identified on two fragments of brick. The first has been made with a fingertip but does not appear to form any easily recognisable characters or words (Fig. 100.33). Indeed, this mark could represent a more elaborate signature mark. The second piece of graffiti (B[646]; B<470>; Fig. 102) is by far the most detailed, represented by three lines of cursive text scored into the brick with a pointed tool or stick. This graffiti is discussed separately below.

Accidental marks

Animal prints represent the most common accidental marks on the bricks and tiles, including the paw prints of cats, dogs, and at least one fox. One *tegula* has dog claw marks down side of the flange (fabric 3006; Fig. 100.13). Two cloven hoof prints, from either deer or goats, were also identified. Other marks include finger marks and hobnail impressions from footwear. Fern leaf and possible raindrop impressions have also been recorded, indicating that the tiles laid were outside to dry and at least some were uncovered.

Fig. 100i   Brick and tile: Hollow voussoir tile and stamped and marked brick and tile (scale 1:4)

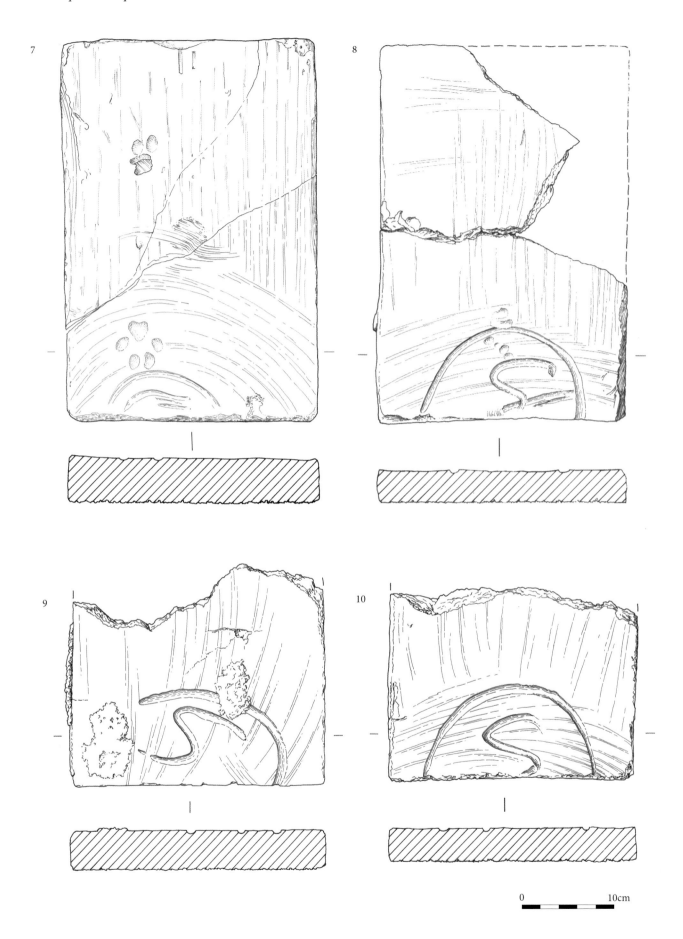

Fig. 100ii   Brick and tile: Signature marks (scale 1:4)

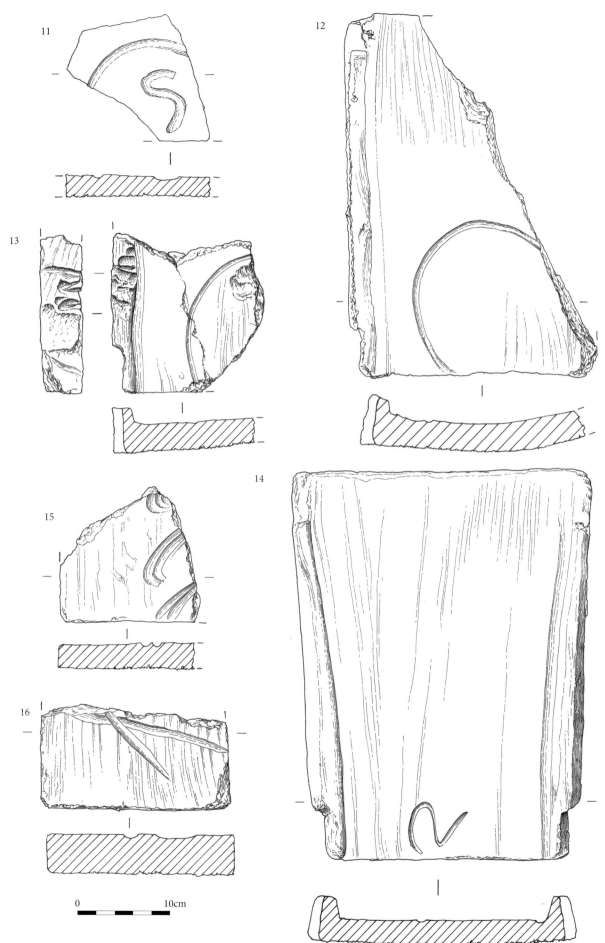

Fig. 100iii   Brick and tile: Signature marks (scale 1:4)

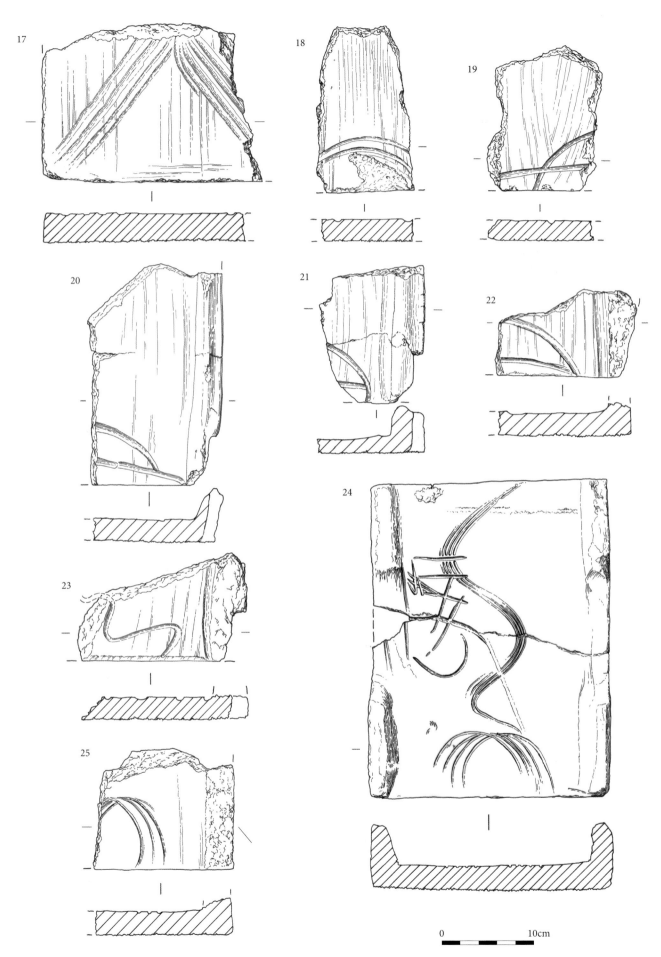

Fig. 100iv   Brick and tile: Signature and batch marks (scale 1:4)

Fig. 100v   Brick and tile: Signature and tally marks (scale 1:4)

Catalogue of signature-marked brick and tile

Fig. 100.1: Hollow voussoir (B[646]/BXC)

Fig. 100.2: Stamped *tegula* (B[466]/
B<477>/3006nr2452)

Fig. 100.3: Signature mark (B[465]/SX13/3006)

Fig. 100.4: Signature mark (B[646]/
SX22/2452nr3006)

Fig. 100.5: Signature mark (B[466]/SX12/2459c?)

Fig. 100.6: Signature mark (B[1177]/
SX26/3006nr2452)

Fig. 100.7: Signature mark (B[921]/SX14/2452)

Fig. 100.8: Signature mark (B[646]/
SX23/2452nr3006)

Fig. 100.9: Signature mark (B[646]/SX23/3006)

Fig. 100.10: Signature mark (B[646]/SX23/2452)

Fig. 100.11: Signature mark (B[607]/SX6/3006)

Fig. 100.12: Signature mark (B[729]/SX17/3006)

Fig. 100.13: Signature mark (B[550]/SX8/3006)

Fig. 100.14: Signature mark (B[640]/
SX21/3006nr2452)

Fig. 100.15: Signature mark (B[595]/SX3/3006)

Fig. 100.16: Signature mark (B[646]/SX24/3006)

Fig. 100.17: Signature mark (B[595]/SX2/3006)

Fig. 100.18: Signature mark (B[728]/SX19 = Type 6
in corpus/3023)

Fig. 100.19: Signature mark (B[467]/SX4/3060)

Fig. 100.20: Signature mark (B[550]/SX4/3023)

Fig. 100.21: Signature mark (B[466]/SX4/3023)

Fig. 100.22: Signature mark (B[595]/SX4/3023)

Fig. 100.23: Signature mark (B[607]/SX7/3023)

Fig. 100.24: Signature mark (B[855]/SX16/3023)

Fig. 100.25: Signature mark (B[265]/SX9/3023b)

Fig. 100.26: Signature mark (B[443]/SX11 near to
Type 15 in corpus/2459b)

Fig. 100.27: Signature mark (B[607]/SX5/ 2459a)

Fig. 100.28: Signature mark (B[646]/SX25/2459b)

Fig. 100.29: Signature mark (B[485]/
SX15/2459bnr2452)

Fig. 100.30: Signature mark (B[595]/SX1/2459b)

Fig. 100.31: Signature mark (B[728]/SX20/2452)

Fig. 100.32: Tally marks (B[379]/3060)

Fig. 100.33: Graffiti (B[1177] B<476>)

3.5 Inscriptions and graffiti

Four examples of writing were found on Site B: a small fragment of an inscribed panel, a near-complete brick bearing three lines of cursive text and two examples of post-firing graffiti on pottery vessels.

Inscription

Roger Tomlin

The top right corner of an inscribed panel, 0.077m by 0.095m, 0.018m thick, made of white marble now discoloured grey and buff. The letters are well-drawn but coarsely incised:

> [...]VS
> [...]ET
> [...]

Only the top-right serif survives of the first letter in line 2, but it does not belong to S, and the sequence FT can be excluded.

Despite being found in a Roman bath house, this is probably part of a tombstone. In which case, line 1 either consisted of the funerary formula *Dis Manibus* ('To the shades of the dead', its unabbreviated use suggesting a date before *c*. AD 125), or ended with part of the name of the deceased, in the masculine nominative case. Line 2 ended with the conjunction *et* ('and') (Tomlin and Hassall 2004, 355, no. 1).

Fig. 101　Detail of inscription, thought to have been part of a funerary monument

Cursive graffiti: the inscribed *pedalis*

A nearly complete brick inscribed with three lines of cursive graffiti was recovered from a layer B[646] associated with the demolition of the bath house. The example is a standard local London product (fabric 2459A) manufactured between *c.* AD 50 to 160 and measures 292mm x 292mm x 46mm, in this case slightly less than one Roman *pes* (0.296m). As with the majority of examples across Roman Britain the graffiti was incised pre-firing, probably in this case with a sharp point or stylus, but more unusually the entire inscription survives (Fig. 102).

The graffiti has proved difficult to translate and could be read in a number of ways, none of which makes obvious sense. Two independent interpretations are presented below, followed by a general discussion.

Roger Tomlin

Fragment of tile broken to top and bottom, but the text is apparently complete. This was inscribed before firing, with a sharp point, in cursive letters unlikely to be much later than the mid second century. They are firmly inscribed and quite well preserved, but in such a small sample of uncertain meaning, some are ambiguous. There is no separation of words. A literal transcript follows, with ambiguous letters identified by subscript dots:

natedeanam

tercaloribuscreper

stum

Notes line by line, identifying letters numerically by line and their position within it:

Fig. 102 *Pedalis* inscribed with cursive graffiti (scale 1:4)

Line 1

1.3 is either T or C. If C is read in line 2 (see below), then C can be rejected here. The letter is perfectly acceptable as T, but differs from T at the beginning of line 2 by the leftward placing of the downstroke, which also curves to the right.

1.5 is certainly D, unless a different D be read later in the line (see below). D in cursive can be difficult to distinguish from B, but in this hand (see line 2), B is distinguished by the conventional sinuous downstroke.

1.7 and 1.8. After the certain E (1.6), the next two letters superficially resemble M, but this reading must be rejected if this line and 3 both end with M (see below); M is unlikely in any case, in view of the short downstroke which immediately follows. This actually cuts the preceding stroke, making it unlikely to be a separate I, let alone the beginning of an interrupted loop of D. It is best seen as completing N, formed rather like 1.1.

1.10. The line ends in the same letter-form as line 3. This is perfectly acceptable as M in itself (although RA would be possible), and is inherently likely in this position as the end of an accusative.

Line 2

1.4 is difficult to read as C, but not impossible, if some distortion is allowed; and almost inevitable in view of the ablative-plural letter-sequence which follows, assuming the text is Latin, *caloribus* would mean 'by [with, from] heats'.

1.13, which consists of a detached horizontal stroke above an L-like downstroke, is apparently also C. The sequence CREPER only suggests the Latin nomen *Crepereius*, but this cannot be continued into line 3. Just possibly the scribe also wrote on a second tile, now lost.

Line 3

1.1 consists of a long diagonal stroke, perhaps curving rightward at the top. It most suggests Q, but there is no sign of the initial loop. Perhaps therefore S, but at a distorted angle.

1.2 is apparently a wide cross-stroke above a short diagonal stroke, perhaps an incomplete T.

1.3 is apparently V, formed in two strokes like 'LI'; it is supported by the final M, since terminal –*um* is so common, whereas (say) TIM is not a possible word-ending.

These ambiguities allow quite a variety of readings, but no combination produces a convincing text. Many graffiti made on tiles before firing relate to the manufacturing process: dates, batch-totals, tilers' names, etc. But some are 'writing-practice' – snatches of verse, and the like – which is what this graffiti must be: the hand is quite sophisticated. However, it remains an enigma. It should be noted that a slightly different reading to this, with less discussion of the letter-forms, appears in Britannia 35 (Tomlin and Hassall 2004, 342, no. 18).

Pierre-Yves Lambert

[..?..]n a cedemiam   n or ai or a

[..?..]tercaloribusereper   -c-, not –g-

[..?..]q(u)ium

Caloribus in the second line: the second stroke of c is no more visible, but we neatly see where it was ending thanks to a "ligature" stroke with the following letter, a.

Caloribus might connect this inscription with the main function of the building.

A rather pedestrian interpretation would be the following:

[I]n ac(c)ede mia m-
A[]ter caloribus erepe r-
[e]q(u)ium

or; Inac(c)ede, mia m(a)ter, caloribus erepe r(e)q(u)ium – "enter, my mother, with (such) heats draw (some) rest"

with typical features of Vulgar Latin:
mia = mea (meus, mea, meum)
erepe = eripe (eripio, eripere)
reqium = requiem (requies)
inacede = accede

Discussion

Berni Sudds

The implicit suggestion in Pierre-Yves Lambert's translation that the brick may have been manufactured as a sign to mark the female changing room in a bath house would imply the tiler, or someone with access to the unfired tiles, knew of the ultimate destination. This would raise questions concerning manufacture and supply, specifically with regard to raising individual batches to order, potentially designated for specific structures. While this is a possibility, it is highly unlikely that the graffiti on the *pedalis* at Shadwell was ever intended for view.

To begin with the tile, dated from the late first to early second century, is evidently reused in the Shadwell baths, constructed sometime around *c*. AD 250. Furthermore, although difficult to substantiate, the mortar identified adhering to the inscribed face may indicate that the tile was reused within a masonry element, for example a wall, and was consequently not on display.

It is evident that much of the building material used in the construction of the bath house was salvaged from an earlier structure containing a substantial hypocaust. This is most likely to have been another bath house but this does not necessarily imply that the tile was originally used as a sign, particularly when no parallel can be sought. The graffiti is fairly well accomplished in execution but is not easily legible, particularly from any

distance, nor is it centrally placed within the brick thus making a very unsuitable sign or plaque.

Alternative explanations may be found by looking at other inscribed tiles from London and across Roman Britain (Brodribb 1979a; 1987; Tomlin 1979; Frere and Tomlin 1993). Evidently, many of the marks on Roman tile relate to the process of production, principally in dating batches, recording quantities and noting makers names or signs (Tomlin 1979, 233). Instruction in literacy also appears, namely in possible reading and writing exercises. Possible proprietors and soldiers names also occur, the latter including individuals thought to have been seconded to legionary brickworks (Tomlin 1979, 236). Other more casual and sometimes superfluous information is recorded which include aphorisms or longer expressions and adages, the latter noted from the continent (Tomlin 1979, 239). Less frequently graffiti refers to a third-person, with an example from London noting that 'Every day for thirteen days Austalis has been wandering by himself' (Frere and Tomlin 1993, 2491.147, 138).

Other interpretations could therefore be suggested, although of course nothing can be proven. Even if the individual who marked the tile, whether or not it was the tiler himself, knew of the ultimate destination the graffiti may not represent a sign but more a dedication to the intended structure or to bring good luck. To be led by the original context of the brick, however, is not advisable especially when this is not known for certain and even if sourced to a bath house the presence of the graffiti could be entirely coincidental. Although used and reused in many ways, both *pedalis* and *bessalis* bricks were chiefly manufactured for the construction of hypocaust *pilae*. It is possible one of the tilers may just have been making a pun or aphorism suitable to the form, but were at the same time entirely unaware of the brick's actual destination. In this way the content and meaning is perhaps akin to other, more arbitrary examples.

The letters themselves, or the phrase 'enter, my mother, with (such) heats draw (some) rest' may also have been amuletic. Letters are symbols and thus 'magic' in many semi-literate societies. Given the reference to heat, perhaps the text was deliberately scrawled into the green tile to ensure a successful firing. Given the significant investment of effort and materials in a single firing a literate individual of particular significance may even have been paid to do so.

Although the translation resembles no adage that the author can parallel, if correctly transcribed it could also possibly represent a writing lesson. It is thought that a tile recovered from Silchester depicting a Virgilian tag might have been used for just this purpose, containing fifteen separate letters (Frere and Tomlin 1993, 2491.148, 138). The brick from the bath house appears to use sixteen separate letters or characters. Alternatively the graffiti may represent a symbolic funerary mark by the tiler after the death of his mother or perhaps even have a more lascivious meaning.

Graffiti on pottery vessels

Roger Tomlin

Two graffiti were found on vessels, both made after firing, and thus relating to the use of the vessel; very likely to be ownership inscriptions consisting of the owner's name perhaps abbreviated.

1. Base sherd of a Nene Valley colour-coated beaker (dated AD 250-370/400) from fill A[1615] of Period 6 well A[1399] (see Fig. 60.9). Scratched underneath:

VI

The graffito is evidently complete, and probably an abbreviated personal name. Inherently likely to be Victor or Victorinus, although there are some other possibilities such as Virilis and Vitalis. A numeral, VI for '6', is unlikely.
2. Wall sherd of an Alice Holt/Farnham ware dish (dated AD 350-420) from Period 7 dumped deposits overlying Building 11 (see Fig. 65.3). Scratched on the outside:

[...]VIC[...]

Probably the name Vic[tor] or Vic[torinus].
Since the vessels overlap in date, and were found at the same site it is quite possible that they both relate to the same owner whose name began with VIC. This would strengthen the likelihood of Victor or Victorinus, both very common names, although there is a much less common cognate name, Victorius, and a few rare names also beginning with VIC.

3.6 Glass

Sarah Carter and John Shepherd

The following report discusses the Roman glass assemblages from Sites A and B. A full catalogue of all Roman glass appears as Appendix 3. The two assemblages have been kept separate, although the numbering is consecutive. A select catalogue of those items illustrated is replicated below.

Site A (nos. 1–63)

The Roman glass from Site A is made up of fifty-four vessel fragments, nine of which are from identifiable forms (nos. 1–9), and forty-five are body fragments from vessels of indeterminate form (nos. 19–63) (n.b. adjoining fragments are catalogued as one example). There are also eight fragments of window glass (nos. 10–17) and one blue glass *tessera* (no. 18). Of the identifiable vessel glass fragments, one (no. 1) is a polychrome fragment dating from the first century (and likely to be an heirloom piece on this site) and six (no. 4–9) are from utilitarian vessels such as bottles and flasks, which are broadly datable from

the first to third centuries. Only two fragments (nos. 2–3) can be identified as tableware and both appear to date to the late third or fourth centuries. A small number of selected pieces have been drawn (Fig. 103).

Site B (nos. 64–142)

In summary, the Roman glass assemblage from Site B ranges in date from the late first century through to the fourth. It is evident, however, that many vessels are residual in their Roman contexts, a feature that is discussed further below.

Only six of the catalogue entries (nos. 88–93) are from standard utilitarian vessels such as bottles, flagons and jars. This compares with twenty-seven entries (nos. 64–87 and 94–96) that come from finer tablewares such as beakers, cups, bowls and flasks. Though small, the fragment of a face flask (no. 87) is a most important item.

Of the seventeen fragments of window glass seven (nos. 126–132) belong to the matt-glossy variety, commonly used from the first to third centuries, and ten fragments come from the double glossy type, which was more prevalent during the third and fourth centuries.

Catalogue of illustrated glass

Cat. no.1 (Fig. 103.1) A[660] A<390>
(Period 7, dumped deposit/open ground.)
Fragment of flat polychrome mosaic glass in translucent green with yellow and red canes; probably the flat part of a plate or tray or a piece of inlay from furniture. First century.

Cat. no. 4 (Fig. 103.2) A[1307]
(Period 5.2, disuse of Building 8)
Neck and rim in natural blue-green glass from an unguent bottle or flask with a flared out and fire rounded rim, or possible unguent bottle with indents? Late first or early second century.

Cat. no. 64 (Fig. 103.3) B[467]
(Period 7, demolition & robbing within Room 14, B4)
Fragment of very thin colourless glass with flaky iridescent surface patina from a cup with wheel-cut decoration of oval facets and wheel-cut lines. Mid to late second century.

Cat. no. 66 (Fig. 103.4) B[140]
(Period 4.3, recut of boundary ditch)
Six fragments from the rim and body of a cup or beaker in thin colourless glass with a slightly out-turned rim, cracked off and ground. Evidence of horizontal wheel-cut lines below the rim and just above the change in angle on the profile. Late first to mid second century.

Cat. no. 80 (Fig. 103.5) B[750]
(Period 3, B3)
Base and eight body fragments of colourless glass from an Airlie cup with a pushed in outer ring and an applied inner ring on the base. (Isings 1957, 85b). Late second or early third century.

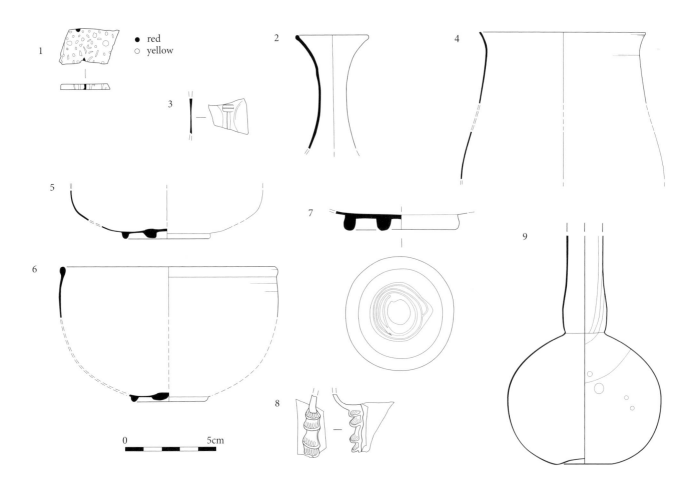

● red
○ yellow

0   5cm

Fig. 103   Glass vessels: (1) polychrome mosaic glass, A<390>; (2) Neck and rim in natural blue-green glass from an unguent bottle or flask; (3) Fragment of very thin colourless glass from a cup with wheel-cut decoration of oval facets and wheel-cut lines; (4) fragments from the rim and body of a cup or beaker in thin colourless glass with a slightly out-turned rim; (5), (6), (7) fragments of colourless glass from three Airlie cusp with a pushed in outer ring and an applied inner ring on the base; (8) fragments of colourless glass from the neck of a flagon with a flattened form (9) fragments of natural pale green, bubbled glass from a globular flask with a cylindrical neck with a vertical, cracked-off rim and a slightly concave base (scale 1:2)

Cat. no. 81 (Fig. 103.6) B[750]
(Period 3, B3)
As for no. 80 above but from a different vessel.

Cat. no. 82 (Fig. 103.7). B[554]
(Period 5.1, Service yard OA 6)
As for no. 80 above but from a different vessel, base only illustrated.

Cat. no. 83 (Fig. 103.8) B[502]
(Period 7, robber trench B4)
Two fragments of colourless glass from the neck of a flagon with a flattened form. Has an applied handle in the same metal, which is very thin and extends into a pinched claw decoration down the body of the vessel. Probably an import from the Rhineland. Late first or early second century.

Cat. no. 94 (Fig. 103.9) B[103] B<1>
(Residual in a post-medieval context)
Forty-six fragments of natural pale green, bubbled glass from a globular flask with a cylindrical neck with a vertical, cracked-off rim and a slightly concave base. (Isings 1957, 103). Mid to late third century.

Discussion

In general, and probably to be expected, the glass from both of these sites is very fragmentary with no complete profiles. The concentration of drinking vessels, some of which have survived in reasonably large fragments, especially the bases, from Site B is worthy of further note (see below) but the general impression is of small fragments of glass that give an indication of the original supply of glass to the site but, in the absence of a more complete assemblage, must represent only a very small proportion of what was originally supplied and in use.

The small fragment of polychrome glass from Site A (no. 1) is without a doubt the earliest identifiable glass vessel, or object, from the site. The multi-coloured pattern is typical of the decoration used in cast and sagged vessels dating from the early to mid first century AD. Similar fragments come from *Londinium* itself, usually in first , or early second century contexts. This item is interesting in that it appears to have survived in use for a considerable period of time. It is just possible that it is a keepsake, of some sort; such colourful glass fragments, if found, might have been regarded as worth keeping by their finder.

This appeared to be the case in Burial 392 in the eastern cemetery of *Londinium* (Barber and Bowsher 2000, 186–189). This grave, untouched by later intrusions, contained a lead coffin, in which were the remains of a young girl. Alongside the coffin were a number of objects including some fragments of multi-coloured glass from a small bowl. Not all the fragments joined, however, so it is just possible that they had been placed, as fragments, into the grave alongside the child because they once meant a great deal to the young girl. Another possibility is that the fragment, being flat, comes from a piece of veneer that once decorated a box or item of furniture. Once again, however, the object itself would have been quite old in its context on this site.

Considering the proximity of a bath house, it is perhaps surprising that there were only two vessels that could be directly associated with cosmetics or oils (nos. 4–5). No. 4 comes from the simple rim of a small phial, a commonplace form in the Roman world, whereas the small looped handle fragment (no. 5) comes from the distinctive two-handled bulbous-bodied oil flask known as an *aryballos*. Such vessels were used in the bath house itself, carried by a handle attached to the two loops.

There are, however, a number of fragments from the standard square-sectioned prismatic bottles (nos. 6–7 and 88–93). These vessels are ubiquitous throughout the Roman Empire, especially from the first to third centuries AD, and would have been used as in transit and storage containers for all manner of liquid or semi-viscous commodities, such as foodstuffs or cosmetics. No. 88 comes from the upper part of a rectangular-sectioned bottle, a less common type than the square-sectioned prismatic form.

The bulbous-bodied flask from Site B (no. 94) is a very poorly made vessel. The glass contains many large bubbles (seed) and a number of pieces of unfused material, showing up as black specks in the glass itself (batch). The presence of a crackle spot on the lip of the vessel indicates also that the rim was left rough once it had been removed from the blowing iron (letting a small drop of water fall onto the hot glass near the blowing iron would cause a crackle spot which, when struck, would be weak enough to gently sever the vessel from the iron). The resulting shape, with a constriction at the base of a neck that tapers slightly upwards, imitates much better made vessels, often in colourless glass, of the third and fourth centuries (eg Isings 1957, form 103).

The two fragments from the neck and body of a flattened flask in a fine colourless glass (no. 83) are from a very finely made vessel. The thin handle has been applied and very finely pinched to form a pinched claw that runs down the side of the vessel. One would suspect that this handle was mirrored by a second on the other side of the body of the vessel.

Flattened flasks are known in late first and second century contexts, but the colourless glass of this example would suggest it belonged to a later vessel. An exact parallel is hard to find, but even more elaborate and highly decorated examples are known. An extreme example of flattened flask is the famous 'Masterpeice' glass from Cologne (Fremersdorf 1959, 56-58, tafel 70 and 71). This flask, with a pedestal knop base, flattened body, slightly flaring neck and two looped handles with pinched spurs down their outsides and down the sides of the body was decorated with an intricate pattern of coloured glass filigree. This, too, is in a fine colourless glass. It was excavated in 1893 in a limestone coffin in Luxemburger Strasse, Cologne, and cautiously dated to the third century AD. There is no evidence that the Shadwell vessel was so elaborately decorated, but the similarity in form and handle finish is worthy of note.

Also from Cologne comes a small flattened ring flask with pinched trailed claws down the sides of the flattened body (Fremersdorf 1959, 58-59). This small flask is dated to the first half of the third century and also came from Luxemburger Strasse.

The fragment of a head-shaped vessel, no. 87, is a particularly interesting piece (though too small for illustration) and comes from a vessel type, the mould-blown head, that is not at all common in Britain, this is only the third example. Unfortunately the fragment is too small to be certain of the type it comes from, showing just the nose, lips and chin of the face. Mould-blown flasks, and occasionally cups, in the shape of human heads are known from first to fourth century AD contexts throughout the Roman Empire but they are not common finds. Being such recognisable items, this category of glass vessel has been the subject of much research (see Stern 1995, 201–215 for a brief study of this vessel type in connection with examples in the Toledo Museum) and so it is not surprising that it is possible to make a few additional comments about this fragment.

Most head-shaped vessels are small bottles or flasks, such as this example, although a few cup examples are also known. There are three main head types, a single head, a 'Janus' type head (two heads joined at the back) and multiple heads (Stern 1995, 202). The subjects of the heads appear to be primarily deities and mythological characters, such as Medusa and Dionysus/Bacchus. Chubby cheeked, child-like characters were also used, although it is not certain whom they are supposed to represent. Ethnic faces are also present, such as the sub Saharan/African example from London, and there are also a few grotesque faces (see below). Also, there are a number of ordinary faces. In general, though, the mythological and child-like heads appear predominantly in the Eastern Mediterranean, whereas the Ethnic types, ordinary faces and caricatures, such as the grotesque heads, appear in Italy and the north-west provinces.

The type is long-lived, being produced in the eastern Mediterranean from the first to third centuries AD. However, it would appear that production in the western provinces, perhaps in Italy, was shorter lived and focused on the first century AD (Stern 1995, 203).

A single sub Saharan/African head from a cup in bluish green glass (extant height 105mm, but probably no more than 120mm complete) with a signature C. CAESI on the nape and BUGADDI under the chin, was found in 1938 in King William Street, London, EC4 (British

Museum, no.P.1973.7-2.386). It also has a radiate bust looking right on the base (Price 1974, 291–292). A near identical example, also an example of an ethnic head with sub Saharan/African features was found associated with Flavian material at Caerleon (Boon 1969, 95-97, fig. 2). These two vessels can be compared with similar examples from *Herculaneum* (Scatozza Höricht 1986, form 33, no. 103, pls. XII and XXXIII) and Pompeii (Isings 1957, 93, form 78a).

Site B produced a very large number of drinking vessel fragments, from two main form types, dating from the middle of the second through to the middle of the third centuries. Cups with cracked off rims, often carinated bodies and wheel-cut horizontal lines are a common feature of sites with evidence of second-century occupation and are well-represented here (nos. 64–73). These were one of the commonest drinking vessel types of the period (Cool and Price 1995, 79).

The 'Airlie' type bowl or cup (Charlesworth 1959, 44–46, pl. I,4), a cylindrical cup on a low base-ring with a smaller applied concentric ring at the centre of the base, is one of the most common drinking vessel types in the north-west provinces during the late second to mid third century (nos. 75–82). Of particular interest here, however, is that many of these cups, all from Site B, come from later contexts, in particular make-up dumps for later buildings. It is a probable indication however of the use of glass on this site during the third century.

Only four small fragments of late third- or fourth-century drinking vessels (nos. 2–3 and 95–96) came from these two sites, two from each. These, again, are standard drinking vessel types for the period.

Finally, the presence of window glass gives an indication of an architectural detail of the buildings on and nearby the site. The fact that so little was found, however, might be an indication that the buildings were stripped of their portable fittings when they had become redundant.

3.7 Timber

Damian Goodburn

Waterlogged woodwork was revealed during excavations on both sites. The woodwork was preserved due to rapid burial and waterlogging, although there was some evidence of recent decay, possibly due to local de-watering.

Archaeological investigations of the waterlogged port area located in the City of London and nearby parts of North Southwark (eg Milne 1985) have revealed much about Roman civil engineering in timber through the recording of quays, jetties, dock inlets and river walls (Brigham 1990a; Goodburn in Brigham and Woodger 2001a). Some evidence of specialised warehouse buildings constructed of timber has also been recovered (Brigham and Goodburn *et al.* 1996). Waterlogged areas away from the main waterfront zones have also provided an increasing volume of diverse evidence for building

carpentry and related structures such as wells, drains and defensive works (Goodburn 1991, 1996; Goodburn in Leary and Butler in prep.; Goodburn in Hill and Rowsome in prep.; Hawkins *et al.* 2008). This large body of evidence for various forms of Roman carpentry allows us to define what is typically 'Roman' in the technology and style of woodworking.

Key features of formal Roman woodworking include the use of regular timbers squared with axes and planks, sawn out to rather standardised sizes, the frequent use of cross-cut and rip-saws, relatively elaborate joints and the widespread use of iron nails. In contrast with earlier and later woodworking, the controlled splitting of timber ('cleft' timber) was generally reserved for specialised purposes such as water pipes, fence and palisade pales and foundation piles. Cleft timber was sometimes very carefully squared-up with axes and used in the same manner as small beams cut from whole logs. The overall impression is of organised, standardised workmanship relying on regularly-sized materials. None of these features is typical of pre- or post-Roman structural woodwork in Britain.

Although we have much material which can be defined as formal 'Romanised' structural woodwork, recent archaeological excavations in the suburbs and hinterland of *Londinium* have provided glimpses of non-standard or 'rustic', woodwork with features more typical of native Iron Age or Saxon work (eg Goodburn in Leary and Butler in prep.; Goodburn in Pickard and Brown in prep.). The woodwork excavated at the Shadwell sites displays features of both formal Roman and rustic woodwork.

Archaeological excavation in the City of London and Southwark as well as in north-western continental Europe has also provided information on the construction of planked ships, boats and barges similar to those that would have been used on the Thames and its tributaries during the Roman period (Marsden 1994). Both the northern Roman or 'Romano-Celtic' and Mediterranean styles of construction, which have been documented, are distinctively different to land carpentry, particularly in the fastening methods used. This allows identification of a nautical origin to quite small fragments of timber in some cases.

Methodology and quantification

The general approach to the recording and sampling of the waterlogged woodwork found during the excavations at Shadwell is broadly that laid down in the Museum of London Archaeological Site Manual second edition (Spence 1990) and commensurate with the English Heritage guidelines on waterlogged wood (Brunning 1996). Standard site recording of woodwork included scale plans, sections and photographs. All but the most decayed material was described in detail and sketched on a 'timber recording sheet'. Where possible a full selection of the more solid items were lifted and cleaned to allow additional detailed recording, often including annotated

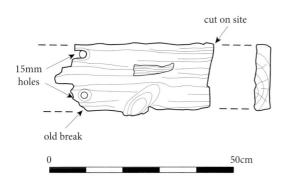

Fig. 104   An oak plank fragment B[1303] found on the Period 2 foreshore, possibly derived from a boat built in the north Roman or 'Romano-Celtic' style (scale 1:10)

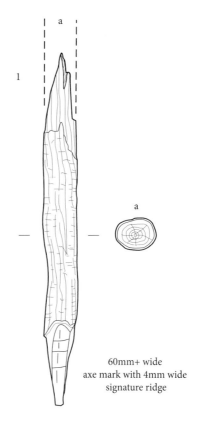

scale drawing. The timber specialist visited the sites during excavation to provide advice on the interpretation, recording, and sampling of the woodwork exposed.

A total of 94 individual items of worked timber or roundwood were recorded from Site A, of which 80 were examined off-site, where the records were up-dated and additional scale drawings made. A total of 13 pieces of worked timber were lifted from Site B, whilst others were examined *in situ*. In some cases timbers could not be safely recovered from areas of deep excavation and were left *in situ*.

Examination of cleaned timbers allows identification of the most diagnostic common native timber species such as the two oaks, ash, beech, elm, yew and box. Other species groups are less diagnostic and require botanical identification, as does small roundwood. Roman regional assemblages are typically dominated by the oaks, so relatively few species samples need to be taken.

A small number of suitable samples were selected for tree-ring dating, and the methodology and results of dendrochronological analysis are reported separately, below (see Chapter 3.8).

Key items of woodwork

A description of key items of woodwork from each period is given below, summarising attributes of groups of worked round wood and timber excavated and lifted. This summary concentrates on the best-preserved and most diagnostic items and describes representative samples where there were several similar examples. A more general description of the material, including some items that could not be lifted, is contained in the chronological narrative (Chapter 2). Records for all of the timbers form part of the site archive.

Woodwork from Period 2

Woodwork recovered from Site A comprised eight roundwood stake tips of oak A[1764] to A[1774]. The tips had been hewn to a square shape from whole stems or cleft ¼ stems around 40mm in diameter. They formed a roughly 'V' shaped alignment *c.* 1m wide by 1.5m long

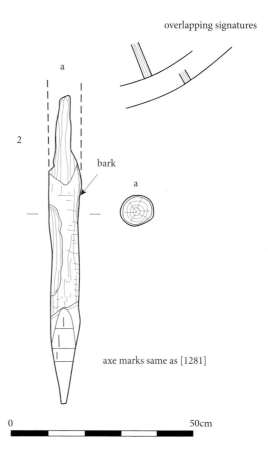

Fig. 105   Period 3 oak roundwood stakes with identical axe signature marks on the tips (1) B[1281]; (2) B[1280] (scale 1:10)

giving the impression that they would have been part of some form of fish or wildfowl trap. The tips were clearly truncated and must have been driven from a level at least 150mm higher. None of the stems had more than 35 annual growth rings.

Period 2 woodwork from Site B solely comprised a weathered and decayed, tangentially faced plank B[1303], which was found lying on what appears to have been a patch of sandy foreshore on the southern edge of the site. The most intact end of the plank contained two round bored holes of *c.* 15mm diameter, surrounded by round nail head impressions (Fig. 104). The plank was 185mm wide and 45mm thick, surviving for a length of 0.43m. It may have been a piece of a Romano-Celtic style ship's plank, which normally had large iron nails which were sometimes associated with rawl plugs and were driven through pre-bored holes cut through the planking and frame and then turned once or twice on the inside of the vessel (Marsden 1994, 50). The tentative identification of a ship's plank might indicate that a ship breaker's lay nearby. The plank fragment was found at +1.79m OD, where we might expect a first-century strand line.

Woodwork from Period 3

Period 3 woodwork comprised a small group of small, round oak piles eg B[1280] and B[1281] from the southwest corner of Site B (see Fig.10). The lack of a clear alignment makes a functional interpretation of the group very difficult, though a support for a building platform may have been likely. The largest and best preserved examples survived to a length of *c.* 0.90m and were up to 105mm in diameter eg. B[1280]. All had surviving bark and were slightly crooked. Most of the piles had tips made by three, wide, flat facets (Fig. 105). The two axe cut tips of piles B[1280] and B[1281] were extremely similar and well preserved, with the 'signature ridges' created by nicks in the axe blade surviving in both cases and being an exact match, indicating that the two piles had been pointed with the same axe. By overlapping the axe stop mark drawings the blade of the axe was reconstructed as being over 85mm wide, with a slight curve. This size is towards the smaller end of the range of recorded Roman axe stop marks (Bateman *et al.* 2008). The piles all had less than 35 annual rings and were not tree-ring sampled.

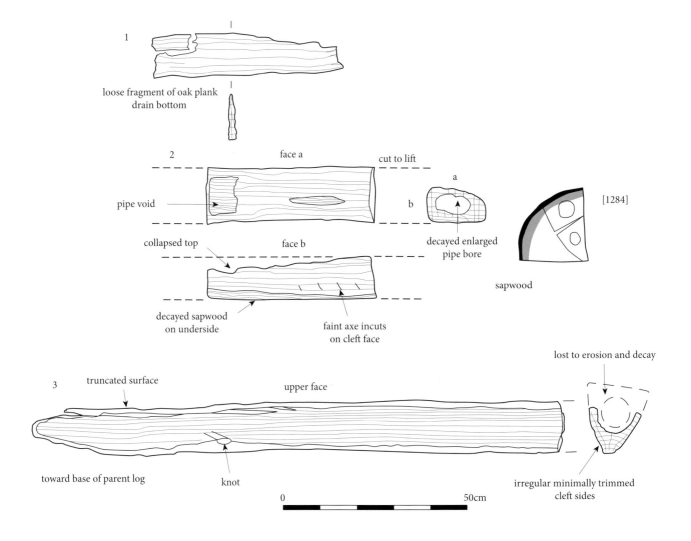

Fig. 106   Oak water pipes from Period 5.1 (1) B[1087] and elements of Structure B[1094]: (2) B[1284]) and (3) B[1283]; diagram shows how a 1/8th split section of a log was split in half to make two water pipes (scale 1:10)

Several larger oak foundation piles formed part of a north–south alignment adjacent to the eastern wall of Building 3, Room 1 (see Fig. 10). These pile tips were typical of Roman foundation piles used in soft ground, such as those found at Drapers' Gardens in the City of London (Hawkins *et al.* 2008). All of the piles had neatly squared, axe-cut tips and most were made from cleft 1/4 or 1/8th logs. The largest surviving example B[869] was nearly 200mm square and hewn from a whole log. These piles are relatively large and may have supported a wide wall made of earth above a timber sill beam.

Three piles, A[1371], A[1352] and A[1362], initially thought to be part of a large timber-lined tank assigned to Period 5.2 (see below), were apparently freshly made and were found to have the same tree-ring felling date of spring AD 228 (see Chapter 3.8). They were in good condition and had bark edge in places (eg A[1352], Fig.107). The structure supported by these foundations was probably built in AD 228 or a few months later at most, as the fresh timber showed little sign of seasoning 'shakes' (drying cracks).

Woodwork from Period 4.1

Surviving Site A woodwork was quite decayed and comprised part of a small drain and a ditch revetment. Oak dugout drain A[1222] was briefly examined on-site and found to be similar to the better preserved example A[1225] (see below). Drain A[1222] was roughly of the proportions of a gutter and would originally have been equipped with a lid. The ditch revetment comprised two oak piles hewn from small whole logs to a boxed heart section measuring *c.* 130mm x 100mm, typical of small Roman building studs (Goodburn 1991). The edge plank which they originally retained was too decayed to lift. The piles had *c.* 45 annual growth rings, which is borderline for tree-ring dating but could not be matched.

Timber from Site B comprised a very decayed, boxed heart oak sill beam B[845]. The decay had created a deep groove along one face of the beam but the timber was a plain unjointed beam *c.* 1.66m+ long by 210mm x 100mm thick. The timber lay roughly in line with the pile group noted above as B[869] etc. It is likely that it was part of a building and may had a mudbrick or *pisé* wall over it.

Woodwork from Period 5.1

Site B produced two groups of woodwork associated with drainage works in OA5, to the south of the bath house. Structure B[1094] includes two lengths of decayed timber pipe, whilst structure B[1087] is a simple stake and plank drain (Fig. 106, see Fig. 44). Both structures ran east–west and may be of slightly different date or function. After cleaning it could be seen that the two oak pipes of structure B[1094] (B[1283], B[1284]) were actually bored out of cleft sections of oak made by cleaving a 1/8th radially split section tangentially (Fig. 106). A pipe section could be made from the inner and outer pieces of the 1/8th section. The bore of the pipes was *c.* 75mm, whilst the

width was *c.* 150mm and the length up to 1.45m. Similar pipes have been found in less decayed condition in the City of London, where sharp iron tubular connectors were driven into the end grain (Goodburn in prep. b). In some cases timber pipes may have carried clean water under pressure rather than waste water (Hawkins *et al.* 2008), though the function of the timber pipe found at Shadwell is unclear. Cleft oak sections were selected for their resistance to further splitting compared with whole small logs. The production of the pipes would have required specialised drilling equipment and must have been skilled work.

The crudely made drain B[1087] was decayed but it could be seen that oak stakes were used to retain sawn oak planks on edge alongside a bottom plank (see Fig. 44). Normally Roman 'box drains' were made as prefabricated square sections held together with nailed joints (eg Goodburn in prep. a). Capacious drain B[1087] could have been made by semi-skilled workers and was able to carry far more liquid than the timber pipes discussed above. A large stake B[1358] associated with this drain provided a tree-ring felling estimate of AD 232–262, or the mid third century AD.

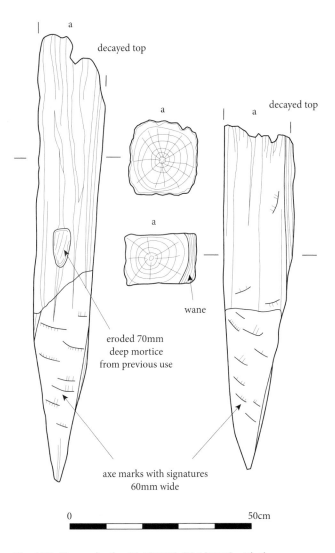

Fig. 107   Two oak piles (1) A[1340]; (2) A[1352] with the same axe signature marks on the tips; pile A[1340] has a relict mortice indicating reuse (scale 1:10)

Woodwork from Period 5.2

Surviving woodwork from Site A comprised lines of oak stake tips from an east–west cut feature A[665]/A[1299], very truncated by rot, all hewn to neat, typically 'Roman', square section points. No surviving point had over 25 annual growth rings and thus were not sampled.

A larger group of more than 20 substantial piles included typically Roman forms hewn to neat rectangular cross sections from small whole or less commonly halved oak logs. The tips were also hewn to neat square sections. Several of the best-preserved examples bore clear axe marks in good condition, which ran up to 85mm wide with a slight curve. The smaller timbers were typically *c.* 140–150mm wide by 90mm thick, common sizes for Roman building studs. Larger examples ran up to *c.* 200mm square, such as pile A[1340], which was weathered and bore an eroded mortice joint on one face showing that it had been reused and that it probably came from a building. Matching axe-mark signatures on several of the fresh pile tips from timbers dated to AD 228 and assigned to Period 3 such as A[1352], and tips of reused timbers including A[1340], indicate that they were hewn at the same time by the same workers (see Fig. 107).

A north–south dugout drain A[1225], found in the southeast corner of the excavation area and very similar to drain A[1222], was examined *in situ* and a section lifted and cleaned off-site. The surviving fragment measured *c.* 170mm wide and 70mm high and was probably cut from a whole log. The central section was hewn out and it is likely that the top of the drain was once covered by a separate lid plank. As with A[1222], the proportions are more appropriate for a gutter than a dugout drain. Experiments with a fresh oak log, using Roman-style tools shows that a 2m length of a drain or gutter could be made in one day; a rate likely to be doubled by an experienced worker.

Woodwork from Period 6

Period 6 woodwork recovered from Site A included parts of a crude timber-lined well A[1399], found along the southern edge of the site in OA12. This structure was very irregular, and some of the eccentrically located piles such as A[1635] may be intrusive and unrelated to its use. The well was *c.* 0.8m square and appeared to have been built of leftover timber and some new roundwood (see Fig. 53). A plan of the well at a low level shows the lining most clearly with at least one square corner pile A[1634]. The well had thin planking on edge on the east, west and south sides, with thicker planking on the north side. Sawn plank A[1724] was only 25mm thick and sawn plank A[1717] was 60mm thick. Small cleft fragments of oak board were also found in the well. Although some chisel-cut recesses had been made in some of the planks around nail holes none appeared to be related to the well's fixing structure, implying that some of the planks were reused, as the well planking was simply wedged behind the uprights. Groups of irregular logs and offcuts were laid around the top of the well as if to form a curb, and included a reused alder(?) stake and a cleft log of beech, the latter being a species very rarely encountered in *Londinium*.

An irregular scatter of small roundwood stakes around the edges of the well may be relics of lightweight wattle fencing that once enclosed the well head, reducing the likelihood of people, livestock or debris falling into the well shaft. The material included horizontal rod elements and a number of species were present, including some oak, such as A[1666]. Some of the stake tips were of 1/4 poles and most had three faceted tips made with an axe or bill hook. Light wattle-work decays rapidly outdoors in Britain and may have required replacement after only 3 years.

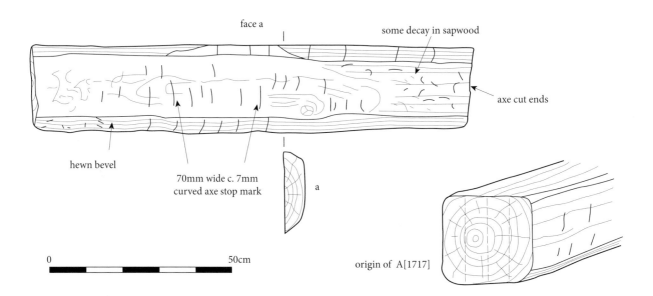

face a

some decay in sapwood

axe cut ends

hewn bevel

70mm wide c. 7mm
curved axe stop mark

a

0   50cm

origin of A[1717]

Fig. 108   Period 6 well plank A[1717] with one hewn face and one sawn, from the outside of the hewn parent baulk

Evidence of sawn hewn baulks in the later Roman hinterland of *Londinium*

Detailed studies of Roman sawn planking from London excavations and elsewhere in Britain (Goodburn 1991; Goodburn 1995; Goodburn 2001) have shown that it was produced by sawing a hewn baulk of timber using one of three trestle sawing methods, so that the planks from the 'outside' of the baulks would have one hewn and one sawn face, whilst the others had both faces sawn. The use of standardized sawn material was one of the key features of formal Roman woodworking. It is also clear that there was a strong increase in the use of smaller, faster-grown oak trees typical of managed woodland in the middle and later Roman periods (Goodburn 1998), when the huge baulks and planks of the early Roman period were far less common. The Shadwell site has produced more clear evidence of this trend, with all its implications for the nature of the regional wooded landscapes and local woodmanship.

Some of the thicker plank well-linings such as A[1717] and A[1691], were very similar and probably derived from similar small parent baulks *c.* 230mm and 250mm (9 and 10 *unciae*) square. Plank A[1717] was 230mm wide and 60mm thick, with one hewn rather waney face and one sawn face (Fig. 108a). On the hewn face a pattern of axe stop marks up to 70mm wide were recorded, showing that the worker had hewn the timber along rather than across the grain, as was typical in medieval times. The parent baulk would probably have provided four planks, with the inner being more regular and *c.* 50mm thick, (Fig. 108b). These planks are very similar to a set studied from a late Roman well-lining excavated at Borough High Street (Brown and Pickard in prep.).

Conclusions

The analysis of the medium-sized assemblage from Shadwell has provided more information of how woodworking was undertaken outside the urban core of *Londinium*. The work of specialised woodworkers such

as pipe makers was used alongside the apparently *ad hoc* rustic work of local labourers or householders. We can also see the use of native traditions such as wattlework, roundwood and cleft board, with reused and left-over timber made in typically Romanised ways. This mixture of traditions may reflect erratic finances and periods of comparative poverty, though this is uncertain.

3.8 Dendrochronology

Ian Tyers

A total of nine samples from seven timbers recovered from excavations at the two Shadwell sites were submitted for dendrochronological assessment and analysis. A summary of the dating results is provided in Table 19 and Fig. 109. The Shadwell sites provide one of the few significant groups of tree-ring data recovered from the area outside the main settlement of Roman London in the City of London and North Southwark.

Each sample was obtained by sawing a cross-section and the samples were obtained from the optimum location for sapwood and bark survival from each timber.

Methodology

Each sample was assessed for species type, number of rings and whether the sequence of ring widths could be reliably resolved. For dendrochronological analysis samples need to be oak (*Quercus* spp.) and to contain 50 or more annual rings, with the sequence free of aberrant anatomical features such as those caused by physical damage to the tree. Standard dendrochronological analysis methods (English Heritage 1998) were applied to each suitable sample.

The sequence of ring widths in each waterlogged archaeological sample were revealed by freezing the sample and then preparing a surface equivalent to the original horizontal plane of the parent tree with a variety of bladed tools. By this method the width of each successive annual tree ring was revealed. The complete

Sample	Size (mm)	Type	Rings	Sap and/or Bark	Date of measured sequence	Interpreted result
A[1313]	130 x 90	Oak	52	3 sap	undated	-
A[1350]	150 x 85	Oak	78	31 sap + bark	undated	-
A[1352]	215 x 120	Oak	68	22 sap + bark	AD 160–227	AD 228 spring
A[1362.1]	150 x 100	Oak	-	-	unmeasured	-
A[1362.2]	150 x 100	Oak	47	17 sap + bark	AD 181–227	AD 228 spring
A[1371]	170 x 125	Oak	53	27 sap + bark	AD 175–227	AD 228 spring
B[1284.1]	140 x 80	Oak	70	40 sap	undated	-
B[1284.2]	140 x 80	Oak	-	-	unmeasured	-
B[1358]	120 x 85	Oak	58	16 sap	AD 175–232	AD 232–262

Table 19 Details of the dendrochronological samples from the Shadwell sites.

sequence of the annual growth rings in the suitable samples were measured to an accuracy of 0.01mm using a micro-computer based travelling stage. The sequence of ring widths were then plotted onto semi-log graph paper to enable visual comparisons to be made between sequences. In addition cross-correlation algorithms (Baillie and Pilcher 1973) were employed to search for positions where the ring sequences were highly correlated (Tyers 2004). Highly correlated positions were checked using the graphs and, if any of these were satisfactory, new composite sequences were constructed from the synchronised sequences.

	A[1362]	A[1371]
A[1352]	6.78	4.72
A[1362]		4.97

Table 20 The t-values (Baillie and Pilcher 1973) between the individual series from Site A Period 5.2; these series were combined into the composite sequence, below.

	B[1358]	A[1362] A[1371]
London, City, Poultry ONE94 (Tyers 2000)	6.16	4.22
London, City, Baynards Castle BC75 (Morgan 1980)	3.08	3.42
London, City, Billingsgate BIG82 (Hillam 1990)	3.91	4.22
London, City, Guildhall GYE92 (Tyers 2001)	3.22	4.95
London, City, New Fresh Wharf NFW74 (Hillam 1987)	5.77	3.89
London, Southwark, Guys GHL89 (Tyers and Boswijk 1996)	3.51	5.38
London, Tower Hamlets, Tower of London (Hillam 1982)	3.15	3.73
Sussex, Pevensey Castle (Tyers 1994)	4.41	3.15

Table 21 Composite sequence of t-values (Baillie and Pilcher 1973) between the datable material from the two sites and reference data.

The *t*-values reported below (Table 20) were derived from the original CROS algorithm (Baillie and Pilcher 1973). A *t*-value of 3.5 or over is usually indicative of a good match, with the proviso that high *t*-values at the same relative or absolute position need to have been obtained from a range of independent sequences and supported by satisfactory visual matching.

The composite *t*-table (Table 21) lists examples of matches for the data from this site against references series. This table is intended to show that there is independent corroboration for the dating given here, the details on which chronologies match best is irrelevant beyond showing the data correlates with material derived from the London area.

Results and discussion

Three samples came from two timbers from the Babe Ruth excavations at Site B (Table 19). Both are from OA5, Period 5.1 (two samples from drain B[1284] and one from stake B[1358]). Sample B[1284.2] was not measured since it was compressed and distorted. Sample B[1284.1] was measured but proved undatable. The sample from B[1358] proved datable (Table 21) and ends in AD 232. This end-date is for a sequence with some surviving sapwood but not bark-edge, and the condition of this sample prevents a certain identification being made. Allowance for missing sapwood suggests sample B[1358] was felled between AD 232 and AD 262.

Six samples came from five timbers from Tobacco Dock Site A (Table 19). One timber was from OA8 in Period 4.1, group 25, A[1313] but the sample proved undatable. The remaining five samples are derived from from four timbers, three of which derive from Period 3, OA4 (A[1352], A[1362.1], A[1362.2] and A[1371]) and a fourth which may derive from this phase, or a later structure in OA11, Period 5.2 (A[1350]). Sample A[1350] had more rings than the rest of the material but proved undatable. Sample A[1362.1] was too distorted to measure. Samples A[1352], A[1362.2] and A[1371] were all measured, cross-matched (Table 20) and found to be datable (Table 21). Each of these sequences contains bark-edge and the results obtained provide a replicated felling date for the timbers of spring AD 228.

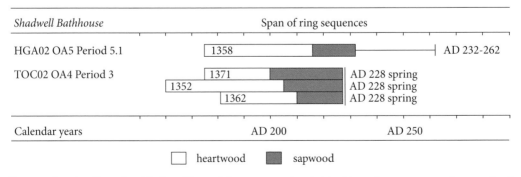

Fig. 109 Bar diagram showing the calendrical positions of the measured and dated tree-ring sequences for samples from the Shadwell sites

3.9 Animal bone

Philip L. Armitage

The data on the two sites presented below represent hand-collected bones as well as those recovered from sieved residues of environmental samples. Apart from a single aurochs humerus from the Period 1 (prehistoric) palaeochannel at Site A, all the bones discussed in this report derive from Roman/sub-Roman deposits of the first century AD to AD 400+.

Numbers of bone elements/fragments and species identified

A total of 2659 animal bones were submitted for analyses and interpretation. Roman deposits (Periods 2–7) at Site A produced a total of 1475 animal bone elements/fragments. Of these, 1228 (83.3%) are identified to taxon/species and anatomy, and 247 (16.7%) remain as indeterminate specimens owing to severe fragmentation and absence of diagnostic features. Overall, the Roman assemblages comprise bones from eleven mammalian species, two bird species, three fish species, and a single amphibian species (Table 22). In addition to the Roman bones, there is a single humerus from a wild ox (aurochs) from the Period 1 (prehistoric) palaeochannel (see below).

Roman deposits (Period 2–7) at Site B produced a total of 1183 animal bone elements/fragments. Of these, 993 (83.9%) are identified to taxon/species and anatomy, and 190 (16.1%) remain as indeterminate specimens owing to severe fragmentation and absence of diagnostic features. Overall, the Roman assemblages comprise bones from fourteen mammal species, seven bird species, eight fish species and a single amphibian species (Table 22; Table 23).

Species/Period	1	2	3	4.1	4.5	5.1	5.1	5.2	5.2	6	6	7	Totals
	H	H	H	H	H	H	S	H	S	H	S	H	
Mammals:													
wild cattle	1												1
domestic cattle		3	10	25	19	93	3	161	1	413	3	237	968
domestic sheep			1	3	2	13	2	17		48	1	46	133
domestic pig			1	4	2	8		7	2	18		14	56
domestic horse			4	3		1		4		13		3	28
red deer						1						1	2
dog				1		1		2		1	1	1	7
black rat											1		1
cf. rat							2		1				3
house mouse							1		2		2		5
mole							1						1
field vole											1		1
Birds:													
domestic fowl				2		2		1		1	1	1	8
woodcock				1									1
Fish:													
herring									1		2		3
plaice							2			1			3
freshwater eel											2		2
Amphibian:													
common frog											6		6
Unidentified species:													
unidentified mammal			8	2	1	22	11	18	10	61	50	55	238
unidentified bird						1	1					1	3
unidentified fish									1		5		6
Totals	1	3	24	40	25	142	23	210	18	556	75	359	1476

Key to the periods for Site A: **H** = hand-collected bones   **S** = bones from environmental samples/sieved residues

Table 22 Site A summary counts (NISP) of the animal bone elements/fragments by taxon/species and site phase.

Preservation

In general, the bone assemblages from both sites exhibit low to moderate frequencies of weathered/leached/burnt/dog-gnawed specimens (Table 24). The relatively high incidence (4.1%) of weathered/eroded/abraded bones recorded from Site B mostly comprises those specimens from make-up layer B[677] to the service yard (Period 4.3), and represents redeposited residual debris. Redeposited debris is also represented at Site B by the scrappy bone fragments in the fills of postholes, which comprised high proportions of broken pieces of the ribs of cattle and sheep. Bone elements/fragments from features associated with waterlain deposits (eg fills in

Species/Period	2	3	3	4.1	4.1	4.2	4.2	4.3	4.3	4.4	4.5	4.5	4	4	5.1	5.1	6	7	Totals
	H	H	S	H	S	H	S	H	S	H	H	S	H	S	H	S	H	H	
Mammals:																			
horse	4					2					2				1		4	3	16
cattle		5		12		37	1	124	2	23	46		4		124	1	129	37	545
sheep				3		16	2	25	1	2	20		2	1	26		32	5	135
pig				5		11		18	1	4	8			2	18	2	10	2	81
dog						2									1				3
cat														1					1
fox																		1	1
hare				2				1			2				1				6
black rat														4					4
house mouse					1		4							10					15
cf. water vole							3												3
cf. field vole														2					2
water shrew														6					6
common shrew														1					1
unidentified mammal		3	7	12		15	6	35	5	1	15			14	24		25		162
Birds:																			
domestic fowl		2	1			8		5		1	25			2	21	3	9		77
grey-lag/domestic goose																	1		1
mallard/domestic duck						2											1		3
cf. tufted duck																	1		1
raven																	1		1
cf. starling			1																1
cf. robin														1					1
unidentified bird								1	1			1				2			5
Fish:																			
plaice					1														1
mackerel					1							1							2
herring							1												1
thin-lipped grey mullet					1														1
cf. black sea bream							1									1			2
freshwater eel							1					1							2
cyprinid (*cf.* roach)									1										1
cyprinid (*cf.* crucian carp)												1							1
cyprinid (indet.)																1			1
unidentified fish					3		1		6	1		5		3		4			23
Amphibian:																			
common frog					1		4							71				1	77
Totals	4	10	9	34	8	93	24	208	18	31	119	9	6	118	216	13	213	49	1183

H = hand-collected bones S = bones from environmental samples/sieved residues

Table 23 Site B summary counts (NISP) of the animal bone elements/fragments by taxon/species and site phase.

ditches) are encrusted with silt/sand and/or dark stained; as for example in the specimens from the fills B[127]/B[134]/B[140] of the recut B[138] of the E/W boundary ditch at Site B (Period 4.3). The 68 frog bones from Site B silt layer B[808] sample B{44} (Period 4.3) exhibit a pattern of breakage and silt/sand encrustation indicating this group of bone represents redeposited skeletal (or decomposing) remains of deceased frogs washed into the hypocaust system when it flooded. There is no reason to suppose these frogs had inhabited the hypocaust system at the time of the flooding incident, unlike the rats and mice whose skeletal remains were present in silt deposit B[809] sample B{46} (Period 4.1) (see below).

	weathered	burnt	dog gnawed
HGA02/'Site B'			
Periods 3, 4.1, 4.2, 4.3, 4.4 (AD 230 – 325)	4.1%	1.1%	0.8%
Periods 5.1 & 6 (AD 325 – 410)	0.2%	0%	1.0%
TOC02 'Site A'			
Periods 4.1, 4.5, 5.1 & 5.2 (AD 275 – 375)	1.0%	0%	1.0%
Period 6 (AD 375 – 410)	1.8%	0.4%	2.7%
Period 7 (AD 410+)	0.3%	0.3%	2.2%

Note: 'weathered' refers to bones exhibiting signs of sub-aerial weathering/erosion/leaching/abrasion

Table 24 Frequencies of weathered, burnt, and dog gnawed bones from each site. Hand collected bone samples.

Period	N	Mean	Min.	Max.	SD
Period 2	1			112.3	
Period 3	1			122.8	
Period 4	1			108.5	
Periods 5 & 6	9	102.4	99.7	123.2	
Overall	12	114.6	99.7	123.2	6.68

Table 25 Cattle heights at the withers (cm). Site A and Site B data combined.

There is no discernible pattern in the discard pattern of the horse bone elements, which were found scattered throughout the deposits at both sites, intermixed with domestic food debris. The only exceptions are the parts of the left fore and right hind legs of an adult horse recovered from Site B, B[1300] (Period 2). These articulated bones perhaps represent the remains of a complete carcass that had been left on the foreshore to decompose, or had been washed up on the foreshore. What is surprising however is the absence of weathering, leaching or erosion in the bones, which are well preserved (apart from very slight post-depositional abrasion) and with no evidence of either chopping (butchery) or knife cuts (skinning). There is, however, evidence of dog gnawing but only on the distal femur.

Descriptions of the animals

Aurochs

At Site A, context A[1657] fill of palaeochannel A[1679] produced the distal portion of a massive bovid humerus identified as an adult wild ox (aurochs) *Bos primigenius*. Measurements (mm) taken on this specimen: greatest breadth of the distal end (Bd) 110mm, and greatest breadth of the trochlea (BT) 105.4mm.

Domestic cattle

Type and stature

Based upon the classification system of Armitage and Clutton-Brock (1976), two types of domestic cattle (short- and medium-horned) are represented by horn cores in the excavated bone samples from Site B (Period 4.2) and from Site A (Period 6). Details of the horn cores are given below (catalogue of waste products from horn and antler working).

From length measurements taken on complete adult long-bones, estimates of withers heights in twelve of the cattle are calculated (using the factors of Fock 1966 and Matolsci 1970, see von den Driesch and Boessneck 1974) as shown in Table 25. These data provide supporting evidence for the co-existence in south-eastern England, in

	N	J	I	SA1	SA2	A1	A2	A3	E
HGA02/Site B									
Periods 3, 4.1 & 4.3 (3rd/early 4th century AD)					1			6	
Period 5.1, 6 & 7 (Later 4th century AD/Sub-Roman)							1	3	
TOC02/Site A									
Period 5.1 (4th century AD)						1		1	
Period 6 (Late 4th century AD)								3	
Overall					1	1	1	13	

Key: N = neonatal; J = juvenile; SA = subadult; A = adult; E = elderly

Table 26 Cattle kill-off profile based on dental eruption and wear in mandibles. Age categories after Bond and O'Connor (1999).

the Roman period, of both dwarf, short-horned (so-called 'Celtic') cattle and larger, medium-horned cattle.

Age profile

With the exception of a single sub-adult individual, all of the cattle represented by mandibles from Site A and Site B seem to have been slaughtered as adults (Table 26), with the majority in age category A3, probably between 5 and 8 years of age. Such mature cattle would have been kept principally as milk cows and plough oxen, and only later on in their lives killed for their meat.

Although the mandibles are noticeable for the absence of calves, evidence for veal consumption (though very limited) is however provided by an isolated unworn,

upper molar tooth from Site B, B[333] (Period 5.1) and two post-cranial elements of calves from Site A: 1 humerus A[935] (Period 5.2) and 1 metacarpal bone A[1537] (Period 6).

Sex ratio

Besides the four male cattle identified from their horn cores (see horn-working waste products below), there are six female cattle represented, which are recognized from their innominate bones (using the criteria of Grigson 1982), as follows:
2 females - Site B - third century AD
1 female - Site A - late third/early fourth century AD
3 females - Site A - late fourth century AD

	element	GL	GLC	Ll	Bp	BFp	SD	Bd	BFd	Dd
Site B Partial skeleton (left foreleg & right hindleg) from B[1300] Period 2										
	radius	328.0		314.0	84.6	79.4	37.0	75.8	65.2	
	radius & ulna	401.0								
	femur	381.0	345.0		114.3		42.6	92.8		
	tibia	342.0		315.0	97.1		41.5	75.4		45.6
Site B 4th/Late 4th century AD contexts										
B[554] Period 5.1	tibia	352.0		326.0			41.6			
B[323] Period 6	radius	336.0		310.0	79.7		37.0			
Site A 3rd century AD context										
A[1526] Period 3	tibia			331.0			44.2	78.2		
Site A Late 4th century AD contexts										
A[451] Period 6	tibia			292.0						
A[1615] Period 6	tibia	328.0		297.0	87.5		37.9	67.7		

Table 27 Horse bone measurements (mm). System of von den Driesch (1976).

		Site B	Site B	Site A
		Periods 3–5.1 (c. AD 230–375)	Period 6 (c. AD 375–410)	Periods 6 & 7 (AD 375 to Sub-Roman)
Wear stage	Age-range			
A	0–2 months			
B	2–6 months	6		
C	6–12 months			
D	1–2 years	2	3	6
E	2–3 years	2	2	1
F	3–4 years			
G	4–6 years	1	3	2
H	6–8 years			
I	8–10 years			

Key: Site B Periods 3–5.1; Site B Period 6; Site A Periods 6 and 7

Table 28 Sheep kill-off profile based on dental eruption and wear in mandibles.

Horse

Stature

Heights at the withers (cm) in six horses may be reconstructed from lateral length measurements taken on their long-bones (Table 27) using the factors of Kiesewalter 1888 (see von den Driesch and Boessneck 1974):

Site A
Period 3 - AD 325–375 - 144.3cm
Period 6 - AD 375–410 - 127.3 & 129cm (MNI = 2)

Site B
Period 2 - AD 50–230 - 135.9cm
Periods 5.1 & 6 - AD 325–410 - 134.5 & 142.1cm (MNI = 2)

Four of the six animals represented (with withers heights 134.5 to 144.3cm) fall within the size-range for horses associated with military sites throughout the Roman north-west Provinces as documented by Prummel (1979, 434) and Lauwerier and Hessing (1992, 92). Such tall horses (for the Roman period) are however also found at villa and farm sites, where they probably proved ideal in connection with rounding up cattle (see Luff 1982, 136).

Ages at death

Using the method of Levine (1982) the ages at time of death in two of the horses represented may be determined from measurements of crown heights in their upper and lower cheekteeth (below):

A[1603] (Period 3, pit A[1611]) - AD 230–275 - adult horse aged 14–15 years
B[379] (Period 6, ditch) - AD 375–410 - adult horse aged 9–10 years

Sheep

Appearance and stature

At least one young adult ram (represented by a horn core from Site B: B[1029] Period 7 robbing of the bath house B4) had horns similar to those seen today in modern male Soay sheep. Withers heights in two sheep may be estimated from lengths of their metapodial bones (after the method of Teichert, see von den Driesch and Boessneck 1974) as follows:
A[1338] (Period 5.2, B8 disuse) - metacarpal bone (GL 123.1mm) withers height 60.2cm
B[457] (Period 4.5, B3) - metatarsal bone (GL 142mm) withers height 64.5cm

These calculated values indicate animals of average and above average height in comparison with other Romano-British sheep documented by Luff (1982, 163). The largest of the two sheep (from Site B) however does not match the exceptionally tall sheep with withers heights between 71.4 and 75.9cm, recorded at Godmanchester and Colchester (Luff 1982), and in London at the General Post Office site (GPO75) (West 1983).

Age profile

Table 28 summarises the ages at death in the Roman sheep from Site A and Site B, as determined from dental eruption and wear in the mandibular teeth (using the criteria of Payne 1973).

	N	J	I1	I2	SA1	SA2	A1	A2	A3	E
Site A										
Period 5.2 (4th century AD)						1				
Period 6 (Late 4th century AD)					1		1			
Site B										
Periods 4.2, 4.5 & 5.1 (*c.* AD 230–375)	2					2				
Period 6 (*c.* AD 375–410)	2									

Key: Age Categories: **N** = neonatal; **J** = juvenile; **I** = immature; **SA** = subadult; **A** = adult; **E** = elderly

Table 29 Pig kill-off profile based on dental eruption and wear in mandibles. Age categories after Bond & O'Connor (1999).

	Black rat	Rat (probably black rat)	House mouse	Water vole	Field vole	Water shrew	Common shrew	Mole	Common frog
Period 5.1 A[1695] <A335> floor make-up Building 6		2 (1)	1					1	
Period 5.2 A[1307] <A235> dump/demolition layer		1	2 (2)						
Period 6 A[369] <A17> upper fill E/W ditch A[391]	1								
Period 6 A[378] <A18> primary fill E/W ditch A[391]			2 (1)		1				6 (1)

Table 30 Site A, small mammal and amphibian bones from sieved residues of environmental samples; summary counts (NISP) of bone elements/fragments and estimated minimum numbers of individuals.

Pig

Size

Using the factors of Cornelia von Becker (1980, 27) the withers heights in three adult pigs are calculated as follows (based on length in the metatarsus III):
A[1060] (Period 7, dump deposit) - 80.5cm
B[255] (Period 5.1, B7) - 81.0cm
B[339] (Phase 5.1, B7) - 77.9cm
All three pigs appear to have been domestic rather than wild animals.

Age profile

Evidence of neonatal (sucking) piglets as well as subadult and young adult pigs in the Site B bone assemblages is provided by analysis of the dental eruption and wear in lower mandibles (Table 29). Additional evidence of (neonatal) sucking piglets is provided at Site B by the following bone elements:
B[477] (Period 4.3, B3c) - 1 metatarsus
B[541] (Period 4.3, B3c) - 1 radius
B[507] (Period 5.1, pit cutting B7) - 1 radius
B[195] (Period 6, pit) - 1 ulna
In marked contrast, the bone assemblages from Site A do not include mandibles or post-cranial elements of neonatal

(sucking) piglets, all the pigs represented are either subadults or young adults (Table 29).

Sex ratio

Eighteen pigs are identified as all males/castrates by the morphology of their lower canine teeth (tusks) (criteria of Mayer and Brisbin 1988), and no female teeth are represented:

Site A
Late third/early fourth century deposits - 2 males
Late fourth century deposits - 8 males
Site B
Third-century deposits - 7 males
Late fourth century deposit - 1 male

Minor mammalian species

Dog

Using the regression equation of Harcourt (1974) the shoulder height of the adult dog represented by the humerus from Site A (A[1323], Period 4.5 eroded gravels) is estimated at 50.2cm (based on length GL 154.2mm). By Roman standards, this animal would have been of average stature (Romano-British dogs documented by Harcourt 1974, 166, ranged in height from 23 to 72cm).

	Black rat	Rat (probably black rat)	House mouse	Water vole	Field vole	Water shrew	Common shrew	Mole	Common frog	Starling	Robin
Period 3 Building 3 B[754] <31> floor make-up										1	
Period 4.1 Building 3a B[605] <35> fill of posthole [B606]			1						1		
Period 4.1 B[809] <46> primary fill of fire-box	3 (1)		10 (3)				1		3 (1)		1
Period 4.1 B[640] <29> dump layer -fire-box goes out of use			4 (1)	3 (1)					4 (2)		
Period 4.2 B[782] <39> secondary fill of rebuilt fire-box	1										
Period 4.3 B[808] <44> silt layer in hypocaust system					2 (1)	6 (1)			68 (9)		
Period 7 B[1021] <49> fill of cut [B1030]- robbing of the bath house									1		

Table 31 Site B, small mammal, bird and amphibian bones from sieved residues of environmental samples; summary counts (NISP) of bone elements/fragments and estimated minimum numbers of individuals.

Cat

A young domestic/feral cat is represented by a lower incisor tooth recovered from the fill of the fire-box B[809] sample B{46} at Site B (Period 4.1).

Fox

Fox (*Vulpes vulpes*) is represented by an isolated radius from a gravelly sandy silt dump layer B[1033] at Site B (Period 7). Measurements (mm): GL 121.3, Bp 12.2, SD 8.1, Bd 15.0.

Hare

Hare (*Lepus europeus*) is represented at Site B by six bone elements:
Period 4.1 B[755] fill of posthole B[756] Building 3a - 1 radius
Period 4.1 B[687] floor layer Building 3a - 1 tibia
Period 4.3 B[477] sample B<9> sandy silt layer Building 3c - 1 jawbone
Period 4.5 B[470] sandy silt layer Building 3e - 1 femur
Period 4.5 B[394] fill of cut B[424] Building 3e - 1 humerus
Period 5.1 B[348] fill of posthole B[349] Building 7 - 1 humerus

Commensal rodents and other small wild mammal species

Bone elements of small wild mammals were recovered from the sieved residues of environmental samples collected from both sites (Table 30, Table 31) and represent the following species: Black rat *Rattus rattus*; House mouse *Mus musculus*; Water vole *Arvicola terrestris*; Field vole *Microtus agrestis*; Water shrew *Neomys fodiens*; Common shrew *Sorex araneus*; mole *Talpa europaea*.

Identification of *Rattus rattus* in the lower jawbone from Site B, B[809] B{46} was made on the basis of the value of the diastema index (78.8) (method of Armitage in Armitage *et al.* 1984, 378), and in the maxilla from the same deposit using dental characters (Armitage *et al.* 1984, 377).

Domestic fowl

Size

Measurements (Table 32) of the domestic fowl (*Gallus gallus* domestic) bones from Site B deposits reveal a wide size-range, with the greatest proportion comparable to modern bantams and only a few representing larger birds similar to modern laying and boiling fowl. No metrical data are available for the Site A domestic fowl bones, owing to a much smaller sample size and higher degree of fragmentation.

Sex ratio

Using the criteria of West (1982; 1985) eleven domestic fowl in the bone assemblages from Site B (see below) are identified as females from the absence of a spur in their tarsometatarsal bones, and a single capon (castrate) (also from Site B) is recognized by the extra large size of its tarsometatarsal bone and presence of a spur scar (criteria of Sadler 1990). The distal breadth (Bd) in the capon bone is 17.6mm, which falls outside the upper range of the females (Bd range 11.1 to 12.1mm, mean 11.5mm, N = 4).
Period 3 to 4.4 AD 230–275 - 1 castrate - 1 adult female
Period 4.5 AD 275–325 - 1 adult female
Period 5.1 AD 325–375 - 6 all adult female
Period 6 AD 375–410 - 2 adult and 1 immature female

Element		No.	Bantam	Modern Laying hen	Boiling fowl
Humerus					
	3rd century AD deposits	57.6–72.4	2	72.8	81.8	82.2
Radius					
	3rd century AD deposits	68.7	1	64.1	71.1	
Ulna					
	3rd century AD deposits	66.4–75.9	2	69.7	80.8	82.1
	Late 3rd/Early 4th century AD deposits	60.9–61.0	2			
	Late 4th century AD deposits	63.6	1			
Femur					
	Late 4th century AD deposits	70.7	1	76.3	90.4	91.8
Tibiotarsus					
	Late 4th century AD deposits	96.8	1	109.7	129.9	129.1
Tarsometatarsus (unspurred)					
	Late 3rd/Early 4th century AD deposits	63.4	1	74.4	85.3	
	Late 4th century AD deposits	62.6–75.5	4			

Comparative modern specimens: Black Minorca bantam, AM Lab. No. 2787; Laying fowl, Booth Museum of Natural History Brighton Acc. No. 102093; Boiling fowl, Armitage collections

Table 32 Site B, measurements of the Gallus gallus (domestic) bone elements in comparison with those from modern domestic fowl. Greatest length (GL) in mm.

Immature birds

Out of the total of 77 domestic fowl bones from Site B, two are from immature individuals (2.6%) and all others are from fully mature birds. All eight domestic fowl bones from Site A represent fully mature birds.

Greylag/domestic goose *Anser anser*/domestic: A single adult goose humerus came from Site B, B[229] fill of cut B[230] (Period 6). It is not possible to determine whether this particular specimen represents a domestic goose or a wild greylag goose.

Mallard/domestic duck *Anas platyrhynchos*/domestic: this bird is represented by three bone elements, from two adults (specimens are listed below) all from the area of the service yard on Site B: Period 4.2, B[644] make up layer produced 1 coracoid (GL 56.7, Lm 53.9, Bb 23.2, BF 21.0mm) and 1 humerus; and Period 6, B[379] fill of cut B[380] produced 1 ulna (GL 81.2mm)

As with geese there are problems in differentiating between domestic and wild ducks from their skeletal remains. It is therefore possible that one or both of the two individuals above represent mallard rather than the domestic duck.

Tufted duck *Aythya fuligula*: this wildfowl species is represented by an isolated carpometacarpus from Site B, B[240] fill of cut B[249] (Period 6).

Woodcock *Scolopax rusticola*: this wild woodland species is represented among the hand-collected bone from Site A by an isolated carpometacarpus from A[1444] a clayey sand dump layer (Period 4.1), dated on the associated pottery to AD 200–250. Other Romano-British sites where this species has been recorded include the first/second-century site at Lincoln Road, London Borough of Enfield (identified by Cowles and Gask, referenced in Armitage 1977, 187), Frocester Villa (Bramwell 1979, referenced in Luff 1982, 131), and in first- to fourth-century deposits at Exeter (Maltby 1979).

Raven *Corvus corax*: this scavenger bird is represented by a single coracoid from Site B, a silty layer B[384] that covered the now redundant service yard (Period 6). Measurements (mm): GL 56.1, Lm 51.9, BF 17.2, Bb 17.4.

Starling *Sturnus vulgaris*: this wild bird is represented by a radius from Site B floor make-up layer B[754] sample B{31} (Period 3).

Robin *Erithacus rubecula*: this wild bird is represented by a tibiotarsus from Site B fill of the fire-box B[809] B{46} (Period 3).

Fish

Freshwater, estuarine, and marine fish species are all represented among the bone assemblages from both sites (see Table 22, Table 23). Of special interest is the cyprinid precaudal (anterior abdominal) vertebra from B[335] sample B{6}, (Period 4.5), a beaten earth floor in Building 3e. This specimen compares closely with Crucian carp *Carassius carassius*, which at the present day is found locally common in lakes, rivers and canals throughout England and Wales, but has been considered by many zoologists as a recent (post-Roman) introduction (see

Jenkins 1925 reptd. 1942, 284 and Newdick 1979, 48). Wheeler (1977) however, suggested Crucian carp in the Thames were "probably indigenous" and owed their occurrence there to former connections of the Thames with Continental European rivers during the period of post-glacial depression (Flandrian land bridge). Another precaudal cyprinid vertebra, from B[477] sample B{9}, a beaten earth floor within Building 3c, (Period 4.3) compares with Roach *Rutilus rutilus*, a common native species in the freshwater reaches of the tidal Thames and other rivers in the London area. These same rivers probably were the sources of the freshwater eel *Anguilla anguilla* consumed at both sites.

Black sea bream *Spondyliosoma cantharus* is represented among the bones from two deposits on Site B: 1 caudal vertebra from layer B[766], sample B{38} (Period 4.2); 1 precaudal vertebra from beaten earth in Building 7, B[316], sample B{5} (phase 5.1). The presence of this particular marine species in Roman deposits at Site B is of interest as possibly indicating transportation of food fish from south coast fishing ports to Roman London, a suggestion made by Wheeler (1980, 161) in regard to his identification of black sea bream from a Roman context at Billingsgate Buildings, Lower Thames Street, London.

The thin-lipped grey mullet *Chelon ramada*, represented by a caudal vertebra from Site B, context B[605], sample B{35}, fill of posthole B[6] and part of Building 3a (Period 4.1), could have been caught in the Thames estuary where it is common today (Wheeler 1979, 160).

Plaice *Pleuronectes platessa* consumed at both sites probably had been caught in the outer estuary of the Thames, where this fish is common today (Wheeler 1979, 196).

The other two marine fish, herring *Clupea harrengus* and mackerel *Scomber scombrus*, consumed at both sites were probably caught in the lower tidal Thames or supplied from coastal fisheries beyond the mouth of the Thames.

Amphibian species

Common frog *Rana temporaria*: skeletal remains of frog came from the sieved residues of environmental samples from both sites (see Table 30; Table 31).

Catalogue of waste products from horn- and antler-working

There is only limited evidence of craft activity using animal products as a raw material from Site A, and even less from Site B.

Horn-working waste

Evidence of the utilisation of the horns of cattle is provided by chopped portions of crania with horn cores attached, recovered from the following deposits:

Fills of timber-lined well A[1399] (Period 6):
A[1281] 1 young adult medium-horned bull & 1 young adult short-horned bull and 1 broken specimen of indeterminate age/type/sex
A[1615] 1 young-adult medium-horned bull

Building 3b sandy silt layer/occupation debris (Period 4.2):
B[704] 1 young adult short-horned bull

Sheep horns also were removed as a raw material, as evidenced by specimens from the following deposits:

Fill of well A[1399] (Period 6.1):
A[1615] 1 sheep cranium with the horn cores chopped off

Fill of robber cut B[1030] (Period 7)
B[1029] 1 horn core of a young adult male, chopped through the base

Antler-working waste

Two waste off-cut pieces of red deer antler tines were recovered from Site A deposits:
Layer A[800] (Period 5.1) and sandy silt layer A[1028] (Period 7).

Interpretation and discussion of the animal bone

Site environment: unwelcome rodent vermin and wild fauna

Our understanding of the fine-scale distribution of Black rat in Roman Britain is still patchy (Armitage 1994). Reumer (1986) believed that *Rattus rattus* during the Romano-British period would have been confined to ports and the larger urban centres, and entirely absent outside these. This assertion is now being questioned by more recent discoveries at such sites as those at Shadwell, TOC02, and HGA02, where the archaeological deposits clearly reveal the presence of this exotic rodent vermin (see Table 30; Table 31). As a warmth-seeking animal (originating from tropical southern Asia, see Armitage *et al.* 1984) the heated rooms/areas near the heating system of the Roman period bath house would have been especially inviting as a habitation. At both sites, rats

would also have benefited from the freely abundant food sources unwittingly provided by the human inhabitants in the form of discarded kitchen/table waste and scraps. Likewise, the provision of shelter, warmth, and sources of food at both sites attracted another unwelcome rodent pest (commensal) species, the house mouse *Mus musculus*, as evidenced by its skeletal remains in the archaeological deposits.

Botanical specimens (see environmental report) obtained from Site A produced evidence showing the types of vegetation cover close to human habitation, indicating the presence of tall grassland, waste/damp ground, as well as cultivated fields nearby. All these sorts of habitats would have attracted field voles, moles, water shrews, common shrews, and common frog, as well as small wild birds such as the robin; whose skeletal remains are represented at Site A and Site B. Semi-aquatic habitats provided by drainage ditches and marshy areas created by localized flooding supported water voles, water shrews, and frogs, as attested by their skeletal remains found on both sites.

By the last quarter of the fourth century AD (Period 6) the Roman period bath house on Site B had gone out of use and subsequently was systematically demolished, and the level of human activity in the area declined. It was at this time that the site apparently attracted passing scavengers such as fox and raven.

Dietary profiles of the inhabitants and food procurement

Relative proportional frequencies of the main meat-yielding species, calculated from the NISP data (Table 33), reveal beef to have been the principal dietary staple at both sites. Mutton and pork supplemented the beef. Based on skeletal part representation in the cattle and sheep bones assemblages, it appears the inhabitants of Site B enjoyed more of the better quality cuts of beef and mutton, in contrast to their neighbours on Site A whose food comprised higher frequencies of heads and feet. In addition to the better meat cuts provided by the mature fully-grown cattle and sheep, the Site B inhabitants consumed newborn lambs and neonatal (sucking) piglets, both of which are absent from the Site A dietary profile.

		Cattle	Sheep	Pig
Site A				
Periods 4.1 to 5.2	AD 275 - 375	83.4%	10.2%	6.4%
Periods 6 & 7	Late 4th century AD/Sub-Roman	83.7%	12.2%	4.1%
Site B				
Periods 3 to 4.4	AD 230 - 325	69.9%	16.8%	13.3%
Periods 4.5 to 5.1	4th century AD	68.9%	19.3%	11.8%
Periods 6 & 7	Late 4th century AD/Sub-Roman	77.2%	17.2%	5.6%

Table 33 Relative proportional frequencies of the main domesticates/meat-yielding species; values based on NISP data.

Also of significance is the discovery that proportionally more domestic fowl appear to have been eaten at Site B than at Site A. This difference is particularly noticeable with reference to the fourth-century AD deposits at Site B, where domestic fowl bones as a percentage of the total bones of all the meat-yielding species (cattle, sheep, pig and fowl) exhibit an extra high frequency (20.1%) (Table 34). This value is close to the frequency (19.8%) recorded for the domestic fowl bones at the Bishopsgate site in London, where the food debris was believed to derive from the kitchen of a substantial private dwelling (Tyers 1984, 374). The large quantities of domestic fowl bones at Site B could therefore also reflect a similar high-status diet. It is important to recognize that the domestic fowl was held in high esteem by Roman epicures and was a luxury food when specially prepared in an elaborate fashion for feasts (see Lauwerier 1993, 79). In addition to its contribution to feasting, domestic fowl was also considered by Romans to be the perfect light snack food. Bathers at the Caerleon Fortress bath house, in the first century AD, appear especially to have relished such food, as evidenced by the extraordinarily high frequency (63.7%) of the bones of domestic fowl represented in the food debris recovered from the frigidarium drain (O'Connor 1983).

Further supporting evidence of a more affluent diet associated with the Roman period bath house site at Site B is provided by the greater variety of fish represented in the food debris deposits, which indicate procurement from freshwater, estuarine, and marine sources (Locker 2007). Hunted game at Site B is represented by the hare bones, which are notably absent from the Site A food debris. At Site A, the carpometacarpal bone of woodcock from a Period 4.1 deposit provides the sole evidence of exploitation of local wild food resources. This particular bird probably had been caught in the open mixed deciduous woodland close to the site, the existence of which was revealed from analyses of the Site A botanical samples.

At Site B, by Period 6 (late fourth century), there is an indication in the food debris that the inhabitants were exploiting local wildfowl (geese and ducks). At the same period, the presence of hens and neonatal (sucking) piglets (despite a general decline in pigs, see Table 33) possibly reflects backyard (subsistence) livestock farming activity. Hens may have been kept as egg-producers as well as for their flesh. Although the consumption of fat (yearling) lambs seems to continue at both sites, newborn lambs no longer feature in the dietary profile (Table 33). Considering all of this evidence, it may be suggested that by the last quarter of the fourth century AD at both sites the inhabitants had adopted a much more self-reliant food procurement/production system than that followed in the earlier Roman period.

		Frequency
Site A		
Periods 4.1 to 5.2	Late 3rd/early 4th century AD	1.4%
Periods 6 & 7	Late 4th century AD/sub-Roman	0.4%
Site B		
Periods 3 to 4.4	3rd century AD	5.8%
Periods 4.5 to 5.1	4th century AD	20.1%
Post-bathhouse		
Periods 6 & 7	Late 4th century AD/sub-Roman	4.2%
London sites		
General Post Office	1st–2nd century AD	0.9%
Billingsgate Buildings	1st –2nd century AD	1.6%
Bishopsgate	1st century AD	19.8%
Southwark sites		
Swan Street	1st–4th century AD	1.2%
Long Lane	2nd/3rd century AD	10.3%
Caerleon (Gwent)		
Caerleon Fortress bathhouse	1st century AD	63.7%

Sources:

General Post Office (GPO75) - West (1983)

Caerleon Fortress Bathhouse - O'Connor (1983)

All others - Armitage

Table 34 Sites A and B, proportional frequencies of the domestic fowl bones as a percentage of the total NISP for all the principal meat-yielding species (cattle, sheep, pig and fowl) in comparison with other Romano-British sites in London, Southwark, and Caerleon (Gwent).

3.10 Environmental analysis of Tobacco Dock (Site A) samples

Nick Branch

Archaeological excavations at Tobacco Dock (Site A) revealed a complex series of Roman deposits and samples were recovered and analysed from six separate phases of activity: Period 2 (*c.* AD 50–230), Period 4.1 (*c* AD 275–325), Period 5.1 and 5.2 (*c.* AD 325–375), Period 6 (*c.* AD 375–410) and Period 7 (*c.* AD 410+). The geoarchaeological findings and the results of both the assessment and analysis of the archaeobotanical remains are summarised below. The results are discussed in the wider context of the environment, economy and diet of Roman London in particular and Roman Britain in general. Analysis of samples from Site B were the subject of a separate report and the results are integrated with the chronological narrative.

Geological and geoarchaeological context

Tobacco Dock lies on the north side of the River Thames at a distance of about 0.65km from the present waterfront and occupies the bluff that separates the floodplain from the Taplow Terrace. The Geological Survey (1:50,000, Sheet 256, North London, 1994) shows the site to be underlain by Alluvium, but the mapped boundary between Alluvium to the south and Taplow Gravel to the north runs along the northern edge of the site. Immediately to the north of the site, brickearth, mapped by the Geological Survey as Langley Silt overlies the Taplow Gravel. In this part of London, Gibbard (1994) terms the sediment underlying the Taplow Terrace, the Mucking Gravel. In Shadwell, Gibbard shows a thickness of *c.* 5m of Mucking Gravel underlying the Taplow Terrace at a level of *c.* 10m OD. In the same area, Gibbard records the surface of the floodplain alluvium at *c.* 1m OD. The sediments investigated at Tobacco Dock occur at levels between 2.70m and 6.22m OD.

During the archaeological excavations, several column samples were recovered to record the main local variations in the sedimentary sequence across the site. Three column samples are of particular relevance here: A{107}, A{106} and A{296} (Fig. 110). Overlying sand and gravel, which can be confidently referred to the Taplow Gravel (Mucking Gravel of Gibbard 1994), sediments of colluvial and/or anthropogenic origin were recorded in column sample A{107} A[1475], Period 5.1 and the upper part of column sample A{106} ditch A[665], context A[576], Period 5.2. They are more or less clayey, gravelly sands and silts, with low organic matter content, and contain charcoal and pieces of brick or tile. They probably represent a mixture of Taplow Gravel and Langley Silt that has moved downslope across the bluff separating the Taplow Terrace from the floodplain alluvium and

anthropogenic 'dump' deposits. Column sample A{107} also provides evidence for a 'stable' occupation surface (possible floor) between 3.41 and 3.60m OD (context A[1427], Period 5.1), and is overlain by further evidence for colluvial deposition and anthropogenic 'dumping'.

A thin layer of peat (170mm, context A[1521], Period 4.1) was recovered in column sample A{296} and found near the southeastern edge of the site at levels between 3.55m and 3.38m OD, underlying sandy gravel (Taplow Gravel). It seems to be at too high a level to have formed as part of the natural aggradation of the Holocene floodplain and instead may have formed during the Roman period in a localised natural or artificial depression just above the edge of the floodplain.

In conclusion, the sedimentary sequences at Tobacco Dock indicate the presence of *in-situ* Quaternary terrace sediment overlain by redeposited sand and gravel. Across the southern end of the site in particular, sediments that are both colluvial and anthropogenic in origin have been recorded. They probably represent a mixture of Taplow Gravel and Langley Silt that has moved downslope across the bluff separating the Taplow Terrace from the floodplain alluvium and anthropogenic 'dump' deposits. Occupation surfaces have been recorded and dated to *c.* AD 325–375 (Period 5.1), whilst peat formation near the south-eastern edge of the site, dated to *c.* AD 275–325 (Period 4.1), is thought to have occurred within a localised natural or artificial depression.

Archaeobotany

Plant macrofossil assessment

During the archaeological excavations, 234 bulk samples were obtained from Tobacco Dock, and a sub-sample of 10 litres was processed by flotation or wet sieving (due to their highly organic, waterlogged nature), with the exception of samples A{26}, A{39} and A{203}, where 20 litres was processed. The residues were scanned 'by eye', and the 'flots' examined using a low power zoom-stereo microscope. Those samples having medium to high recovery of charred and waterlogged seeds were then submitted for a more detailed assessment, and the results are presented here (Table 35).

Period 2 (AD 50–230)

Sample A{333} context A[1458] was taken from a posthole. It provided a small but rich flot, in terms of both quantity and diversity of material. The assemblage was dominated by *Sambucus nigra* (elder) and *Carex* sp. (sedges).

Period 4.1 (AD 275–325)

Sample A{295} context A[1517] was sampled from posthole A[1518], and sample A{334} context A[1648] from a possible floor over-lying timber beams. Both were relatively rich, with a range of well-preserved fruit seeds including *Rubus* sp. (brambles), *Ficus carica* (fig) and *Sambucus nigra*, along with *Ranunculus* sp. (buttercup) and species from the Apiaceae (carrot) family.

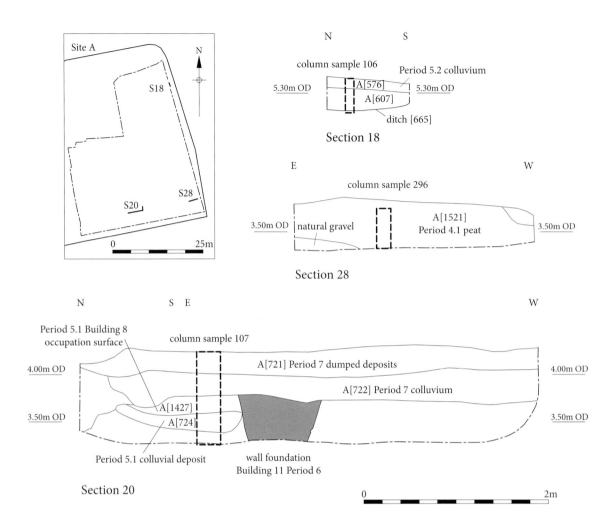

Fig. 110   Location of column samples A{106}, A{107} and A{296} (scale 1:40)

Period 5.1 (AD 325–375)

Eight samples presented assemblages worthy of detailed assessment from this phase:- A{257} context A[1425], A{259} context A[1427], A{264} context A[1451], A{273} context A[1481], A{282} context A[1515], A{304} context A[1533], A{325} context A[858] and A{335} context A[1695]. Samples A{257}, A{259} and A{282} are all from layers. Their assemblages contained a range of species including charred *Hordeum* sp. (barley) grains, waterlogged *Rubus* sp., *Sambucus nigra*, and Chenopodiaceae (goosefoot) species. Sample A{273} was taken from posthole A[1482]; Sample A{304} was from a ditch A[1534]; and the remainder were from fills of sub-circular or rectangular pits. These all provided rich assemblages, with samples A{264} and A{325} having particularly good preservation. Fruit seeds are the most prevalent species in all of these samples, and charcoal was present in all but sample A{325}. Waterlogged wood occurred in all but samples A{273}, A{325} and A{335}.

Period 5.2 (AD 325–375)

Sample A{38} context A[467] was taken from the fill behind the lining of ditch A[665], and presented a rich and relatively diverse assemblage including species from the Lamiaceae (dead-nettle) family, and other grassland species along with occasional charcoal and frequent wood. Sample A{101} context A[750] was sampled from ditch A[751], and provided a varied assemblage with charred grain, *Sambucus nigra*, *Carex* sp. and other fruit seeds. Sample A{235} context A[1307] was predominantly *Sambucus nigra* and *Carex* sp., whilst sample A{307} context A[1535] contained purely *Sambucus nigra*.

Period 6 (AD 375–410)

Samples A{17} context A[369] and A{18} context A[378] are from a Roman ditch A[391]. Both contain charred wheat grains, along with waterlogged *Sambucus nigra* and seeds from the Lamiaceae family. Samples A{185} context A[1028], A{203} context A[722] and A{245} context A[1372] come from layers; Sample A{58} context A[553] was from a posthole; Samples A{221} context A[1269] and A{225} context A[1259] were both sampled from slot A[1279]. Sample A{24} context A[414] is from ditch A[415]. They all contain frequent *Sambucus nigra*, along with other wild fruit seeds and grassland species.

Pollen analysis

Following the assessment of 40 pollen samples (Branch *et al.* 2004a), extracted from both the column and small bulk samples, four samples were selected from the Roman deposits for pollen analysis (Table 36; Fig. 111 – Fig. 114). In addition, the pollen assessment data from column sample A{296}, a shallow peat sequence assigned to Period 4.1 (*c.* AD 275–325) are presented (Table 37).

The pollen was extracted using modified, standard procedures involving: (1) dispersion in 1% Sodium pyrophosphate; (2) sieving to remove the coarse mineral and organic fractions (>125μ and <10μ); (3) removal of finer minerogenic fraction using Sodium polytungstate (specific gravity of 2.0g/cm³), and (4) mounting of the sample in glycerol jelly. Each stage of the procedure was preceded and followed by thorough sample cleaning in filtered distilled water. Pollen grains and spores were

Phase	Context number	Sample number	Plant material				Wood		Preservation	Information
			<10	10-30	30-50	50+	Charcoal	Water-logged		
	2181	275		*			F		**	elder, sedge, fruit seeds
3.1	1458	333				*			**	elder, sedge
4.1	1517	295				*	F	O	***	bramble, fig, elder, carrot, goosefoot family, sedge, buttercup
4.1	1648	334			*		A	O	***	sedge, elder, bramble
5.1	414	24				*	F		*	waterlogged elder, occasional dock, dead nettle family
5.1	1425	257				*	F	A	***	charred barley grain, waterlogged elder, sedge, bramble, nettle family
5.1	1427	259				*	F	F	***	elder, occasional nettle family
5.1	1451	264			*		F	F	***	elder, bramble
5.1	1481	273				*	F		**	bramble, fig, elder, carrot, goosefoot family, sedge
5.1	1515	282				*	F	O	***	bramble, fig, elder, carrot, goosefoot family, sedge, buttercup
5.1	1533	304				*	O	O	***	buttercup, carrot, goosefoot, sedge, knotgrass, strawberry
5.1	858	325		*					***	elder, sedge, fruit seeds
5.1	1695	335				*	F		**	elder, sedge, fruit seeds
5.2	467	38				*	O	F	***	dead nettle family, sedge, knotgrass
5.2	750	101				*			***	charred grain, elder, sedge, fruit
5.2	1307	235				*		O	***	elder, sedges
5.2	1535	307			*		F		***	elder
6	369	17		*			F	O	**	elder, charred wheat grain, dead nettle
6	378	18		*			F	F	**	elder, charred wheat grain, dead nettle
6	553	58		*			F	O	**	elder, knotgrass
6	1028	185		*			F	O	**	elder, fig, goosefoot, sedge, buttercup
6	722	203				*	A		***	elder, sedge, fruit seeds
6	1269	221				*	F		**	elder, sedge, fruit seeds
6	1259	225			*		F		**	elder, sedge, fruit seeds
6	1372	245		*			F	A	**	carrot family, sedge, fruit seeds

Key: A = Abundant F = Frequent O = Occasional *** = Good ** = Average * = Poor

Table 35 Plant macrofossil assessment, Site A.

identified using the Royal Holloway (University of London) pollen type collection and the following sources of keys and photographs: Moore *et al.* (1991); Reille (1992). Plant nomenclature follows the Flora Europaea as summarised in Stace (1997). For each sample, pollen and spore counts of 200–300 were attained (pollen sum), and the counts are expressed as a percentage of total pollen (Table 36; Fig. 111 – Fig. 114). For the pollen assessment (Table 37), the procedures consisted of scanning the prepared slides at 2mm intervals along the whole length of the coverslip and recording the concentration and state of preservation of pollen grains and spores, and principal pollen taxa.

Pollen samples at 3.40–3.39m OD and 3.24–3.23m OD were extracted from column sample A{107}, which was taken through an occupation floor, assigned to Building 8, Period 5.1 (*c.* AD 325–375) (Table 36; Fig. 111; Fig. 112). The assemblages are dominated by non-arboreal pollen, notably Poaceae (36–46%), Lactuceae (19–22%) with Cyperaceae (4%), *Centuarea nigra* (4%), *Sinapis* type (3–5%), *Cirsium* type (2–3%), *Serratula* type (2%) and *Chenopodium* type (4%). Lesser herbaceous taxa include *Plantago lanceolata*, Caryophyllaceae undiff, *Stellaria* type and *Ranunculus* type. Cereal type pollen is present at 2–4%. Tree and shrub taxa include *Alnus, Betula, Fraxinus, Quercus, Corylus* type and Rosaceae. Aquatic and spore taxa include *Oenanthe* type, *Dryopteris* type and *Pteridium*.

The pollen assemblages in both samples are broadly consistent and suggest that during the mid fourth century AD the woodland and shrubland cover was sparse, and comprised birch, ash, oak and hazel. The presence of alder and semi-aquatic pollen taxa such as Cyperaceae (sedge) and *Oenanthe* type (eg water dropwort), possibly indicate nearby wetland vegetation on the Thames floodplain. The depositional context represented by column sample A{107} needs to be considered however when interpreting the possible plant communities represented by the pollen taxa. This is particularly important with respect to the non-arboreal taxa, which dominate the assemblages. Although they may be indicative of the local flora, they may be derived from material brought onto site during domestic and/or industrial activities by the occupants, and added or trampled into the floor layer. For example, cereal pollen (*Cereale* type) may be transported to occupation sites as part of the unprocessed or partly processed crop. Alternatively, if cultivation is taking place nearby, the cereal pollen may be transported by wind to the site and deposited naturally. The same may apply to pollen from plants found in meadows eg *Centaurea nigra* (black knapweed), which could be transported and deposited naturally if the meadow is nearby, or alternatively it could arrive on site within materials collected for animal fodder or bedding. In conclusion, it is difficult to ascertain whether the cultivated fields or grassland suggested by the pollen assemblages is local or extra-local/regional to the site. Nevertheless, the pollen record provides unequivocal evidence for their presence and likely utilisation during the fourth century AD.

Pollen taxa/ Depth m OD	5.52-5.51	5.22-5.21	3.40-3.39	3.24-3.23
	<106>	<106>	<107>	<107>
Alnus	1.0	0.0	0.4	0.4
Betula	0.0	0.0	0.4	0.0
Fraxinus	0.5	0.0	0.4	0.0
Pinus	0.0	0.6	0.0	0.0
Quercus	2.6	1.7	1.7	0.4
Corylus type	0.0	0.0	0.4	0.4
Rosaceae undiff.	0.0	0.0	0.4	0.0
Anthemis type	0.5	0.0	0.0	0.0
Apiaceae undiff.	2.1	0.6	0.4	0.4
Centaurea nigra	4.7	5.6	4.6	4.2
Centaurea cyanus	0.0	0.0	0.0	0.4
Cereale type	2.1	0.6	4.2	2.3
Cirsium type	0.0	0.6	2.5	3.1
Cyperaceae	5.7	3.4	4.2	0.8
Poaceae	24.4	24.7	36.8	46.2
Caryophyllaceae undiff.	0.5	0.0	0.8	1.5
Chenopodium type	1.6	2.2	4.6	4.2
Filipendula	0.5	1.1	0.8	1.1
Heracleum type	0.0	0.0	0.4	0.4
Lactuceae undiff.	38.3	48.9	22.6	19.8
Melampyrum	0.5	0.6	0.0	0.0
Plantago lanceolata	0.5	1.1	1.3	1.1
Plantago media/major	0.0	0.0	0.4	0.0
Papaver type	0.0	0.0	0.4	0.0
Polygonum type	0.0	0.0	0.4	0.4
Poterium	1.0	0.0	0.0	0.0
Ranunculus type	1.0	1.1	0.8	0.4
Serratula type	1.0	1.1	2.5	1.9
Sinapis type	6.7	3.4	3.3	5.0
Stellaria type	0.0	0.0	1.3	0.4
Succisa	0.0	0.6	0.0	0.8
Trifolium type	0.0	0.0	0.4	0.4
Oenanthe type	0.0	0.0	0.4	0.4
Sparganium type	0.0	0.0	0.0	0.4
Typha latifolia	0.5	0.0	0.0	0.0
Dryopteris type	0.5	0.6	0.4	0.0
Pteridium	3.1	1.1	2.5	0.8
Unknown/Obscured	0.5	0.6	0.0	2.7
Total %	**100**	**100**	**100**	**100**

Table 36 Pollen analysis, Site A.

Pollen samples at 5.52–5.51m OD and 5.22–5.21m OD were extracted from column sample A{106}, ditch A[665], which has been assigned to Period 5.2 (AD 325–375) (Table 36; Fig. 113; Fig. 114). The assemblages are dominated by non-arboreal pollen, notably Lactuceae (28–48%) and Poaceae (24%) with Cyperaceae (3–5%), *Centaurea nigra* (4–5%), *Sinapis* type (3–6%), Apiaceae

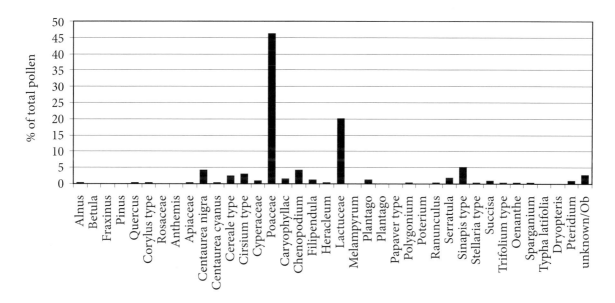

Fig. 111   Pollen sample 3.24–3.23m OD, from column sample A{107}, occupation floor, Period 5.1 (AD 325–375)

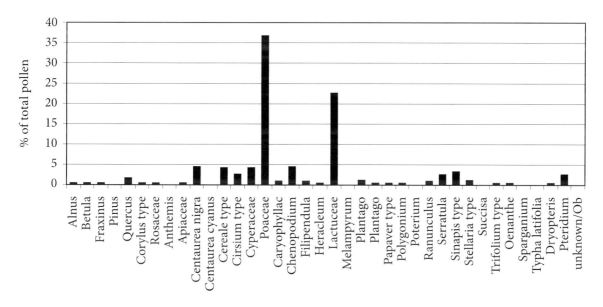

Fig. 112   Pollen sample 3.40–3.39m OD, from column sample A{107}, occupation floor, Period 5.1 (AD 325–375)

(2%) and *Chenopodium* type (2%). Lesser herbaceous taxa include *Plantago lanceolata*, *Ranunculus* type and *Serratula* type. Cereal type pollen is present at 2%. Tree and shrub taxa include *Alnus* (1%), *Fraxinus*, *Pinus* and *Quercus* (1–2%). Aquatic and spore taxa include *Typha latifolia*, *Dryopteris* type and *Pteridium*.

The results of the pollen analysis of the Period 5.2 samples are broadly in agreement with Period 5.1. This is particularly important with respect to our understanding of pollen taphonomy and for addressing the issues outlined above because the depositional context here is a ditch rather than an occupation layer. Based upon the assumption that the ditch sediments are likely to have been receiving much of their pollen by wind from plants growing locally and extra-locally to the site, the assemblages provide an important insight into the vegetation cover at Tobacco Dock during the Roman period. Like the Period 5.1 samples, they indicate five

broad vegetation communities:
(1) Grassland (Poaceae), including meadow taxa, such as *Centaurea nigra* (black knapweed), (2) Waste/disturbed ground dominated by Lactuceae (*Taraxacum* type - dandelion) and *Plantago lanceolata* (ribwort plantain), (3) Cultivated fields with *Cereale* type (cereals) and an associated weed flora eg *Sinapis* type (eg charlock), (4) Dryland scattered woodland comprising ash, pine and oak, and (5) Wetland scattered woodland and grassland with aquatic/semi-aquatic taxa, including alder and *Typha latifolia* (reedmace).

In conclusion, although differential preservation has undoubtedly affected the composition of the pollen assemblages, and may account for the enhanced levels of Lactuceae pollen in both phases due to its resistance to decay, the range of taxa represented does provide a valuable contribution to our understanding of the Roman vegetation cover in London. In particular, the pollen taxa have provided an insight into the vegetation composition of the dryland and wetland, as well as human activities, which appear to include both cultivated fields and meadows.

Column sample A{296} (Period 4.1, *c.* AD 275–325) contains well-preserved pollen grains and spores. Unfortunately, they were not in sufficiently high concentration to justify full analysis (Table 37). A diverse range of arboreal and non-arboreal taxa dominates the pollen assemblage, including Poaceae, Lactuceae (*Taraxacum* type), *Quercus*, *Ulmus*, *Betula* and *Corylus*, indicating the presence of open, dryland woodland in close proximity to the site. The presence of *Alnus* pollen and *Sphagnum* moss spores is extremely important since they provide some indication of the type of vegetation growing on the nearby river floodplain at the end of the third century. The non-arboreal pollen record also includes *Cereale* type, *Plantago lanceolata* and *Cirsium* type, and provides unequivocal evidence for the presence of grassland, disturbed/waste ground and cereal cultivation.

Discussion

Roman environment

There are no direct proxy records from London, or southeast England, for climatic conditions during the Roman period. However, by using a range of information derived from documentary and palaeoenvironmental (eg ice cores, dendroclimatology, peat stratigraphy) sources it is possible to provide a broad insight into climatic conditions during the 350–400 years of occupation at Tobacco Dock. Of particular importance is the transition from colder and wetter climatic conditions, which persisted across north-west Europe during the Iron Age, to a warmer and milder climate at approximately 150 BC. Therefore, during the Roman period, Britain experienced ameliorating climatic conditions, which created favourable conditions for settlement and agriculture, and which lasted until approximately AD 400 (Lamb 1981).

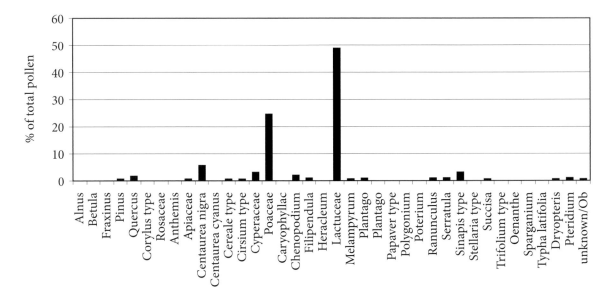

Fig. 113　Pollen sample 5.22–5.21m OD, from column sample A{106}, ditch A[665], Period 5.2 (AD 325–375)

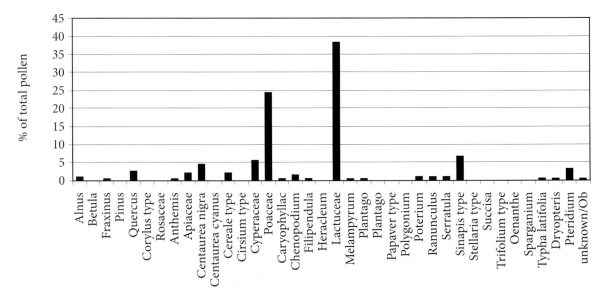

Fig. 114　Pollen sample 5.52–5.51m OD, from column sample A{106}, ditch A[665], Period 5.2 (AD 325–375)

Although Tobacco Dock is situated in close proximity to the River Thames floodplain, unfortunately no detailed information exists on the wetland environment during the Roman period. Therefore, it is unclear whether deposition of peat or alluvial sediments, or both, was occurring, and whether the primary forcing factor was a regional reduction or increase in relative sea level, human activities in the Thames Valley catchment or localised natural changes in the fluvial system. Research in the East Anglian Fens suggest that marine inundation of coastal wetlands during the Iron Age and Early Roman period was succeeded by a regional reduction in relative sea level for much of the Roman occupation, which led to extensive peat formation (Waller 1994). The discovery of peat deposits at Tobacco Dock possibly supports this finding but, as noted earlier, the elevation of the peat indicates that it may have formed as a response to local impeded drainage or even human activities. In the Middle and Upper Thames Valley there is good evidence for alluvial

deposition during the Roman period that may reflect erosion of catchment soils due to agricultural practices. The effect of this activity on the Lower Thames Valley is uncertain, although an increase in sediment accumulation in the lower reaches of the Valley seems likely. Therefore at present, it is not possible to determine whether the nearby floodplain at Tobacco Dock was accreting alluvial sediments or peat, or both, during the Roman period.

Our knowledge and understanding of the vegetation history of London, and southeast England in general, is poor for the Roman period. The general picture we have of London is of scattered wetland woodland comprising *Salix* (willow) and *Alnus* (alder), with *Quercus* (oak) and *Corylus* (hazel) growing on adjacent dryland. Therefore, the vegetation cover was dominated by grassland, pasture, meadow, together with arable fields, and managed woodland (eg fruit trees), and ornamental shrubs (eg box). The pollen records from Tobacco Dock enhance this picture and indicate that the woodland also comprised

Depth (m OD)	Pollen taxa	Common name	Preservation	Concentration
3.69–3.68	*Pinus* Poaceae *Ulmus* *Chenopodium* type Caryophyllaceae undiff. *Plantago lanceolata* *Alnus* *Taraxacum* type *Quercus* *Cereale* type *Cirsium* type *Filipendula*	Pine Grass Family Elm Goosefoot Family Campion Family Ribwort plantain Alder e.g. Dandelion Oak Cereal Thistle Meadowsweet	Good	Medium
3.60–3.59	Poaceae *Sphagnum* Filicales *Artemisia* *Ulmus* *Chenopodium* type Caryophyllaceae undiff. *Plantago lanceolata* *Alnus* *Taraxacum* type *Cereale* type *Cirsium* type	Grass Family Moss e.g. Male fern Mugwort Elm Goosefoot Family Campion Family Ribwort plantain Alder e.g. Dandelion Cereal Thistle	Good	Medium
3.53–3.52	Poaceae *Cereale* type	Grass Family Cereal	Good	Medium
3.46–3.45	Poaceae *Cereale* type	Grass Family Cereal	Good	Medium
3.33–3.32	Filicales *Betula* *Corylus* type *Sphagnum* *Taraxacum* type	e.g. Male fern Birch Hazel Moss Dandelion	Good	Medium

Table 37 Pollen assessment, column sample <296> (peat sequence), Site A.

birch, ash and pine. Otherwise, the picture from Tobacco Dock is broadly consistent with records from Roman Britain, suggesting an overall reduction in woodland cover, by comparison with the Iron Age. However, there was clearly regional variation in the extent and nature of the woodland cover, and in some instances woodland expanded during the Roman occupation (Dark 2000), and therefore it is difficult to evaluate the situation in London because of the paucity of pollen records. As Dark states "A wider coverage of well-dated pollen sequences with closely sampled Roman-period deposits is needed before pollen analysis can shed further light on the environmental consequences of the Roman Conquest" (Dark 2000, 188–119). This is especially true for the London area and southeast England in general.

Roman economy and diet

It is generally accepted that during the Roman period in southeast England, sub-urban and rural residential complexes, eg villas, would have been surrounded by extensive field systems, enclosed by boundary ditches. This agricultural land would have been important for supplying a range of products for urban centres, such as London, including grain, legumes and animal fodder/bedding (hay). In addition, there is good archaeological evidence for watermills, corn driers and granaries, suggesting a well-developed infrastructure for the storage and processing of cereal grain. Whether the floodplain of the River Thames in East London was brought into agricultural production is unclear, but such was the demand for land during the Roman period it is highly likely that areas accumulating alluvium may have been suitable for drainage and cultivation. Certainly, there is archaeological evidence from the East Anglian Fens and Severn Estuary Levels, and parts of the Upper Thames Valley, for extensive drainage and cultivation during the Roman period (Dark 2000).

The range of crops being either cultivated in southeast England or imported from the continent was extensive (see Table 38). The most commonly occurring cereals were *Triticum spelta* (spelt wheat), *Hordeum vulgare* (barley) and *Secale cereale* (rye), also *Triticum aestivum* (bread wheat) and *Secale cereale* (oats), *Triticum dicoccum* (emmer wheat) and *Triticum compactum* (club wheat). *Triticum aestivum* in particular is known to have been cultivated on clay and silt-rich soils (Dark 2000), such as alluvial floodplains, and therefore may have formed an important crop at Tobacco Dock. Unfortunately, it has not been possible to ascertain whether the charred wheat grains found at Tobacco Dock were of *Triticum spelta* or *T. aestivum,* or another species. However, along with the charred remains of *Hordeum* (barley), it indicates the utilisation of both wheat and barley at this time. Whether wheat and barley were being cultivated locally, rather than simply processed and stored, is an important issue and is often difficult to resolve based solely upon plant macrofossil remains. At Governor's House, London, for example, *Triticum spelta* was recorded in Roman deposits along with glume bases and rachises,

which suggest that crop processing may have been taking place within an urban context (Brigham and Woodger 2001). At Tobacco Dock, however, the presence of cereal pollen together with charred grains tends to imply that cereals were being cultivated in the local area, perhaps to supply the urban centre.

It is also apparent from archaeobotanical assemblages that crops such as *Vicia faba* (Celtic bean) and *Pisum sativum* (pea) were becoming more important during the Roman period, as were herbs like *Anethum graveolens* (dill) and *Coriandrum sativum* (coriander) (see Table 38). Although these plants were not recorded at Tobacco Dock, they undoubtedly contributed to the Roman diet of London (see Table 38). In many archaeobotanical assemblages, plants commonly associated with arable land are also recorded, providing a valuable insight into the composition of fields and soil status in which these crops were being grown during the Roman period. For example, at Governor's House, London, *Agrostemma githago* (corncockle), was present suggesting nutrient rich agricultural soils (Brigham and Woodger 2001). At Tobacco Dock, the pollen of *Centaurea cyanus* (cornflower), and the pollen and plant macrofossils of *Chenopodium, Lamium, Polygonum* and *Ranunculus*, all provide possible evidence for the composition of arable fields (see Table 38). Although evidence from the adjacent site of LD74 is sparse, samples taken from a water storage tank were found to contain a rich collection of agricultural weeds, though little evidence of cultivated plants (Willcox 1977).

The use, cultivation and/or import of 'exotic' products, such as *Vitis vinifera* (grapes), are widely recognised, and there are excellent examples from Roman London (Willcox 1978; Tyers 1988; Pearson and Giorgi 1992). However, it is often difficult to establish whether these plants were being cultivated, imported or both. For example, although there is no known evidence for grape cultivation in the southeast England during the Roman period, a record does exist for Northamptonshire (Meadows 1996), which suggests that it was entirely likely that vineyards existed in the southeast but that perhaps cultivation was small scale and localised. Nevertheless, grape seeds are a common occurrence in archaeobotanical assemblages from Roman deposits together with coriander, dill, *Ficus carica* (fig), *Olea europea* (olive), *Pinus pinea* (stone pine) and *Juglans regia* (walnut). In the absence of extensive evidence for cultivation, these remains suggest that many of these products were probably imported (eg Governor's House, London; Brigham and Woodger 2001; see Table 38). At Tobacco Dock, fig seeds are present, which suggests that imported 'exotic' products were eaten. The amphorae recovered suggest the importation of a range of goods including olive-oil, wine, fish products and olives (see Chapter 3.1).

The use of hay is recorded on some urban archaeological sites by the presence of specific hay meadow plants, such as *Leucanthemum vulgare* (ox-eye daisy), *Rhinanthus minor* (yellow rattle), *Centaurea nigra* (knapweed), *Linum catharticum* (fairy flax) and

Scientific name	English name	Habitat and use codes
Trees		
Juglans regia	Walnut	FHI
Olea europaea	Olive	FGHI
Pinus pinea	Stone pine	FHI
Shrubs		
Corylus avellana	Hazel	CF
Ficus carica	Fig	FGI
Prunus avium/cerasus	Sloe/cherry	CFGI
Rubus fruticosus/idaeus	Blackberry/raspberry	CFGH
Sambucus nigra	Elder	BCFGH
Vitis vinifera	Grape	Fl
Grasses and Herbs		
Triticum spelta	Spelt wheat	Fl
Hordeum sativum	Barley	Fl
Agrostemma githago	Corncockle	AB
Apium sp.	Marshwort	EFI
Brassica sp.	Cabbage	ABFGHI
Chenopodium album	Fat hen	ABFH
Chenopodium murale	Nettle-leaved goosefoot	AB
Conium maculatum	Hemlock	CEG
Coriandrum sativum	Coriander	FGI
Hyoscyamus niger	Henbane	BDG
Lamium sp.	Deadnettle	ABC
Leontondon sp.	Hawkbit	BDF
Linum sp.	Flax	ADHI
Lycopus europaeus	Gipsy-wort	EH
Malva sylvestris	Mallow	BCDF
Polygonum sp.	Knotgrass	ABCDEFG
Polygonum aviculare	Knotgrass	ABG
Potentilla erecta	Tormentil	CDEGH
Prunella vulgaris	Self-heal	BCDG
Ranunculus acris/repens/bulbosus	Buttercup	ABCDEG
Ranunculus scleratus	Celery-leaved crowfoot	E
Raphanus raphanistrum	Wild radish	A
Reseda luteola	Dyer's rocket	ABGHI
Rumex acetosella	Sheep's sorrel	AD
Silene sp.	Campion	ABCDF
Stellaria graminea	Lesser stitchwort	CD
Solanum nigrum	Black nightshade	BF
Sonchus asper	Sow-thistle	AB
Urtica dioica	Stinging nettle	BCDEFGH
Viola sp.	Violet	ABCDG
Aquatics		
Carex sp.	Sedge	CDEH
Eleocharis sp.	Spike rush	E
Juncus sp.	Rush	ADEH
Mentha sp.	Mint	ABCEFGI
Ferns e.g. *Pteridium*		
Unknown		
Mosses e.g. *Sphagnum*		
Indeterminate		

Habitat and use codes:
A – Weeds of cultivated land
B – Ruderals, weeds of waste places and disturbed ground
C – Plants of woods, scrub and hedgerow
D – Open grassland/heath
E – Plants of damp/wet environment and aquatics
F – Edible plants
G – Medicinal and poisonous plants
H – Commercial/industrial use
I – Cultivated plants

Table 38 Plants commonly occurring in Roman deposits in London; recorded as charred and waterlogged macro-remains.

Trifolium pratense (red clover), as well as *Filipendula ulmaria* (meadowsweet), *Prunella vulgaris* (self heal) and *Lotus corniculatus* (bird's foot trefoil) (see Table 38). However, in many instances it is difficult to establish the specific habitat represented by plants recorded in an archaeobotanical assemblage, either due to the plant's growth in more than one habitat, such meadowland and woodland edges eg *Rumex acetosa* (common sorrel), or the level of taxonomic precision attained by the identifications. For example, *Linum usitatissimum* (common flax) is found in Roman deposits and may indicate its cultivation; alternatively, it may have simply been a weed of arable fields or grassland. At Shadwell several pollen taxa suggest the presence of tall herb grassland eg *Centaurea nigra*. Although it is not possible to establish whether these meadow plants were being used for hay, their presence in the local area provides a record of their availability that may be confirmed by future archaeobotanical work.

The utilisation of woodland for industrial and domestic purposes was also clearly of importance during the Roman period. Indeed archaeological records indicate that a wide range of taxa were exploited, including *Quercus* (oak), *Corylus* (hazel), *Alnus glutinosa* (alder), *Acer campestre* (field maple), *Fraxinus excelsior* (ash), *Ulmus glabra* (elm), *Salix* (willow), *Euonymus europaeus* (spindle), *Betula* (birch) and *Ilex aquifolium* (holly). Dark (2000) highlights several important foci for industrial activities, especially iron and pottery production eg the Weald. This would have resulted in a major impact on woodland resources unless methods of management, such as coppicing, were employed; a suggestion supported by some charcoal data from archaeological sites. Domestic use of wood would have also placed a strain on resources, especially for bath houses, hypocausts and hearths, such as those uncovered at Shadwell. Again, woodland management may have been important in this context, especially given the large amounts of oak (preserved as waterlogged wood and charcoal) known to have been managed. The use of woodland resources for animal fodder and for human consumption has also been recorded in the Roman period, with the use of *Ulmus* (elm) leaves and branches (Fowler 2002), *Corylus* (hazel) nuts, and *Rubus fruticosus/Rubus idaeus* (blackberry/raspberry) and *Sambucus nigra* (elder) fruit (see Governor's House, London; Brigham and Woodger 2001) well known. At Tobacco Dock, despite the presence of pollen records for woodland, and charcoal records for fuel wood utilisation, it has not been possible to identify evidence for woodland management (Branch *et al.* 2004a). The identification of elder seeds at Tobacco Dock is of some interest and may, rather tentatively, indicate the use of the berries from this tree for human consumption.

Finally, a variety of plants associated with medicinal or industrial activities are also found in Roman deposits. For example, at Governor's House, London, *Reseda luteola* (weld/dyer's rocket) was recorded (Brigham and Woodger 2001; see Table 38); this plant produces a yellow dye and has strong association with the dyeing industry (Willcox 1977), as well as being used as a sedative and treatment for bruises. Unfortunately, at Tobacco Dock there is no direct evidence from the archaeobotanical remains for medicinal plants.

Chapter 4 Thematic aspects

4.1 Alternative interpretations of the bath house

James Gerrard

Building 4 was a large heated masonry structure that during excavation was interpreted as a bath house. This is an interpretation to which we hold and with which other commentators are in broad agreement (Peter Rowsome, pers. comm.; Martin Millett, pers. comm.). However, the structure presents a number of difficulties that highlight its somewhat abnormal nature. It has an unusually high number of heated rooms (and by Period 4.2 all but one or possibly two of the excavated rooms were heated), evidence for baths was slight (Room 3 and, less plausibly, 5 may have been cold plunges and either Room 11 or 14 may have been additional small hot plunge bath) and the building is of a size that falls uncomfortably between those of excavated public and private baths. Due to this, at various stages of the post-excavation analysis we rigorously questioned the primary interpretation of the structure as a stand-alone bath house. This section discusses some alternative (but unconvincing) interpretations of the structure that can be summarised as follows:

1) An official/public building
2) Part of a high status domestic complex (villa)
3) Part of a *mansio*
4) Part of a military establishment
5) Part of a religious complex

This list of five alternative explanations embodies a number of different interpretive elements. The first option would suggest that Building 4 may not have been a bath house at all. Options two and three assume that Building 4 may have been a bath house but was integral to another structural complex. Finally, options four and five see the bath house as a stand alone building associated with other, specialised activities. The following discussion looks briefly at each of these options in turn.

The late Roman period is generally characterised by the decline of large public buildings and in London, for instance, the forum-basilica was demolished by c. AD 300 (Brigham 1990b, 77–79). There are, however, traces of late Roman structures that are best explained as performing public functions. In the City a large mid fourth-century aisled building at Colchester House has been interpreted

variously as a major late Roman cathedral, a state granary or an imperial treasury (Sankey 1998). Similarly, at Colchester the Temple of Claudius seems to have been demolished in the early fourth century and replaced with a structure whose plan is only partially discernible beneath the later Norman castle (Drury 1984). The building seems to have been lavishly appointed and its fragmentary plan recalls that of the imperial audience-hall at Trier (Drury 1984, fig 13). None of these buildings share any similarities in plan with Building 4, nor were they heated.

The heated building excavated at the Old Station Yard, York was originally interpreted as a bath house but has recently been argued to be a late Roman *aula* (official reception hall) (Bidwell 2006, 34). Superficially, this structure offers a parallel for Building 4. It is late Roman, heated and was originally interpreted as a bath house. However, *aulae* were apsed, aisleless halls and this is a description that hardly fits Building 4 in any of its phases.

The late Roman countryside was dominated by large and richly appointed domestic structures that are usually termed 'villas' and these building complexes often had extensive bath suites. Such baths were usually connected to the main building complex either directly or by a corridor. At Shadwell Building 4 seems to have a direct, formal access facing south and this makes its interpretation as a villa bath suite unlikely. The lack of any evidence (such as substantial numbers of *tesserae*) for mosaic flooring, the limited evidence for the use of wall plaster and the fact that in its primary phase the structure may have been double suited makes its interpretation as part of a villa complex improbable. A large villa in such close proximity to *Londinium* would also be remarkable (Millett 1990, 193).

The idea that the complex formed a *mansio* (stopping place on a highway used by the imperial post) is thwarted by both the site's close proximity to London and the fact that it does not lie on a major Roman road. Furthermore, the best-known *mansio* from Britain is a building excavated in the nineteenth century at Silchester. Its identification as a *mansio* remains uncertain given the absence of epigraphic evidence but it seems clear that its bath suite was intended to be entered *via* a corridor connecting it to the main building complex (Wacher 1995, fig 124). This was not the case at Shadwell where access to Building 4 seems to have been through a main entrance.

A military interpretation of Building 4 is essentially a development of the argument that the building must, in some way, have been 'official' and is largely connected to Shadwell's own peculiar history of archaeological interpretation (see Chapter 5 below). Baths within the Saxon Shore forts of Richborough, Lympne (Johnson 1979, fig 55) and Reculver (Philp 2005, fig 25) are the closest military baths but are smaller than Building 4. Furthermore, it seems inconceivable that a structure as large as Building 4 could have been required to service the bathing needs of a handful of soldiers stationed in a watchtower (*contra* Bird 2008, 100).

Finally, there is the possibility that the baths formed part of a religious complex. The close association between baths and religious sites in the Roman Empire is well known and needs no reiteration here. The spring line at Shadwell could have offered a series of ritual *foci* and Building 4 could represent a set of baths attached to a religious establishment. Bath is the most grandiose example of this phenomenon in Britain (Cunliffe 1969) but the temple and baths at Lydney might offer a better parallel (Casey and Hoffman 1999). There is, however, no unambiguous evidence to support the notion that the Shadwell sites were some type of religious complex.

In conclusion, Building 4 is best interpreted as a stand-alone bath house that formed part of a wider settlement of indeterminate character. Future excavations may reveal new evidence to alter our interpretation of the structure and its local context. However, until that evidence is excavated from beneath modern Shadwell's streets and buildings it is impossible to be able to choose between the myriad of interpretive options available. Given this, the building is assumed to have been a stand-alone bath house and this interpretation has guided our interpretations and the reconstruction of the building proposed in the following section.

The Shadwell Tower as a *castellum aquae*

The excavations at Sites A and B are the remit of this volume and early in the post-excavation process it was decided that there would be no explicit attempt to reinterpret the function of the adjacent tower (LD74/LD76). Therefore we have followed Lakin *et al.*'s (2002) view of this enigmatic structure and accepted that it may have functioned as an early Roman mausoleum. In this section we tentatively suggest an alternative hypothesis. We do so partly out of sheer devilry – the tower is so poorly recorded that it is impossible to definitively establish its real function – but also because the alternative interpretation offered here may be considered plausible.

In an interim press release regarding the site, circulated by PCA in 2003, an off-the-cuff reinterpretation of the tower was offered when it was suggested that it may have functioned as a 'water tower'. Bird, in his reappraisal of the site, dismissed this interpretation in no uncertain terms:

> One rather curious suggestion was use as a 'water tower'... but in the absence of any parallels (except settling tanks on raised aqueducts like that at Segovia) this is unlikely. (David Bird 2008, 98)

The literary and archaeological evidence for Roman period 'water towers' (*castellum aquae* or *castellum divisiorum*) is indisputable. Even a cursory review of the published literature regarding Roman water management will reveal examples at Rome (Aicher 1993; Evans 1994; Taylor 1997), Pompeii (Ohlig 2001, Adams 2005, fig 589), Nîmes (Evans 1982, 402) and Petra (Bedal 2002) and ancient sources such as Frontinus (Evans 1994, 7–8) and Vitruvius (Vitruvius *De arch.* 8.6; Rowland 1994, 104) describe such structures. In Britain examples have been postulated at a number of sites, including London (Blair *et al.* 2006, 46). However, the best example may be described in an antiquarian account of the Lincoln aqueduct (Burgers 2001, 35). The Vitruvian description of a *castellum aquae* states:

> When it [an aqueduct] reaches the walls of the city, make a reservoir (castellum aquae)... (Vitruvius De arch. 8.1, Rowland 1994, 104)

followed by:

> If water is going to be conducted in systems of lead pipes, first a castellum aquae *should be constructed at the source and then the diameter of the pipes should be fixed on the basis of this supply.* (Vitruvius De arch. 8.4, Rowland 1994, 104)

At Shadwell the presence of wooden water pipes points to the piping of water under pressure. The place name Shadwell indicates that a naturally available spring line was available for modification. It seems possible that the difference in elevation between the springs and the baths may have been enough to supply the necessary water pressure. However, if this was not the case then a *castellum aquae* may have been necessary. Presumably the water would have been lifted into the tower's reservoir using a water lifting machine like those identified at Gresham Street and the Cheapside baths in London (Blair *et al.* 2006).

The tower at Shadwell may have served as an *castellum aquae* for the baths complex and the presence of a number of ditches, drains and tanks in association with the structure may heighten this possibility. Indeed, one might argue that the tower is far more likely to have performed a function related to water management (given its close juxtaposition to the baths) than have served as a military watchtower or signal station (*contra* Bird 2008).

4.2 Reconstruction of the bath house

Berni Sudds

The first attempt to reconstruct the appearance of Building 4 was prompted by the client, who was interested in having an image for display on a plaque at the new development, where the bath house remains have been preserved *in situ* (Fig. 115). The initial reconstruction exercise was useful on a broader level, as it spurred research into the likely scale, decoration and physical appearance of the baths. The extent to which archaeological evidence can provide answers to these questions is not entirely straightforward, particularly given the truncation of much of the bath's superstructure in antiquity, although some general reconstruction suggestions are possible. A second and equally interesting aspect of reconstructing the physical appearance of the bath house is consideration of what this might tell us about who built it and what this might reveal about its status.

The greatest obstacle to a factual reconstruction of the bath house is the general absence of upstanding masonry, an incomplete ground plan and limited excavation due to preservation of the remains *in situ*. The bath house remains survived only to sub-floor level and continued both beyond the eastern and western limits of excavation of Site B. The structure was also probably stripped of valuable fixtures and fittings shortly after disuse, and extensive robbing of building materials followed in the sub-Roman or post-Roman period.

A reconstruction based on such limited evidence is not only difficult but also potentially misleading. The results are inevitably highly conjectural, but can give the impression of certainty to the viewer. It should thus be reiterated at this point that the reconstruction presented here is only one of a wide range of possibilities and that the initial reconstruction exercise (Fig. 115) was undertaken at a very early stage in the post-excavation process. A range of alternative possible options are presented and discussed further below (Fig. 118).

The original and simplest phase of the bath house was chosen to form the focus of reconstruction. In addition to the limited *in-situ* evidence, information from the demolition debris overlying the baths and directly related to the structure, was also taken into account. Although much of the building material was evidently reused from other structures, it is clear that the builders of the baths followed standard principles of Roman construction. Bath houses often demonstrate a close similarity in the presence, sequence, function and relative dimension of rooms and in the layout of sub-floor areas and hypocaust design.

Layout of the Shadwell bath building

The arrangement of the heated and non-heated sub-floor areas within the primary phase of the bath house (Period 3) indicates that it probably contained two suites from the outset, ie two separate sets of hot rooms. The excavated evidence also suggests that these suites were unlikely to have been symmetrical. For the purpose of reconstruction the ground plans of both the eastern and western ranges were completed in the simplest way possible, with the minimum number of rooms required for a fully functioning bathing suite (Fig. 116).

A typological classification of baths was developed

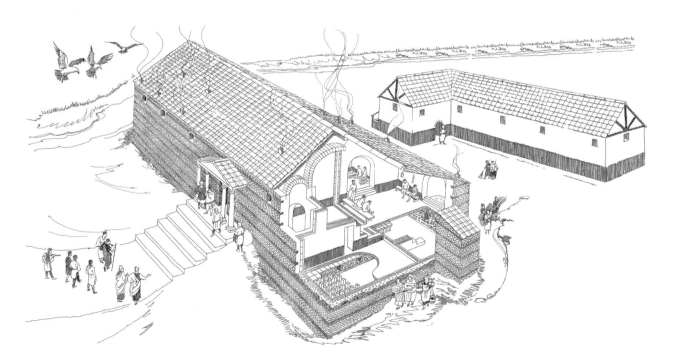

Fig. 115   Artist's reconstruction view of the bath house, looking north-west; this reconstruction is highly conjectural but suggests a south-central entranceway as well as three east–west barrel vaults covered by a pitched tile roof; accommodation block Building 3 in the background, by Sarah Kensington

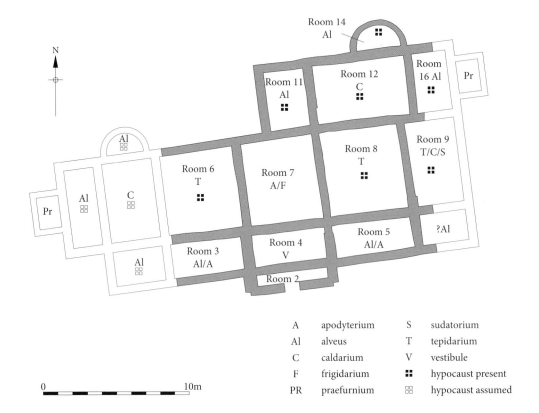

Room 14
Al

Room 12
C

Room 11
Al

Room
16 Al

Pr

Al

Room 6
T

Room 7
A/F

Room 8
T

Room 9
T/C/S

Al

C

Pr

Al

Room 3
Al/A

Room 4
V

Room 5
Al/A

?Al

Room 2

A	apodyterium	S	sudatorium
Al	alveus	T	tepidarium
C	caldarium	V	vestibule
F	frigidarium	▪▪	hypocaust present
PR	praefurnium	▦	hypocaust assumed

0   10m

Fig. 116   Diagrammatic ground plan of the Shadwell bath house, showing the room layout and function of excavated Period 3 building and proposed overall layout as a double suite bath house (scale 1:250)

by Krencker (Krencker *et al.* 1929) and identified three types: row, ring and imperial. Row type baths were by far the most common in the western and northern border provinces of the Roman empire, providing the simplest type of installation suitable for small and medium-sized baths (*balnea*), and defined by the fact that the bather followed the same route through the rooms, retracing their steps at the end of the procedure (Nielsen 1990, 4). Amongst recorded row type baths, sub-types are identified according to the layout of the principal room areas, with the most common sub-type being the axial row. An axial row bath would normally be recognisable by its cold, warm and hot rooms being sited on a single axis (Nielsen 1990, 67). The axial row type usually had a single furnace, adjacent to the *caldarium* also sharing the same axis. However, these baths were not always truly symmetrical and could include two suites and other variations due to restraints caused by the topography or shape of the available construction area whilst still being classified as an axial row type in terms of basic design.

A closely related sub-type is the angular row bath, where the layout of the principal rooms is L-shaped or dog-legged. The angular row bath was potentially the most compact in terms of the size of the building plot used, and thus it was often the least monumental and smallest (Nielsen 1990, 69).

Although the Shadwell bath house extends beyond the limits of excavation and its primary phase was partially obscured by later alterations, its east–west aligned southern range of rooms could be categorised as a pure

axial row type, perhaps with two suites or rooms, running west and east from a centrally located entranceway on its southern side (Fig. 116). However, it would appear that the adjacent northern range of rooms is also part of the primary phase of construction perhaps suggesting an angular row type or something less suitable for precise categorisation.

The layout and use of the extant rooms is discussed in detail in the chronological narrative but, in summary, it is thought that the bather may have entered the baths from the south, via Room 2. It is not clear if this space represents a porch with a doorway to the north wall offering access to Room 4 or an enclosed room with a doorway to the south wall. If entrance was obtained from the south it is likely that Room 2 or Room 4 incorporated a vestibule and possible changing room (*apodyterium*) and the larger area of Room 7 to the north a cold room (*frigidarium*). To the west and east of Room 7 were Rooms 6 and 8 respectively, which were of similar dimensions and originally heated, probably representing warm rooms (*tepidaria*).

An alternative interpretation is that Rooms 3 and 5, respectively lying to the west and east of Room 4, may represent two separate changing rooms, although they may also have held unheated plunge baths accessed from Rooms 6 and 8.

In the postulated eastern suite of the baths, the bather may then have continued north into Room 12 (later divided into Rooms 12 and 13) or east to Room 9, either of which may have been *caldaria*. A furnace area may have lain to the east of Room 9 or east of Room 12 and north of Room 9, though these areas lay beyond the limits of excavation.

The scorched, arcaded sub-floor wall flanking the east side of Room 12/13 suggests that the furnace (*praefurnium*) supplying heat to the eastern bathing suite was located nearby. The scale of Room 12/13 makes it perhaps the most likely candidate for identification as a *caldarium*, and this interpretation is supported by the presence of a small ancillary furnace, which butted onto the north wall of the bath house at the north-western corner of Room 12. The furnace may have helped to boost heat within the room and could also have incorporated an overhead tank used for the supply of hot water to a hot plunge bath (*alveus*). The nearby apse (Room 14) also had underfloor heating and may have contained a plunge bath (Yegül 1992, 376).

At Winchester Palace in Southwark a similar apsidal room was identified, the small size and sunken sub-floor of which were taken to suggest the possible presence of a plunge bath (Yule 2005, 66). Room 14, measuring *c.* 3.00m by 1.35m, is of a very similar dimension to the apse at Winchester Palace but does not demonstrate the same relative difference in sub-floor height. At Winchester Palace the sub-floor was between 0.6m and 0.7m below the main build whereas at Shadwell a variation of just 0.08m was recorded. This nominal difference is not considered significant and the presence of the flue linking Room 12 to 14, rising almost to floor level would further preclude the likelihood of a sunken plunge. This, however, is not to say that a plunge did not exist. One may have been present above floor level, accessed over a raised, stepped masonry division (Adam 2001, 270; Nielsen 1990, fig 13, 14, 17 & 27; Yegül 1992, 365).

Interpretation of the Shadwell bath's partially excavated western suite is more difficult. It can be reconstructed along a single axis, with a hot room, plunges and *praefurnium* added on sequentially and neatly fitting within the available space before hitting a postulated north–south access road to the west. A more complex arrangement of rooms is also possible, similar to that seen in the eastern suite, but the overall evidence indicated that the northern range of rooms to the west and north of Room 11 was not constructed until a later date (see below and Periods' 4 and 5 chronological narrative). The implication is that the primary ground plan of the baths was that of an 'L' shaped building, with two heated suites of rooms sharing the same entranceway and unheated rooms in the south-central part of the complex.

Mixed bathing was prohibited from the time of Hadrian and a two-suite layout might be thought to reflect such an arrangement, but the apparent existence of a single *frigidarium* would appear to rule out the provision of separate suites for males and females. In any case, it is known that many bath houses coped with the prohibition of mixed bathing, whose earlier prevalence may anyway have been exaggerated, by simply allotting different bathing times (Nielsen 1990, 147; Merrifield 1983, 85; Yegül 1992, 33). The incorporation of two suites of rooms

in the primary phase, and the overall total size of the bath building, might therefore imply that it served a large number of users.

As discussed in the chronological narrative the layout proposed is not without problems and in the absence of a complete ground plan may be entirely erroneous. Assuming the entrance is to the south the change in level from the contemporary external ground surface to the south of Building 4 and the level of the floor in the hot rooms to northeast is somewhere between 1.50m (based on the level of surviving foundation wall offsets on the south wall of the building) and 1.80m (based on a surviving contemporary ground surface to the south-east). It is not clear from the surviving evidence how access was obtained and specifically how a bather rose to the level of the hot rooms. If entrance was obtained via Room 2 and the floor was level throughout the building, with the cold rooms filled in to the level of the adjacent heated rooms, a substantial external staircase to the south would have been required. Alternatively, incremental floor rises may have existed internally towards the north of the building with a series of smaller staircases. No evidence exists to support either suggestion although the existence of a level floor surface throughout is both more practical and better-paralleled. It is just possible that Room 4 housed a substantial staircase. There may have been steps in Room 2 and there would almost certainly have been at least one step externally to the south of Room 2, but evidence in support of any of these scenarios is lacking. The possibility that the entrance existed in another location has also been considered but the arrangement of heated rooms in the Period 3 bath house makes this unlikely. Access to the northeast is precluded by the presence of the hot rooms and is unlikely to have been to the west if, as suggested, Room 6 was originally heated and Room 7 unheated as the sequence of cold to hot would be interrupted.

The possibility was also considered that Rooms 4 and 7 were heated from the outset, although this is considered unlikely given an absence of evidence and fact that the original build had clearly been truncated and modified to incorporate a hypocaust in these areas at a later date. Certainly by Period 4.2 and Period 5, however, most of the excavated rooms of Building 4 were heated and issues of layout and use become even more complicated and conjectural. Indeed, although the later phases of the bath house do not form the basis of the reconstruction discussed below they are briefly worth considering as they are difficult to interpret and do not necessarily fit easily with the interpreted function of the structure.

By Period 5 at least 11 of the 14 excavated rooms of Building 4 were heated with evidence for two more continuing beyond the limits of excavation to the east. When compared to other Roman bath houses in Britain this is an unusually high number. It is possible, however, that the alterations at sub-floor level reflect changes to the spaces above creating a fairly small number of large open heated areas. Rather than there being 11 or more small heated rooms therefore, there were perhaps three

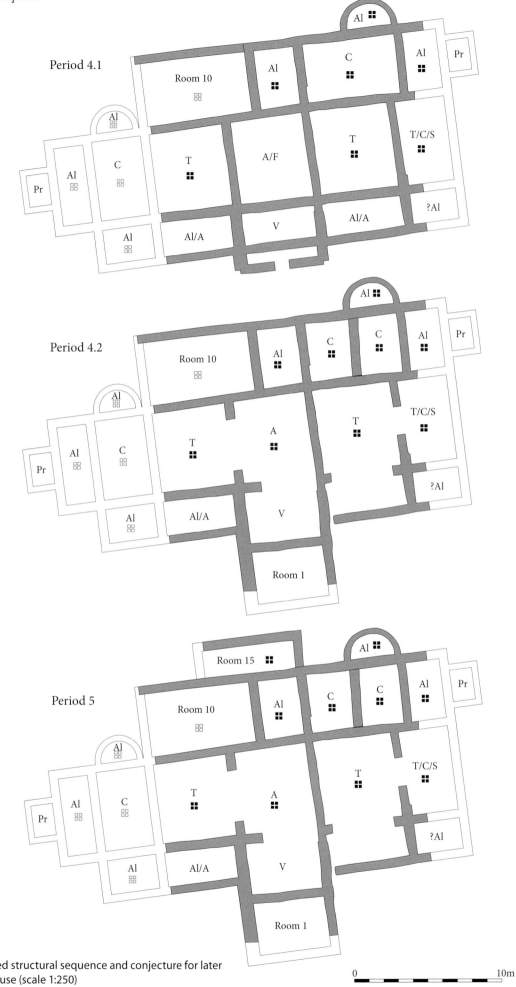

Fig. 117   Simplified structural sequence and conjecture for later phases of bath house (scale 1:250)

or four large heated spaces including warm areas 2/4/6/7 and 5/8/9 and hot rooms 11–15). It is not clear how the hot rooms were divided above the floor, particularly following the addition of a sub-floor arcaded wall in Room 12 (Period 4.2), but it is possible the sub-floor walls in this area reflect both above floor walls and stepped masonry partitions to separate wet from dry, including plunge pools and perhaps even a *laconicum* (hot dry room).

The expansion of the heated spaces within the building may have been necessitated by a growing demand for the facilities offered but the original cold rooms evidently became heated in the process. If Building 4 was operating as a bath house during these phases it might be assumed that cold rooms would have been a necessity. The provision of a new entrance to service the new arrangement may also have been required. It is possible the bath house still incorporated two suites with a shared entrance, changing room and cold room but relocated into the extension to the south of the building. It is also possible, however, that they remained in the same place but simply became heated. The idea of a heated changing room is not unusual in a cold climate, and although the idea of a heated *frigidarium* might seem contradictory, parallels can be found (Nielsen 1990, 153–4).

Another possibility is that two separate sets of cold rooms may have existed beyond either limit of excavation but obviously this cannot be proven. Alternatively, the bath house may have been modified to function as a single large suite. In this case, given the location of the hot rooms, cold rooms and an entranceway may have existed to the west or north-west, although the available space between bath house and the access road and channel is fairly limited. Clearly more of Building 4 would need to be excavated to draw any firm conclusions concerning the development of the ground plan.

Appearance of the bath house

External walls and entranceway

The walls were built of stone with tile lacing courses. The southern wall, containing the proposed entrance, proves no exception, although the stone used is of a single type (Kentish ragstone) and demonstrates more regular dimensions and coursing. It is possible that the external walls were rendered, although no evidence survived and the absence of any render or plaster that can directly attributed to the bath house is notable. No render was recorded *in situ*, and though this might be explained by the general truncation of the building's superstructure, none at all was identified within the bath's demolition horizon.

Many more masonry buildings in Roman Britain may have been externally rendered and painted than is evident from the surviving remains (de la Bédoyère 2001, 26–7). In *Londinium*, surviving render recorded at the mid third-century temple of Mithras was scored to resemble dressed masonry (Shepherd 1998, 61) and plaster render

on a late Roman building at Lloyd's Register painted with lines to imitate ashlar masonry (Bluer *et al.* 2006, 41). The British climate may have been responsible for decay and loss of render in most cases, but the absence of any traces of render on the Shadwell bath building implies that the masonry courses were left exposed. This might account for a deliberate attempt to construct the southern face of the bath house with more regularity, as it would have been displayed prominently to approaching users and visible from the Thames.

As noted above, Room 2, projecting from the south wall of the building, may represent the remains of a porch or small vestibule with steps at the entranceway to the bath house, although far too little survived to allow us to determine the appearance of this structure. Given that much of the building was constructed from salvaged material and that there is little evidence for any ostentatious appointment or decoration it is perhaps more likely that the entranceway was relatively plain in appearance, perhaps taking the form of double wooden doors topped by a simple pediment, rather than a colonnaded portico as depicted in the original reconstruction drawing. The Carrara marble architectural moulding recovered from demolition debris may have been part of a door surround but could easily have been used or reused internally as a moulding, in paving or in reverse as a veneer.

Roofs, vaults and ceilings

One of the most difficult and contentious aspects of bath building reconstruction relates to the design of roofs, vaults and ceilings. A great many bath house reconstructions have been attempted on paper and a full-scale working example has been constructed at *Segedunum* Roman Fort and Museum at Wallsend, based upon the remains of the legionary bath house at Chesters. Very few Roman roofs survive intact, even in a collapsed state, and the variation represented in the various reconstructions is unsurprising. The most common suggestions for roofing are exposed barrel-vaulting; standard pitched tile roofs with tie beams, either with or without a barrel vault below; and vaulted ceilings set directly under a pitched tile roof. In many cases a combination of more than one of these techniques has been suggested for different elements of the same bath building.

The reconstructions of exposed barrel vaults with a curved *extrados*, including those for Cheapside (Blair *et al.* 2006, fig 5; Hall and Merrifield 1986, 20) and Billingsgate (Marsden 1980, 152–154), are influenced by the well-preserved Roman bath houses in North Africa (Ward-Perkins and Toynbee 1949). The strongest argument against this arrangement is perhaps the British climate, primarily frost and rain. The durability of a lime-based concrete, even if the water-resisting properties are increased by the addition of a pozzolanic substitute such as crushed tile (*opus signinum*), may be called into question. Analysis of the roof tile from the bath house at Beauport Park, Sussex has led to the suggestion that

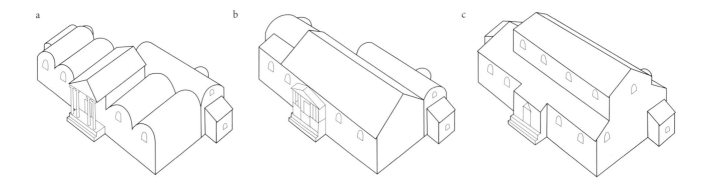

Fig. 118 Diagrammatic views of the possible superstructure and arrangement of vaults and pitched roofs; view looking north-west: (a) a series of north–south exposed barrel vaults to the east and west of a central pitched roof and an east–west exposed barrel vault to the north; (b) three east–west aligned barrel vaults, with the two vaults making up the southern range covered by a pitched roof; (c) three east–west aligned barrel vaults each covered by a tiled roof with a central clerestory (not to scale)

curved *tegulae* were produced to cover the surface of vaulted roofs and provide extra protection (Warry 2006, 111–118). No curved *tegulae* or domed sections of concrete were identified in the demolition debris overlying the Shadwell bath house, however, suggesting that exposed barrel vaulting, or vaulting covered with curved tile may both be unlikely roofing arrangements here.

Environmental conditions, this time within the bath house, are also likely to have caused problems with the use of a simple pitched tile roof. The warm, damp conditions of the *tepidarium* and *caldarium* would have quickly rotted exposed timberwork, as apparently occurred at Bath (Cunliffe 1995, 71). One solution to this problem may have been to suspend *bipedales* on iron hooks below the joists, in order to protect the wood from the steam (Brodribb 1987, 41). Few *bipedales* were identified in the Shadwell demolition deposits, and those that were appear to have been set aside for use to bridge the *pilae* of the hypocaust. Metal hooks are also absent, although these may have been salvaged for reuse.

The use of internal vaulting does represent the most efficient way to cover the heated rooms of a bath house and is common in surviving structures on the continent (Yegül 1992, 365–368; Adam 2001, 274). Vaults were constructed in a variety of ways, either of solid concrete or ceramic or stone voussoirs, or else using armchair or hollow voussoirs to create hollow rib vaulting (Cunliffe 1969; Brodribb 1987; de la Bédoyère 2001, 30–31; Adam 2001). Hollow voussoir tiles (*tubulus cuneatus*) are similar to box-flue tiles, but tapered to one end and linked to form arched ribs connecting with the wall flues and the hypocaust, allowing for the transfer of heat through the ceiling. The space between the ribs was then filled with concrete or mortared rubble. Collapsed sections of vaulting constructed with hollow voussoirs have been observed at Bath, and fragmented hollow voussoirs, indicating the presence of a heated vault, recovered from demolition debris at several sites in Britain, including Beauport Park in Sussex, and Winchester Palace in Southwark (Brodribb 1979b; 1987, 80; Crowley 2005, 96–97).

The demolition deposits associated with Building 4 contained both hollow voussoirs and roof tile. The hollow voussoirs indicate that some heated vaulting is likely to have existed at the Shadwell baths. The total number is relatively small, although likely to be under-represented, perhaps suggesting they were used intermittently, as with the wall flues, or that their use was restricted to the hot rooms. The larger assemblage of roof tile is comprised of *tegulae* and *imbrices*, although a single possible ridge tile was also identified. Some of this material would have been reused in general construction, but the presence of late Roman examples would suggest that the building had a pitched tile roof. As with the hollow voussoir tiles, the relative quantity of late Roman tile is quite small. Later robbing may have affected the totals but it is possible that early roof tile, where salvaged whole, was also reused in the roof, though early roof tiles were larger than later types and they could not have been used together on the same section of roof.

It is not clear precisely how vaulted ceilings and tiled roofs may have worked in combination. Vaulting may have been structurally independent of the pitched roof above, sitting below the tie beam, as suggested for the Phase II roof at the legionary fortress baths at Chester (Mason 2005, 38-9). In this arrangement the timber framework of a conventional pitched roof would be raised on wall plates. This would transfer the weight of the tiled roof from the vault to the side walls but add extra height. Alternatively, a conventional tiled roof could be placed directly over a vault, with the rafters resting on a secondary wall behind the one supporting the vault, as seen at the legionary fortress baths at Exeter, although no secondary walls are evident there (Warry 2006, 113; de la Bédoyère 2001, pl.15). Another solution would be to set the roof tiles directly onto the extrados of the vault, as found at the Bewcastle bath house in Cumbria and at many sites on the continent (Gillam *et al.* 1993, 14; Adam 2001, 208). At Bewcastle concrete was found on the outer curve of a group of surviving ribs of the vault with roofing slates adhering to the outer surface forming an angled pitch (Gillam *et al.* 1993).

The last of these designs is considered the most plausible for the Shadwell baths and fits best with the available evidence, although such an arrangement is not without its problems. The simplest way in which to roof the Shadwell bath's known ground plan is with three vaults, each orientated along the long east–west axis, and with a single pitched roof then covering all three vaults (Fig. 115; see Fig. 20). A single pitched roof close above the vaulting would have required less material than some other designs, though the weight and thrust of a single roof span on the outer walls would have been a structural concern. At Bath, even though hollow voussoir tiles were utilised to reduce the weight, the addition of the Period III vault required the existing piers to be strengthened to withstand the extra force (Warry 2006, 113).

Additional structural supports, such as buttresses, were not identified in the extant excavated area of the Shadwell bath house where the wall superstructure was only 0.60m thick. In contrast, the Huggin Hill baths had walls up to *c.* 0.85m thick and internal buttresses (Rowsome 1999). At Shadwell, the smaller dimensions of the rooms to the north and south of the large central suite may have provided its walls and roof with structural support against lateral forces. It is also possible that parts of the building beyond the excavated area were provided with buttresses. At Bewcastle it has been argued that the extra concrete required to construct a vault with a pitched tile covering, as opposed to a curved extrados, did not add signficant weight to the overall roof structure (Gillam *et al.* 1993, 14). The technique of placing extra mass on the sides of the vault to counteract lateral thrust can also be seen in Roman barrel vaults (Gillam *et al.* 1993, 14). This was usually achieved by building the external walls to a height above the springing point of the vault, and is not detectable in the archaeological record.

At Chester another alternative to the problem of lateral thrust was proposed with the Phase I roof reconstruction where the vault sits directly beneath the pitch (Mason 2005, 39; III40). As observed at Bath, it was argued that the vault is almost certain to have contained reinforcing ribs every few metres, constructed of brick voussoirs, and that these may have been topped by brickwork extending above the concrete vault (Mason 2005, 40). The purpose of this brickwork was to act as the principal rafters, or the base for such, supporting the timber purlins and common rafters carrying the tiles. It was suggested that this would transfer the weight of the pitch roof to the outer walls but as resting directly on the ribs, and in absence of a tie beam, this arrangement would still generate some lateral thrust. Having the timber framework supported on raised ribs would create a lighter roof as the entire space between vault and pitch would not need to be filled. At Bewcastle it is not clear if the concrete filled the entire gap between the top of the vault and the pitched roof, or only where the vault and roof came into close contact. It has, however, been argued that the buttressing identified supporting the warm rooms at Bewcastle and other bath houses on Hadrian's Wall may only have been necessary because the concrete

did not consolidate the roof sufficiently to contain the lateral forces produced (Gillam *et al.* 1993, 14; Warry 2006, 113).

A second concern in proposing a solid pitched and vaulted roof at Shadwell is the apparent absence of any evidence for surviving fragments of curved plaster or concrete vaulting. However, the near complete absence of plaster and concrete from the bath's demolition horizon, including sections of *suspensura* (other than in Room 5), is an unusual feature of the site and is discussed further below.

Given the weakness of the archaeological evidence directly related to the bath house superstructure, the reconstruction options presented must remain highly speculative. Indeed, other roofing arrangements remain possible, a few of which are presented here (Fig. 118). The first depicts a series exposed barrel vaults covering the warm and hot rooms and a central pitched roof over the unheated spaces of the building. Similarly to the reconstruction shown in Figure 114, the second option has three east-west aligned barrel vaults but only the two vaults making up the southern range are covered by a pitched tile roof, the hot rooms to the north and west being covered with exposed barrel vaults. The last option also has three east-west barrel vaults covered with pitched or sloping tiled roofs but has a central clerestory. This would allow the internal rooms to receive direct light but would make the building very tall. Each of these reconstructions present difficulties but without a clearer understanding of the full layout of the structure little more can be concluded.

Irrespective of the roofing design, chimneys must have pierced the roof, venting the combustion gases from the box-flues and possibly hollow voussoirs, thus maintaining the circulation of hot air through the hypocaust system (Yegül 1992, 357). Chimneys were usually placed at the springing point of the vaults and were often formed of round or square pipes, although no doubt other forms, including *imbrices* and *tubuli*, would have also been used (Yegül 1992, 357).

Cavity walling

The quantity of box-flues (*tubulationes*) used in a wall influence the level of insulation and heat. The high percentage of box-flue tiles recovered from the demolition of the Winchester Palace baths has led to the suggestion that a continuous cavity wall was constructed (Yule 2005, 68), although this would appear to be relatively rare in London, where box-flues were usually used to line only small areas (Betts 2003, 113). Too few box-flue tiles were recorded *in situ* in the Shadwell bath building to be certain of their arrangement. By number box-flue tiles represent nearly a fifth of the building material related directly to the bath house although there were at least five heated rooms excavated as part of the original phase, perhaps suggesting they were used intermittently in cells, or potentially more continuously in the hot rooms than the warm.

Internal walls

The internal walls of the Shadwell bath house would almost certainly have been plastered, although none survived *in situ* or was recovered. Where small sections of wall survived above the foundations, even the wall-jacketing, over which the plaster would have been applied, was missing. The absence of wall plaster from the demolition deposits is more surprising. Plain and painted wall plaster was recovered from demolition layers elsewhere on the site primarily from Site B but relating to Building 3. A single fragment of *opus signinum* with a lime top coat (*intonaco*), recovered from the yard area B[825], may have been derived from the bath house but could equally have come from Building 3 to its north. The general absence of wall plaster seems anomalous and it is unlikely that it would have been removed from site attached to robbed building materials. It is possible that the particularly wet ground conditions on the site of the baths had caused its disintegration over time.

Flooring and veneer

Very little flooring survived *in situ* in Building 4, represented singularly by a section of the collapsed *opus signinum suspensura* in Room 5, though it is not clear whether this represents the floor surface itself or a bedding layer. The surface was fairly smooth and appeared finished however, and this type of floor is often found in structures associated with the use of water, being similar to floors in the Cheapside and Winchester Palace baths (P. Roberts, pers. comm.; Ian Betts, pers. comm.; Yule 2005, 69).

Opus spicatum bricks and cut tile *tesserae* were found in demolition layers at Shadwell, but were spread across the site and occur infrequently. At least one worn *opus spicatum* brick was retrieved from the demolition horizon above the bath house. One room in the baths may have had herringbone flooring in addition to *opus signinum*, also found at the Cheapside baths (Ian Betts, pers. comm.), but most of the *tesserae* found at Shadwell were recovered from deposits directly associated with Building 3 to the north.

Large fragments of imported white Carrara marble and indigenous dark greenish-grey Forest marble paving slabs were also retrieved from the demolition horizons that sealed the bath building. The fragments recovered appear to have derived from one or two larger slabs and had been reused in the bath house in a fragmented state. It is possible that they were reused as flooring or, perhaps more likely, as a lining for plunge pools.

Windows and doors

The position of windows and doorways in the bath house is unknown as all of the upper superstructure was truncated. Evidence for their appearance is scanty, with no chamfered plaster and very little window glass identified in the demolition debris, although glass is likely to have been salvaged in antiquity. The few fragments of glass recovered are typical, being cast and blue-green in colour. It may be speculated that the enlarged sub-floor openings created during the remodelling of the baths in Period 4.2 are likely to have mirrored enlarged arched openings between the corresponding rooms above.

Water supply and drainage

The Shadwell bath house was located on the north bank of the Thames at the base of a slope, allowing it to tap into the hillside spring line. In this regard the Shadwell baths were closely comparable to the Huggin Hill public baths (Rowsome 1999) as well as the smaller bath houses excavated at Billingsgate and Pudding Lane (Rowsome 1996, 421). Securing a constant supply of fresh spring water was an essential prerequisite when choosing the site of a bath house (Rowsome 1999), and Shadwell's geological and topographical setting met these requirements.

Storage tanks holding spring water were established up the slope from the baths, with water pipes delivering a constant supply of fresh water, whilst drains carried away excess water and grey water, as well as providing surface drainage. No ceramic water pipes were identified at Shadwell and it may be that timber bored pipes were a simpler and effective alternative. The tank identified at LD74 (see Fig. 38) may have been part of the water supply to the baths. It is even considered possible that the 'tower' functioned as a *castellum aquae*.

Parts of the internal water supply of the bath house are likely to have been provided by lead pipes and iron boilers but no evidence survived for metal fixtures or fittings, as these would almost certainly have been salvaged and removed from site in antiquity, probably immediately after the decommissioning of the baths.

Sources of salvage

The *in-situ* remains of Building 4 are constructed primarily from first- and second-century local tile and brick in fabric group 2815, although both the building and demolition rubble also contain later brick and roof tile dated to the mid or late second to third century. The bath house has a suggested construction date of between AD 230–260, indicating that the majority of the brick and tile was reused, although some of the later tile would still have been in production at this time and possibly sourced as new. A considerable proportion of the building material used in Roman Britain was manufactured during the first and second centuries AD, and late Roman structures were often built from tile and brick salvaged from earlier buildings. This material would have been supplemented where necessary, particularly with new, later Roman roof tile, as the roof represents one part of the building in which the reuse of fragmented material is less viable.

The building materials used in the Shadwell bath house were common types which could have been salvaged from many other sites in *Londinium*. The apparently selective use of combed flues and *bessales*, largely in fabric 3006, might suggest a significant proportion originated from a heated building of late first- to mid second-century date, possibly even a defunct bath house. The presence of material of a later date and different fabric composition in sections of the original build, including fabrics post-dating *c.* AD 120, AD 140 and AD 170, would suggest, however, that more than one structure is likely to have been quarried for reuse, even in the primary phase.

The variation in the material reused becomes more pronounced during remodelling of the baths in Periods 4 and 5, no doubt reflecting the changing availability of salvaged material during each stage. The use of first-century Kentish fabrics and first-century half-box-flue tiles from Hertfordshire can be observed alongside the standard local 2815 fabric group and later second and third-century tile fabrics. No evidence was found to suggest that any of the material was on its second reuse at Shadwell. The absence of procuratorial stamps from the assemblage may indicate that the main source of salvage is unlikely to have been a public building, though the presence of reused Carrara and Forest marble may suggest that at least one of the original sources was well-appointed.

Unfortunately, it is not possible to determine whether the materials used at Shadwell were salvaged directly from the earlier structures or if a more organised procurement system involved material arriving at Shadwell *via* a salvage yard. Given the paucity of late Roman tileries in the London area and a dependence on the reuse of earlier material, it seems reasonable that to expect that the builders would have gathered and stockpiled building material in advance of the start of work, perhaps purchasing it from an intermediary specifically dealing with salvage. Preparation of this kind may have been

particularly likely in the early third century, when there was an apparent increase in building work, principally involving the construction of masonry buildings (Perring 1991, 98–105).

The later Roman tile from the 2453 fabric group was still in production during the period of construction of the Shadwell baths and may therefore have been sourced directly from the tilery. As a non-local product, however, supply to London may also have been controlled by a middle-man, or perhaps even a salvage yard.

Comparative structures

Local parallels to the Shadwell baths, in terms of design and function, include the bath houses identified at Huggin Hill, Cheapside, Pudding Lane, and Billingsgate, all within the main settlement, and Winchester Palace in Roman Southwark south of the Thames. A summary of these and other possible bath house structures in *Londinium* has been drawn together and presented elsewhere (Rowsome 1999), but a map of their locations is included below (Fig. 119).

A survey of these other baths appears to indicate that there was a change from the largely public provision of bathing facilities up until the mid second century to private baths after that date (Rowsome 1999, 274–277). The large first-century bath house at Huggin Hill represents a true public bath or *thermae*, whilst the late Roman structures at Pudding Lane, Poultry, Billingsgate and Winchester Palace were interpreted as smaller, privately owned bath houses or *balnea*. Although an important factor, this decrease in scale is not likely

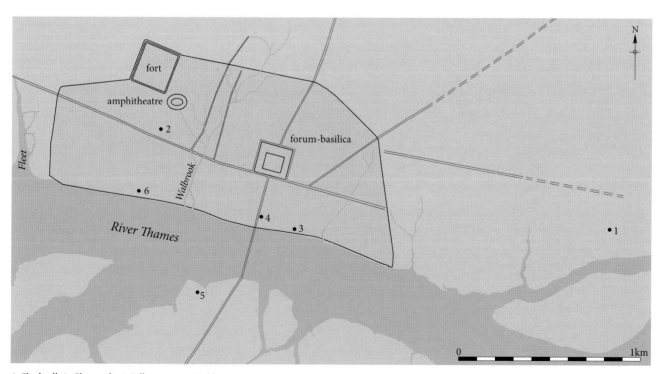

1 Shadwell; 2 Cheapside; 3 Billingsgate; 4 Pudding Lane; 5 Winchester Palace; 6 Huggin Hill

Fig. 119   Map showing location of other known and possible bath houses in *Londinium* and Southwark

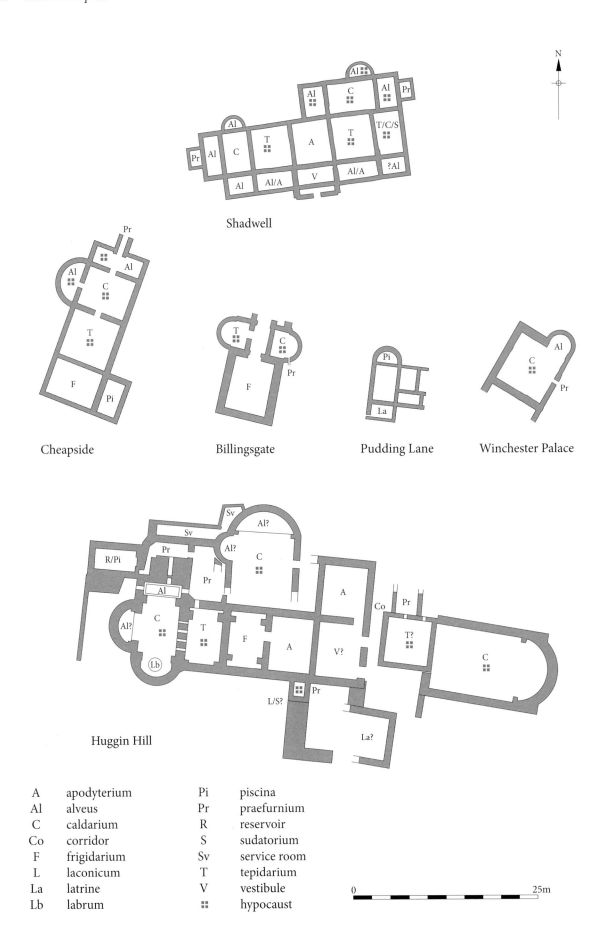

Shadwell

Cheapside   Billingsgate   Pudding Lane   Winchester Palace

Huggin Hill

A	apodyterium	Pi	piscina
Al	alveus	Pr	praefurnium
C	caldarium	R	reservoir
Co	corridor	S	sudatorium
F	frigidarium	Sv	service room
L	laconicum	T	tepidarium
La	latrine	V	vestibule
Lb	labrum	▦	hypocaust

0   25m

Fig. 120   Comparative ground plans of some of the main London bath houses compared to the Period 3 Shadwell bath house: Cheapside, Billingsgate, Pudding Lane, Winchester Palace and Huggin Hill (scale 1:500)

to relate solely to a suspected decline in *Londinium*'s economy and population from the mid second century, but also to reflect a change in the social context of bathing (Rowsome 1999, 274–277).

Even with the apparent resurgence of private and public building in the third century, there is as yet no evidence for a large late Roman public bath in the town, perhaps reflecting a change to private bathing related to a suggested increase in personal modesty amongst the wealthy (Thebert in Rowsome 1999, 277). This is not to say that all late Roman baths were constructed by the wealthy solely for their own use, or that public bathing ceased. Indeed, although privately owned or commissioned, sometimes perhaps with the involvement of authority, the various *balnea* are likely to have been used by all members of society, including the owners, the military, members of *collegia*, officials and paying customers (Rowsome 1999, 277).

If constructed around the middle of the third century, the Shadwell bath building represents the latest bath house to be established in the vicinity of *Londinium*. Billingsgate bath house is the nearest in terms of date, possibly built in the early third century (Perring 1991, 101), although the baths at Pudding Lane, Winchester Palace and Poultry all date from the mid or late second to fourth century and were evidently in operation at the same time as the baths at Shadwell (Rowsome 1999, 275–276).

The topographic situation of Shadwell is similar to Huggin Hill, Pudding Lane and Billingsgate, with all of these baths lying on the same terrace below the hillside spring-line, adjacent to the north bank of the Thames. The scale of the Shadwell bath building is closest to that of Cheapside, Pudding Lane, Billingsgate and Winchester Palace. Few complete Roman London bath house ground plans are known, making comparison of overall dimensions difficult. A comparison of the size of the various *caldaria*, as undertaken in the Winchester Palace volume (Yule 2005, 70), is possible and has proved more useful. The caldarium at Shadwell is closest in size to Cheapside and Winchester Palace, at 42m² (Fig. 120).

The overall quality of construction at Shadwell was markedly different from that of the early Roman *thermae* at Huggin Hill but similar to contemporary late Roman baths which were probably privately constructed *balnae* built of reused materials. Whilst similar to some other London bath houses in siting, scale or construction, the Shadwell baths are unique in other ways. Even without knowing the full ground plan, it is evident that Shadwell had many more rooms than any of the other known late Roman baths in London. It may also have been unique in London in potentially having two suites of heated rooms from the outset. Billingsgate baths, the nearest in date to Shadwell, may have served a private town house or an inn for wealthy travellers and had only three rooms (Rowsome 1999, 275; Marsden 1980, 152–155). By contrast the first baths at Shadwell had at least eleven rooms, six of which were heated, making it far too large for domestic use, even before its subsequent expansion in Period 4.

The general appointment and status of the Shadwell

baths is difficult to place in context when so few of its fixtures and fittings survived robbing and truncation in antiquity. Many of the comparative baths are equally incomplete or remain largely unstudied or only partially published. A clue to the Shadwell bath's status might be found in its use of timber water pipes, which may have been a cheaper alternative to ceramic pipes (Ian Betts, pers. comm.). The latter represent relatively rare fittings when manufactured in the early Roman period, largely restricted to high status structures, and may have been difficult to source as salvage. The use of box-flue tile is also thought to represent a less expensive form of cavity walling, as it could be used to heat smaller sections of wall, in contrast to wall tiles that were used to create one continuous cavity. Once again though, the selection of the former may simply reflect the available salvage, and box-flue tiles were far more widely used than other types of wall jacketing. The use of *opus signinum* and possible *opus spicatum* flooring, the latter also observed at Cheapside (Ian Betts, pers. comm.), is also considered to be more utilitarian than ostentatious.

The late date, combined with the vagaries imposed by salvage, could therefore explain the more functional appearance of the Shadwell building and a relative absence of embellishment, but this is evidently not the case in other contemporary masonry structures. For instance, the late Roman bath suite forming part of the palatial complex at Winchester Palace in Southwark is of a similar size to the Shadwell bath and constructed largely from reused building material, but included continuous wall jacketing, imported marble veneers and decorated wall plaster (Yule 2005, 68–69). Elsewhere, the mid second and third-century Period I complex of buildings in the south-west quarter of the City of London, perhaps representing a temple or religious site of public or official construction, was also largely built of reused material but opulently appointed with newly-sourced marble veneers, paving, mosaics and finely painted wall plaster (Sudds 2008, 39–40). Perhaps the partial cavity walling, functional flooring and small-scale and selective reuse of indigenous Forest marble and plain white Carrara at the Shadwell baths reflects a smaller construction budget. One might speculate that this implies a private builder at Shadwell, rather than an official or public purse.

Despite being constructed with more limited funds the Shadwell bath house was competently designed and built, and was ambitious in scale. The size and layout of the baths suggests an intention to impress and to provide bathing facilities for a large number of users. It is certainly too big for purely domestic use but may be too small to represent a true *thermae* or public baths. Associated finds assemblages point to luxurious hospitality and feasting in the vicinity of the baths and perhaps they are best seen as part of a private commercial venture aimed at a paying clientele. Whether this establishment took the form of an 'inn' or had a wider function as part of the immediate settlement is difficult to determine and is discussed further in Chapter 5.

4.3 The Shadwell sites and the Thames

James Gerrard

Today Tobacco Dock lies hundreds of metres north of the course of the Thames as it meanders past Wapping and Rotherhithe. The identification of possible 'foreshore' deposits, associated with the partially articulated remains of a horse carcass and a ship's timber (see Chapter 2.2), in the current excavations raised the possibility that the Thames passed close by the site's southern boundary during the Roman period. Establishing this with certainty has proven difficult. What is needed is a full-scale geoarchaeological research project to examine the historic topography of the Shadwell-Wapping area but such a project was beyond the means and remit of this publication. However, nineteenth-century sources do provide some hints about the make-up of the geological deposits in this area.

A basic understanding of the functioning of river-systems would suggest that the Thames has moved south at Wapping. The meander at Wapping is eroding the south bank of the Thames at Rotherhithe, but depositing silt on the north bank. Thus the course of the Thames would be predicted to be further to the north in historic times. The question is how far further north? Much of the Shadwell-Wapping area was excavated in the nineteenth century during the construction of the London Docks complex. It was hoped that geological descriptions of these excavations might survive and that they could answer this question.

In the event the only easily obtainable information was contained in Whitaker's (1889a; 1889b) *The Geology of London and Part of the Thames Valley*. There are summary descriptions of the geology encountered at the 'London Docks' (Whitaker 1889b, 131), the 'New London Docks (Shadwell Basin)' (Whitaker 1889a, 458) and the 'London Docks: eastern dock' (Whitaker 1989b, 308). Whitaker's sources for this information seem to have been drawn largely from personal communications to either himself or the *Royal Geological Society* (*RGS*). The Shadwell Basin account (Whitaker 1889a, 458) references a manuscript section presented to the *RGS* by a Mr Ridsdale. Unfortunately, enquiries at the *RGS* revealed that this document is no longer extant.

It is difficult to draw definitive conclusions from these accounts. However, it seems clear that in all of the dock excavations heterogeneous deposits were encountered overlying the London Clay. These were variously described as 'made ground', 'alluvium' or 'river drift' and were consistently 30–40ft thick (see Appendix 4). In some cases clear stratigraphy appears to have been visible and specific observations were made about particular layers, with 'human bones' being noted and 'prostrate trees' observed in a peat deposit. Similar sequences of deposits were encountered during the construction of a well in 1888 for the British Linde Refrigeration Company's Factory at the entrance to the Shadwell Basin, although no London Clay was encountered. However, the deposits encountered during the dock construction differ from those encountered during the construction of the Low Level Sewer (North Side), which ran for part of its course along Cable St, a little to the north of The Highway. Here gravels of the Taplow Terrace overlay the London Clay (Whitaker 1889a, 249) and no trace of alluvium was found. This is unsurprising, but it does confirm that deposits to the south of Taplow Terrace edge are significantly different and of more recent, riverine origin.

There is thus strong circumstantial evidence to support the contention that a channel ran to the south of the excavated sites during the Roman period. This may have been the main Thames channel, or a subsidiary channel as shown in some MoLAS publications (eg Barber and Bowsher 2000, fig 3). Clearly, a full geoarchaeological study of this area is needed.

It is perhaps worth noting that during the excavation of the Shadwell Basin large quantities of spoil, amounting to hundreds of thousands of cubic metres of material, were taken upstream and dumped in Wandsworth and Battersea and used for land reclamation and other purposes (Cotton 1996). In fact, a layer of presumably prehistoric peat 10ft thick dug from the Shadwell Basin was used as mulch in Battersea Gardens (Cotton 1996, 93)! The movement of this material from the Shadwell area to Battersea raises an uncomfortable possibility. The Thames foreshore at Battersea has produced an important series of late fourth-century pewter ingots stamped with Chi-Rhos and the name 'Syagrius' (for instance Thomas 1981b, 102). These finds are usually seen as a cargo lost from a late Roman trading vessel (Milne *et al.* 1997, 140). However, it may be no coincidence that the first ingot was found in 1859 and the expanded Shadwell basin was constructed in 1854–1858. Thus we may have to consider that these items originated from Shadwell (either as a lost 'cargo' or as a 'hoard') and were subsequently transferred to their 'findspot' by Victorian engineering and spoil disposal.

Chapter 5 Discussion and conclusions

James Gerrard

Fig. 121   View looking north-west from Greenwich showing the commanding views afforded from the top of Greenwich hill and the relatively low-lying position of Shadwell. The arrow indicates St George in the East, to the north of the sites.

In the introduction to this monograph a number of key themes were highlighted. Having presented the chronological narrative (Chapter 2), the artefactual and ecofactual data (Chapter 3) and discussed aspects relating to the reconstruction of the bath house itself (Chapter 4), this final chapter is concerned with drawing those sometimes disparate threads together. To this end many of the themes raised in earlier chapters are revisited here in order to develop an interpretation of the evidence from Shadwell that attempts to place it in an over-arching interpretive framework for the late Roman settlement.

The 'military' argument revisited: interpretation versus evidence

The Roman army was an important social, economic and political force within the late Roman Empire and, by extension, Britain (Heather 2005; Ward-Perkins 2005). The impact of the army on *Londinium* in the third and fourth centuries is an important area of research (Nixon *et al.* 2002, 39) and Shadwell has traditionally been seen as a key 'military' site (Johnson 1975; Johnson 1979, 128). The publication of the 'tower' site (Lakin 2002) shed considerable doubt on the military interpretation but it has

recently been forcefully restated (Bird 2008) so it is worth briefly looking at this vexing issue again.

The first published interpretation of the 'tower' (LD74/LD76) as a military installation (a watchtower or signal station) was made in a short interim note on the excavations, but presented no compelling evidence to support the interpretation (Johnson 1975). Within four years the tower was accepted as part of late Roman London's defences (Johnson 1979, 128). The site's military status seems to have gained credence and acceptance through repetition of the interpretation, rather than a presentation of the supporting empirical evidence (for instance Sheldon 1995, 66–67; Pearson 2002, 62). When that evidence was belatedly presented (Lakin 2002) there was nothing that could conclusively and explicitly be used to demonstrate a military presence, as there were no explicitly military buildings or finds assemblages from the sites (Lakin 2002, 26–27).

The more recent excavations at Sites A and B confirm this non-military pattern. The relatively small finds assemblage is negative militarily: it has less military equipment than one might find on an intramural *Londinium* site as a matter of course (see Chapter 3.3 above; also Lakin 2002, 26–27). The supposed 'military' East Gaulish samian from the site would appear to have more to do with the site's chronology and location rather than a military use (see Chapter 3.1 above). In fact the only 'military' evidence from the site's finds and environmental assemblages seems to be that some of the horse bones were from large animals (see Chapter 3.9 above), though this could be explained by the use of big horses in agriculture or hunting. The absence of clear evidence for the Roman army at Shadwell might be most easily explained by arguing that the army was not stationed there, and that the 'tower' was not a military installation but a mausoleum in a civilian settlement (Lakin 2002).

Much has been made of Shadwell's supposed strategic position overlooking the Thames. Yet at *c.* 9m OD the prospect up and downriver from Shadwell is hardly comparable with that from Greenwich at *c.* 43m OD. Greenwich possesses commanding views to the east at least as far as Woolwich Reach, as well as good upriver views towards the City of London and Southwark. Greenwich is also well connected to the Roman road system, particularly Watling Street, which connected *Londinium* with Kent and the military installations of Reculver and Richborough on the Wantsum Channel. Excavations at Greenwich have also recovered finds indicative of an official Roman presence, in the form of procuratorial tiles (Wallower 2002a; 2002b). Topographically, Shadwell would appear to be a poor candidate for the location of a watchtower or signal station when compared to Greenwich.

It is also worth considering the practicalities of how a chain of watchtowers or signal stations would function. Donaldson (1988) and Southern (1990), in a cogently argued review of this topic, questioned whether Roman signalling could have successfully and quickly communicated any but the most brief and simple message. Donaldson (1988, 356) concluded that:

… the Roman imperial command system can only have met their strategic communications requirements by using the most reliable, fastest, all-weather means available, namely the written word carried by fast-riding couriers. As far as visual systems are concerned, the effects of inclement weather on visibility, the inevitable garbling in the retransmission of a message by operators at every relay-post, and the limitations on the quantity and quality of transmittable information imposed by the nature of the systems available, effectively exclude their use except for the transmission and reception of the simplest tactical material…

Supposing that the Shadwell tower did form part of a chain of beacons relaying a simple message, such as 'the enemy is coming up the Thames', then one must ask who was going to react to the message. Other than the Cripplegate fort, which was abandoned by the fourth century (Howe and Lakin 2004, 53) and the unusual building complex at Winchester Palace in Southwark (Yule and Rankov 1998) there is little evidence for a substantial military presence in *Londinium*. Any suggestion that a late Roman fleet was based in London is also

speculative, unsupported by any late Roman epigraphic or documentary sources. We should also consider what type of force would be capable of challenging the largest walled, defended urban centre and seat of the late Roman administration (including at various times an imperial mint and treasury) in the Diocese of the Britains. In the late fifth century, during the twilight of Roman military power in the West, the Visigoths still struggled to capture towns (Heather 2005, 416). It seems inconceivable that the third- and fourth-century Saxons could have mustered and transported a force large enough to lay siege to and capture *Londinium* (Cotterill 1993; Pearson 2005).

The only force capable of militarily threatening a defended town such as *Londinium* would have been the Roman army itself. It is worth noting that Constantius Chlorus' fleet was able to sale up the Thames estuary and into London unopposed in AD 296 – an event commemorated on the Beaurains/Arras medallion (Hartley *et al.* 2006, 115). Unless one is to suppose a specific historical context, such as the Carausian/Allectan usurpation (which the site chronology does not allow), for the construction of the signal tower, then it would seem to have had little use in relation to external threats.

Beyond the army: new interpretive horizons

Given that the empirical evidence for the presence of the Roman army at Shadwell is virtually non-existent we are left with a difficult question: why is there a complex of buildings, including a large bath house, in this unusual extra-mural Thameside location? What follows is an attempt to answer this question using the available evidence.

It seems reasonable to begin with a consideration of Sites A and B and their immediate hinterland. It is likely that a major Roman road ran just to the north of the sites and it is suggested that this ran along the approximate line of The Highway (Barber and Bowsher 2000, 52), although an extrapolation eastwards of a road extending from the eastern cemetery would place this somewhat further north, nearer Cable Street. It also seems possible that the modern Wapping Lane, a street that used to be known, perhaps significantly, as Old Gravel Lane (George Foster's *Map of London* 1738) and which probably has medieval origins (Croot 1997), may have formed a subsidiary street running south from the main road to the Thames. Evidence of Roman period activity is slight, but the intense post-medieval development of the area is likely to have destroyed or masked such remains. The presence of ephemeral traces of activity at 172–176 The Highway (HIH95) and the Roman burials from the north side of the Shadwell basin (see Chapter 1) arguably indicate a more extensive settlement. This is supported by the statistical interpretation of coin loss at Sites A and B, which suggests the site shares a pattern of loss with some 'small towns' (Burnham and Wacher 1990) and the butchery evidence, which is considered to be characteristic of urban sites (see Chapter 3.9; Lakin 2002, 62–63). Finally, the baths building (B4) at Site B should be considered. The baths were too large to be associated with a domestic residence (see Chapter 4.1) and their size implies that they were built to service the needs of a reasonably large population.

It is suggested that Shadwell be interpreted as a small 'nucleated settlement'. This is a neutral term and we have deliberately avoided labels such as 'small town' or 'village' as too value-laden. It joins a large number of small nucleated satellite settlements around *Londinium* (Sheldon 1971, 1972; Bird 1996; Brown *et al.* in prep.). Shadwell would be by far the closest such settlement to *Londinium* and would be unusual in being sited on a minor road rather than an important arterial route linking major urban centres.

The overall evidence leaves Shadwell's *raison d'être* as something of a mystery. One tentative interpretation has been that Shadwell functioned as a 'port' for late Roman London. This suggestion has proved controversial (Bird 2008) and it seems worth digressing here to clarify this argument.

It has long been recognised that the accession of Diocletian in the late third century marks the end of a complex series of processes that had altered many of the structures of Classical antiquity and produced something rather different: 'late antiquity' (Jones 1964; Brown 1971). Late third- and fourth-century Britain (*c.* AD 250–410) differed substantially from early Roman Britain. One of the fundamental shifts that occurred saw a substantial decline of identifiable long-distance trade into the province, and the emergence of largely self-sufficient regional economies within Britain (Millett 1990, 157–180). At the same time the nature of Britain's urban centres began to change, with an apparent increase in elite dwellings, a decline in investment in public infrastructure (Reece 1980) and the shrinking of 'industrial' production, which appears to have been relocated to so-called 'small towns' (Millett 1990, 147).

London was not immune to these changes. In the first and second century *Londinium* was the heart of the province, centre of the imperial administration and the major port and consumer city in Britain (Perring 1991). However, a combination of factors may have made its special economic status vulnerable. Roman York's growth as an important military and administrative centre during the third century (Ottaway 1993) and its status on occasion as the imperial seat (Birley 1999, 178; Bidwell 2006) may have meant that some of London's state-sponsored trade was redirected north as the centre of power in the province shifted. The archaeological evidence from London seems to confirm this, with an apparent decline in activity from the late second century onwards only partially reversed by renewed prosperity in the late Roman period (Perring 1991, 84–89). As *Londinium*'s imperial patronage and economic pre-eminence declined, another factor, completely beyond the control of *Londinium*'s inhabitants, struck. The arguments are complex but it appears that London suffered from

the effects of falling sea level and a tidal regression of the Thames as far inland as the Roman port. From the mid first to the mid third century there were repeated shifts in the location of the city's waterfronts and quays in an attempt to compensate for these changes (Brigham 1990a). However, no quays later than the mid third century have yet been identified and Brigham (1990a, 147) has suggested that by that date the river at high water would barely have exceeded the first-century low water mark, and at low water the third-century river would have lain 30–40m from the earlier quay front, exposing a shallow, shelving foreshore. The combination of a decline in the volume of trade (Millett 1990, 162–163) and the change in river level meant that expensive and complex quays were no longer warranted (Brigham 1990a). Riverine trade may now have been conducted through the creeks and inlets of North Southwark and the Thames estuary, with Shadwell and the mouth of the Lea selected as locations for dispersed 'ports' or beachmarkets (Brigham 1990a, 159–160).

The archaeological evidence from the Shadwell sites that would support this hypothesis remains ambiguous. At no point was the late Roman foreshore conclusively identified, although there was some evidence that it lay nearby in the early Roman period (see Chapter 2). The river frontage, with 'port buildings' (jetties, wharves and warehouses) may have lain just to the south of the limit of excavation (see Chapter 4.3; Fig. 5). However, such structures may not have been needed if the level of trade was much lower in the late Roman period. Instead of a formal 'port', like New Fresh Wharf (Miller *et al.* 1986), we may need to consider that trading centres more akin to beachmarkets were established. These are a well-known feature of the early Middle Ages (Hodges 1982, 50–51) but are also known from the Roman period (McCormick 2001, 84–85; Houston 1988, 560–561). Some of these 'ephemeral' beachmarkets could handle surprising quantities of traded goods (Gardiner and Mehler 2007).

If Shadwell were a port or 'gateway community' then the settlement's existence and apparent growth does become more explicable. The Thames links the site to the interior of Britain. The navigable Lea, to the east, would probably have allowed access north as far as Hertford and the Thames estuary offered easy access for coastal vessels to Kent and Essex. Finally, for sea-going vessels, the Scheldt estuary and the Rhine corridor were only a short crossing away. Pottery (see Chapter 3.1) links Shadwell to these regions: Oxfordshire wares were transported along the Thames, Hadham products down the Lea and BB1 from Dorset. Pottery from Essex and Kent attest to coastal trade and the East Gaulish samian, mortaria and exotic amphorae indicate links to the Rhine and wider Empire. There are also a handful of coins from Sites A and B (see Chapter 3.2), as well as the 'tower' site (Bird 2008), that are unusual and could have been dropped by travellers from distant regions. Furthermore, it seems clear that the Shadwell baths faced the river to the south, rather than the road to the north, suggesting that the building was designed to impress river traffic or those arriving at the site by river.

Fig. 122 Reconstructed view looking south-west across the service yard for the bath house. Set around Period 4.2, the rear of the bath house building can be seen on the left with Building 3b on the right, by Jake Lunt-Davies

Shadwell's location appears to be a good indicator that it served as a trading centre. However, the archaeological evidence to support this hypothesis, in particular the pottery assemblages (see Chapter 3.1), is far from conclusive and can be interpreted in a number of ways. It should also be noted that our understanding of the chronology of changes in the Thames' river level is far from perfect (Brigham 1990a).

Power, patronage and people at Shadwell

This discussion has so far concentrated on general issues relating to the Shadwell settlement. It has examined the military hypothesis and gone on to suggest that the site can probably best be classed as a 'nucleated settlement'. A further consideration of the changing nature of the Thames and the late Roman economic situation, combined with an appreciation of Shadwell's geographical situation, suggests that this 'nucleated settlement' may have been a gateway community or riverside trading centre. This final section builds on these interpretive foundations and seeks to explain some of the more unusual aspects of the site and its finds assemblages.

During the early Roman period (Period 2) the evidence for occupation at Shadwell is restricted to low intensity activities such as gravel extraction and wild fowling. The environmental evidence suggests the presence nearby of mixed agriculture and Building 1 may even have functioned as a granary, perhaps serving as a temporary

store for local agricultural surpluses that were destined for shipment to consumers in *Londinium*.

More intense activity began during the middle decades of the third century with the construction of the bath house (B4) and nearby clay-and-timber buildings (B2 and B3). This may mark the creation of a greatly expanded settlement at Shadwell, and the following discussion attempts to explain how and why it sprang into existence at this time.

The first point that needs to be made concerns the site chronology. The structural remains of the bath house were left largely *in situ* and as a result very few datable artefacts associated with the bath's construction were recovered. Nevertheless, the beginning of intensive activity can be fixed with some precision.

Intense coin loss began in the years after *c.* AD 260. This phenomenon is typical of many British sites and says more about the problems of third-century coin supply than the intensity of occupation on the site. The first- and second-century bronze issues could still have been circulating in the third century and a handful of coins of the earlier third century may suggest that increased activity began after *c.* AD 200 and before *c.* AD 260.

This date range can be narrowed further by consideration of the pottery evidence. Most of the pottery associated with the earliest phases of Buildings 2 and 3 was of mid third-century date. However, the groups were small, occasionally contaminated by intrusive material and on occasions not susceptible to detailed chronological analysis. Fortunately the controversial samian assemblage provides an important and relatively fixed chronological point. Joanna Bird (see Chapter 3.1) has argued that the East Gaulish samian reached the site as a single shipment in the middle third of the third century (*c.* AD 230–AD 260). The virtual absence of Central Gaulish samian would suggest that there was no substantial activity on site prior to the cessation of exports from the Central Gaulish kilns in *c.* AD 200.

Furthermore, Hartley's analysis of the German mortaria has revealed that some of the vessels used on site had terminal production dates of *c.* AD 230 and that the subsequent mortarium form is unrepresented in the Shadwell assemblage. If the samian and mortaria travelled together from the Rhineland to Britain (as seems likely given that they were produced in kilns located in relatively close proximity) then one might suggest that activity at Shadwell began towards the beginning of the AD 230–260 date range indicated by the samian.

Finally, samples obtained from three piles from Site A all returned tree-ring dates of spring AD 228. Goodburn notes that the condition of these timbers clearly demonstrates that they had been driven into the ground within a year, at most, of felling and that they had not been reused in any later structure.

The 30 years from AD 230–260 fall within the worst of the so-called third-century crisis. It can be dangerous to associate archaeological evidence with major historical events but it would be foolish to completely disregard the historical context. Britain largely escaped the vicissitudes of the third century but its continental neighbours did not (Salway 1981, 275–278) and this may be of relevance to our interpretation of the Shadwell settlement.

Several strands of evidence can be brought together to suggest that in its early phases the Shadwell settlement may have been inhabited by a migrant population (Heather 2009) who either originated within Gaul or were at least supplied with goods that originated there. The evidence is tenuous but nonetheless deserving of attention. Firstly, there is the unusual 'samian' assemblage. The full arguments concerning this point have been presented in Chapter 3.1 but are summarised here. The almost total absence of Central Gaulish samian is unusual. If the site had been populated by a 'local' British population who were able to move their goods and chattels with them one might expect heirloom Central Gaulish samian to have been used on the site (Wallace 2006). Its absence may indicate either that a population was brought to the site without their property or that the population originated somewhere closer to where the East Gaulish samian was produced.

The second point concerns the slight evidence from early occupation deposits associated with the use of Building 3 in Period 4.1 (see Chapter 3.1, Key Group 1). This material is almost exclusively formed of imported pottery and the absence of Romano-British wares may tentatively support the idea of a migrant population, though the coin evidence remains ambiguous on this point (Chapter 3.2). There are a number of coins that could be direct imports from the Continent but all are too late to fit within the early third-century time bracket under consideration. The small finds assemblage (Chapter 3.3) remains firmly Romano-British, with no obvious imported objects, which is somewhat surprising as personal adornments and possessions are generally considered to be more sensitive to issues of identity than other categories of objects (for instance Swift 2000).

It is difficult to suggest a convincing interpretation based on the relatively tenuous evidence outlined above. However, it is possible to suggest that what occurred at Shadwell in the period *c.* AD 230–260 was related to the movement of people into the new settlement from another region of Britain or the Western Empire. Interpretations centred on migration have long been unfashionable in British archaeology but should not be discounted out of hand (Heather 2009). If the new inhabitants of Shadwell originated on the Continent then they seem to have brought with them few archaeologically visible possessions other than pottery. If they originated in Britain then those first inhabitants of Shadwell may have brought little more than a few personal possessions and seemingly little or no local pottery.

Why this population settled at Shadwell remains a mystery. A purely local and economic explanation seems unlikely. The lack of Central Gaulish samian suggests an incoming population without goods (but with unusual trading connections) rather than local traders establishing a new settlement in close proximity to *Londinium*. The lack of slow growth, organic development also seems unusual. The bath house was not an addition to a modest settlement that had developed over several decades but a relatively large building established where there had been little activity beforehand.

It is perhaps tempting to see the hand of the state at work creating a new settlement for a population displaced by conflict elsewhere in the empire. The historical context would fit and third-century Gallic refugees are thought to have existed (Mattingly 2007, 374, although see Smith 1982 for a sceptical view). We also know that the Roman state was quite willing to move populations around the empire, as with the Sarmatians who were moved to Britain in the late second century (Salway 1981, 207–208). Yet the sponsoring of migration by the state and emperor was usually (as with the Sarmatians) for military reasons and these seem to be absent at Shadwell. Furthermore, the settlement and bath house seem too modest for a piece of imperial altruism. Another explanation is needed.

Rather than seek an 'organic' explanation for the Shadwell settlement's appearance in the mid third century we might instead suggest the involvement of a powerful individual or group. It is generally accepted that the third century saw the beginnings of a process that led to the creation of a two tier social system. As power, wealth and influence became increasingly concentrated in the hands of the few, the many sought security through the patronage of a lord (for instance Brown 1971, 34–38; Esmonde Cleary 1989, 15; Faulkner 2001, 131–157; Kelly 2006; Wickham 2010, 36–37). At Shadwell we may be seeing the beginnings of such a system.

The preparation of the site area with new terraces and boundaries, the possible establishment of streets and the construction of the baths required access to considerable quantities of labour and materials. The construction of a large bath house requires particular explanation, given that the third century is a time when the construction of public buildings (other than defences) was on the wane. The bath house is too large to have functioned as a purely domestic establishment and must have been intended to serve a relatively large population.

The creation of the Shadwell settlement may indicate the bringing together of people, money and resources at a previously under-utilised or unexploited point, perhaps by a powerful individual or private group (Millett 1990, 195; Mattingly 2007, 289). We may assume that the motives were primarily economic. The changing river levels may have made Shadwell attractive as a landing place for coastal and cross-channel shipping and an opportunity to hold markets and fairs. The bath house might represent a development of this core economic activity as a provider of services, offering respite and entertainment to travellers. Aside from bathing, the Shadwell baths might have offered other pleasures for a price.

It would be wrong, however, to see the relationship between the people who lived and worked at Shadwell and their putative lord or lords as simply one of exploitation. No matter how 'oppressive' late Roman society was, those at the top and bottom were still tied together by a web of relationships that governed the patron and client's behaviour. The bath house may have been symbolic of the lord's benevolence and munificence – such motives no doubt played a part in Julianus and his wife Domna's decision to build a bath house in the Syrian villa of Serjilla in AD 473 (Kennedy 1985, 9; Foss 2002, 92). An explanation for the unusual imported pottery (samian and mortaria) can even be found in this concept. If the inhabitants were brought to the site with few possessions then it is possible that material culture used in those first years was largely supplied by the patron or his agents (Whittaker 1983). One might even speculate that the new inhabitants of Shadwell, working for their patron, may have been reminded on a day-to-day basis of their lord's benevolence by the bath house and by being overlooked by a mausoleum associated with the patron's ancestors.

A thriving community

The period from *c*. AD 275–375 (Periods 4 and 5) represents a time of consolidation, modification and intense activity at Shadwell, but apparently punctuated by a significant flood. The overall evidence suggests that the settlement and its inhabitants were thriving and well resourced.

At the heart of the settlement were the baths. Bath houses were large consumers of resources, including timber for fuel, labour for maintenance and day-to-day running, as well as commodities like oil and food for the customers. From the settlement's earliest days the baths must have placed considerable demands on its rural hinterland, and we may suppose that some supplies, particularly the hundreds of tons of fuel (Blyth 1999) were supplied by the owner's estates. The lack of quern stones at the site and the presence of a fragment of possible millstone may suggest that the inhabitants were not grinding grain themselves but had access to cereals grown and ground elsewhere.

What is most striking about Periods 4 and 5 is that the baths, with their appetite for resources, not only continued in use but underwent substantial modifications and expansion. These modifications included the rearrangement of the bath's internal space and the addition of new hypocaust systems in previously unheated rooms. In Period 4.3 the bath's hypocausts were flooded – a not unusual event in a bathing establishment (see for instance Cunliffe 1969, 131). The flood silts contained fragmentary and concreted frog bones (see Chapter 3.9) that may have been redeposited, suggesting a fairly severe flooding event that carried sediments into the baths from another water source.

In Period 5 the baths were restored and at least one new heated room was added to the structure, demonstrating that they were still actively required and used beyond the mid fourth century (*c*. AD 325–375). The sequence of modifications and the addition of heated rooms would appear to indicate that the baths were not only being used but that use was increasing. It is also clear that the necessary resources were available to support the bath's extension, remodelling and related running costs.

The ancillary building (B3), located to the north of the bath house, was also subject to repeated alterations and rebuilding during Period 4. Building 3a was, like its predecessor, a clay-and-timber construction but a relatively well-appointed building, interpreted as a possible accommodation block. During the course of Period 4 this property underwent a total of five modifications and renovations (Buildings 3a–3e), an average of once every decade. In Period 5 a new building, B7, was constructed in much the same position.

Extensive truncation means that the function and layout of Buildings 3a–3e is poorly understood. Nevertheless, the rapid pace at which the alterations were made is surely significant. They not only indicate that clay-and-timber structures were vulnerable to decay and had a comparatively short life, but that the use of the internal room areas and spaces in the building were subject to repeated change and that resources remained available to repeatedly modify the building.

A large assemblage of wall plaster recovered from Buildings 3a–3e and Building 7 shows that in at least some, if not all, of the property's phases, the walls were internally rendered and painted. Fragments of plaster from Building 3d demonstrate that the plaster and paint scheme had been replaced at least once. Furthermore, although many of the rooms had beaten earth floors, in some phases of the structure's use rooms were given mortar or *opus signinum* floors. The overall impression is of a relatively high-status building or a structure intended to emulate one. The buildings were also furnished with heating, albeit in the form of open hearths rather than hypocausts, indicating an attempt to make the structures comfortable.

There were few finds from Buildings 3a–3e or Building 7 that could be categorically related to its internal furnishing (see Chapter 3.3). The recovery of a small bronze foot B<302> and a small piece of bone inlay B<349>, both of which may have been decorative elements on furniture, suggests that parts of the property were reasonably well appointed. The recovery of a shale tabletop fragment from Site A might indicate that good quality furniture adorned some of the rooms of buildings at Shadwell.

The function of Buildings 3a–3e and Building 7 is uncertain, though the rapid modifications and rebuildings seem unusual for a domestic residence and a connection with the nearby bath house seems likely. The overall artefactual and ecofactual evidence from Site B indicates a place of consumption. Better quality joints of meat were consumed including young pigs, lamb, beef and surprisingly large quantities of chicken (see Chapter 3.9). The pottery and glass also seems to indicate a bias in favour of consumption, with drinking vessels seeming to be over-represented in the assemblage (see Chapter 3.1 and 3.6). This might suggest that Buildings 3a–3e and Building 7 were primarily sites of consumption and leisure. It is notable that almost one in five of the hair pins recovered from Site B came from either the floors or demolition layers associated with these buildings (see Chapter 3.3), suggesting that women were present. Although it certainly cannot be proven, one might speculate that amongst the entertainments available at the baths, prostitution may have been part of the life of the settlement, and Buildings 3a–3e could have contained rooms available for casual or short-term use.

Activity at Site A, to the west of the bath house, was superficially similar to the sequence recorded at Site B during Periods 4 and 5. Building 2 was demolished and its site taken by a clay-and-timber replacement, Building 5. This building was associated with a possible oven. External activity and a fragmentary building (B6) followed, but a subsequent reconstruction of the same property in Period 5.1 repeated a similar pattern of clay-and-timber building (B8) and nearby oven. In Period 5.2 the property was again rebuilt as Building 9.

The Site A building sequence, situated at the southern end of the site on the lower terrace and interspersed with evidence of external activity and repeated downslope erosion, may have been different in function to Buildings 3a–3e and Building 7 to the north of the bath house on Site B. The pottery evidence from Site A (see Chapter 3.1) seems to indicate an emphasis on domestic vessels for cooking and storage. The evidence for at least two ovens may suggest that this was generally an area where food and drink was prepared rather than eaten. A fragment of flat polychrome mosaic glass probably derived from a plate or tray or a piece of inlay from furniture, although from a Period 7 dumped deposit, may be related to the presentation or serving of food. The recovery of fig seeds

from Building 5 may also be of significance, as the animal bone evidence suggests that the 'high status' foods were being consumed on Site B. The presence of an exotic and imported fruit may indicate not its consumption but its preparation for consumption elsewhere. One might speculate that the Site A buildings dating from Periods 4 and 5 were involved in the preparation of food for consumption at the bath complex to the east, though this cannot be proven. The Site A buildings may also have provided living space for people who worked at the baths.

The overall evidence from Periods 4 and 5 is of a thriving community by the banks of the Thames. At the heart of the settlement were the baths, built for communal use and a focus for a variety of leisure activities. Close to the baths were clay-and-timber buildings used for associated activities, perhaps including the consumption of food, entertainment, accommodation and the other demands of the baths' customers. Further away on Site A, to the west, were buildings of a more domestic nature associated with the preparation of food. Some of the foodstuffs were exotic imported commodities like figs, oil and wine and these may have been offloaded from ships beached on the nearby foreshore. The users of the Shadwell baths and consumers of these commodities may have been visitors from the nearby city or travellers arriving by road or river.

Although the settlement apparently thrived from the late third until the late fourth century, the buildings at Shadwell required frequent repairs and their provision suggests not only that adequate resources were available throughout the period but that the Shadwell settlement and its baths were a commercial success.

Realignment and retrenchment: the end of the Roman period

Our understanding of the latest Roman activity at Sites A and B (Periods 6 and 7) is hampered by an uncertain chronology that goes hand-in-hand with the 'end of Roman Britain' (Esmonde Cleary 1989, 141–142). The latest artefact from either site is a copper-alloy coin of Honorius A<341>, struck between AD 394 and AD 402 (see Chapter 3.2). No Anglo-Saxon finds were recovered and any activity that took place in the fifth century is effectively undatable and therefore largely unidentifiable. However, the phase of activity that began in the last quarter of the fourth century, and probably continued into the early fifth century, provides a final and fascinating chapter in the history of the Shadwell settlement.

By the last quarter of the fourth century the two monumental structures that had dominated life in the settlement, the baths and the 'tower' up the hill to the northeast, were in decline. The 'tower' appears to have been demolished sometime after AD 365 (Lakin 2002, 24) and this must have represented a discordant break with the Romano-British past if it was an early Roman mausoleum. The baths may have been abandoned and stood disused before being stripped of valuable scrap materials. The two buildings that could be seen as the embodiment of late Roman secular power – the private mausoleum and the semi-public baths – were gone. The social system that had bound the settlement together in earlier phases was changing.

This impression is reinforced by other activity at Site B. Clay-and-timber building B7 was demolished and its remains levelled. The fragmentary remains of a later building (B10) occupied the same location but this was built with earth-fast posts and appeared quite different in construction. Building 10 was associated with the latest extant Roman finds and may be of late fourth or even fifth century date. The building was separated from the disused baths by the cobbled service yard OA6, that had long been maintained to the north of the bath complex. The surface of the yard was now allowed to become buried beneath a layer of silt and sediment, which was cut by drainage ditches on different alignments from the earlier building phases, suggesting that the long-standing property layout and ownership had ended.

At Site A to the west, the last quarter of the fourth century saw the demolition of Building 9 and its replacement with Building 11, which was also located on the southern part of the area and looks, superficially at least, like the continuity of a well-established pattern. However, Building 11 differed from its predecessors by being built, at least in part, with mortared stone walls. Some of the stone may have been robbed and reused from either the 'tower' or the nearby baths. The ground plan of Building 11 was incomplete but it appears to have been a substantial structure with several rooms, and may have been served by a timber-lined drain. The building lay near a crudely built well whose construction at such a late date might indicate that a piped water supply had failed.

The overall impression is that activity continued on both Sites A and B until the very end of the Roman period, though substantial changes had clearly already occurred. The disuse and abandonment of the baths suggests that the resources to maintain and run it had failed, perhaps suddenly. The demolition of the 'tower' might indicate a breakdown in other long-standing arrangements that had helped to underpin the settlement, although people continued to live at Shadwell for a while longer.

The end of Roman activity at Shadwell seems to have come sometime in the early fifth century. The evidence from the well suggests formal abandonment, with the large assemblage of pottery from its fills containing a high percentage of tablewares including high status items or vessels used in feasting (see Chapter 3.1). This interpretation is reinforced by the recovery of a copper-alloy bowl, a valuable and easily recycled object (see Chapter 3.3). The presence of African amphorae in the well may also be significant, particularly if they indicate the consumption of imported commodities during Roman Shadwell's final days. The dumping of this large collection of pottery and other material in the well may have had a ritualistic motive, serving as a 'closing' deposit and can be compared with the well and hoard at Drapers' Gardens in the City (Gerrard 2009). The presence of 'ritual' pits to the north, one of which contained an intact pot, might be related to these activities.

Once the settlement had been abandoned the extant remains of buildings were sealed beneath layers of clay and silt. The baths appear to have been systematically robbed, although when this occurred is a matter for debate. There is no definitive evidence that the robbing occurred later than the Roman period, though it is difficult to believe that there was a substantial demand for building stone in the early fifth century, and the robbing might not have taken place until seventh century or later. By the time of the Domesday Survey in the 11th century Shadwell was part of the *vill* of Stepney and owned by St Paul's (Baker 1998). If the land had been granted to the church earlier, perhaps in the middle Saxon period (Bailey 1989, 117), then the ruined baths could have been robbed and the stone reused in a 7th- or 8th-century ecclesiastical context (Eaton 2000). The robbing brought the Roman influence at the site to a close and a marsh developed which was not reclaimed for new development until the post-medieval period.

Concluding remarks

It is hoped that this monograph has succeeded in its aim to describe the findings at Shadwell and address associated issues of local, regional and national significance. The findings from the Shadwell sites have allowed the development of a new interpretive framework for understanding the late Roman settlement, moving the debate beyond the military hypothesis.

The empirical data, presented in some detail, provides a record of an important and unusual site sequence and provides a pathway to its extensive archive. It is also our hope that the substantial assemblage of late Roman pottery, coins, small finds, building materials and faunal remains from Shadwell will be a resource of use to other researchers interested in the nature of late Roman London and its environs. Much of the material, in particular the samian and amphorae, has significance far beyond its local context.

It is worth ending with something of an archaeological cliché. The interpretations presented in this volume are not the final word on the settlement and its function. The challenge now is to take these interpretations and hypotheses forward and test them as new data becomes available. We look forward to seeing those challenges tackled, our interpretations challenged and the understanding of late Roman Shadwell further extended and clarified.

Specialist appendices

Appendix 1:

Catalogue of samian pottery

Site B

B[103]

Drag 33, East Gaul, probably Rheinzabern; seven sherds, approximately two-thirds of the vessel. No stamp; base raised in centre. Early to mid third century. Slip almost completely lost, foot worn.

B[127]

Drag 53, East Gaul, Rheinzabern; four sherds, including those from B[134], B[140] and B[171]. The stump of one handle is present and a small amount of barbotine decoration, including what is probably a tendril, on the body. Early to mid third century.

Drag 31/Lud Sa, East Gaul, probably Trier; four sherds, including those from B[134] and B[140]. The slip is fired black over most of what survives, except where it is thinner over the potter's fingermarks; the fabric is still completely red. This is not a form which is normally made in a black-slipped version, while samian that has been burnt in a fire usually shows some blackening of the core (cf. Jope 1945); perhaps some feature of the firing is responsible, such as the bowl's position in the kiln. Early to mid third century.

B[134]

Drag 53 = pot in B[127], *q.v.*

Drag 31R, Central Gaul, Lezoux; two sherds. Mid to late Antonine.

Drag 31/Lud Sa = pot in B[127], *q.v.*

Drag 37, East Gaul, Trier; two sherds. The ovolo, straight border, cockerel and rosette are on a bowl in the style of Criciro from the St Magnus House quay (Bird 1986, no. 2.71); the other motifs are a tripod surmounted by a bird (Fölzer 1913, taf. 30, type 690) and a crater (Gard 1937, type V27). The tripod, cockerel and crater are on an unattributed bowl from Niederbieber which has an ovolo recorded for Amator and Atillus-Pussosus (Oelmann 1914, taf. 6, 27). The surfaces are abraded and the fabric is very friable, a drab yellowish brown in colour, with traces of orange slip; this unusual fabric may be due to some contamination in the nearby soil. Early to mid-third century. (Fig. 123.1)

Drag 18/31, Central Gaul, Lezoux. Hadrianic–Antonine

B[135]

Drag 37, East Gaul, Rheinzabern; three sherds. The ovolo is not very clear but is probably Ricken and Fischer 1963, type E2, used by several potters but particularly Cerialis I. Below is a scroll or medallion. Rim 45mm high, slightly flared. Cerialis was active *c.* AD 170–200, but the rim suggests later use of the mould.

Drag 37, East Gaul, Rheinzabern. Fragment of decoration. Early to mid third century.

B[140]

Drag 37, a frieze of animals in the style of Dubitus of Trier. The motifs are all recorded elsewhere in Dubitus' work: ovolo Gard 1937, type R22, bull T54, dog T86, bear T35, large and small boars T37 and T43, and rosettes V55 and V100. Some of the elements are on a similar bowl in his style from Colchester (Bird 1999, fig 2.60, 1191). *c.* AD 225–245. Badly abraded on both surfaces. (Fig. 123.2)

Drag 53 = pot in B[127], *q.v.*

Drag 31/Lud Sa = pot in B[127], *q.v.*

B[152]

Drag 37, an arena scene of *damnatio ad bestias* in the style of Comitialis of Trier; four sherds, including that from B[406]. The prisoner, Fölzer 1913, type 517, and the leaf type 762 are on a mould-stamped bowl from Niederbieber (Oelmann 1914, taf. 8, 10), the prisoner and the lion type 585 on a mould-stamped bowl from Utrecht (Brunsting and Kalee 1989, afb. 84, 98). Other bowls in his style from Niederbieber have the ovolo, prisoner, leaf and lion (taf. 8, 11) and the prisoner, leaf, lion and bear (taf. 8, 12). Comitialis was active *c.* AD 160–190, but this is probably from a later use of his mould. Despite the difference in colour and finish, the sherd from B[406] joins, and the levels of ovolo and internal turning lines match; the sherds from B[152] now have a thin and only partly glossy slip, worn to a lighter orange shade B<565>. (Fig. 123.3)

B[171]

Drag 53 = pot in B[127], *q.v.*

B[180]

Drag 31 or 31R, Central Gaul, Lezoux. Mid- to late Antonine

B[195]

Drag 45, East Gaul, Trier; three sherds, including those from B[250]. Early to mid third century. The interior, of which only the top of the grits is present, shows little sign of wear.

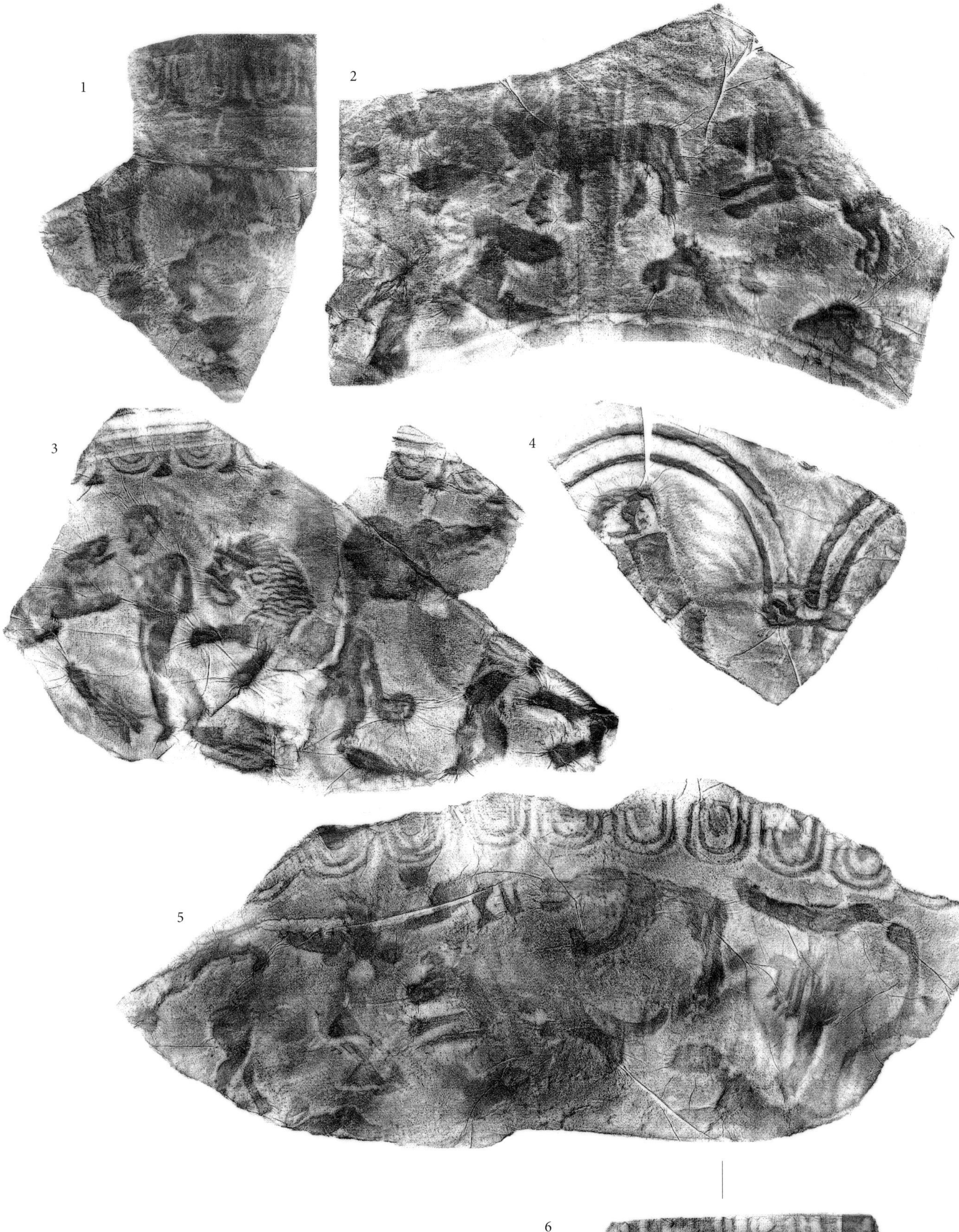

0   2cm

Fig. 123   Decorated samian

B[203]

Drag 45, East Gaul, Trier; two sherds. Early to mid third century. Worn interior.

B[214]

Drag 37, East Gaul, Trier, a thick heavy rim. Second quarter third century.

B[224]

Drag 31R/Lud Sb, East Gaul, Trier. Early to mid third century.

B[240]

Mortarium base, East Gaul, Trier; two sherds. Early to mid third century. The interior and foot are worn.

B[250]

Drag 37 in the style of Julius II–Julianus I of Rheinzabern. The arcade, Ricken and Fischer 1963, type KB72, is on a mould-stamped Julianus bowl in the Museum of London (accession no. S649G); the gladiator is type M227, the stand O179. Bowls in similar style are on Ricken and Thomas 2005, taf. 207. *c.* AD 225–245. The relief is abraded. (Fig. 123.4)

Drag 37, East Gaul, Rheinzabern. The ovolo, Ricken and Fischer 1963, type E1, was used by several potters. Rim 51mm high and rather flared; the slip is now matt and light orange in colour. Early to mid third century.

Drag 45 = pot in B[195], *q.v.*

B[281]

Sherd, East Gaul, Rheinzabern. Late second to mid third century.

B[284]

Drag 37, East Gaul, Rheinzabern. The ovolo, Ricken and Fischer 1963, type E25, was used by several potters; the motif beneath is too broken to identify. Early to mid third century.

B[296]

Drag 37, an animal scene in the style of Afer of Trier; two sherds. The ovolo, Gard 1937, type R18, bear T31, lion T4, leopards T21 and T24, hound T79, hare T108 and peacock T129 are all recorded for Afer, while the ovolo, stag T58, crayfish T182 and the snake or s-shaped ornament V49 are recorded for Dubitatus, who shared a number of motifs with Afer. Afer was active *c.* AD 200–220, but this bowl is probably somewhat later, especially if the footring below belongs with it. Shallow relief, abraded over it. (Fig. 123.5, Fig. 123.6)

Drag 37 footring, East Gaul, Trier. Thick heavy foot of late type; this may be the foot to the Afer bowl, despite its darker colour, as footrings were added after removal from the mould. Second quarter third century. Heavily worn.

B[301]

Drag 37, East Gaul, Rheinzabern. Early to mid third century.

B[305]

Drag 37, East Gaul, Rheinzabern. The ovolo is badly modelled and finished but is probably Ricken and Fischer 1963, type E26; the little dog is T138a, and the two motifs were shared by several potters. Early to mid third century.

B[339]

Drag 33, East Gaul, Trier. Late second to mid third century.

B[340]

Drag 33, East Gaul, Trier. The base is conical underneath, raised on the interior; no stamp though there may be some ?deliberate impression there. Second quarter third-century.

B[385]

Drag 37, East Gaul, Rheinzabern. The ovolo, Ricken and Fischer 1963, type E17, was used by several potters but particularly the Julius II-Julianus I group. Rim 50mm high and flared. *c.* AD 225–245.

Mortarium sherd, East Gaul, Trier. Early to mid third century. Little wear.

B[392]

Drag 37, East Gaul; the fabric and finish suggest Trier but neither the leaf nor the small crane can be paralleled there. The ovolo is too smudged to identify certainly but may be Huld-Zetsche 1993, type E11, used by potters of Werkstatt II Serie B. The crane is the reverse of Gard 1937, type T123, which is recorded for Atillus; the other motifs, a rosette and perhaps small animals, are not identifiable. The Werkstatt II potters are Antonine in date but this bowl dates from the early to mid third century. (Fig. 123.7)

B[396]

Drag 30 or 37, East Gaul, probably Rheinzabern. Early to mid third century.

Mortarium sherd, East Gaul, Trier. Early to mid third century. Worn interior.

B[400]

Drag 38, East Gaul, Rheinzabern; almost exactly half the vessel. Shallow bowl with small foot; two rings round the centre of the floor but any stamp has gone. Second quarter third century. Worn foot.

B[402]

Dish base, East Gaul, Rheinzabern. Stamped SIIVIIRIANVSF , with blind A and both the letters S reversed; die 3e of the potter identified in the Leeds Index of Potters' Stamps as Severianus ii (Brenda Dickinson, pers. comm.). Severianus was one of the latest

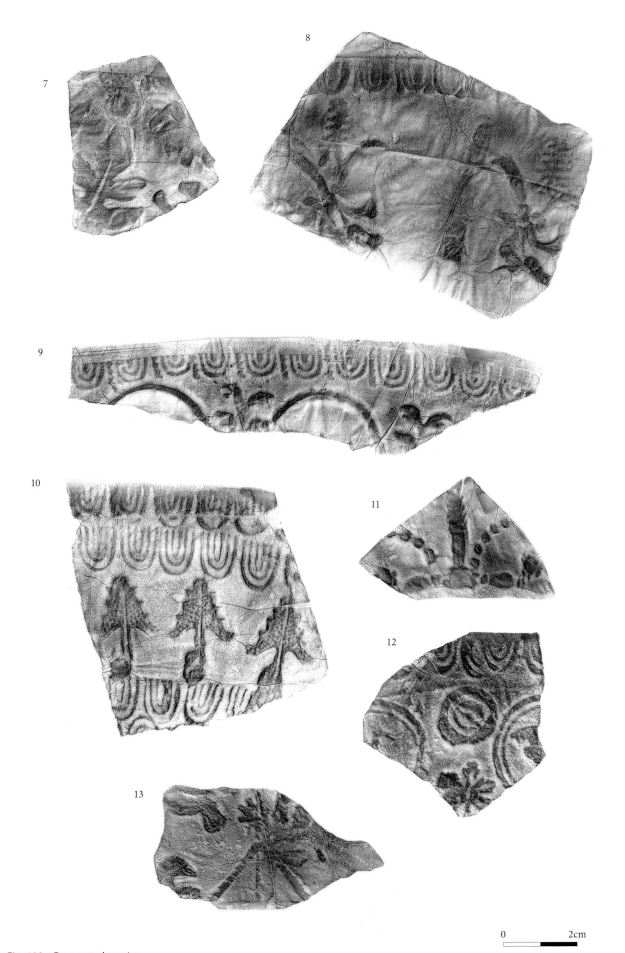

Fig. 123   Decorated samian

Rheinzabern potters exporting to Britain (cf. Bird 1993, 3), and this dish dates towards the middle of the third century, probably *c*. AD 235–250.

B[406]

Drag 37 = pot in B[152], *q.v.*
Drag 36, East Gaul, Trier. Later second to early third century, on rim form. Slightly burnt.

B[412]

Drag 37 in the style of the anonymous Werkstatt II Serie A at Trier. The ovolo is Huld-Zetsche 1993, type E13, and the figure is probably the victorious charioteer, type M103. Taf. 20, A145, has the ovolo and charioteer with a different border; for the plain border here, with the ovolo partly impressed over it, cf. taf. 22, A158. The potters of Werkstatt II A were active in the early to mid-Antonine period; this sherd is too small to show if it is contemporary or from later reuse of the mould, but the other Werkstatt II bowls from the site would suggest the latter. Abraded.

B[432]

Mortarium, East Gaul, Trier; very thick and heavy vessel. Early to mid-third century. Heavy wear inside.

B[435]

Drag 37, East Gaul, Rheinzabern. Probably by a potter of the Julius I-Lupus group, who used the cornucopia ornament, Ricken and Fischer 1963, type O160a, and the medallion K20. *c*. AD 210–235. Slip now orange and matt on the exterior.

B[445]

Drag 33 base, East Gaul, Rheinzabern. The base is nearly conical underneath; no stamp. Second quarter third century.

B[453]

Dish, Lud Tg or Walters 79, East Gaul, Trier. Later second to mid-third century.

B[477]

Sherd, probably upper wall of Drag 37; East Gaul, Trier. Early to mid-third century.

B[485]

Foot, beaker/small jar, East Gaul, Rheinzabern. Base almost conical underneath. Second quarter third century.

B[488]

Drag 37, East Gaul, Trier. The lion, Gard 1937, type T3, was shared by Censor, Atillus and Dubitus, and is on a Dubitus bowl from A[357]. So much space around the figure would be unusual for a bowl by Censor. Fabric and finish characteristic of the second quarter of the third century.

B[489]

Drag 37, Central Gaul, Lezoux; two sherds. Antonine.
Drag 38, East Gaul, Trier. Early to mid third century.

B[496]

Drag 37, East Gaul, Trier. Early to mid third century.
Drag 37, East Gaul, Rheinzabern. Early to mid third century.
Drag 38, East Gaul, Rheinzabern; two sherds. Early to mid third century.
Drag 45, East Gaul, Trier. Early to mid third century.

B[517]

Drag 37, East Gaul, Rheinzabern. Early to mid third century.
Drag 45, East Gaul, Trier. Early to mid third century. Heavily worn interior.

B[518]

Drag 37, East Gaul, Trier. Basal wreath of paired hollow leaves, damaged in finishing the base; such leaves were mainly used by potters of the anonymous Werkstatt II. Early to mid third century. Late ware, abraded relief.

B[563]

African Red Slip ware dish, Hayes (1972) form 50A; three sherds, including those from B[649] and B[740]. Despite differential wear, all three sherds have a slight lilac tinge to the core of the fabric and are likely to come from the same vessel; a base sherd of what is probably form 50 was found in 1974, and may be another piece of this dish (Bird 2002, 31–32; the sherd came from Phase 7, Structure 8, LD74.18). *c*. AD 230/240–325. The piece from B[563] has lost most of its slip, those from B[649] and B[740] have not, while the sherd from B[740] is slightly burnt.

B[582]

Dr 31R/Lud Sb, East Gaul, Rheinzabern; four sherds. Early to mid third century.

B[592]

Drag 37, East Gaul, Trier. Top of ovolo. Early to mid third century.

B[595]

Drag 37, East Gaul, probably Trier. First half third century.

B[608]

Sherd, probably Drag 37, East Gaul, Trier. First half third century. Abraded on exterior.

B[642]

Bowl, probably Drag 38 with a small foot; East Gaul, Rheinzabern. The base is conical underneath. Second quarter third century. Worn interior and foot.

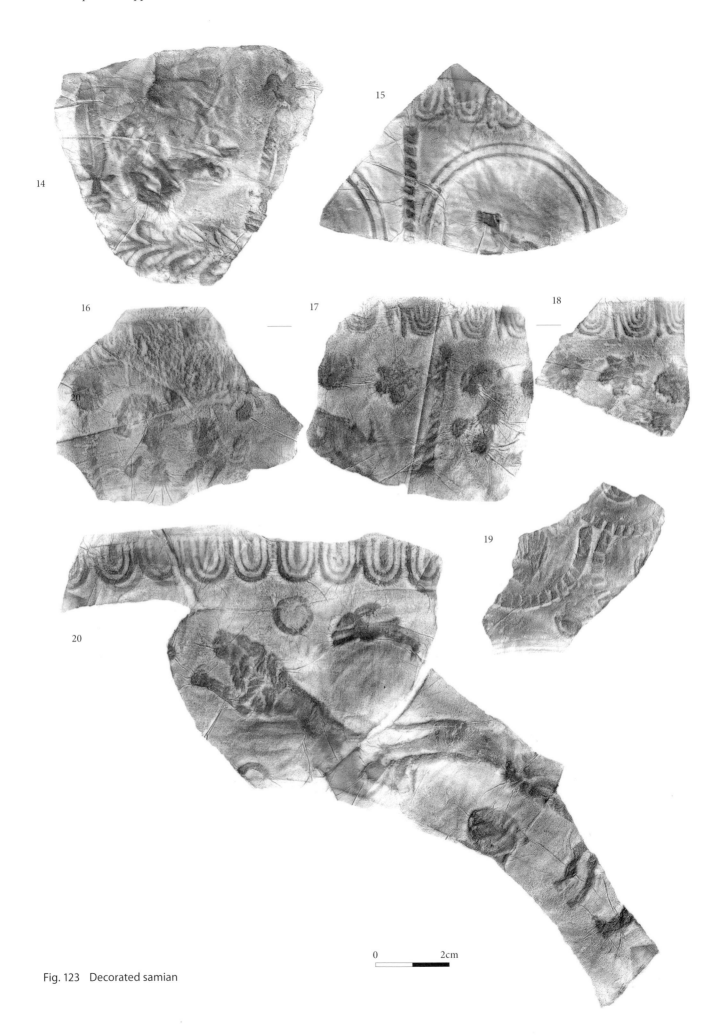

Fig. 123   Decorated samian

B[643]

Mortarium, East Gaul, Trier. Late second to mid-third century. Little sign of wear on grits.

B[644]

Drag 37, East Gaul, Rheinzabern. Large single medallion with a rosette at the base; the rosette is similar to Ricken and Fischer 1963, type O71, but too indistinct to be certainly identifiable. Late second to mid-third century.

Drag 37, East Gaul, Trier. Early to mid-third century

B[649]

African Red Slip ware form 50: = pot in B[563], *q.v.*

Sherd, probably Drag 37, East Gaul, Rheinzabern. The fragment of decoration is too small to identify. Late second to first half third century.

B[677]

Curle 15, the variant with a straight hanging lip; Central Gaul, Lezoux. Antonine.

Drag 45, East Gaul, Trier. The edge of the applied mask is present round the spout. Early to mid-third century.

B[687]

Drag 37 in the style of Dexter of Trier. The 'vase' ovolo, Gard 1937, type R5, column V10 and floral festoon P6 are on a similar mould-stamped bowl from Trier (Fölzer 1913, taf. 15, 14); the same decoration is on another Shadwell bowl (Bird 2002, fig 18, SAM 25) and this may be a sherd of the same bowl. Dexter was active *c.* AD 160–190 but this bowl probably dates from the early to mid third century.

Drag 37 with mould-stamp of Victorinus II of Rheinzabern; three sherds. The retrograde stamp reads VICTORINVSF, and is die 4b of the potter identified as Victorinus ii in the Leeds Index of Potters' Stamps (Brenda Dickinson, pers. comm.). The design consists of a cupid, Ricken and Fischer 1963, type M144a, supporting an ornament O169 (the five-sprigged version). There are no close parallels to the design in Ricken and Thomas 2005; the stamp is on taf. 218, 1–3, 5, 6, 13. *c.* AD 225–245. (Fig. 123.8)

B[721]

Drag 37, East Gaul, Trier. The broken ovolo has a hollow core and is probably one of the Werkstatt I E6 series (Huld-Zetsche 1972). Rim 36mm with heavy lip. The Werkstatt I potters worked in the Hadrianic–early Antonine period, but this is probably a later use of the mould: early to mid third century. Worn orange slip.

Drag 37, East Gaul, Trier, probably by Dubitatus. The figure is probably a *bestiarius*, Gard 1937, type M63, the boar is T43; both are recorded for Dubitatus. *c.* AD 225–245.

Drag 37, East Gaul, Rheinzabern. The ovolo is Ricken and Fischer 1963, type E3, the rosette probably O37; both were used by Cerialis IV. The fabric has a lilac tone in the core

and is probably over-fired. Probably a later use of a Cerialis mould, early to mid third century.

Drag 37, East Gaul, Trier; two sherds. Rim at least 60mm high. Early to mid third century.

Drag 45, Central Gaul, Lezoux. Later second century.

Drag 45, East Gaul, Trier. Early to mid third century. Little or no wear at top of grits.

B[726]

Drag 37 in the style of the Primanus group of Trier. The ovolo is Gard 1937, type R23; the motif beneath may be a poor impression of the rosette V120. The rim is at least 60mm high, turned somewhat inwards above the decoration, and roughly finished above the ovolo. *c.* AD 235–250. Slightly burnt.

Drag 37, East Gaul, Trier; two sherds. Early to mid third century.

Drag 31R/Lud Sb, East Gaul, Trier. Early to mid third century.

B[737]

Drag 37 in the style of Primitivus IV of Rheinzabern; five sherds, including that from B[750]. The ovolo, Ricken and Fischer 1963, type E11, acanthus P148 and medallion K10 are on Ricken and Thomas 2005, taf. 200, 8, which has the same vertical arrangement of the leaves. Rim 37mm high. *c.* AD 215–240. (Fig. 123.9)

B[740]

African Red Slip ware form 50: = pot in B[563], *q.v.*

B[750]

Drag 37 in the style of the anonymous Werkstatt II Serie B of Trier; four sherds, including that from B[800]. Huld-Zetsche 1993, taf. 27, B26, is the same design and may be from the same mould: the ovolo type E13 impressed in two rows over guidelines, above a band of trees O149b standing on roundels O107; the second double row of ovolos has the lower one inverted. The fabric, finish and height of the rim (55mm) suggest a late date: early to mid third century. Abraded over relief. (Fig. 123.10)

Drag 37, East Gaul, Trier. The ovolo is too incomplete to identify certainly, but is probably Huld-Zetsche 1993, type E16, used by Werkstatt II Serien E and F. Rim 67mm, indicating late use of the mould: early to mid third century, and if the base below belongs to it, second quarter of the third century. The slip is worn to thin orange, only slightly glossy. A rim sherd from B[800] is probably the same bowl.

Drag 37 in the style of Dexter of Trier. The column Gard 1937, type V10, is flanked by arches of large beads K51 with pine-cones V56 inside; the wreath of astragalus motifs round the base is R43 or 45. Similar bowls are on Gard taf. 13, 7 and 8. Dexter dates *c.* AD 160–190, but this bowl is probably early to mid third century. (Fig. 123.11)

Drag 37 = pot in B[737], *q.v.*

Drag 37, East Gaul, Trier; two sherds. This is probably the

base of the Werkstatt II bowl; the footring scar is of thick late type, dating to the second quarter of the third century.

Drag 37, East Gaul, Rheinzabern. Early to mid third century.

Sherd, probably Drag 31/Lud Sa or Dr 31R/Lud Sb, East Gaul, Rheinzabern. Early to mid third century.

Drag 31R/Lud Sb, East Gaul, Rheinzabern; five sherds. Second quarter third century.

Bowl sherd, East Gaul, Trier. Early to mid third century.

B[752]

Drag 37, East Gaul, Trier. Part of a small double medallion: cf Gard 1937, type K8, recorded for Victor, though this may have an outer third ring. First half third century.

Drag 38, East Gaul, Rheinzabern; two sherds, probably the same vessel. Late second to mid-third century.

Drag 37 probably, East Gaul, Trier. Late second to mid-third century.

Mortarium base, East Gaul, Trier. Late second to mid-third century. Heavily worn.

Four small East Gaulish sherds, three from Trier, one from Rheinzabern.

B[754]

Drag 37 in the style of the anonymous Werkstatt II Serie B of Trier. The same decoration is on Huld-Zetsche 1993, taf. 28, B38, and this may be from the same mould. The ovolo, here overlapped at the end of the run, is type E13, impressed over a guideline; the medallion is K2, the crane inside the medallion T104, the ring motif O102, and the leaf O130. Clearly late moulding, early to mid third century. Abraded on relief; slip not very good. (Fig. 123.12)

B[780]

Drag 37, East Gaul, Rheinzabern; two sherds. The rosette Ricken and Fischer 1963, type O48, was used by several potters, including the Julius I-Lupus group who used it with a similar arrangement of corded rods, as on Ricken and Thomas 2005, taf. 154, 12. The small animal may be the sea-horse on taf. 157, 10; the other motifs are not identifiable. *c.* AD 210–235. Very abraded relief. (Fig. 123.13)

B[800]

Drag 37 = pot in B[750], *q.v.*

Drag 37, probably = pot in B[750]. (Fig. 123.10)

Dr 33, East Gaul, Trier. Early to mid third century.

B[878]

Drag 31R/Lud Sb, East Gaul, Trier. First half third century

B[883]

Drag 37 in the style of the anonymous Werkstatt II Serie F of Trier; two sherds. The tree, Huld-Zetsche 1993, type O148, bird T105 and wreath O124 are in a similar arrangement on taf. 73, F112; the figure of Actaeon attacked by his hounds was used occasionally by the Serie

F potters. Very late moulding, early to mid third century. Slip now dull and abraded on relief. Slightly burnt. (Fig. 123.14)

B[909]

Drag 37 in the style of Primitivus IV of Rheinzabern; three sherds. The ovolo, Ricken and Fischer 1963, type E11, medallion K19 and corded rod O232 are on Ricken and Thomas 2005, taf. 202, 13, the little dog on taf. 202, 19. *c.* AD 215–240. (Fig. 123.15)

unstratified

Drag 33, East Gaul, Trier. No stamp; base nearly conical underneath. Second quarter third century. Worn foot.

Bowl/dish, East Gaul, Rheinzabern. Early to mid third century. Worn foot and interior.

Site A

A[38]

Drag 31R/Lud Sb, East Gaul, Rheinzabern. Early to mid third century.

A[357]

Drag 37 in the style of Dubitus of Trier; six sherds, including those from A[578], A[750], A[862]. The motifs, ovolo Gard 1937, type R25, here overlapped, lion T3, boar T37 and rosettes V55 and V100, are all recorded for him, and some of them only for him. The corded upright is probably the rod used as a lower border on bowls in Dubitus' style from Keller 1 at Langenhain (Simon and Köhler 1992, nos C I 163, 167, 183 and 184). *c.* AD 225–245. Abraded relief. (Fig. 123.16)

A[403]

Jar base, probably Déch 72 series, East Gaul, Rheinzabern. The slip is incomplete on the interior. Late second to early-third century, on the profile of the foot.

A[524]

Drag 37, Central Gaul, Lezoux. The tier of cups, Rogers 1974, type Q53, is recorded for Quintilianus, Austrus and Secundinus II; the fine finish would suggest Quintilianus. The figures are not certainly identifiable; the one on the left, wearing buskins, is probably the one on Rogers 1999, pl. 94, 37. *c.* AD 125–150.

A[529]

Drag 33, South Gaul, Montans. Stamped Q.V.C , die 1e of this particular reading in the Leeds Index of Potters' Stamps. Almost all the recorded examples of the die come from Britain, including several from St Katherine Coleman in the City of London (Brenda Dickinson, pers. comm.). *c.* AD 120–145.

A[578]

Drag 37 = pot in A[357]. (Fig. 123.17)

A[722]

Mortarium, Central Gaul, Lezoux. Late second century. Heavily worn inside

A[750]

Drag 37, Central Gaul, Lezoux. Not attributable; a small panel containing a naked warrior, Oswald 1936–37, type 202. Antonine.

Drag 37 = pot in A[357]. (*q.v.* Fig. 123.18)

A[847]

Drag 33, East Gaul, Rheinzabern. Base conical underneath, no stamp, and very thick wall and foot. Second quarter third century.

Dish, East Gaul, Rheinzabern.

A[851]

Drag 33, East Gaul, Rheinzabern. Late second to mid-third century.

A[862]

Drag 37 = pot in A[357].

Drag 37, East Gaul, Trier. Late second to mid-third century.

Sherd, East Gaul, Trier.

A[1028]

Drag 37 in the style of Afer of Trier. An arrangement of corded half-medallions, Gard 1937, type K60, containing shells T172 and roundels V106 or small busts M1. Two Afer bowls from St Magnus House have a similar arrangement: Bird 1986, nos 2.78, with a different arcade but the same shell, and 2.79, the same arcade but inverted and empty. *c.* AD 200–220, but probably moulded somewhat later. Relief abraded. (Fig. 123.19)

Drag 45, East Gaul, Trier; two sherds. First half third century. Worn interior.

Mortarium, East Gaul, Trier. Late second to mid-third century. Little wear on interior.

A[1045]

Drag 37 in the style of a potter associated with the Reginus II-Julius I-Lupus group; five sherds, including those from A[1612], A[1619] and A[1627]. The ovolo, Ricken and Fischer 1963, type E51, the ring O148 and the prisoner M229b are on Ricken and Thomas 2005, taf. 161, 17, the lion to left T8, on Taf 161, 14, both bowls in this style. The second lion T14 is recorded for Reginus II and the hare T154d for Lupus and the Julius I-Lupus group. The foot may belong to a gladiator; the motif at the base has no apparent parallel, but may be a basket of fruit, a variant of O25. Rim 67mm high. *c.* AD 210–235. (Fig. 123.20)

A[1131]

Drag 45, East Gaul, probably Trier; three sherds. First half third century.

A[1139]

Drag 37, East Gaul, Trier. Tip of ovolo above a wavy line border; below is a small arcade of long narrow beads and an unidentifiable motif. First half third century.

Sherd, East Gaul, Trier.

A[1214]

Base, cup form Drag 41; no decoration survives. East Gaul, Rheinzabern. First half third century. Worn base.

A[1219]

Drag 37 probably, East Gaul, Trier. First half third century.

A[1227]

Drag 31R/Lud Sb, East Gaul, Trier. Second quarter third century.

Dish sherd, East Gaul, Rheinzabern. Late second to mid-third century.

A[1249]

Round-bodied beaker or jar, or small version of the handled crater Drag 53, decorated with barbotine scrolls. East Gaul, Rheinzabern. Second quarter third century.

A[1276]

Dr 37, East Gaul, Rheinzabern; two sherds. Broken ovolo. Rim 50mm high.

Drag 45 with applied lion-head spout, East Gaul, Trier. The spout is similar to one found at St Magnus House (Bird 1986, no. 2.215), but the ears on the two bowls have been placed differently after the mask was applied and certain identification is not possible. The St Magnus mask is dated to the first half of the third century. Worn interior.

Dr 31R/Lud Sb, East Gaul, Trier. Early to mid third century.

A[1307]

Drag 30 or 37 base, Central Gaul, Lezoux. Mid- to late Antonine. Some wear on foot, the interior heavily burnt.

A[1323]

Drag 38, East Gaul, Trier; two sherds. A shallow version of the form, similar to the Trier 'Massenfund' type 15 (Bird 1993, fig 3), which could have served as a lid. Second quarter third century. The flange is broken off, and the slip almost completely gone.

Drag 31/Lud Sa or Dr 31R/Lud Sb, East Gaul, Trier. Early to mid third century.

Drag 31R/Lud Sb, East Gaul, Trier; seven sherds, probably all the same vessel. Early to mid third century.

Mortarium sherd, East Gaul, Rheinzabern. A very red fabric. The main trituration grits appear to be red-brown grog, as some contain quartz grains; the others are smaller, consisting of white, grey and pink quartz grains and a black grit, possibly also grog. Early to mid third century. Worn interior.

A[1338]

Drag 38, East Gaul, Trier. Shallow version of the form, with angular flange. Second quarter third century.

Drag 38, East Gaul, Trier. Shallow version, with angular flange. Second quarter third century.

A[1444]

Drag 45, East Gaul, Trier. Lower wall with at least six relatively deep and narrow grooves. Early to mid-third century. Grits heavily worn, most of them missing.

A[1447]

Drag 30, East Gaul, Rheinzabern. Parallel upright lines, probably z-corded: cf. Ricken and Thomas 2005, taf. 190, 4, 6 and 9, by Primitivus I. *c.* AD 215–240.

Drag 31R/Lud Sb, East Gaul, Trier; two sherds. Second quarter third century.

Drag 38, East Gaul, Trier; seven sherds. Early to mid third century. The flange has broken off; the slip is worn away except at the rim and the foot is worn.

A[1487]

Drag 37, East Gaul, Rheinzabern. The ovolo, Ricken and Fischer 1963, type E46, and rosette O48 were used by the Julius I-Lupus group. *c.* AD 210–235.

A[1511]

Drag 31R/Lud Sb, East Gaul, Rheinzabern. First half third century.

A[1515]

Drag 37 probably, East Gaul, Trier. First half third century.

A[1517]

Dish, Central Gaul, Lezoux, Hadrianic–Antonine.

A[1521]

Drag 30 or 37, Central Gaul, probably Les Martres-de-Veyre rather than one of the early Lezoux workshops. Trajanic–Hadrianic.

A[1525]

Drag 31R/Lud Sb, East Gaul, Trier. Early to mid third century.

Drag 38, East Gaul, Trier; three sherds. Early to mid third century. Worn interior.

East Gaulish sherd.

A[1526]

Drag 31R, Central Gaul, Lezoux. Mid to late Antonine. Slightly burnt.

Drag 31R/Lud Sb, East Gaul, Rheinzabern; two sherds. Later to mid third century.

A[1532]

Drag 33, East Gaul, Trier. Late second to mid third century.

Drag 33, East Gaul, Rheinzabern. Base conical underneath, no stamp. Second quarter third century.

A[1573]

Drag 18/31, Central Gaul, Lezoux. Hadrianic–Antonine.

A[1603]

Drag 45, Central Gaul, Lezoux. Late second century. Little wear on interior.

A[1610]

Drag 45, East Gaul, Trier. Early to mid-third century.

A[1612]

Drag 37 = pot in A[1045]. *q.v.* (Fig. 123.20)

A[1613]

Drag 31R/Lud Sb, East Gaul, Trier; two sherds. Wide band of feathered rouletting on the floor. Early to mid third century.

Drag 38, East Gaul, Trier; three sherds. Early to mid third century. Heavily worn inside; one sherd slightly burnt.

A[1615]

Wall-sided bowl, with the lower edge of the wall everted. This belongs to a series of late third- to fourth-century bowls, variant forms of Drag 44/Lud SMb with the straight upper wall of the mortarium Drag 45: cf Gose (1950) form 63, from Trier, and Chenet (1941) form 324, from the Argonne. The fabric, together with the regular occurrence on British sites of plain and roller-stamped Argonne vessels of late third- to fourth-century date (e.g. Bird 1995, 775), would suggest the Argonne as the source of this bowl. Poorly turned on the interior. Burnt.

A[1617]

Drag 37 probably, East Gaul, Rheinzabern; a small bowl. Late second to mid-third century

Drag 37 probably, East Gaul, Trier. First half third century

A[1619]

Drag 37 = pot in A[1045], *q.v.*

A[1627]

Drag 37 = pot in A[1045], *q.v.*

A[1628]

Dish form, East Gaul, Trier. Late second to mid-third century.

A[1762]

Drag 38, East Gaul, Trier; three sherds. Early to mid third century. Heavily worn interior; slightly burnt.

unstratified

Drag 37, East Gaul, Trier. The broken ovolo may be one used by the Afer-Marinus group (cf Bird 1986, nos. 2.73, 2.75-76). First half third century.

Drag 38, East Gaul, Trier. Second quarter third century.

Sherd, East Gaul, Trier.

Appendix 2: Summary list of Roman coins

The coins from Tobacco Dock (Site A) as identified by James Gerrard

Context	Small Find	Obverse	Reverse	Date	Comments
+	59	Illegible	Illegible	C3/C4	
+	359	Barb Rad	Illegible	270–290	
+	360	Illegible	Illegible	C3/C4	
+	569	Illegible	Illegible	C1/C2	
42	6	Illegible	Illegible	C3/C4	
45	320	Barb Rad	Illegible	270–290	Copy
110	76	Illegible	Illegible	C1/C2	
130	14	Illegible	CONSECRATIO, altar	270–290	
130	15	Valentinianic	GLORIA ROMANORUM	364–378	
130	16	Magnus Maximus/Flavius Victor	SPES ROMANORUM, camp gate	383–388	
130	18	Constantinian	GLORIA EXERCITUS, 2 soldiers, 1 standard	335–341	
130	19	Illegible	Illegible	C3/C4	
130	47	Constantinian	FEL TEMP REPARATIO, Emperor and 2 captives	348–350	
130	167	Illegible	Illegible	C3/C4	
195	64	Illegible	Illegible	296–318?	
195	67	Illegible	Illegible	296–318?	
195	68	Illegible	Illegible	C1/C2	
195	69	Illegible	Illegible	C1/C2	
195	71	Illegible	Illegible	C3/C4	
195	72	Illegible	Illegible	294–324	
205	104	Constantinian	GLORIA EXERCITUS, 2 soldiers, 1 standard	335–341	Copy
250	108	Constantinian	GLORIA EXERCITUS, 2 soldiers, 2 standards	330–335	
250	150	Illegible	Illegible	C3/C4	
285	217	Illegible	Illegible	C3/C4	
292	418	Constantinian	Wreath	318–324	MM: LON
319	361	Constantius II	FEL TEMP REPARATIO, falling horseman	354–364	
325	45	Constantinian	VICTORIAE DDAVGQNN	343–348	
325	46	Constantinian	FEL TEMP REPARATIO, falling horseman	354–364	
325	51	Barb Rad		270–290	
325	169	Illegible	Illegible	C3/C4	
369	178	Radiate	Horse	Late C3	
371	1770	Illegible	Illegible	C3/C4	
378	185	Barb Rad	Illegible	270–290	
378	186	Illegible	Illegible	C3/C4	
384	184	Constantine I	Wreath?	318–324	
384	190	Illegible	Illegible	C3/C4	
403	191	Illegible	Illegible	C3/C4	
403	312	Illegible	Illegible	C3/C4	
451	210	Barb Rad		270–290	
451	211	Illegible	Illegible	C3/C4	
451	215	Illegible	Illegible	C3/C4	
456	216	Illegible	Illegible	C3/C4	
496	214	Claudius II	SALVS AVG	268–270	
529	321	Illegible	Illegible	C3/C4	
529	326	Illegible	Illegible	C3/C4	
529	428	Nuremburg Jeton		1500–1600	
545	218	Barb Rad	Illegible	270–290	
576	204	Maximinus	GENIO POPULI ROMANI	294–307	
607	207	Illegible	Illegible	C3/C4	
609	275	Illegible	Illegible	C3/C4	
618	276	Tetricus I		270–273	
618	277	DIADEM	Illegible	324+	Copy

Context	Small Find	Obverse	Reverse	Date	Comments
618	278	Illegible	Illegible	C3/C4	
618	395	Illegible	Illegible	C3/C4	
654	208	Diadem		324+	
654	254	Illegible	Illegible	C3/C4	
657	230	Urbs Roma	Wolf and Twins	330–335	
660	389	Constantinian	FEL TEMP REPARATIO, Emperor with 2 captives	348–350	Copy
660	410	Barb Rad		270–290	Copy
660	712	Valentinianic	GLORIA ROMANORUM	364–378	
668	324	Illegible	Illegible	C3/C4	
676	442	Barb Rad	Illegible	270–290	
676	443	Barb Rad		270–290	
698	241	Carausius	LAETITIA	286–293	
698	242	Illegible	Illegible	C3/C4	
718	301	Constantinian	GLORIA EXERCITUS, 2 soldiers, 1 standard	335–341	Copy
718	313	Constantine I	PROVIDENTIA AVG. camp gate	324–330	MM: PTR~.
718	314	Helena	SECURITAS REIPUBLICAE	324–330	
718	315	Illegible	Illegible	C3/C4	
718	316	Constantinian	FEL TEMP REPARATIO, falling horseman	354–361	
718	317	Illegible	Illegible	C3/C4	
718	318	Illegible	Illegible	C3/C4	
719	337	Illegible	Illegible	C3/C4	
719	338	Valentinianic	GLORIA ROMANORUM	364–378	
719	339	Constantinian	GLORIA EXERCITUS, 2 soldiers, 2 standards	330–335	MM: TR
719	340	Constantinian	GLORIA EXERCITUS, 2 soldiers, 1 standard	335–341	
719	341	Honorius	VICTORIA AVGGG	394–402	MM: PCON, LRBCII, 570
719	342	Barb Rad		270–290	Copy
719	343	Illegible	Illegible	C3/C4	
719	344	Valentinianic	GLORIA ROMANORUM	364–378	
719	345	Constantinian	FEL TEMP REPARATIO, Falling horseman	354–361	
719	346	Postumus	standing figure	259–268	
719	347	Illegible	Illegible	C3/C4	
719	348	Barb Rad?	CONSECRATIO, altar	270–290	Copy
719	349	Barb Rad		270–290	Copy
719	350	Constantinian	VICTORIAE DDAVGGQNN	343–348	Copy
719	351	Radiate		260–296	
719	352	Illegible	Illegible	C3/C4	Copy
719	353	Illegible	Illegible	C3/C4	
722	431	Constantinopolis	Victory on prow	330–335	
722	433	Illegible	Illegible	C3/C4	
722	434	Illegible	Illegible	C3/C4	
722	435	Illegible	Illegible	C3/C4	
722	436	Illegible	Illegible	C3/C4	
722	437	Illegible	Illegible	C3/C4	
722	438	Illegible	Illegible	C3/C4	
722	439	Constantinian	GLORIA EXERCITUS, 2 soldiers, 1 standard	335–341	
722	440	Illegible	Illegible	C3/C4	
722	441	Illegible	Illegible	C3/C4	
722	543	Constantinian	GLORIA EXERCITUS, 2 soldiers, 2 standards	330–335	
722	605	Illegible	Illegible	C3/C4	
728	325	Illegible	Illegible	C3/C4	
731	240	Illegible	Illegible	C1/C2	
750	393	Illegible	Illegible	C3/C4	
800	362	Valens	SECURITAS REIPUBLICAE	364–378	
800	367	Diadem	Illegible	324+	
820	373	Barb Rad	Illegible	270–290	
846	384	Illegible	Illegible	270–290	
846	385	Illegible	Illegible	C3/C4	
846	386	Illegible	Illegible	C3/C4	

Context	Small Find	Obverse	Reverse	Date	Comments
846	387	Illegible	Illegible	C3/C4	
846	391	Illegible	Illegible	C3/C4	
846	486	Illegible	Illegible	C3/C4	
846	487	Barb Rad, Tetricus II	Illegible	270–290	Copy
846	489	Illegible	Illegible	C3/C4	
848	375	Illegible	Illegible	C3/C4	
856	411	Diocletianic follis	Illegible	294–307	
856	412	Illegible	Illegible	C3/C4	
856	413	Barb Rad		270–290	
856	414	Constantinian	GLORIA EXERCITUS, 2 soldiers, 1 standard	330–335	MM: CONST
856	415	Tetricus		270–273	
856	416	Illegible	Illegible	C3/C4	
856	419	Illegible	Illegible	C3/C4	
862	401	Illegible	Illegible	270–290	
862	402	Illegible	Illegible	C3/C4	
864	488	Illegible	Illegible	C3/C4	
904	409	Valentinianic	SECURITAS REIPUBLICAE	364–378	MM: Arles
908	408	Constantine I	SOLI INVICTO COMITI	316–317	MM: T/F/PLN
909	483	Illegible	Illegible	C3/C4	
1028	424	Constantinian	Illegible	318–324	
1028	429.1	Follis		296–318	
1028	429.2	Follis		296–318	
1028	429.3	Follis		296–318	
1028	430	Illegible		C1–C2	
1060	445	Carausius	Pax	286–293	
1060	462	Illegible	Illegible	C3/C4	
1060	463	Illegible	Illegible	C3/C4	
1060	464	Illegible	Illegible	C3/C4	
1060	465	Illegible	Illegible	C3/C4	
1060	466	Barb Rad	Illegible	270–290	Copy
1060	467	Constantinian	GLORIA EXERCITUS, 2 soldiers, 1 standard	335–341	Copy
1060	468	Illegible	Illegible	C3/C4	
1060	469	Illegible	Illegible	C3/C4	
1060	470	Illegible	Illegible	C3/C4	
1060	471	Illegible	Illegible	C3/C4	
1060	472	Illegible	Illegible	C3/C4	
1060	473	Illegible	Illegible	C3/C4	
1060	475	Illegible	Illegible	C3/C4	
1060	490	Illegible	Illegible	270–290	
1060	491	Victorinus?		268–270	
1131	506	Illegible	Illegible	C3/C4	
1139	447	Claudius II	Eagle, CONSECRATIO	268–270	
1139	448	Constantinian	PROVIDENTIAE CAES, camp gate	324–330	MM: SMANTE
1139	449	Constantinian	FEL TEMP REP FH	354–364	copy
1139	450	Illegible	Illegible	C3/C4	
1139	451	Illegible	Illegible	C3/C4	
1139	452	Magnentius	VICTORIAE DDNNAVGETCAES	350–353	
1139	454	Illegible	Illegible	C3/C4	
1139	455	Barb Rad		270–290	
1139	457	Barb Rad	Victory	260–290	Copy
1139	461	Illegible	Illegible	C3/C4	
1139	494	Barb Rad	Illegible	270–290	Copy
1139	495	Illegible	Illegible	C3/C4	
1139	497	Illegible	Illegible	C3/C4	
1154	492	Barb Rad	Illegible	270–290	Copy
1214	484	Illegible	Illegible	C3/C4	
1249	499	Illegible	Illegible	C1/C2	
1259	498	Barb Rad	Illegible	270–290	Copy
1269	493	Constantinian	GLORIA EXERCITUS, 2 soldiers, 1 standard	335–341	

Context	Small Find	Obverse	Reverse	Date	Comments
1276	503	Alexander Severus	Illegible	222–235	
1276	580	Illegible	Illegible	C3/C4	
1281	527	Constantinian	VICTORIAE DDNNAVGQNN	350–353	
1307	510	Illegible	Illegible	C3/C4	
1307	511	Illegible	Illegible	C3/C4	
1307	512	Barb Rad	Illegible	270–290	
1307	513	Illegible	Illegible	C3/C4	
1307	514	Radiate	Illegible	238–260	
1307	515	Carausius	Pax?	286–293	
1307	516	Tetricus?	Standing fig	270–273	
1307	517	Illegible	Illegible	C3/C4	
1307	518	Illegible	Illegible	C3/C4	
1307	519	Barb Rad	Illegible	270–290	
1307	520	Illegible	Illegible	C3/C4	
1307	521	Illegible	Illegible	C3/C4	
1307	522	Illegible	Illegible	C3/C4	
1307	523	Illegible	Illegible	C3/C4	
1307	533	Illegible	Illegible	C3/C4	
1307	534	Illegible	Illegible	C3/C4	
1307	535	Illegible	Illegible	C3/C4	
1307	536	Illegible	Illegible	C3/C4	
1307	537	Illegible	Illegible	C3/C4	
1307	538	Illegible	Illegible	C3/C4	
1307	539	Radiate	Illegible	238–290	
1307	540	Radiate	Illegible	238–290	
1307	541	Illegible	Illegible	C3/C4	
1307	688	Illegible	Illegible	C3/C4	
1308	504	Gallienus?	VIRTVS	253–268	
1308	505	Illegible	Illegible	C3/C4	
1341	560	Claudius II	CONSECRATIO, altar	268–270	
1372	544	Constantinian	VICTORIAE DDAVGQNN	343–348	Copy
1379	551	Illegible	Illegible	C1/C2	
1427	552	Constantinian	VICTORIAE DDAVGGQNN	343–348	
1444	582	Constantinian	FEL TEMP REPARATIO, falling horseman	354–361	Copy
1449	555	Illegible	Illegible	C3/C4	
1449	556	Barb Rad	Illegible	270–290	Copy
1449	557	Barb Rad	Illegible	270–290	
1449	558	Barb Rad		270–290	
1449	559	Barb Rad	Illegible	270–290	
1473	561	Magnentius	VICTORIAE DDNNAVGETCAES	350–353	MM: TRS copy
1473	565	Barb Rad	Illegible	270–290	
1473	566	Illegible	Illegible	C3/C4	
1473	567	Constantinian	FEL TEMP REPARATIO, falling horseman	354–361	
1473	570	Illegible	Illegible	C3/C4	
1474	573	Barb Rad	Illegible	270–290	
1515	689	Illegible	Illegible	C3/C4	
1515	690	Illegible	Illegible	C3/C4	
1515	703	Constantinian	GLORIA EXERCITUS, 2 soldiers, 1 standard	335–341	Copy
1517	571	Illegible	Illegible	C3/C4	
1517	572	Aurelian	Sol?	270–275	
1535	307	Illegible	Illegible	C3/C4	
1610	588	Barb Rad	Illegible	270–290	
1616	585	Illegible	Illegible	C3/C4	
1646	663	Barb Rad	Illegible	270–290	
1648	593	Claudius II	CONSECRATIO altar	268–270	
1648	597	Barb Rad	Illegible	270–290	
1676	595	Magnentius	VICTORIAE DDNNAVGETCAES	350–353	Copy

Table 39 The coins from Site A (Tobacco Dock)

The coins from the Babe Ruth site (Site B) as identified by Mike Hammerson

Context	SF	Identification	Date
+	20	Irreg. Gallic Empire	260–285
+	111	Illeg.	?
+	112	Sestertius, ?Trajan	?96–117
+	113	Sestertius, ?Antoninus Pius	?140–180
+	114	Irregular AE 15mm	270–285 or 340–365
+	115	Irregular Urbs Roma, TRS	340–350
+	116	Irreg. Claudius II, rev. CONSECRATIO, rev. Altar	260–285
+	117	Irreg. Gallic Empire	260–285
+	118	Gallienus, Ant., DIANAE CONS AVG, Deer L, /XII	259–268
+	119	Irregular Urbs Roma, TRS.	340–350
+	120	Irreg. Gallic Empire, AE 17mm	260–285
+	121	Gratian, poss. cast copy, SECVRITAS REIPVBLICAE, K A-F/ASISCP	367–375
+	122	Irreg. Tetricus I	260–285
+	123	Irreg. Gallic Empire	260–285
+	124	Probus, Ant., rev. un	276–282
+	125	Irreg. Gallic Empire,	260–285
+	126	Irregular AE 18mm, prob. cast copy 270-285 or 340-365	270–285 or 340–365
+	127	Sestertius, Flavian-Trajanic	80–120
+	129	Irreg. Gallic Empire	260–285
+	136	Irreg. Gallic Empire	260–285
+	207	Illegible	260–295
+	435	Irreg.,prob. Gallic Empire	?270–285
+	519	Gallienus, 259-268, apparently part-overstruck by ?Gallic Empire	270–285
+	520	As/Dup., illegible	40–120
+	521	Gratian, VOT XV MVLT XX	378–383
+	522	Gratian, VICTORIA AVGGG, Emperor l with wreath & palm	378–383
+	523	Irreg. Gallic Empire	260–285
+	524	Gallic Empire	259–273
+	525	poss. Carausius	?287–293
+	526	Carausius	287–293
+	527	Valens	364–378
+	528	Tetricus I, poss. irregular	270–285
+	529	Valentinianic,GLORIA ROMANORVM, prob. cast copy	365–375
+	530	Two ants. One Tetricus I, overlapping & fused together	?270–273
+	531	Septimius Severus, AR den. (or AR plated copy on AE core?),]ERVS PI[, cut in half in antiquity	195–210
+	532	poss. AR plated copy of den., 200-250, or Gallic empire.	200–250 or 260–285
+	533	Gallic Empire, poss. Irreg.	260–285
+	534	Irregular Constantius II, fallen horseman, well made	355–365
+	535	Postumus, prob. Irregular	270–285
+	536	Irreg. Gallic Empire, broken	260–285
+	537	Gallienus, Ant., DIANAE CONS AVG, Deer L, /XII	259–268
+	538	Irreg. Gallic Empire	260–285
+	539	Irreg. prob. Gallic Empire	?270–285
+	541	Claudius II, GENIO AVG, poss. irregular	268–285
+	542	Gallienus, DIANAE CONS AVG, Deer L, /XII	259–268
+	543	Irreg. prob. Gallic Empire	?270–285
+	544	Constantinopolis, poss. irregular	330–350
+	545	Illeg. ant.	260–295
+	546	As/Dup., illegible	40–120
+	566	Irreg. Gallic Empire	260–285
+	567	Un Folles	310–320
+	142	Irreg. Gallic Empire, crude	270–285
+	143	Claudius II, Ant., rev. FELICITAS	268–270
+	144	Gallienus, Ant., SALVS	259–268
+	145	Tetricus I, poss. irreg.	270–285

Context	SF	Identification	Date
+	146	Gallic Empire, poss. irregular	270–285
+	147	Irreg. Gallic Empire,	270–285
+	148	Irreg. Gallic Empire,	270–285
+	149	Irreg. Tetricus II, PIETAS AVGG	270–285
+	500	Irregular, broken	270–285 or 340–365
+	501	Irreg. Gallic Empire	270–285
+	502	Licinius I, follis, IOVI CONSERVATORI, ( ) III/]ARL	315–320
+	503	Irregular	270–285 or 340–365
+	504	Irregular	270–285 or 340–365
+	505	Postumus, Antoninianus	259–268
+	513	Irreg. Gallic Empire,	270–285
+	514	Constantinian, Two Victories poss. irregular	348–350
+	515	Claudius II, Ant., AEQVITAS AVG	268–270
+	516	Valentinianic, Cast copy, GLORIA ROMANORVM, ( )/)CONST	365–375
+	517	Illegible	270–275
+	518	Illegible	270–275
+	554	Irregular, broken	270–285 or 340–365
+	137	Irregular Constantinopolis	340–350
+	138	Irregular Constantinian, two standards	340–350
1	464	Illegible	270–275
180	26	Valentinianic, GLORIA ROMANORVM, poss. cast copy	365–380
180	27	Illegible	320–375
180	43	Tetricus II	260–273
180	44	Illeg. irregular	270–285 or 340–365
180	45	Claudius II, Ant., rev. CONSECRATIO, eagle	270
180	46	Illeg.	260–295 or 330–365
180	47	Illeg.	260–285
180	48	Illeg. Irregular	270–285 or 340–365
180	55	Claudius II, Ant., rev. CONSECRATIO, altar	270
180	59	Crispus, VOT X/CAESARVM NOSTRORVM, RIC (Trier) 440	323–324
182	106	As./Dup.	40–140
184	100	Irregular	340–365
184	104	Irreg.	270–285 or 340–365
184	130	Illeg.	270–285 or 340–365
184	34	Illeg.	270–275
186	36	Irregular Constantine II	340–350
190	54	Illeg, prob. irreg.	270–285 or 340–365
190	56	Valentinian I, SECVRITAS REIPVBLICAE, OF - II/LVGP, poss cast copy	364–78
190	57	Illeg. prob. irregular 270–285 or 340–365	270–285 or 340–365
190	58	Irreg. Gallic Empire, v. crude	270–285
192	37	Valentinianic, GLORIA ROMANORVM, cast copy	365–375
194	107	Irreg. Gallic Empire	270–285
194	108	Gallienus	259–268
194	38	Irreg. Gallic Empire	270–285
194	78	Tacitus, AEQVITAS AVG	275–276
196	65	Valentinianic, SECVRITAS REIPVBLICAE, thin cast copy	365–380
196	66	Irregular	270–285 or 340–365
196	67	Ant., poss. Valerian I	?253–260
196	68	prob. Ant., badly broken	260–295
196	69	Irreg. Gallic Empire	270–285
196	70	Gallic Empire, AE Ant. poss. irreg.	260–285
2	467	Illeg. irregular	270–285
2	468	Irregular Gallic Empire	270–285
202	75	Illeg. irregular 270-285 or 340-365	270–285 or 340–365
210	150	Illeg.	260–275
210	80	Diocletian or Maximian, follis, VOT/XX/S, Ticinum, unusual British site find	299
210	81	Cast copy, Gallic empire	270–285
216	82	Illeg. Irregular	270–285 or 340–365
216	83	Carausius or Allectus, frag. of Ant., broken in antiquity, (ML)	287–296

Context	SF	Identification	Date
222	85	Valentinianic, GLORIA ROMANORVM OF-II/LVGP, prob. cast copy	365–375
224	86	Irregular Constantinian, two standards, TRS	340–350
224	87	Irregular Gallic empire,	270–285
227	88	Irreg. Gallic Empire,	270–285
232	91	Tetricus II, Ant., SPES AVGG	270–273
234	96	Irregular Tetricus II	270–285
235	93	Illeg.	270–285 or 340–365
240	151	Irregular Constantinian, one standard	340–350
240	152	Illeg.	260–285
240	154	Illeg.	260–285
240	155	Irreg. Gallic Empire	270–285
240	157	AE fragment, coin?	?
240	99	Claudius II, Ant.	268–270
243	153	Irreg. Gallic Empire	270–285
247	171	Illeg. irregular,	270–285 or 340–365
250	156	Carausius, Ant., trace of silver wash?	287–293
250	163	Urbs Roma, Wolf and Twins	330–335
250	164	Irregular Constantinian, one Standard,)LG	340–350
250	165	Irregular Tetricus II	270–285
252	200	Constantinian, VICTORIA AVGVSTORVM, LRBC1.254-5, v. unusual British find	341
252	201	Gallienus, Ant.	259–268
254	172	Constantinian, poss. irreg.	330–365
256	176	prob. Ant.	260–280
256	177	Illeg. prob. Ant	?260–280
256	178	Illeg. prob. Ant	?260–280
256	182	Illeg. Prob. irreg	270–285 or 340–365
264	187	prob. Ant.	260–285
264	188	Illeg. irregular	270–285 or 340–365
264	189	Irreg. Gallic empire	270–285
264	190	Irregular Constantinian, Two Standards	340–350
266	199	Illeg. prob. Ant.	260–285
283	206	Tacitus, Ant.	275–276
305	214	Irregular Urbs Roma	340–350
314	220	Irregular Constantine II, Two Standards, TRP	340–350
326	229	Irregular Gallic Empire	270–285
339	232	Urbs Roma, poss. irregular,)SIS(	330–350
386	270	Illeg.	270–285
390	244	Illeg.	260–285
390	245	Illeg.	270–285 or 330–365
390	246	Sestertius, illeg.	140–190
390	248	Ant., illegible	260–285
390	249	Illegible, prob. Gallic Empire	260–285
435	281	Prob. irregular	prob. 270–285
435	282	Postumus, Ant., broken	259–268
445	288	Cast copy, Constantinian	340–350
445	289	Irregular	270–285 or 330–365
453	291	Irregular Fallen Horseman, cast flan	355–365
453	292	Carausius, Ant.	287–293
453	293	Postumus, Ant., VIRTVS AVG	259–268
453	294	Irregular Fallen Horseman, cast flan	355–365
453	295	Irregular Gallic Empire, poss. Tetricus II rev. Pietas	270–285
46	311	Tetricus II, Ant.	270–273
465	318	Uncertain. Poss. Constantinian AE3, 330-340, but could possibly be a plated AE copy	?
466	303	Claudius II, prob. irregular	prob. 270–285
466	304	Illeg., some lettering on x-ray	prob. 260–285
466	305	Irregular Gallic Empire, crude, rev. fig. w/spear & cornucopiae?	270–275
466	306	Irregular Gallic Empire, v. crude	270–275
466	307	Irregular Claudius II, rev. animal	270–275
466	308	Irregular Gallic Empire, v. crude design and flan	270–275

Context	SF	Identification	Date
466	309	Irregular Tetricus II	270–275
466	310	Illeg. broken	270–285 or 330–365
466	312	Irregular Gallic Empire	270–275
470	135	Illeg. prob. irregular Gallic Empire	?270–285
470	321	Illeg. irregular	270–285 or 340–365
470	322	Irregular Tetricus I	270–285
470	323	Irregular Gallic Empire, broken	270–285
470	324	Illeg. Ant., possibly Allectus	?293–296
470	325	Illeg., irregular	
470	326	Illeg., irregular	270–285 or 340–365
470	327	Illeg. AE, irregular	270–285 or 340–365
470	330	Irregular Gallic Empire	270–285
470	331	Probus, Ant., RIC 752, rev. SALVS AVG	276–279
470	332	Illeg. irregular	270–285 or 340–365
470	334	Irregular Gallic Empire	270–285
496	400	Irregular Constantinian	340–365
496	401	Illeg. irregular	270–285 or 340–365
500	339	Irregular Gallic Empire	270–285
541	351	Illegible Ant.	260–275
549	363	Illeg, irregular	270–285 or 340–365
575	365	Irregular Gallic Empire	270–285
579	366	Constantine I, Follis, MARTI CONSERVATORI	313–316
580	369	Prob. Ant.	prob. 260–275
586	371	Irreg. Gallic Empire	270–285
586	372	Irregular Claudius II, rev. CONSECRATIO, eagle	270–285
586	373	Claudius II, Ant., DIANAE CONS AVG, deer	268–270
588	381	Claudius II, Ant., Sol stg. l.	268–270
595	376	Constantine I, follis, rev. BEATA TRANQVILLITAS, probably an irregular copy	340–350
595	377	Prob. irregular Constantinian	340–365
648	388	Irregular Gallic Empire.	270–285
658	390	Sestertius, poss. Antonine (Faustina II?)	140–180
679	396	Irregular V. corroded	270–285 or 340–365
704	406	Irregular Gallic Empire, rev. VIRTVS, v. crude	270–285
704	407	Gallienus, Ant., VBERITAS AVG	259–268
704	408	Irregular Gallic Empire, struck off flan, broken	270–285
721	412	Sestertius, Hadrian or Antoninus Pius	120–160
862	568	Claudius II, Ant.	268–270
386	268.1	Postumus, Ant	259–268
386	268.2	Postumus, Ant	259–268
386	268.3	Postumus, Ant	259–268

Table 40 The coins from site B (Babe Ruth site)

Appendix 3:
Full catalogue of Roman glass

Site A

Polychrome

1. A[660] A<390> Fig. 103.1
Period 7, dumped deposit/open ground.

Fragment of flat polychrome mosaic glass in translucent green with yellow and red canes; probably the flat part of a plate or tray or a piece of inlay from furniture. First century.

Colourless glass

2. A[660]
Period 7, dumped deposits/open ground.

Fragment of colourless, bubbled glass with a green tint and faint wheel-cut horizontal lines in a band. Probably from a bowl, cup or beaker. Late third or fourth century.

3. A[1608]
Period 5.2, Building 9.

Fragment from the rim of a beaker in colourless, bubbled glass with a green tint. Has a cracked off, slightly out-turned rim with faint wheel-cut horizontal lines in bands immediately under the rim and further down the vessel. Late third or fourth century.

Naturally coloured glass

4. A[1307] Fig. 103.2
Period 5.2, disuse of Building 8.

Neck and rim in natural blue-green glass from an unguent bottle or flask with a flared out and fire rounded rim, or possible unguent bottle with indents? Late first or early second century.

5. A[657]
Residual in post-medieval context.

Two adjoining fragments of natural, pale green glass from the handle of a bath flask. *c.* AD 75–250.

6. A[1613]
Period 5.1, dumped deposit.

Fragment of natural blue-green, slightly bubbled glass from a square-sectioned bottle or flask. First or second century.

7. A[846]
Period 5.2, slope erosion.

Fragment of natural blue-green glass from a ribbed ribbon handle. First to third century.

8. A[846]
Period 5.2, slope erosion.

Fragment of natural blue-green glass from the base of a bulbous vessel. First to third century.

9. A[1449] A<554>
Period 5.1, Building 8.

Fragment of natural blue-green glass from a ribbon handle with three broad ribs. First to third century.

Window Glass

10. A[849]
Period 5.1, fill of E/W revetted ditch.

Fragment of natural pale blue-green matt-glossy window glass. First to third century.

11. A[849]
Period 5.1, fill of E/W revetted ditch.

Fragment of natural pale blue-green matt-glossy window glass. First to third century.

12. A[1145]
Period 6, Building 11.

Fragment of natural pale green matt-glossy window glass. First to third century. 5 x fragments of pale green window glass with surface weathering.

13. A[667]
Residual in post-medieval context.

Fragment of pale green window glass with surface weathering

14. A[667]
Residual in post-medieval context.

Fragment of pale green window glass with surface weathering

15. A[667]
Residual in post-medieval context.

Fragment of pale green window glass with surface weathering

16. A[667]
Residual in post-medieval context.

Fragment of pale green window glass with surface weathering

17. A[667]
Residual in post-medieval context.

Fragment of pale green window glass with surface weathering

Tessera

18. A[1307] A<531>
Period 5.2, disuse of Building 8.

A dark blue *tessera*.

Natural blue indeterminate vessel fragments

Six fragments of natural blue glass from free-blown vessels of indeterminate form. Roman.

19. A[357]
Residual in post-medieval context.

Fragment of natural blue glass from free-blown vessels of indeterminate form. Roman.

20. A[722]
Period 7, dumped deposits/open ground.

Fragment of natural blue glass from free-blown vessels of indeterminate form. Roman.

21. A[1139]
Period 6, Building 11.

Fragment of natural blue glass from free-blown vessels of indeterminate form. Roman.

22. A[1214]
Period 5.1, dumped deposits.

Fragment of natural blue glass from free-blown vessels of indeterminate form. Roman.

23. A[1307]
Period 5.2, disuse of Building 8.

Fragment of natural blue glass from free-blown vessels of indeterminate form. Roman.

24. A[1307]
Period 5.2, disuse of Building 8.

Fragment of natural blue glass from free-blown vessels of indeterminate form. Roman.

Natural blue green indeterminate vessel fragments

Eight fragments of natural blue green glass from free-blown vessels of indeterminate form. Roman.

25. A[568]
Residual in post-medieval context.

Fragment of natural blue green glass from free-blown vessel of indeterminate form. Roman.

26. A[660]
Period 7, dumped deposit/open ground.

Fragment of natural blue green glass from free-blown vessel of indeterminate form. Roman.

27. A[667]
Residual in post-medieval context.

Fragment of natural blue green glass from free-blown vessel of indeterminate form. Roman.

28. A[846]
Period 5.2, slope erosion.

Fragment of natural blue green glass from free-blown vessel of indeterminate form. Roman.

29. A[1028]
Period 7, dumped deposit/open ground.

Fragment of natural blue green glass from free-blown vessel of indeterminate form. Roman.

30. A[1060]
Period 7, dumped deposit/open ground.

Fragment of natural blue green glass from free-blown vessel of indeterminate form. Roman.

31. A[1060]
Period 7, dumped deposit/open ground.

Fragment of natural blue green glass from free-blown vessel of indeterminate form. Roman.

32. A[1307]
Period 5.2, disuse of Building 8.

Fragment of natural blue green glass from free-blown vessel of indeterminate form. Roman.

Natural blue-green, fire distorted, indeterminate vessel fragments

34. A[722]
Period 7, dumped deposit.

A fragment of fire-distorted natural blue glass from a vessel of indeterminate form. Roman.

Colourless indeterminate vessel fragments

Six fragments of colourless glass from free-blown vessels of indeterminate form.

35. A[849]
Period 5.1, E/W revetted ditch.

A fragment of colourless glass from free-blown vessel of indeterminate form.

36. A[1060]
Period 7, dumped deposit/open ground.

A fragment of colourless glass from free-blown vessel of indeterminate form.

37. A[1060]
Period 7, dumped deposit/open ground.

A fragment of colourless glass from free-blown vessel of indeterminate form.

38. A[1139]
Period 6, Building 11.

A fragment of colourless glass from free-blown vessel of indeterminate form.

39. A[1281]
Period 6, well.

A fragment of colourless glass from free-blown vessel of indeterminate form.

40. A[1433]
Period 5.1, Building 8.

A fragment of colourless glass from free-blown vessel of indeterminate form.

Colourless with green tint indeterminate vessel fragments

Twenty-three fragments of colourless glass, with green tints, from free-blown vessels of indeterminate form.

41. A[378]
Period 6, ditches.

A fragment of colourless glass, with green tints, from free-blown vessel of indeterminate form.

42. A[529]
Period 6, dumped deposit.

A fragment of colourless glass, with green tints, from free-blown vessel of indeterminate form.

43. A[529]
Period 6, dumped deposit.

A fragment of colourless glass, with green tints, from free-blown vessel of indeterminate form.

44. A[529]
Period 6, dumped deposit.
A fragment of colourless glass, with green tints, from free-blown vessel of indeterminate form.

45. A[660]
Period 7, dumped deposit/open ground.
A fragment of colourless glass, with green tints, from free-blown vessel of indeterminate form.

46. A[660]
Period 7, dumped deposit/open ground.
A fragment of colourless glass, with green tints, from free-blown vessel of indeterminate form.

47. A[660]
Period 7, dumped deposit/open ground.
A fragment of colourless glass, with green tints, from free-blown vessel of indeterminate form.

48. A[722]
Period 7, dumped deposit/open ground.
A fragment of colourless glass, with green tints, from free-blown vessel of indeterminate form.

49. A[722]
Period 7, dumped deposit/open ground.
A fragment of colourless glass, with green tints, from free-blown vessel of indeterminate form.

50. A[722]
Period 7, dumped deposit/open ground.
A fragment of colourless glass, with green tints, from free-blown vessel of indeterminate form.

51. A[722]
Period 7, dumped deposit/open ground.
A fragment of colourless glass, with green tints, from free-blown vessel of indeterminate form.

52. A[722]
Period 7, dumped deposit/open ground.
A fragment of colourless glass, with green tints, from free-blown vessel of indeterminate form.

53. A[722]
Period 7, dumped deposit/open ground.
A fragment of colourless glass, with green tints, from free-blown vessel of indeterminate form.

54. A[846]
Period 5.2, slope erosion.
A fragment of colourless glass, with green tints, from free-blown vessel of indeterminate form.

55. A[1060]
Period 7, dumped deposit/open ground.
A fragment of colourless glass, with green tints, from free-blown vessel of indeterminate form.

56. A[1139]
Period 6, Building 11.
A fragment of colourless glass, with green tints, from free-blown vessel of indeterminate form.

57. A[1139]
Period 6, Building 11.
A fragment of colourless glass, with green tints, from free-blown vessel of indeterminate form.

58. A[1139]
Period 6, Building 11.
A fragment of colourless glass, with green tints, from free-blown vessel of indeterminate form.

59. A[1139]
Period 6, Building 11.
A fragment of colourless glass, with green tints, from free-blown vessel of indeterminate form.

60. A[1139]
Period 6, Building 11.
A fragment of colourless glass, with green tints, from free-blown vessel of indeterminate form.

61. A[1281]
Period 6, well.
A fragment of colourless glass, with green tints, from free-blown vessel of indeterminate form.

62. A[1535]
Period 5.2, post demolition pitting.
A fragment of colourless glass, with green tints, from free-blown vessel of indeterminate form.

63. A[1615]
Period 6, well.
A fragment of colourless glass, with green tints, from free-blown vessel of indeterminate form.

Site B

Colourless Glass

64. B[467] Fig. 103.3
Period 7, demolition and robbing.
Fragment of very thin colourless glass with flaky iridescent surface patina from a cup with wheel-cut decoration of oval facets and wheel-cut lines. Mid to late second century.

65. B[726]
Period 4.2, service yard.
Three adjoining fragments from the rim of a cup in colourless glass with a green tint. Knocked-off rim. Mid to late second century.

66. B[140] Fig. 103.4
Period 4.3, recut of boundary ditch.
Six fragments from the rim and body of a cup or beaker in thin colourless glass with a slightly out-turned rim, cracked off and ground. Evidence of horizontal wheel-cut lines below the rim and just above the change in angle on the profile. Late first to mid second century.

67. B[272]

Residual in post-medieval context.

Two adjoining fragments of very thin colourless glass from the rim and body of a cup with a cracked off and ground rim which is slightly out-turned. Decorated with horizontal wheel-cut lines. Second or third century.

68. B[752]

Period 3, service yard.

Fragment as for no.67 above but from a different vessel.

69. B[140]

Period 4.3, recut of boundary ditch.

Two body fragments of colourless glass with a green tint from a cup, beaker or small bowl. One fragment has a band of horizontal wheel-cut lines. Second century.

70. B[247] B<167>

Residual in post-medieval context.

Three body fragments of very thin colourless glass with iridescent surface patina from a cup or beaker. One fragment has evidence of wheel-cut horizontal lines. *c.* AD 140–180.

71. B[339]

Period 5.1, Building 7.

Fragment of very thin colourless glass from a cup or beaker with faint wheel-cut horizontal lines. Second or third century.

72. B[407]

Period 5.1, Building 7.

Three fragments of thin colourless glass probably from the same cup or beaker. Two fragments have faint wheel-cut horizontal lines. Second or third century.

73. B[553]

Period 4.2, Building 3b.

Fragment of thin colourless glass from the body of a cup decorated with faint wheel-cut horizontal lines. Second or third century.

74. B[726]

Period 4.2, service yard.

Two adjoining fragments of colourless glass from a cup or beaker with horizontal wheel-cut decoration. Late first to fourth century.

75. B[518]

Period 4.5, pitting.

Fragment from the rim of an 'Airlie' type cup. Free-blown; colourless glass. Rim fire-rounded and sloping slightly inwards. Late second or early third century.

76. B[518]

Period 4.5, pitting.

As for no.75 above, but from a different vessel.

77. B[400]

Period 5.1, dump layers.

As for no. 75 above but from a different vessel.

78. B[485]

Period 4.3, Building 3c.

As for no. 75 above but from a different vessel.

79. B[214]

Period 6, E/W ditch.

As for no. 75 above but from a different vessel.

80. B[750] Fig. 103.5

Period 3, Building 3.

Base and 8 body fragments of colourless glass from an Airlie cup with a pushed in outer ring and an applied inner ring on the base. (Isings 85b). Late second or early third century.

81. B[750] Fig. 103.6

Period 3, Building 3.

As for no.80 above but from a different vessel.

82. B[554] Fig. 103.7

Period 5.1, service yard.

As for no. 80 above but from a different vessel.

83. B[502]

Period 7, robber trench.

Two fragments of colourless glass from the neck of a flagon with a flattened form. Has an applied handle in the same metal which is very thin and extends into a pinched claw decoration down the body of the vessel. Probably an import from the Rhineland. Late second or third century.

Natural Coloured Glass

84. B[750]

Period 3, Building 3.

Fragment from the rim of a bowl or dish in natural green glass with an everted and tubular rim. Second to fourth century.

85. B[190]

Residual in a post-medieval context.

Fragment of natural pale green, slightly bubbled glass from a cylindrical beaker with a slightly concave base. Possibly first half of fourth century.

86. B[284]

Period 6, E/W ditch.

The base of a beaker or jar. Free-blown; natural green glass. Flat base, body cut out above the edge of the base. Third or fourth century.

87. B[453] B<296>

Period 4.5, dump layers.

Fragment showing the nose, lips and chin of a mould-blown face flask in natural green glass. (Isings 78) Late first to third century.

88. B[485]

Period 4.3, Building 3c.

Five fragments of natural, slightly bubbled, blue glass from the neck and shoulder of a rectangular-sectioned bottle. One fragment shows evidence of a handle. Late first to second century.

89. B[470]
Period 4.5, Building 3e.

The rim and neck of a small flask or bottle. Free-blown; natural green blue glass. Rim fire-rounded and folded inwards. Late first or second century.

90. B[140]
Period 4.3, recut of boundary ditch.

Fragment of natural pale blue, slightly bubbled glass from a square sectioned jar or bottle. Mid first to second century.

91. B[113]
Residual in a post-medieval context.

Fragment of natural blue-green glass from the handle of a jug or bottle. Second to third century.

92. B[517] B<343>
Period 5.5, dump layers.

Fragment from a combed angular ribbon handle of a bottle in natural pale blue glass. First to fourth century.

93. B[640]
Period 4.1, Bath house 4a fire-box disuse.

Fragment from the side of a barrel-shaped bottle (Isings form 89/128). Mould-blown; natural green blue glass. Body decorated with three high relief ribs, depicting the hoops of a barrel. Third to fourth century.

94. B[103] B<1>
Residual in a post-medieval context.

Forty-six fragments of natural pale green, bubbled glass from a globular flask with a cylindrical neck with a vertical, cracked-off rim and a slightly concave base. (Isings 103). Mid to late third century.

95. B[283]
Period 5.1, pitting.

Fragment from the rim of a beaker or bowl. Free-blown; natural green glass. Rim outsplayed and knocked-off. Late third or fourth century.

96. B[305]
Period 5.1, dump layers.

Fragment of natural yellow-green glass from the body of a beaker, cup or bowl with shallow horizontal wheel-cut decoration. Fourth century.

Natural blue indeterminate vessel fragments

Four fragments of natural blue glass from free-blown vessels of indeterminate form. Roman.

97. B[283]
Period 5.1, pitting.

Fragment of natural blue glass from free-blown vessel of indeterminate form. Roman.

98. B[379]
Period 6, E/W ditch in service yard.

Fragment of natural blue glass from free-blown vessel of indeterminate form. Roman.

99. B[412]
Period 4.5, Building 3e.

Fragment of natural blue glass from free-blown vessel of indeterminate form. Roman.

100. B[631]
Period 4.3, Building 3c.

Fragment of natural blue glass from free-blown vessel of indeterminate form. Roman.

Natural blue green indeterminate vessel fragments

Two fragments of natural blue green glass from free-blown vessel of indeterminate form. Roman.

101. B[127]
Period 4.3, recut of boundary ditch.

Fragment of natural blue green glass from free-blown vessel of indeterminate form. Roman.

102. B[432]
Period 4.1, Bath house 4a/service yard.

Fragment of natural blue green glass from free-blown vessel of indeterminate form. Roman.

Natural green indeterminate vessel fragments

Three fragments of natural green glass from free-blown vessels of indeterminate form. Roman.

103. B[198]
Period 6, pitting.

Fragment of natural green glass from free-blown vessel of indeterminate form. Roman.

104. B[283]
Period 5.1, pitting.

Fragment of natural green glass from free-blown vessel of indeterminate form. Roman.

105. B[467]
Period 7, demolition and robbing of bath house.

Fragment of natural green glass from free-blown vessel of indeterminate form. Roman.

Colourless indeterminate vessel fragments

Fourteen fragments of colourless glass from free-blown vessels of indeterminate form. Roman.

106. B[292]
Period 5.1, posthole in service yard.

Fragment of colourless glass from free-blown vessel of indeterminate form. Roman.

107. B[339]
Period 5.1, Building 7.

Fragment of colourless glass from free-blown vessel of indeterminate form. Roman.

108. B[377]
Period 5.1, pitting.

Fragment of colourless glass from free-blown vessel of indeterminate form. Roman.

109. B[377]

Period 5.1, pitting.

Fragment of colourless glass from free-blown vessel of indeterminate form. Roman.

110. B[377]

Period 5.1, pitting.

Fragment of colourless glass from free-blown vessel of indeterminate form. Roman.

111. B[377]

Period 5.1, pitting.

Fragment of colourless glass from free-blown vessel of indeterminate form. Roman.

112. B[377]

Period 5.1, pitting.

Fragment of colourless glass from free-blown vessel of indeterminate form. Roman.

113. B[406]

Period 4.3, service yard.

Fragment of colourless glass from free-blown vessel of indeterminate form. Roman.

114. B[406]

Period 4.3, service yard.

Fragment of colourless glass from free-blown vessel of indeterminate form. Roman.

115. B[488]

Period 4.5, Building 3e.

Fragment of colourless glass from free-blown vessel of indeterminate form. Roman.

116. B[541]

Period 4.3, Building 3c.

Fragment of colourless glass from free-blown vessel of indeterminate form. Roman.

117. B[579]

Period 4.5, robber trench, part of demolition of Building 3d.

Fragment of colourless glass from free-blown vessel of indeterminate form. Roman.

118. B[809]

Period 4.1, Bath house B4, primary fill of fire-box.

Fragment of colourless glass from free-blown vessel of indeterminate form. Roman.

119. B[809]

Period 4.1, Bath house B4, primary fill of fire-box.

Fragment of colourless glass from free-blown vessel of indeterminate form. Roman.

Colourless with green tint indeterminate vessel fragments

Six fragments of colourless glass with green tints from free-blown vessels of indeterminate form. Roman.

120. B[135]

Period 4.3, recut of boundary ditch.

Fragment of colourless glass with green tints from free-blown vessel of indeterminate form. Roman.

121. B[323]

Period 6, E/W ditch in service yard.

Fragment of colourless glass with green tints from free-blown vessel of indeterminate form. Roman.

122. B[496]

Period 4.1, Building 3a.

Fragment of colourless glass with green tints from free-blown vessel of indeterminate form. Roman.

123. B[496]

Period 4.1, Building 3a.

Fragment of colourless glass with green tints from free-blown vessel of indeterminate form. Roman.

124. B[543]

Period 4.3, Building 3c.

Fragment of colourless glass with green tints from free-blown vessel of indeterminate form. Roman.

125. B[631]

Period 4.3, Building 3c.

Fragment of colourless glass with green tints from free-blown vessel of indeterminate form. Roman.

Window Glass

126. B[654]

Period 4.1, Building 3a.

Fragment of natural pale green matt-glossy window glass with thumb edge. Badly weathered on both sides. First to third century.

127. B[658]

Period 4.2, Building 3b

Fragment of natural pale green matt-glossy window glass with thumb edge and visible tool marks. First to third century.

128. B[590]

Period 4.1, Bath house 4a, service yard.

Fragment of natural pale green matt-glossy window glass with thumb edge. First to third century.

129. B[579]

Period 4.5, robber trench, part of demolition of Building 3d.

Fragment of natural pale green matt-glossy window glass with thumb edge. First to third century. Three fragments of cast, matt/glossy natural green-blue window glass.

130. B[140]

Period 4.3, recut of boundary ditch.

Fragment of cast, matt/glossy natural green-blue window glass.

131. B[272]
Residual in a post-medieval context.
Fragment of cast, matt/glossy natural green-blue window glass.

132. B[640]
Period 4.1, Bath house 4a, fire-box disuse.
Fragment of cast, matt/glossy natural green-blue window glass.

133. B[234]
Period 6, hearth.
Fragment of slightly bubbled, natural pale green double-glossy window glass. Fourth century.

134. B[157]
Residual in a post-medieval context.
Fragment of very thin natural pale green window glass. Evidence of grozing along one edge. Six fragments of double glossy, cylinder blown natural pale green window glass.

135. B[155]
Period 4.3, recut of boundary ditch.
Fragment of double glossy, cylinder blown natural pale green window glass.

136. B[266]
Residual in post-medieval context.
Fragment of double glossy, cylinder blown natural pale green window glass.

137. B[379]
Period 6, E/W ditch in service yard.
Fragment of double glossy, cylinder blown natural pale green window glass.

138. B[470]
Period 4.5, Building 3.
Fragment of double glossy, cylinder blown natural pale green window glass.

139. B[554]
Period 5.1, service yard.
Fragment of double glossy, cylinder blown natural pale green window glass.

140. B[644]
Period 4.2, service yard.
Fragment of double glossy, cylinder blown natural pale green window glass. Two fragments of double glossy, cylinder blown colourless window glass.

141. B[432]
Period 4.1, Bath house 4a/service yard.
Fragment of double glossy, cylinder blown colourless window glass.

142. B[470]
Period 4.5, Building 3e.
Fragment of double glossy, cylinder blown colourless window glass.

Appendix 4: Geological observations made during construction of the London Docks and associated works

Location	Page ref	Description	Thickness ft
London Docks	131*	Made ground	31
		Blue London clay	17
		Mottled clay (Reading & Thanet Beds)	28
		Mottled sand (Reading & Thanet Beds)	61
		Flint (Reading & Thanet Beds)	1.5
London Docks (Eastern Docks: N. Side)	308*	Made ground	14.5
		Alluvium: peat	3.5
		Alluvium: clay	5.5
		Alluvium: clay & gravel	2
		Gravel (river drift)	13.5
		London clay?: Blue clay	13
		London clay?: silt ?loamy bed	3
		London clay?: clay	7
London Docks (Eastern Docks): S. Side	308*	Made ground	14.5
		Alluvium: black mud	8.5
		River drift: gravel	7
		River drift: clay	5
		River drift: gravel	3
		London clay	27
New London Docks (Shadwell basin)	456**	?Made ground	9
		Alluvium (river deposit: silt, human bones)	6
		Peat: prostrate trees	5.5
		Light-blue clay	1
		Flint gravel	14
		London clay: hard brown clay	1.5
		London clay: yellow clay	12.5
		Reading beds: hard, close sand	3
Shadwell Linde Well	156*	Thames mud, peat and made ground	16
		River drift: loamy sand, sand and ballast	22.5
		Woolwich and Reading Beds	54.5
		Woolwich Beds and Thanet Sand	52
		Chalk	274

* Whitaker 1889a

** Whitaker 1889b

Table 41 Geology encountered during construction of the London Docks and the Linde Well, Shadwell.

Résumé

Nathalie Barrett

Sept périodes d'activités préhistoriques et romaines ont été identifiées à deux fouilles voisines en 2002 à Shadwell, sur la rive nord de la Tamise à l'est de la Cite de Londres et du site de *Londinium*. Les sites, des chantiers de construction, se trouvent au sud de la rue «The Highway» et de chaque cote de Wapping Lane, Tobacco Dock à l'ouest (Site A, code TOC02) et le restaurant «Babe Ruth» à l'est (Site B, code HGA02). Des fouilles qui ont eu lieu juste au nord-est du Site B dans les années 1970 (LD74/LD76) avaient découvert des indices d'activité de période romaine y compris une construction en maçonnerie près de la crête de la colline, d'abord identifiée comme une tour à signal militaire, mais plus récemment réinterprétée comme un mausolée.

Apres une introduction générale à l'ensemble des travaux à Shadwell (Chapitre 1) le récit chronologique des Sites A et B est présenté en ordre de l'usage du terrain (Chapitre 2). Les traces d'activité préhistorique sur le terrain en pente abrupte, où le niveau descend d'une altitude d'environ 7m au nord à 1,6m au sud, était limités à un petit assemblage de silex et des indices d'un paléo-chenal orienté nord-sud, situé entre les deux sites (Période 1, 50 après J.-C.). Les vestiges d'activité de Haut Empire (Période 2, vers 50–230 après J.-C.) comprennent des carrières, des fosses à déchets, du drainage en surface et du terrassement de l'escarpement. Un bâtiment en bois construit dans le quartier sud-ouest était peut-être une grange ou un grenier (B1). Cette activité de Ière et IIème siècle était généralement sur une petite échelle et sporadique.

Vers le début ou milieu du IIIème siècle après J.-C. un changement a eu lieu aux deux sites quand des nouvelles divisions du terrain ont été créées et des bâtiments ont été construits sur les terrasses inférieures au sud, à coté du cours conjecturé de la rivière (Période 3, vers 230–275 après J.-C.). Des grands thermes (B4) construites en pierre sur la partie sud du site B avaient au moins dix salles en première phase, y compris deux salles de bain d'eau tiède (*tepidarium*) et chaude (*caldarium*) accédées d'un vestibule et vestiaire (*apodyterium*) en commun ou d'une salle froide (*frigidarium*). Les thermes peuvent être décrits en style comme une rangée axiale ou anguleuse, avec l'axis longitudinal aligné est-ouest et avec une entrée centrale côté rivière au sud. Une cour de service au nord du bâtiment était délimitée à l'ouest et au nord par les ailes d'un bloc d'hébergement construit en argile et en bois (B3). Un petit bâtiment en bois (B2) a été constaté au sud d'une terrasse sur le Site A, côté ouest.

Il y a eu encore plus d'activité à forte intensité au cours de la Période 4, environ 275–325 après J.-C. et cette période a donc été divisée en 5 phases basées sur une étude stratigraphique très détaillée de la partie du site au nord des thermes où le bloc d'hébergement a été modifié à plusieurs reprises (B3a-e, Période 4.1–4.5). Les thermes eux-mêmes ont été modifiés et agrandis avec de nouvelles salles ajoutées au nord-ouest (B4) et de la modification des hypocaustes sous-sol (Période 4.1). A l'ouest à l'extérieur des thermes au Site A de l'activité de la même phase a été découverte, y compris un nouveau bâtiment en bois (B5) et des fours. Dans une autre réorganisation des thermes des murs intérieurs ont été enlevés et la porte d'entrée a été agrandie vers le sud (Période 4.2). Les hypocaustes ont ensuite été inondés et remplis de vase, ce qui indique une interruption dans l'usage du site vers la fin de la Période 4. L'érosion de la colline et quelques traces fragmentaires de bâtiments (B6) sur le Site A peuvent être plus ou moins contemporain avec cet épisode d'inondation (Période 4.5).

En Période 5, vers 325–375 après J.-C., les thermes sont utilisés à nouveau et agrandis en même temps qu'un nouveau bâtiment (B7) ait été construit au nord de la cour de service. A l'ouest des thermes un revêtement important pour de nouvelles terrasses a été créé, avec un nouveau bâtiment en bois (B8) au sud (Période 5.1). L'usage a continué jusqu'à la fin du IVème siècle, représenté par un nouveau bâtiment (B9) et des fossés de drainage à l'ouest ainsi que la continuation de l'utilisation des thermes à l'est (Période 5.2).

Les thermes ont été abandonnés à la fin du IVème siècle et ont probablement vite été dévalisés de matériaux de valeur pour des travaux de récupérations (Période 6, environ 375–410 après J.-C.). La cour de service au nord des thermes en ruines est également abandonnée et a été tranchée par des fossés de drainage (OA13), mais une construction en poteaux (B10) fut bâtie au nord. A l'ouest sur le Site A un bâtiment en maçonnerie de taille importante (B11) fut construit et sur la pente il y avait un puits et des fosses (OA12). Les derniers indices d'activité à Shadwell ne peuvent pas être datés avec précision à cause des peu d'objets retrouvés mais l'usage du site est probable jusqu'au Vème siècle. Le vol répandu de la superstructure des thermes y compris l'enlèvement des murs et pierres de fondation aurait pu avoir lieu plus tard, même si ceci ne peut pas être daté (Période 7, à partir de 410 après J.-C.).

Les fouilles à Shadwell ont aussi produit des assemblages importants de trouvailles, surtout de l'époque d'Antiquité tardive. Chapitre 3 comprend des rapports de spécialistes sur la poterie romaine, les pièces de monnaie, petits objets, matériaux de construction, inscriptions, le verre et le bois dont certains morceaux ont donné des dates de dendrochronologie (3.1–3.8). La poterie comprend des assemblages de céramiques sigillés et d'amphores qui sont d'importance locale et nationale à cause de leur date tardive. Des articles de décoration personnelle comprennent non seulement des bijoux mais un grand nombre d'épingles à cheveux qui pourraient être associés à l'usage des thermes. Il y a aussi d'importantes collections d'os d'animaux et d'indices archéo-botaniques qui expliquent l'environnement et l'économie locale (3.9–3.10).

L'importance globale des conclusions est ensuite discutée. Chapitre 4 examine l'interprétation des thermes, suggère une reconstruction de son aménagement et aspect et considère le rapport du site avec la Tamise. Un dernier chapitre (5) présente une discussion sur le statut du site d'occupation à Shadwell.

Ce rapport est soutenu par des annexes, y compris des données sous forme de tables, et les archives complètes peuvent être examinées à LAARC.

Zusammenfassung

Sylvia Butler

Bei zwei neben einander liegenden Ausgrabungen in Shadwell an der nördlichen Flussseite der Themse östlich der City of London und der Stätte von *Londinium* wurden im Jahre 2002 sieben Perioden von prähistorischer und römischer Aktivität aufgedeckt. Die Sanierungsgebiete, in der sich die Stätten befanden, lagen zum Süden von The Highway und an beiden Seiten der Wapping Lane, zum Westen von Tobacco Dock (Stätte A; Stätten Code TOC02) und Babe Ruth Restaurant zum Osten (Stätte B; HGA02). Ausgrabungen hatten bereits in den 70er Jahren zum Nordosten der Stätte B (LD74/LD76) stattgefunden und offenbarten Beweise von römischen Aktivitäten. Diese beinhalteten in der Nähe des Hanggipfels eine große Mauerwerkstruktur von welcher man ursprünglich angenommen hatte, dass sie einen militärischen Signalturm darstellte. Sie wurde aber jüngst als Mausoleum neu interpretiert.

Einer generellen Einführung zu der allgemeinen Arbeit an Shadwell (Kapitel 1) folgt eine chronologische Beschreibung der Stätten A und B. Sie wird präsentiert als eine einzelne Flächen-Nutzungssequenz (Kapitel 2). Prähistorische Aktivitäten auf dem steil abschüssigen Gelände, wo die Bodenoberfläche von ca. 7m OD im Norden auf 1.6m OD im Süden abfällt, waren beschränkt auf den Fund einer kleinen Feuersteinansammlung und Anzeichen eines Nord-Süd ausgerichteten Paläo-Flussbettes, welches sich zwischen den beiden Stätten befindet (Periode 1; bis AD 50). Die frührömische Aktivität (Periode 2; ca. AD 50-230) bestand aus Kiesabbau, Abfallgruben, Oberflächenentwässerung und der Terrassierung des Steilgeländes. Ein Holzgebäude wurde im Südwesten errichtet und könnte eine Scheune oder einen Getreidespeicher dargestellt haben (B1). Diese Aktivitäten im ersten und zweiten Jahrhundert waren generell in kleinem Umfang und sporadisch.

Im frühen bis zur Mitte des dritten Jahrhunderts AD fand an beiden Stätten ein Sprung in der Entwicklung statt, als das Land neu aufgeteilt wurde und Gebäude auf den unteren Terrassen zum Süden hin errichtet wurden, angrenzend an die vermutete Strecke des Flusses (Periode 3; ca AD 230-275). Ein großes Steinbadehaus (B4), errichtet auf der südlichen Seite der Stätte B, bestand in seiner anfänglichen Phase aus wenigstens zehn Räumen, einschließlich zweier Bade-Suiten mit Warm- (*Tepidaria*) und Heiß-Räumen (*Caldaria*), die über einen gemeinsamen Vor- und Umkleideraum (*Apodyterium*) oder Kaltraum (*Frigidarium*) zugänglich waren. Die Bauart des Badehauses kann mit seiner nach Ost-Westen hin ausgerichteten langen Achse und einem südlich, zentral liegenden Eingang zur Flussseite hin als axialreihenartig oder winkelreihenartig bezeichnet werden. Ein nördlich des Badegebäudes gelegener Wirtschaftshof war zum Westen und Norden von den Flügeln eines Lehm- und Holz-Wohnblockes (B3) eingegrenzt. Zum Süden einer der Terrassen an der Stätte A zum Westen wurde ein kleines Holzgebäude (B2) verzeichnet.

Während der Periode 4 zwischen ca. AD 275-325 wurden weitere, intensive Aktivitäten an der Stätte verzeichnet, welche in 5 individuelle Phasen unterteilt wurden. Diese Phasen basierten auf der ausführlichsten, stratigraphischen Sequenz zum Norden des Badehauses hin, wo der Wohnblock wiederholt abgewandelt wurde (B3a-e; Periode 4.1-4.5). Das Badehaus selbst war umfangreichen Veränderungen und Erweiterungen unterlegen, wobei zu seiner nordwestlichen Seite (B4) neue Räume angebaut wurden und Veränderungen an dem Unterboden-Hypokaustum (Periode 4.1) vorgenommen wurden. Zum Westen des Badehauses an der Stätte A wurden neuzeitliche externe Aktivitäten, ein neues Holzgebäude (B5) und Öfen für die Nahrungszubereitung verzeichnet. Eine weitere Umgestaltung der Bäder involvierte die Entfernung von Unterboden-Trennwänden und die Erweiterung des Eingangsweges südwärts (Periode 4.2). Jedoch wurden die Hypokausten anschließend überflutet und mit Schlick gefüllt, was zu einer Pause in der Nutzung zum Ende der Periode 4 führte. Hangerosion und lückenhafte Anzeichen von jeglichen Bauarbeiten (B6) an der Stätte A könnten etwa zeitnah mit der Überflutungsepisode gelegen haben (Periode 4.5).

In Periode 5 zwischen ca. AD 325-375 wurde das Badehaus (B4) wieder genutzt und erweitert, während ein neues Gebäude (B7) zum Norden seines Wirtschaftshofes hin errichtet wurde. Zum Westen der Bäder wurde eine bedeutende neue Terrassenverkleidung konstruiert einschließlich eines neuen Holzgebäudes (B8) zur Südseite (Periode 5.1). Die Besiedlung wurde bis in das späte vierte Jahrhundert fortgesetzt, repräsentiert von einem neuen Gebäude (B9) und Kanalisation zum Westen hin und dem fortlaufenden Gebrauch des Badekomplexes im Osten (Periode 5.2).

Das Badehaus wurde im späten vierten Jahrhundert aufgegeben und alle nützlichen Materialien wurden wahrscheinlich schnell geplündert und wieder verwertet (Periode 6, ca. AD 375-410). Der Wirtschaftshof zum Norden der zerfallenen Bäder hin wurde ebenfalls nicht mehr genutzt und wurde von Entwässerungsgraben durchschnitten (OA13). Es wurde jedoch eine Pfostenstruktur (B10) zum Norden hin errichtet. Zum Westen der Stätte A wurde ein relativ großes Mauerwerkgebäude (B11) errichtet und der externe Hang verzeichnete einen Brunnen und Pitting (OA12). Die spätesten Anzeichen von Aktivitäten bei Shadwell können nicht akkurat datiert werden, da nur relativ wenige Funde ausgegraben wurden. Es ist aber wahrscheinlich, dass Aktivitäten bis zum frühen fünften Jahrhundert fortgesetzt wurden. Umfangreiche Plünderung des Oberbaus des Badehauses, einschließlich der Entfernung der Wände und Fundamente, könnte eventuell später stattgefunden haben, aber man ist nicht in der Lage dies zu datieren (Periode 7; ca. AD 410+).

Die Shadwell Ausgrabung lieferte auch wichtige Fundansammlungen, insbesondere von den späteren römischen Perioden. Kapitel 3 umfasst Spezialistenberichte über römische Töpferwaren, Münzen, Kleinfunde, Baumaterial, Inschriften, Glass und Nutzholz, von welchem manches eine dendrochronologische Datierung möglich machte (3.1–3.8). Die Töpferwaren beinhalten Gruppen von ungewöhnlichen Terra Sigillata und Amphoren, welche angesichts ihrer späten Datierung sowohl von örtlicher als auch nationaler Bedeutung sind. Gegenstände der persönlichen Dekoration beinhalten nicht nur Schmuck sondern auch eine große Anzahl von Haarnadeln, welche vielleicht mit der Nutzung der Bäder verbunden sein könnte. Es wurden ebenfalls bedeutende Ansammlungen von Tierknochen gefunden und bedeutendes archäobotanisches Beweismaterial für das örtliche Umfeld und die Wirtschaft (3.9–3.10).

Der allgemeine Stellenwert der Funde wird dann behandelt. Kapitel 4 untersucht die Interpretation des Badehauses, schlägt vor wie das Layout und Design rekonstruiert werden könnte und betrachtet die Stätte in Bezug auf ihren Zusammenhang mit der Themse. Das letzte Kapitel (5) diskutiert den Status der Ansiedlung bei Shadwell.

Der Report wird von Appendices unterstützt, die tabellierte Date beinhalten. Das komplette Archiv für diese Ausgrabung ist bei dem London Archaeological Archive and Research Centre (LAARC) zur Studie erhältlich.

Bibliography

Adam, J. P. 2001 *Roman building: Materials and techniques*. London: Routledge

Aicher, P. 1993 Terminal display fountains and the aqueducts of Rome. *Phoenix* 47 (4), 339–352

Alcock, J. 1996 *Life in Roman Britain*. London: Batsford

Alcock, J. P. 2001 *Food in Roman Britain*. Stroud: Tempus

Allason-Jones, L. 1989 *Ear-rings in Roman Britain*. Oxford: British Archaeological Reports British Series 201

Allason-Jones, L. 1996 *Roman jet in the Yorkshire Museum*. York: Yorkshire Museum

Allason-Jones, L. 1999 What is a military assemblage? *Journal of Roman Military Equipment Studies* 10, 1–4

Allen, M. and Fulford, M. 1996 The distribution of south-east Dorset Black Burnished Category 1 pottery in south-west Britain. *Britannia* 27, 223–281

Armitage, P. L. 1977 The faunal remains. In J. Ivens and G. Deal Finds and excavations in Roman Enfield. *London Archaeologist* 3 (3), 59–65

Armitage, P. L. 1994 Unwelcome companions: Ancient rats reviewed. *Antiquity*, 68 (259), 231–240

Armitage, P. L. and Clutton-Brock, J. 1976 A system for classification and description of the horn cores of cattle from archaeological sites. *Journal of Archaeological Science* 3, 329–348

Armitage, P. L., West, B. and Steedman, K. 1984 New evidence of black rat in Roman London. *London Archaeologist* 4 (14), 375–383

Arthur, P. 1987 Precisazioni su di una forma anforica medio-imperiale dalla Campania. *El vi a l'antiguitat. Economia, producció i comerç al Mediterrani occidental. Actes I Col.loqui d'arqueología romana*. Monografíes Badalonines 9, 401–406

Arthur, P. and Williams, D. 1992 Campanian wine, Roman Britain and the third century AD. *Journal of Roman Archaeology* 5, 250–260

Arup Geotechnics, 2001, *Bisley Properties SA, Tobacco Dock development: Archaeological mitigation strategy report*. Unpublished Ove Arup Report

Atkinson, R. J. C. 1941 A Romano-British potters' field at Cowley, Oxon. *Oxoniensia* 6, 9–21

Bailey, K. 1989 The Middle Saxons. In S. Bassett (ed.) *The origins of Anglo-Saxon Kingdoms*. Leicester: Leicester University Press, 108–122

Baillie, M. G. L. and Pilcher, J. R. 1973 A simple crossdating program for tree-ring research. *Tree Ring Bulletin* 33, 7–14

Baker, T. (ed.) 1998 Stepney: Early Stepney. *A history of the County of Middlesex: Volume 11: Stepney, Bethnal Green*, 1–7, http://www.british-history.ac.uk/report.aspx?compid=22731. Date accessed: 19 June 2008

Barber, B. and Bowsher, D. 2000 *The Eastern cemetery of Roman London: Excavations 1983–1990*. London: Museum of London Archaeology Service Monograph 4

Barker, P. and White, R. 1998 *Wroxeter: Life and death of a Roman City*. Stroud: Tempus

Barnes, T. D. 1998 *Ammianus Marcellinus and the representation of historic reality*. New York: Cornell University Press

Bateman, N., Cowan, C. and Wroe-Brown, R. 2008 *London's Roman amphitheatre, Guildhall Yard, City of London*. London: Museum of London Archaeology Service Monograph 35

von Becker, C. 1980 Untersuchungen an Skelettresten von Haus- und Wildschweinen aus Haithabu. Neumunster: Karl Wachholtz Verlag

Bedal, L. 2002 Desert oasis: Water consumption and display in the Nabataean capital. *Near Eastern Archaeology* 65 (4), 225–234

de la Bédoyère, G. 2001 *The buildings of Roman Britain*. Stroud: Tempus.

Betts, I. 2002 The ceramic and stone building material. In E. Howe *Roman defences and medieval industry: Excavations at Baltic House, City of London*. London: Museum of London Archaeology Service Monograph 7, 74–81

Betts, I. M. 2003 Stone and ceramic building materials. In C. Cowan, F. Seeley, A. Wardle, A. Westman and L. Wheeler *Urban development in north-west Roman Southwark: Excavations 1974–90*. London: Museum of London Archaeology Service Monograph 16, 105–119

Betts, I. M. and Foot, R. 1994 A newly identified late Roman tile group from Southern England. *Britannia* 25, 21–34

Bidwell, P. 2006 Constantius and Constantine at York. In E. Hartley, J. Hawkes, M. Henig and F. Mee *Constantine the Great: York's Roman Emperor*. York: York Museums and Galleries Trust, 31–40

Bird, D. 1996 The London region in the Roman period. In J. Bird, M. Hassall and H. Sheldon (eds.) *Interpreting Roman London: Papers in memory of Hugh Chapman*. Oxford: Oxbow Monograph 58, 217–232

Bird, D. 2008 "The rest to some faint meaning make pretence, but Shadwell never deviates into sense" (further speculation about the Shadwell 'tower'). In J. Clark, J. Cotton, J. Hall, R. Sherris and H. Swain (eds.) *Londinium and beyond. Essays on Roman London and its hinterland for Harvey Sheldon*. York: Council for British Archaeology Research Report 156, 96–101

Bird, J. 1986 Samian wares. In L. Miller, J. Schofield and M. Rhodes *The Roman quay at St Magnus House, London: Excavations at New Fresh Wharf, Lower Thames Street, London, 1974–78*. London: London and Middlesex Archaeological Society Special Paper 8, 139–185

Bird, J. 1993 3rd-century samian ware in Britain. *Journal of Roman Pottery Studies* 6, 1–14

Bird, J. 1995 The samian and other imported red-slipped wares: Summary. In K. Blockley, M. Blockley, P. Blockley, S. Frere and S. Stow, *Excavations in the Marlowe car park and surrounding areas*. Canterbury: Archaeology of Canterbury 5, 772–775

Bird, J. 1999 Decorated Central and East Gaulish samian. In R. P. Symonds, and S. Wade, *Roman pottery from excavations in Colchester 1971–86*. Colchester: Colchester Archaeological Report 10, 75–119

Bird, J. 2002 Samian wares. In D. Lakin with F. Seeley, J. Bird, K. Rielly and C. Ainsley *The Roman tower at Shadwell, London: A reappraisal*. London: Museum of London Archaeology Service Archaeology Study Series 8, 31–48

Bird, J. 2005 The samian ware. In B. Philp, *The excavation of the Roman fort at Reculver, Kent*. Dover: Kent Monograph Series 10, 143–159

Bird, J, forthcoming Decorated East Gaulish samian. In M. J. Darling and B. J. Precious, *A corpus of Roman pottery from Lincoln*. Lincoln: Lincoln Archaeological Studies forthcoming

Bird, J. and Young, C. 1981 Migrant potters – the Oxford connection, with appendix by K. F. Hartley on Hartshill Kiln 6. In A.C. Anderson and A.S. Anderson (eds.) *Roman pottery research in Britain and north-west Europe: Papers presented to Graham Webster* Part ii. Oxford: British Archaeological Reports International Series 123 (ii), 295–312

Birley, A. 1999 *Septimius Severus: The African Emperor*. London: Routledge

Bishop, B. 1996 *An archaeological evaluation at Coopers Yard, Shadwell*. Unpublished Pre-Construct Archaeology Report

Blagg, T. F. C. 1990 Building stone in Roman Britain. In D. Parsons (ed.) *Stone: Quarrying and building in England AD 43–1525*. Stroud: Phillimore, 33–50

Blair, I., Spain, R., Swift, D., Taylor, T. and Goodburn, D. 2006 Wells and bucket-chains: Unforeseen elements of water supply in early Roman London. *Britannia* 37, 1–52

Bluer, R., Brigham, T. and Nielsen, R. 2006 *Roman and later development east of the forum and Cornhill: Excavations at Lloyd's Register, 71 Fenchurch Street, City of London*. London: Museum of London Archaeology Service Monograph 30

Blyth, P. 1999 The consumption and cost of fuel in hypocaust baths. In J. DeLaine and D. E. Johnston (eds.) *Roman baths and bathing: Proceedings of the First International Conference on Roman Baths, held at Bath, England, 30 March–4 April 1992*. Portsmouth, Rhode Island: Journal of Roman Archaeology Supplementary Series 37, 87–98

Bond, J. M. and O'Connor, T. P. 1999 *Bones from medieval deposits at 16–22 Coppergate and other sites in York. The Archaeology of York*, 15/5. York: York Archaeological Trust and Council for British Archaeology

Bonifay, M. 2003 La ceramique Africaine, un indice du developpement economique? *Antiquité Tardive* 11, 113–128

Bonifay, M. 2004 *Études sur la céramique romaine tardive d'Afrique*. Oxford: British Archaeological Reports International Series 1301

Bonifay, M. 2005 Observations sur la typologie des amphores Africaines de l'antiquité tardive. In J. M Gurt i Esparraguera, J Buxeda i Garrigós and M. A. Cau Ontiveros (eds.) *LRCW 1. Late Roman coarse wares, cooking wares and amphorae in the Mediterranean*. Oxford: British Archaeological Reports International Series 1340, 451–472

Boon, G. C. 1969 *Roman glass in Wales*. Annales du 4e Congrès des Journées Internationales du Verre, 93–102

Branch, N. P., Green, C. P., Palmer, A. P., Swindle, G. E., Vaughan-Williams, A. and Wyatt, C. 2004a The environmental assessment. In A. Douglas *Phased summary and assessment document of the excavations at 130–162 The Highway, London Borough of Tower Hamlets.* Unpublished Pre-Construct Archaeology Report

Branch, N. P., Green, C. P., Kemp, R. A., Swindle G. E. and Vaughan-Williams, A. 2004b The environmental assessment. In A. Douglas *Phased summary and assessment document of the excavation at 172–176 The Highway, London Borough of Tower Hamlets E1.* Unpublished Pre-Construct Archaeology Report

Branigan, K. 1976 Villa settlement in the West Country. In K. Branigan and P. Fowler (eds.) *The Roman West Country.* London: David and Charles, 120–141

Brickstock, R. 2004 The production, analysis and standardisation of Romano-British coin reports. London: English Heritage

Brigham, T. 1990a The late Roman waterfront in London. *Britannia* 21, 99–183

Brigham, T. 1990b A reassessment of the second basilica in London AD100–400: Excavations at Leadenhall Court 1984–86. *Britannia* 21, 53–98

Brigham, T., Goodburn, D., Tyers, I. and Dillon, J. 1995 A Roman timber building on the Southwark waterfront. London. *Archaeological Journal* 152, 1–72

Brigham, T. and Woodger, A. 2001 *Roman and medieval townhouses on the London waterfront: excavations at Governor's House, City of London.* London: Museum of London Archaeology Service Monograph 9

Brodribb, G. 1979a Markings on tile and brick. In A. McWhirr (ed.) *Roman brick and tile.* Oxford: British Archaeological Reports International Series 68, 211–220

Brodribb, G. 1979b A survey of tile from the Roman bath house at Beauport Park, Battle, E. Sussex. *Britannia* 10, 139–156

Brodribb, G. 1987 *Roman brick and tile.* Gloucester: Alan Sutton Publishing

Brown, G. 2008 Archaeological evidence for the Roman London to Colchester road between Aldgate and Harold Hill. In J. Clark, J. Cotton, J. Hall, R. Sherris and H. Swain (eds.) *Londinium and Beyond. Essays on Roman London and its hinterland for Harvey Sheldon.* York: Council for British Archaeology Research Report 156, 82–89

Brown, G. and Moore, P. 2001 *Written scheme of investigation for an archaeological mitigation at Bisley Properties SA Tobacco Dock development.* Unpublished Pre-Construct Archaeology Report

Brown G., Bishop B., Douglas A., Leary J., Ridgeway V. and Taylor-Wilson R. forthcoming *Excavations at Old Ford, London.* Pre-Construct Archaeology Monograph

Brown G. and Pickard, C. in prep. *Excavations at Borough High Street, Southwark.* Pre-Construct Archaeology Monograph

Brown, P. 1971 *The world of late antiquity: From Marcus Aurelius to Muhammed.* London: Thames and Hudson

Brunning, R. 1996 *Waterlogged wood: Guidelines on the recording, sampling, conservation, and curation of waterlogged wood.* London: English Heritage

Brunsting, H. and Kalee, C. 1989 Terra sigillata met reliëfversiering In L. R. P. Ozinga, T. J. Hoekstra, M. D. de Weerd and S. L. Wynia (eds.) *Het Romeinse Castellum te Utrecht.* Utrecht: Albert Egges van Giffen Institut voor Prae- en Protohistorie, Studies in Prae- en Protohistorie 3, 121–138

Burgers, A. 2001 *The water supplies and related structures of Roman Britain.* Oxford: British Archaeological Reports British Series 324

Burnham, B. and Wacher, J. 1990 *The small towns of Roman Britain.* London: Batsford

Cameron, A. 1993 *The later Roman Empire.* London: Fontana

Carreras, C. and Williams, D. 2003 Spanish olive-oil trade in late Roman Britain: Dressel 23 amphorae from Winchester. *Journal of Roman Pottery Studies* 10, 64–68

Casey, J. and Hoffman, B. 1999 Excavations at the Roman temple in Lydney Park, Gloucestershire in 1980 and 1981. *Antiquaries Journal* 79, 81–144

Charlesworth, D. 1959 Roman glass from northern Britain, *Archaeologia Aeliana*, 4, 37, 33–58

Chenet, G. 1941 *La céramique sigillée d'Argonne du IVme siècle et la terre sigillée décorée à la molette.* Mâcon

Clarke, G. 1979 *Pre-Roman and Roman Winchester, part 2: The Roman cemetery at Lankhills.* Oxford: Oxford University Press

Coombe, P. C., Grew, F. G., Hayward, K. M. J. & Henig, M. in prep. *Corpus Signorum Imperii Romani. Great Britain i. 10. London and the South-east.* Oxford

Cool, H. 1990 Metal hairpins from southern Britain. *Archaeological Journal* 147, 148–182

Cool, H. and Baxter, M. 2002 Exploring Romano-British finds assemblages. *Oxford Journal of Archaeology* 21 (4), 365–380

Cool, H. E. M. and Price, J. 1995 *Roman vessel glass from excavations in Colchester, 1971–85.* Colchester: Colchester Archaeological Report 8

Cotterill, J. 1993 Saxon raiding and the role of the late Roman coastal forts of Britain. *Britannia* 24, 227–240

Cotton, J. 1996 A miniature chalk head from the Thames at Battersea and the cult of the head in Roman London. In J. Bird, M. Hassall and H. Sheldon (eds.) *Interpreting Roman London: Papers in memory of Hugh Chapman.* Oxford: Oxbow Monograph 58, 85–96

Cowan, C. 1993 A possible mansio in Roman Southwark: excavations at 15–23 Southwark Street, 1980–86. *Transactions of the London and Middlesex Archaeological Society* 43, 3–192

Croot, P. 1997 Settlement, tenure and land use in medieval Stepney: Evidence of a field survey *c.* 1400. *London Journal* 22, 1–15

Crowley, N. 2005 Building materials. In B. Yule *A prestigious Roman building complex on the Southwark waterfront: Excavations at Winchester Palace, London, 1983–90.* London: Museum of London Archaeology Service Monograph 23, 90–100

Crummy, N. 1983 *The Roman small finds from excavations in Colchester 1971–9.* Colchester: Colchester Archaeological Report 2

Crummy, N. 2007 Six honest serving men: A basic methodology for the study of small finds. In R. Hingley and S. Willis (eds.) *Roman Finds.* Oxford: Oxbow, 59–66

Cuming, S. 1858 Roman coffin from Shadwell. *Journal of the British Archaeological Association* 16

Cunliffe, B. 1969 *Roman Bath.* London: Reports of the Research Committee of the Society of Antiquaries of London 24

Cunliffe, B. 1975 *Excavations at Portchester Castle Volume 1: Roman.* London: Reports of the Research Committee of the Society of Antiquaries of London 32

Cunliffe, B 1980, 'Excavations at the Roman fort at Lympne' in *Britannia XI*, 227–288

Cunliffe, B. 1995 *Roman Bath.* London: English Heritage, Batsford

Dark, K. 1996 *Civitas to Kingdom: British political continuity AD 300–800.* Leicester: Leicester University Press

Dark, P. 2000 *The environment of Britain in the first millennium AD.* London: Duckworth

Darling, M. and Gurney, D. 1993 *Caister-on-Sea: Excavations by Charles Green 1951–1955.* Dereham: East Anglian Archaeology 60

Davey, N. and Ling, R. 1981 *Wall-painting in Roman Britain.* London: Britannia Monograph Series 3

Dickinson, B. M. 1993 The samian ware. In M. J. Darling and D. Gurney, *Caister-on-Sea: Excavations by Charles Green, 1951–55.* Dereham: East Anglian Archaeology 60, 154–160

Dickinson, B. 1997 Samian. In J. Monaghan, *Roman pottery from York.* York: Archaeology of York 16/8, 943–966

Dickinson, B. and Bird, J. 1985 The samian ware. In J. Hinchliffe and C. J. Sparey Green, *Excavations at Brancaster 1974 and 1977.* Dereham: East Anglian Archaeology 23, 74–82

Dixon, K. and Southern, P. 1992 *The Roman Cavalry.* London: Batsford

Dixon, P. 2007 Reaching beyond the clearances: Finding the medieval – based upon recent survey by the RCAHMS in Strath Don, Aberdeenshire. In M. Gardiner and S. Rippon (eds.) *Medieval Landscapes.* Macclesfield: Windgather, 153–169

Donaldson, G. 1988 Signalling communications and the Roman Imperial Army. *Britannia* 19, 349–356

Dore, J., Greene, K. and Johns, C. 1979 The decorated ware. In J. N. Dore and J. P. Gillam, *The Roman fort at South Shields.* Newcastle: Society of Antiquaries of Newcastle upon Tyne Monograph Series 1, 107–127

Douglas, A. 1997 *An archaeological evaluation at 130–162 The Highway (Tobacco Dock factory shops Phase 2 – New building).* Unpublished Pre-Construct Archaeology Report

Douglas, A. 2007 An excavation at 5–27 Long Lane, London Borough of Southwark, London SE1. *Transactions of the London and Middlesex Archaeological Society* 58, 15–51

Drummond-Murray, J., Thompson, P. and Cowan, C. 2002 *Settlement in Roman Southwark: Archaeological investigations (1991–8) for the London Underground Limited Jubilee Line extension project.* London: Museum of London Archaeology Service Monograph 12

Driesch, A., von den and Boessneck, J. A. 1974 Kritische Anmerkungen zur Widerristhöhenberechnung aus Längenmaßen vor- und frühgeschichtlicher Tierknochen. *Saugetierkundliche Mitteilungen* 22, 325–348

Driesch, A. von den 1976 *A guide to the measurement of animal bones from archaeological sites.* Harvard University: Peabody Museum of Archaeology and Ethnology, Peabody Museum Bulletin 1

Drury, P. 1984 The temple of Claudius reconsidered. *Britannia* 15, 7–50

Eaton, T. 2000 *Plundering the past: Roman stonework in medieval Britain.* Stroud: Tempus

Ellis, P. (ed.) 2000 *The Roman baths and Macellum at Wroxeter: Excavations by Graham Webster, 1955–85.* London: English Heritage Archaeological Report 9

Ellis, S. P. 2000 *Roman housing.* London: Duckworth

English Heritage 1998 *Dendrochronology: Guidelines on producing and interpreting dendrochronological dates.* London: English Heritage

Esmonde Cleary, A. S. 1989 *The ending of Roman Britain.* London: Batsford

Esmonde Cleary, A. S. 2003 Civil defence in the West under the High Empire. In P. Wilson (ed.) *The Archaeology of Roman Towns.* Oxford: Oxbow Books

Evans, H. 1982 Agrippa's water plan. *American Journal of Archaeology* 86 (3), 401–411

Evans, H. 1994 *Water Distribution in Ancient Rome.* Michigan: Ann Arbor, University of Michigan Press

Farwell, D. and Molleson, T. 1993 *Poundbury Volume 2: the cemeteries.* Dorchester: Dorset Natural History and Archaeological Society Monograph 11

Faulkner, N. 2001 *The decline and fall of Roman Britain.* Stroud, Tempus

Fölzer, E. 1913 *Die Bilderschüsseln der ostgallischen Sigillata-Manufakturen*, Bonn: Römische Keramik in Trier 1

Foss, C. 2002 Life in city and country. In C. Mango (ed.) *The Oxford history of Byzantium*, Oxford: Oxford University Press

Fowler, P. 2002 *Farming in the first millennium AD.* Cambridge: Cambridge University Press

Fremersdorf, F. 1959 *Römische Gläser mit Fadenauflage in Köln. Schlangenfadengläser und Verwandtes.* Köln: Die Denkmäler des Römischen Köln 5

Frere, S. S. 1972 *Verulamium excavations Volume 1.* Oxford: Reports of the Research Committee of The Society of Antiquaries of London 28

Frere, S. S. 1984 *Verulamium excavations, Volume III.* Oxford: Oxford University Committee for Archaeology Monograph 1

Frere, S. S., and Tomlin, R. S. O. (eds.), 1993 Tile-stamps of the Classis Britannica; Imperial, procuratorial and civic tile-stamps; stamps of private tilers; inscriptions on relief-patterned tiles and graffiti on tiles (RIB 2481–2491). In R. G. Collingwood and R. P. Wright *The Roman inscriptions of Britain, Volume II: Fascicule 5.* Gloucestershire: Alan Sutton Publishing

Fulford, M. 1978 Coin circulation and mint activity in the late Roman Empire: Some economic implications. *Archaeological Journal* 135, 67–134

Fulford, M. and Bird, J. 1975 Imported pottery from Germany in late Roman Britain. *Britannia* 6, 171–182

Fulford, M., Champion, T. and Long, A. (eds.) 1997 *England's coastal heritage: A survey for English Heritage and the RCHME.* London: English Heritage Archaeological Report 15

Gard, L. 1937 *Reliefsigillata des 3. und 4. Jahrhunderts aus den Werkstätten von Trier.* Unpublished thesis, University of Tübingen

Gardner, A. 2007 *An archaeology of identity: Soldiers and society in late Roman Britain.* Walnut Creek, California, Left Coast Press

Gardiner, M. and Mehler, N. 2007 English and Hanseatic trading and fishing sites in medieval Iceland: report on initial fieldwork. *Germania* 85, 385–427

Gerrard, J. 2004 How late is late? Black Burnished ware and the fifth century. In R. Collins and J. Gerrard (eds.) *Debating late antiquity in Britain AD 300–700.* Oxford: British Archaeological Reports British Series 365, 65–75

Gerrard, J. 2007 Roman small finds. In J. Taylor *An assessment report of the archaeological investigations at the former Shippam's factory and Shippam's social club, East Walls, Chichester, West Sussex.* Unpublished Pre-Construct Archaeology Report, 245–247

Gerrard, J. with Major, H. 2007 Roman small finds assessment. In D. Killock *An assessment of an archaeological excavation at Tabard Square, 34–70 Long Lane & 31–47 Tabard Street, London SE1, London Borough of Southwark.* Unpublished Pre-Construct Archaeology Report, 240–278

Gerrard, J. 2008 Demolishing Roman Britain. In L. Rakoczy (ed.) *The archaeology of destruction.* Cambridge: Scholars Press, 176–194

Gerrard, J. 2009 The Drapers' Gardens hoard: A preliminary account. *Britannia* 40, 163–183

Gerrard, J. and Gaimster, M. 2007 The metal and small finds. In G. Seddon *An assessment of an archaeological excavation at Grange Farm, Gillingham, Kent.* Unpublished Pre-Construct Archaeology Report

Gerrard, J. and Lyne, M. forthcoming. The pottery. In G. Brown, B. Bishop, A. Douglas, J. Leary, V. Ridgeway and R. Taylor-Wilson *Excavations at Old Ford, London.* Pre-Construct Archaeology Monograph

Gerrard, J. with Anderson, I., Crummy, N. and Hammerson, M. forthcoming. The coins. In G. Brown, B. Bishop, A. Douglas, J. Leary, V. Ridgeway and R. Taylor-Wilson *Excavations at Old Ford, London.* Pre-Construct Archaeology Monograph

Ghalia, T., Bonifay, M. and Capelli, C. 2005 L'atelier de Sidi-Zahruni: Mise en evidence d'une production d'amphores de l'antiquité tardive sur le territoire de la cité de Neapolis (Nabeul, Tunisie). In J. M. Gurt i Esparraguera, J Buxeda i Garrigós and M. A. Cau Ontiveros (eds.) *LRCW I. Late Roman Coarse Wares, Cooking Wares and Amphorae in the Mediterranean: Archaeology and Archaeometry. Oxford:* British Archaeological Reports International Series 1340, 495–516

Gibbard, P. L. 1994 *Pleistocene history of the lower Thames Valley.* Cambridge: Cambridge University Press

Gillam, J. P. 1970 *Types of Roman coarse pottery vessels in Northern Britain.* 3rd. edn. Newcastle upon Tyne

Gillam, J. P., Jobey, I. M. and Welsby, D. A. 1993 *The Roman bath-house at Bewcastle, Cumbria.* Cumberland and Westmorland Antiquarian and Archaeological Society Research Series 7

Giorgi, J. and Pearson, E. 1992 The plant remains. In C. Cowan (ed) A possible mansio in Roman Southwark: Excavations at 15-23 Southwark Street, 1980–86, *Transactions of the London and Middlesex Archaeology Society* vol 43 (1992), pp. 165–70

Going, C. J. 1987 *The Mansio and other sites in the south-eastern sector of Caesaromagus: The Roman pottery.* Chelmsford Archaeological Trust Report 3.2/Council for British Archaeology Research Report 62

Goodburn, D. 1991 A Roman timber-framed building tradition. *Archaeological Journal* 148, 182–204

Goodburn, D. 1995 From tree to town. In T. Brigham, D. Goodburn, I. Tyers and J. Dillon A Roman timber building on the Southwark waterfront, London. *Archaeological Journal* 152, 33–59

Goodburn, D. 1998 The death of the wildwood and birth of woodmanship in SE England. In C. Bernick (ed.) *Hidden Dimensions.* Vancouver: University of British Columbia Press, 130–138

Goodburn, D. 2001a The Roman and post-Roman timber technology. In T. Brigham and A. Woodger *Roman and medieval townhouses on the London waterfront. Excavations at Governor's House, City of London.* London: Museum of London Archaeology Service Monograph 9, 78–85

Goodburn, D. 2001b Wooden remains as an archaeological resource: Some insights from the London wetlands. In S. Rippon (ed.) *Estuarine archaeology: The Severn and Beyond.* Archaeology in the Severn Estuary 11, 187–196

Goodburn, D. in prep. a The wood assemblage. In J. Leary and J. Butler *Excavations at Tokenhouse Yard, City of London.* Pre-Construct Archaeology Monograph

Goodburn, D. in prep. b The timber. In J. Hill and P. Rowsome, *Roman London and the Walbrook stream crossing: Excavations at 1 Poultry and vicinity, City of London.* Museum of London Archaeology Service Monograph 37

Goodburn, D. in prep. c The timber. In G. Brown and C. Pickard *Excavations at Borough High Street, Southwark.* Pre-Construct Archaeology Monograph

Gose, E. 1950 *Gefässtypen der römischen Keramik im Rheinland*, Bonn: Bonner Jahrbuch Beiheft 1 (reprinted 1975)

Green, C. 1980 The Roman pottery. In D. M. Jones and M. Rhodes (eds.) *Excavations at Billingsgate Buildings, Lower Thames Street, London, 1974.* London: London and Middlesex Archaeological Society Special Paper 4, 39–79

Greep, S. 1986 The coarse pottery. In D. Zienkiewicz (ed.) *The legionary fortress baths at Caerleon II: The Finds.* Cardiff: CADW, 50–96

Greep, S. 1995 Objects of bone, antler and ivory from C.A.T. sites. In K. Blockley *Excavations in the Marlowe car park and surrounding areas.* Canterbury: The Archaeology of Canterbury 5, 1112–1152

Grigson, C. 1982 Sex and age determination of some bones and teeth of domestic cattle: A review of the literature. In B. Wilson, C. Grigson and S. Payne (eds.) *Ageing and sexing animal bones from archaeological sites.* Oxford: British Archaeological Reports British Series 109, 7–23

Guiraud, H. 1989 Bagues et anneaux à l'époque romaine en Gaule. *Gallia Prehistoire* 46, 173–211

Haley, E. 2003 *Baetica Felix.* Austin: University of Texas Press

Hall, J. and Merrifield, R. 1986. *Roman London.* London: HMSO

Hamilton, W. (trans) 1986 *Ammianus Marcellinus: The later Roman Empire.* Harmondsworth: Penguin

Hammerson, M. 1978 Excavations under Southwark Cathedral. *London Archaeologist* 3 (8), 206–212

Hammerson, M. 1996 Problems of coin interpretation in Roman London. In J. Bird, M. Hassall and H. Sheldon (eds.) *Interpreting Roman London: Papers in memory of Hugh Chapman.* Oxford: Oxbow monograph 58, 153–164

Hammerson, M. 2002 Roman coins. In D. Lakin with F. Seeley, J. Bird, K. Rielly and C. Ainsley *The Roman tower at Shadwell, London: A reappraisal.* London: Museum of London Archaeology Service Archaeology Study Series 8, 53–56

Hammerson, M. 2004 Roman coins. In A. Douglas *Phased summary and assessment document of the excavation at 172–176 The Highway, London Borough of Tower Hamlets, E1.* Unpublished Pre-Construct Archaeology Report, 273–279

Harcourt, R. A. 1974 The dog in prehistoric and early historic Britain. *Journal of Archaeological Science* 1, 151–175

Hardy, A. and Goodburn, D. in prep. *Report on the woodwork of the mid Saxon tidal mill found at Ebbsfleet, Kent*

Hartley, B. R 1960 *Notes on the Roman pottery industry in the Nene Valley.* Peterborough Museum Society: Occasional Papers, No.2.

Hartley, K. F. 1973 The Kilns at Mancetter and Hartshill, Warwickshire. In A. Detsicas (ed.), *Current research in Romano-British coarse pottery.* London: Council for British Archaeology Research Report 10, 143–147

Hartley, K. 1995 Mortaria. In D. Phillips and B. Heywood *Excavations at York Minster Volume I, Part 2: The finds.* London: HMSO, 304–323

Hartley, K. 1998 The incidence of stamped mortaria in the Roman Empire with special reference to imports to Britain. In J. Bird (ed.) *Form and fabric: Studies in Rome's material past in honour of B. R. Hartley.* Oxford: Oxbow Monograph 80, 199–217

Hartley, K. F. 2007 Mortaria. In W. S. Hanson *Elginhaugh: a Flavian fort and its annexe, Volume II.* London: Britannia Monograph 23, 326–378

Hartley, B. R. and Dickinson, B. 1979 The potters' stamps. In J. N. Dore and J. P. Gillam, *The Roman fort at South Shields.* Newcastle: Society of Antiquaries of Newcastle upon Tyne Monograph Series 1, 100–106

Hartley, B., Hawkes, J., Henig, M. and Mee, F. 2006 *Constantine the Great: York's Roman Emperor.* York: York Museums and Galleries Trust

Hassall, M. and Tomlin, R. 1979 Inscriptions. *Britannia* 10, 339–356

Haupt, D. 1981 Von Birgel nach Silchester. *Bonner Jahrbuch* 181

Haupt, D. 1984 Römischer Töpfereibezirk bei Soller, Kreis Düren. Beitrage zur Archaologie des Römischen Rheinlands 4. *Rheinische Ausgrabungen* 23, 391–476.

Hawkes, S. and Dunning, G. 1961 Soldiers and settlers in Britain: fourth to fifth century. *Medieval Archaeology* 5, 1–70

Hawkins, D. and Meager, R. 2002 *An archaeological desk based assessment for land at 172–176 The Highway, London Borough of Tower Hamlets, E1.* Unpublished CgMs Report

Hawkins, N., Brown, G. and Butler, J. 2008 Drapers' Gardens. *British Archaeology* 98, 12–17

Hayes, J. W. 1972 *Late Roman pottery: A catalogue of fine wares*. London: British School at Rome

Hayward, K. M. J. 2008 Petrological analysis. In N. Bateman, C. Cowan and R. Wroe-Brown *London's Roman amphitheatre: Excavations at the Guildhall Yard, City of London*. London: Museum of London Archaeology Service Monograph 35, 168–169

Heard, K. 1989 Excavations at 10–18 Union Street, Southwark. *London Archaeologist* 6 (5), 126–131

Heather, P. 2005 *The fall of the Roman Empire: A new history*. London: Macmillan

Heather, P. 2009 *Empires and Barbarians: Migration, development and the birth of Europe*. London: Pan

Henig, M. 1985 Roman small finds. In B. Cunliffe and P. Davenport *The Temple of Sulis Minerva at Bath Volume I: The site*. Oxford: Oxford University Committee for Archaeology Monograph 7, 136–140

Hillam, J. 1990 The dendrochronology of the late Roman waterfront at Billingsgate lorry park and other sites in the City of London. In T. Brigham The Roman Waterfront in London. *Britannia* 21, 164–170

Hillam, J. 1982 *Tree-ring analysis of oak timbers from the 1979 excavations at the Tower of London*. Ancient Monuments Laboratory Report 3756

Hillam, J. 1987 *Tree-ring analysis in the City of London. The dating of Roman timbers from Billingsgate and New Fresh Wharf*. Ancient Monuments Laboratory Report 66/87

Hinchliffe, J. and Sparey Green, C. 1985 *Excavations at Brancaster 1974 and 1977*. Dereham: East Anglian Archaeology 23

Hodges, R. 1982 *Dark Age economics: The origins of towns and trade AD 600–1000*. London: Duckworth

Holbrook, N. and Bidwell, P. 1991 *Roman finds from Exeter*. Exeter: Exeter Archaeological Reports 4

Houston, G. W. 1988 Ports in perspective: Some comparative materials on Roman merchant ships and ports. *American Journal of Archaeology* 92 (4), 553–564

Howe, E. and Lakin, D. 2004 *Roman and early medieval Cripplegate, City of London: Archaeological excavations 1992–8*. London: Museum of London Archaeology Service Monograph 21

Howe, M., Perrin, J. and Mackreth, D. 1980 *Roman pottery from the Nene Valley: A guide*. Peterborough: Peterborough City Museum Occasional Paper 2

Huld-Zetsche, I. 1972 *Trierer Reliefsigillata Werkstatt I*. Bonn: Materialen zur römisch-germanischen Keramik 9

Huld-Zetsche, I. 1993 *Trierer Reliefsigillata Werkstatt II*. Bonn: Materialen zur römisch-germanischen Keramik 12

Isings, C. 1957 *Roman glass from dated finds*. Groningen/Djakarta: J. B. Wolters

Jackson, R. 1999 Spas, waters and hydrotherapy in the Roman world. In J. DeLaine and D. Johnston (eds.) *Roman baths and bathing: Proceedings of the First International Conference on Roman Baths, held at Bath, England, 30 March–4 April 1992*. Portsmouth, Rhode Island: Journal of Roman Archaeology Supplementary Series 37, 130–135

Jenkins, J. T. 1925 reptd. 1942 *The fishes of the British Isles both freshwater & salt*. London: Frederick Warne & Co Ltd., Second Edition

Johnson, S. 1979 *The Roman forts of the Saxon shore*. London: Book Club Associates

Johnson, T. 1975 A Roman signal-tower at Shadwell, E1, an interim note. *Transactions of the London and Middlesex Archaeological Society* 26, 278–280

Jones, A. 1964 *The Later Roman Empire: A social, economic and administrative study*. Oxford: Oxford University Press

Jones, M. and Rodwell, W. 1973 The Romano-British pottery kilns at Mucking. *Essex Archaeology and History* 5, 13–47

Jope, E. M. 1945 The action of fire on samian. In G. C. Dunning The two fires of Roman London. *Antiquaries Journal* 25, 76–77

Keay, S. 1984 *Late Roman amphorae in the Western Mediterranean. A typology and economic study: The Catalan evidence*. Oxford: British Archaeological Reports International Series 136

Keily, J. 2007 The accessioned finds. In R. Bluer, T. Brigham and R. Nielsen *Roman and later development east of the forum and Cornhill*. London: Museum of London Archaeology Service Monograph 30, 142–159

Kelly, C. 2006 *Ruling the later Roman empire*. Harvard: Harvard University Press

Kennedy, H. 1985 From Polis to Madina: Urban change in late antique and early Islamic Syria. *Past and Present* 106, 3–27

Kennett, D. 1969 Late Roman bronze vessel hoards in Britain. *Jahrbuch des Römisch-Hermanischen Zentralmuseums Mainz*, 16 Jahrgang 1969, 123–148

Keys, L. and Gaimster, M. 2004 Assessment of the metal and non-metal small finds. In A. Douglas *Phased summary and assessment document of the excavations at 130–162 The Highway, London Borough of Tower Hamlets.* Unpublished Pre-Construct Archaeology Report, 317–327

King, A. 1984 The decline of Central Gaulish sigillata manufacture in the early third century. *Acta Rei Cretariae Romanae Fautores* 23–24, 51–59

King, A. 1985 *The decline of samian ware manufacture in the north-west provinces of the Roman Empire.* Unpublished University of London PhD thesis

Krencker, D., Kruger, E., Lehman, H. and Wachtler, H. 1929 *Die Trierer Kaiserthermen.* Augsburg: B. Filser

Ladstätter, S. 2000 Consumer Cities – the case of Ephesos. In *The economy of Roman pottery. Approaching production mechanisms and exchange patterns. Second International ROCT conference, Leuven, 19–20 May 2000*

Lakin, D. with Seeley, F., Bird, J., Rielly, K. and Ainsley, C. 2002 *The Roman tower at Shadwell, London: A reappraisal.* London: Museum of London Archaeology Service Archaeology Studies Series 8

Lamb, H. H. 1981 Climate from 1000 BC to 1000 AD. In M. Jones and G. Dimbleby (eds.) *The environment of man: The Iron age to the Anglo-Saxon period.* Oxford: British Archaeological Reports British Series 87, 53–65

Lang, M. 1955 Dated jars of early imperial times. *Hesperia* 24, 277–285

Laubenheimer, F. 1985 *La production des amphores en Gaule Narbonnaise.* Paris: Les Belles Lettres

Laubenheimer, F. and Schmitt, A. forthcoming *Amphores vinaires de Narbonnaise, Production et grand commerce. Création d'une base de données géochimique des ateliers*

Lauwerier, R. C. G. M. 1993 Bird remains in Roman graves. *Archaeofauna* 2, 75–82.

Lauwerier, R. C. G. M. and Hessing, W. A. M. 1992 Men, horses and the Miss Blanche effect: Roman horse burials in a cemetery at Kesteren, The Netherlands. *Helinium* 32 (1–2), 78–109

Leach, P. 1982 *Excavations at Ilchester Volume 1.* Bristol: Western Archaeological Trust Excavation Monograph 3

Leach, P. and Evans, J. 2001 *Fosse Lane, Shepton Mallet, 1990: The excavation of a Romano-British roadside settlement and cemetery.* London: Britannia Monograph Series 18

Levine, M. A. 1982 The use of crown height measurements and eruption-wear sequences to age horse teeth. In B. Wilson, C. Grigson and S. Payne (eds.) *Ageing and sexing animal bones from archaeological sites.* Oxford: British Archaeological Reports British Series 109, 223–250

Ling, R. 1985 *Romano-British Wall Painting.* Buckinghamshire: Shire Archaeology

Lloyd-Morgan, G. 1994 Copper-alloy objects excluding brooches. In S. Cracknell and C. Mahany (eds.) *Roman Alcester: Southern extramural area 1964–1966 excavations: Part 2: Finds and discussion.* York: Council for British Archaeology Research Report 97, 177–194

Lockyear, C. 2007 Where do we go from here? Recording and analysing Roman coins from archaeological excavations. *Britannia* 38, 211–224

Luff, R. M. 1982 *A zooarchaeological study of the Roman north-western Provinces.* Oxford: British Archaeological Reports International Series 137

Lyne, M. 1994 *Late Roman handmade wares in south-east Britain.* University of Reading PhD thesis

Lyne, M. and Jefferies, R. 1979 *The Alice Holt/Farnham Roman pottery industries.* London: Council for British Archaeology Research Report 30

McCarthy, M.R. 1990 *A Roman, Anglian and Mediaeval site at Blackfriars Street.* Cumberland and Westmorland Antiq and Arch Soc Res Ser No. 4.

McCormick, M. 2001 *Origins of the European economy: communications and commerce AD 300–900.* Cambridge: Cambridge University Press

MacGregor, A. 1976 *Finds from a Roman sewer and an adjacent building in Church Street* York: York Archaeological Trust, The Archaeology of York 17/1

Major, H. 2004 An assessment of the small finds. In A. Douglas *Phased summary and assessment document of the excavation at 172–176 The Highway, London Borough of Tower Hamlets, E1.* Unpublished Pre-Construct Archaeology Report, 261–272

Maltby, M. 1979 *The animal bones from Exeter 1971–1975.* University of Sheffield: Exeter Archaeological Reports 2

Manning, W. 1985 *Catalogue of the Romano-British iron tools fittings and weapons in the British Museum.* London: British Museum Press

Marsden, P. 1967 *A Roman ship from Blackfriars, London.* London: Guildhall Museum

Marsden, P. 1980 *Roman London.* London: Thames and Hudson

Marsden, P. 1994 *Ships of the port of London first to eleventh centuries AD.* London: English Heritage Archaeological Report 3

Martin, S. 2004 *'Latest' Roman Essex: Chronology and pottery supply and use c. AD 350–450.* Unpublished and revised manuscript of a paper given to the Study Group for Roman Pottery in 2000

Mason, D. J. P. 2005 *Excavations at Chester, the Roman Fortress baths: Excavation and recording 1732–1998.* Chester City Council Archaeological Service Excavation & Survey Report 13

Mattingly, D. 2007 *An Imperial possession: Britain in the Roman Empire.* Harmondsworth: Penguin

Mayer, J. J. and Brisbin, I. L. 1988 Sex identification of *sus scrofa* based on canine morphology. *Journal of Mammalogy* 69 (2), 408–412

Meadows, I. 1996 Wollaston: The Nene Valley, a British Moselle? *Current Archaeology* 150, pp 212-15

Merrifield, R. 1983 *London: City of the Romans.* London: Batsford

Miller, L., Schofield, J. and Rhodes, M. 1986 *The Roman quay at St Magnus House, London: Excavations at New Fresh Wharf, Lower Thames Street, London, 1974–78.* London: London and Middlesex Archaeological Society Special Paper 8

Millett, M. 1990 *The Romanization of Britain.* Cambridge: Cambridge University Press

Mills, J. and Woodward, P. 1993 Shale and jet. In P. Woodward, S. Davies and A. Graham *Excavations at Greyhound Yard, Dorchester 1981–4.* Dorchester: Dorset Natural History and Archaeological Society Monograph 12, 139–145

Milne, G. 1985 *The port of Roman London.* London: Batsford

Milne, G. 1992 *From Roman basilica to medieval market, Archaeology in Action in the City of London.* London: HMSO

Milne, G., Bates, M. and Webber, M. 1997 Problems, potential and partial solutions: An archaeological study of the tidal Thames. *World Archaeology* 29 (1), 130–146

Milne, J. 1907 Surgical instruments in Greek and Roman Times. Oxford: Clarendon Press

Monaghan, J. 1987 *Upchurch and Thameside Roman pottery: A ceramic typology for northern Kent.* Oxford: British Archaeological Reports British Series 173

Monaghan, J. 1997 The distribution of samian ware. In J. Monaghan, *Roman pottery from York.* York: Archaeology of York 16/8, 948–950

Moore, P. D., Webb, J. A. and Collinson, M. E. 1991 *Pollen analysis.* Oxford: Blackwell

Morgan, R. A. 1980 The carbon 14 and dendrochronology. In C. Hill, M. Millett and T. Blagg *The Roman riverside wall and monumental arch in London.* London: London and Middlesex Archaeological Society Special Paper 3, 88–94

Nenova-Merdjanova, R. 1999 Roman bronze vessels as part of *instrumentum balnei*. In J. Delanie and D. Johnston (eds.) *Roman baths and bathing: proceedings of the First International Conference on Roman Baths, held at Bath, England, 30 March–4 April 1992.* Portsmouth, Rhode Island: Journal of Roman Archaeology Supplementary Series 37, 130–135

Newdick, J. 1979 *The complete freshwater fishes of the British Isles.* London: Adam & Charles Black

Nielsen, I. 1990 *Thermae et Balnea: The architecture and cultural history of Roman public baths.* Aarhus University Press

Nixon, T., McAdam, E., Tomber, R. and Swain, H. (eds.) 2002 *A research framework for London Archaeology 2002.* London: English Heritage and the Museum of London

O'Connor, T. P. 1983 Aspects of site environment and economy at Caerleon Fortress Baths, Gwent. In B. Proudfoot (ed.) *Site, Environment and Economy.* Oxford: British Archaeological Reports International Series 173, 105–113

Oelmann, F. 1914 *Die Keramik des Kastells Niederbieber.* Frankfurt am Main: Materialen zur römisch-germanischen Keramik 1

Ohlig, C. 2001 De Aquis Pompeiorum: Das Castellum Aquae in Pompeji: Herkunft, Zuleitung und Verteilung des Wassers. Nijmegen: *Circumvesuviana 4*

Olivier, A. 1996 Brooches of silver, copper-alloy and iron from Dragonby. In J. May *Dragonby*. Oxford: Oxbow Monograph 61, 231–264

Orton, C., Tyers, P. and Vince, A. 1993 *Pottery in archaeology*. Cambridge: Cambridge University Press

Oswald, F. 1936–1937 *Index of figure-types on terra sigillata ('samian ware')*. Liverpool: Annals of Archaeology and Anthropology Supplement 23.1–4, 24.1–4

Ottaway, P. 1993 *Roman York*. London: Batsford and English Heritage

Ove Arup & Partners 1994 *A desktop assessment, Tobacco Dock factory shops Phase II – New building*. Unpublished Ove Arup Report

Panella, C. 1982 Le anfore africane della prima, media e tarda età imperiale, tipologia e problemi. *Actes du colloque sur la céramique antique (Carthage, 23–24 juin 1980). CEDAC. Dossier* 1, 171–186

Payne, S. 1973 Kill-off patterns in sheep and goats: the mandibles from Asvan Kale. *Anatolian Studies* 23, 281–303

Peacock, D. P. S. 1978 The Rhine and the problem of Gaulish wine in Roman Britain. In J. du Plat Taylor and H. Cleere (eds.) *Roman shipping and trade: Britain and the Rhine provinces*. London: Council for British Archaeology 24, 49–51

Peacock, D. 1977 Pompeian red ware. In D. P. S. Peacock (ed.) *Pottery and early commerce*. London: Academic Press, 147–162

Peacock, D. and Williams, D. 1986 *Amphorae and the Roman economy*. London: Longmans

Pearce, S. 2004 *South-western Britain in the early Middle Ages*. Leicester: Leicester University Press

Pearson, A. 2002 *The Roman Shore Forts – coastal defence of southern Britain*. Stroud: Tempus

Pearson, A. 2005 Barbarian piracy and the Saxon shore: A reappraisal. *Oxford Journal of Archaeology* 24 (1), 73–88

Perring, D., Roskams, S. and Allen, P. 1991 *Early development of Roman London west of the Walbrook. The Archaeology of Roman London Vol. 2*. London: Council for British Archaeology Research Report 70

Perring, D. 1991 *Roman London*. London: Seaby

Philp, B. 2005 *The excavation of the Roman fort at Reculver, Kent*. Dover: Kent Monograph 10

Plouviez, J. 2004 Review of Caister-on-Sea excavations by Charles Green 1951–1955. *Journal of Roman Pottery Studies* 11, 119–120

Pollard, R. 1988 *The Roman pottery of Kent*. Maidstone: Kent Archaeological Society Monograph 5

Pomel, M. 1984 *A study of later Roman pottery groups in Southern Britain: Fabrics, forms and chronology*. Unpublished University of London M. Phil thesis

Ponsich, M. 1974 *Implantation Rurale Antique sur le Bas-Guadalquivir, Vol. I*. Madrid

Ponsich, M. 1979 *Implantation Rurale Antique sur le Bas-Guadalquivir, Vol. II*. Paris

Ponsich, M. 1991 *Implantation Rurale Antique sur le Bas-Guadalquivir, Vol. III*. Paris

Price, J. 1974 A Roman mould-blown negro-head glass beaker from London. *Antiquaries Journal* 14, 291–292

Pringle, S. 2002. The building materials. In J. Drummond-Murray and P. Thompson *Settlement in Roman Southwark: Archaeological excavations (1991–8) for the London Underground Limited Jubilee Line extension project*. London: Museum of London Archaeology Service Monograph 12, 151–161

Pringle, S. 2007 London's earliest Roman bath-houses? *London Archaeologist* 11 (8), 205–209

Pritchard, F. A. 1986 Ornamental stonework from Roman London. *Britannia* 17, 169–189

Prummel, W. 1979 The size of Dutch horses and Labouchere's theory on the origin of the Frisian horse. In M. Kubasiewicz (ed.) *Archaeozoology Volume I*. Szczecin, 431–438

Rayner, L. and Seeley, F. 1998 Pottery, publications and research in Roman London. In B. Watson (ed.) *Roman London: Recent archaeological work*. Portsmouth, Rhode Island: Journal of Roman Archaeology Supplementary Series 24, 90–94

Rayner, L. and Seeley, F. 2008 The Southwark pottery type-series: 30 years on. In J. Clark, J. Cotton, J. Hall, R. Sherris and H. Swain (ed.) *Londinium and Beyond: essays on Roman London and its hinterland for Harvey Sheldon.* London: Council for British Archaeology Research Report 156, 184–193

RCHM(E) 1928 *An inventory of the historical monuments in London: Vol III Roman London.* London: HMSO

Reece, R. 1980 Town and country: The end of Roman Britain. *World Archaeology* 12, 77–92

Reece, R. 1991 *Roman coins from 140 sites in Britain.* Cirencester: Cotswold Archaeological Studies 4

Reece, R. 1993 British sites and their Roman coins. *Antiquity* 67, 863–869

Reece, R. 1995 Site finds in Roman Britain. *Britannia* 26, 179–206

Reece, R. 2005 The coins. In B. Philp (ed.) *The excavation of the Roman fort at Reculver, Kent.* Dover: Kent Monograph 10, 103–112

Reille, M. 1992 *Pollen et Spores d'Europe et d'Afrique du Nord.* Marseille: Laboratoire de Botanique Historique et Palynologie

Remesal, J. 1986 *La Annona militaris y la exportacion de aceite bitico a Germania.* Madrid

Reumer, J. W. F. 1986 Note on the spread of the black rat, *Rattus rattus. Mammalia* 50, 118–119

Reutman, M. 1995 *Two late Roman wells at Sardis, preliminary excavation reports: Sardis, Idalion and Tell el-Handaquq North.* Atlanta: AASOR

Ricken, H. and Fischer, C. (ed.) 1963 *Die Bilderschüsseln der römischen Töpfer von Rheinzabern. Textband mit Typenbildern zu Katalog VI der Ausgrabungen von Wilhelm Ludowici in Rheinzabern 1901–1914.* Bonn: Materialen zur römisch-germanischen Keramik 7

Ricken, H. and Thomas, M. (ed.) 2005 *Die dekorationsserien der Rheinzaberner Reliefsigillata. Textband zum Katalog VI der Ausgrabungen von Wilhelm Ludowici in Rheinzabern 1901–1914.* Bonn: Materialen zur römisch-germanischen Keramik 14 (2 vols)

Richmond, I. A., Romans, T. and Wright, R. P. 1944 A civilian bath-house of the Roman period at Old Durham. *Archaeologia Aeliana* 22, 1–25

Ridgeway, V. 2009 (ed) *Secrets of the gardens. Archaeologists unearth the lives of Roman Londoners at Drapers' Gardens.* London: Pre-Construct Archaeology

Rodriguez-Almeida, E. 1989 *Los Tituli Picti de las Anforas Olearias de la Betica.* Madrid: Universidad Complutense

Rogers, G. B. 1974 *Poteries sigillées de la Gaule Centrale, I - les motifs non figures.* Paris: Gallia Supplement 28

Rogers, G. B. 1999 *Poteries sigillées de la Gaule Centrale, II - les potiers.* Lezoux: Cahiers du Centre Archéologique de Lezoux 1/Revue Archéologique SITES Hors-série 40 (2 vols)

Rook, T. 1979 Tiled roofs. In A. McWhirr *Roman brick and tile.* Oxford: British Archaeological Reports International Series 68, 295–301

Rowland, I. (trans.) 1999 *Vitruvius: Ten books on Architecture.* Cambridge: Cambridge University Press

Rowsome, P. 1996 The Billingsgate Roman house and bath – conservation and assessment. *London Archaeologist* 7 (16), 415–423

Rowsome, P. 1999 The Huggin Hill baths and bathing in London: Barometer of the town's changing circumstances? In J. DeLaine and D. Johnston (eds.) *Roman baths and bathing: Proceedings of the First International Conference on Roman Baths, held at Bath, England, 30 March–4 April 1992.* Portsmouth, Rhode Island: Journal of Roman Archaeology Supplementary Series 37, 262–277

Rowsome, P. 2000 *Heart of the City: Roman, medieval and modern London revealed by archaeology at 1 Poultry.* London: English Heritage and Museum of London Archaeology Service

Sadler, P. 1990 The use of tarsometatarsi in sexing and ageing domestic fowl (Gallus gallus L.) and recognising five toed breeds in archaeological material. *Circaea* 8 (1), 41–48

Salway, P. 1981 *Roman Britain.* Oxford: Oxford University Press

Sankey, D. 1998 Cathedrals, granaries and urban vitality in late Roman London. In B. Watson (ed.) *Roman London: Recent archaeological work.* Portsmouth, Rhode Island, Journal of Roman Archaeology Supplementary Series 24, 78–82

Scatozza Höricht, L. A. 1986 *I Vetri Romani di Ercolano.* Roma: Erma Bretschneider

Schiffer, M. 1972 Archaeological context and systematic context. *American Antiquity* 37, 156–165

Schiffer, M. 1985 Is there a "Pompeii premise" in archaeology? *Journal of Anthropological Research* 41, 18–41

Sciallano, M. and Sibella, P. 1991 *Amphores: Comment les identifier?* Aix-en-Provence: Edisud

Seeley, F. and Drummond-Murray, J. 2005 *Roman pottery production in the Walbrook valley: Excavations at 20–28 Moorgate, City of London, 1998–2000.* London: Museum of London Archaeology Service Monograph 25

Shaffrey, R. 2006 *Grinding and milling: A study of Romano-British rotary querns and millstones made from Old Red Sandstone.* Oxford: British Archaeological Reports British Series 409

Sheldon, H. 1971 Excavations at Lefevre Road, Old Ford, E3, September 1969–June 1970. *Transactions of the London and Middlesex Archaeological Society* 23 (1), 43–77

Sheldon, H. 1972 Excavations at Parnell Road and Appian Road, Old Ford, E3, February–April 1971. *Transactions of the London and Middlesex Archaeological Society* 23 (2), 101–147

Sheldon, H. 1995 London and the Saxon Shore. *Transactions of the London and Middlesex Archaeological Society* 46, 59–68

Sheldon, H. and Yule, B. 1979 Excavations in Greenwich Park 1978–9. *London Archaeologist* 3 (12), 311–317

Shepherd, J. 1998 *The Temple of Mithras, London: Excavations by W. F. Grimes and A. Williams at the Walbrook.* London: English Heritage Archaeological Report 12

Simon, H-G. and Köhler, H-J. 1992 *Ein Geschirrdepot des 3. Jahrhunderts: Grabungen im Lagerdorf des Kastells Langenhain.* Bonn: Materialen zur römisch-germanischen Keramik 11

Smith, J. 1982 Flight of capital or flight of fancy? The supposed continental connexions of late Roman villas. *Oxford Journal of Archaeology* 2, 239–246

Southern, S. 1990 Signals versus illumination on Roman frontiers. *Britannia* 21, 233–242

Spence, C. 1990 *Archaeological site manual. 2nd edition.* London: Museum of London

Stace, C. 1997 *New flora of the British Isles.* Cambridge: Cambridge University Press

Stern, E. M. 1995, *Roman mold-blown glass: The first through sixth centuries.* Roma: Erma Bretschneider

Sudds, B. 2008 Ceramic and stone building material and structural remains. In T. Bradley and J. Butler *From Temples to Thames Street: 2000 years of riverside development. Archaeological excavations at the Salvation Army International Headquarters.* London: Pre-Construct Archaeology Monograph 7, 34–40

Swan, V. 2009 'Drinking, ethnicity, troop transfers, and the Classis Britannica. In V. Swan *Ethnicity, Conquest and Recruitment: two case studies from the northern military provinces.* Portsmouth, Rhode Island, Journal of Roman Archaeology Supplementary Series 72, 67–95

Swift, E. 2000 *Regionality in dress accessories in the late Roman west.* Montagnac: editions Monique Mergoil, Monographies Instrumentum 11

Symonds, R. 2000 *Recording Roman pottery: A description of the methodology used at Museum of London Specialist Services (MoLSS) and Museum of London Archaeology Service (Museum of London Archaeology Service).* Unpublished document available from Museum of London Archaeology Service.

Symonds, R. 2001 The Roman pottery. In T. Brigham and A. Woodger *Roman and medieval townhouses on the London waterfront: Excavations at Governor's House, City of London.* London: Museum of London Archaeology Service Monograph 9, 85–92

Symonds, R. and Tomber, R. 1991 Late Roman London: an assessment of the ceramic evidence from the City of London. *Transactions of the London and Middlesex Archaeological Society* 42, 59–100

Symonds, R. P. and Wade, S. 1999 *Roman pottery from excavations in Colchester 1971–86.* Colchester: Colchester Archaeological Report 10

Taylor, H. M. and Taylor, J. 1980 *Anglo-Saxon architecture, Volume 1.* Cambridge: Cambridge University Press

Taylor, R. 1997 Torrent or trickle? The *Aquae Alsietina*, the *Naumachia Augusti*, and the *Transtiberim*. *American Journal of Archaeology* 101 (3), 465–492

The Geographical Survey 1994 (1:50 000) Sheet 256, North London

Thomas, C. 1981a *A provisional list of imported pottery in post-Roman Western Britain and Ireland.* Redruth: Institute of Cornish Studies Special Report 7

Thomas, C. 1981b *Christianity in Roman Britain to AD 500*. London: Batsford

Timby, J. 2000 The Roman pottery. In P. Ellis (ed.) *The Roman baths and Macellum at Wroxeter: Excavations by Graham Webster, 1955–85*. London: English Heritage Archaeological Report 9, 193–312

Tomber, R. and Dore, J. 1998 *The National Roman fabric collection*. London: Museum of London Archaeology Service Monograph 2

Tomlin, R. 1979. Graffiti on Roman bricks and tiles found in Britain. In A. McWhirr (ed.) *Roman brick and tile*. Oxford: British Archaeological Reports International Series 68, 231–251

Tomlin, R. and Hassall, M. 2004 Inscriptions. *Britannia* 35, 335–349

Tuffreau-Libre, M. 1980 *La Ceramique Commune Gallo-Romaine dans le Nord de la France (Nord, Pas-de-Calais)*, Lille

Tyers, I. 1988 Environmental evidence in Southwark and Lambeth. In P. Hinton (ed.) *Excavations in Southwark 1973–76 Lambeth 1973–79*. London: London and Middlesex Archaeological Society/Surrey Archaeological Society Joint Publication 3, 443–477

Tyers, I. 1994 *Tree-ring analysis of Roman piles from Pevensey Castle, East Sussex*. Unpublished Ancient Monuments Laboratory Report 65/94

Tyers, I. 2000 *Archive report on the tree-ring analysis of Roman timbers from Number 1 Poultry, City of London*. Unpublished ARCUS Report 517

Tyers, I. 2001 *Interim report on the tree-ring analysis of timbers excavated at Guildhall, City of London*. Unpublished ARCUS Report 518

Tyers, I. 2004 *Dendro for Windows program guide 3rd edn*. Unpublished ARCUS Report 500b

Tyers, I. and Boswijk, G. 1996 *Dendrochronological spot dates for 82 timbers from Suffolk House (SUF94), City of London, Three Ways Wharf (LTS95), City of London, Guys Hospital (GHL89 & GHD90), Southwark, Lafone St (LAF96), Southwark, Jacob's Island (JAC96), Southwark, and Atlantic Wharf (FTW96), Tower Hamlets*. Unpublished ARCUS Report 286

Tyers, P. 1984 An assemblage of Roman ceramics from London. *London Archaeologist* 4 (14), 367–374

Vermeesch, D. 1993 La céramique à pâte claire du vicus routier de Taverny (Val-d'Oise). In *SFECAG: Actes du Congrès de Versailles 1993*, 117–135

Wacher, J. 1995 *The towns of Roman Britain*. London: Batsford

Wallace, C. 2006 Long-lived samian? *Britannia* 37, 259–272

Waller, M. 1994 *The Fenland Project Number 9: Flandrian environmental change in Fenland*. Cambridge: East Anglian Archaeology Report 70

Wallower, B. 2002 Roman temple complex in Greenwich Park? Part 1. *London Archaeologist* 10 (2), 46–53

Wallower, B. 2002b Roman temple complex in Greenwich? Part 2. *London Archaeologist* 10 (3), 76–81

Ward, M. 2008 The samian ware. In H. E. M. Cool and D. J. P. Mason (eds) *Roman Piercebridge: Excavations by D. W. Harding and Peter Scott 1969–1981*, Durham: Architectural and Archaeological Society of Durham and Northumberland Monograph 7, 169–296

Ward-Perkins, B. 2005 *The fall of Rome and the end of civilisation*. Oxford: Oxford University Press

Ward-Perkins, J. B. and Toynbee, J. M. C. 1949 The hunting baths of Lepcis Magna. *Archaeologia* 93, 165–195

Warry, P. 2006 *Tegulae: Manufacture, typology and use in Roman Britain*. Oxford: British Archaeological Reports British Series 417

Watson, B., Brigham, T. and Dyson, T. 2001 *London Bridge: 2000 years of a river crossing*. London: Museum of London Archaeology Service Monograph 8

Werff, J. van der 2003 The third and second lives of amphoras in Alphen aan den Rijn, The Netherlands. *Journal of Roman Pottery Studies* 10, 109–116

West, B. A. 1982 Spur development: Recognising caponised fowl in archaeological material. In B. Wilson, C. Grigson and S. Payne (eds.) *Ageing and sexing animal bones from archaeological sites*. Oxford: British Archaeological Reports British Series 10, 255–261

West, B. A. 1983 *The Roman buildings west of the Walbrook project: Human and animal bones*. Unpublished Museum of London Archival Report.

West, B. A. 1985 Chicken legs revisited. *Circaea* 3 (1), 11–14

Wheeler, A. 1977 The origin and distribution of the freshwater fishes of the British Isles. *Journal of Biogeography* 4, 1–24

Wheeler, A. 1979 *The tidal Thames the history of a river and its fishes*. London: Routledge & Kegan Paul

Wheeler, A. 1980 Fish remains. In D. M. Jones *Excavations at Billingsgate Buildings, Lower Thames Street, London, 1974*. London: London and Middlesex Archaeological Society Special Paper No. 4, 161–162

Whitaker, W. 1889a *The geology of London and part of the Thames Valley: Vol I descriptive geology*. London: HMSO

Whitaker, W. 1889b *The geology of London and part of the Thames Valley: Vol II Appendices*. London: HMSO

Whittaker, C. 1983 Late Roman trade and traders. In P. Garnsey, K. Hopkins and C. Whittaker (eds.) *Trade in the ancient economy*. London: Chatto and Windus, 163–180

Wickenden, N. 1988 *Excavations at Great Dunmow, Essex: a Romano-British small town in the Trinovantian Civitas*. Chelsmford: Chelmsford Archaeological Report 7/East Anglian Archaeology 41

Wickham, C. 2010 *The inheritance of Rome: A history of Europe from 400–1000*. London: Penguin

Willcox, G. H. 1977 Exotic plants from Roman waterlogged sites in London. *Journal of Archaeological Science* 4, 269–282

Willcox G. H. 1978 Seeds from the late 2nd century pit F28. In J. Bird, A. H. Graham, H. Sheldon and P. Townend (eds.) *Southwark Excavations 1972–74, Volume II*. London: London and Middlesex Archaeological Society/Surrey Archaeological Society Joint Publication 1, 291–422

Williams, D. and Peacock, D. 1983 The importation of olive-oil into Roman Britain. In J. M. Blazquez and J. Remesal (eds.) *Produccion Y Comercio del Aceite en la Antiquedad. II Congresso. Madrid, 63–280*

Williams, D. F. and Keay, S. J. 2006 *Roman amphorae: A digital resource*, http://ads.ahds.ac.uk/catalogue/archive/amphora_ahrb_2005/index.cfm

Williams, J. and Brown, N. 1999 *An archaeological research framework for the greater Thames estuary*. Chelmsford: Essex County Council

Williams, R. J. and Zeepvat, R. J. 1994 *Bancroft, the late Bronze Age and Iron Age settlements and Roman temple-mausoleum*. Aylesbury: Buckinghamshire Archaeological Society Monograph 7

Williams, T. 1993 *The archaeology of Roman London Volume 3: Public buildings in the south-west quarter of Roman London*. London: Council for British Archaeology Research Report 88

Williams, D. and Carreras, C. 1995 North African amphorae in Roman Britain: A reappraisal. *Britannia* 26, 231–252

Willis, S. 2004 Samian pottery, a resource for the study of Roman Britain and beyond: the results of the English Heritage funded project. *Internet Archaeology* 17 http://intarch.ac.uk

Wilmott, T. 1982 Excavations at Queen Street and Roman wells in London. *Transactions of the London and Middlesex Archaeological Society* 33, 1–78

Woodward, A. 1992 *Shrines and sacrifice*. London: English Heritage

Woodward, A. and Leach, P. 1993 *The Uley Shrines*. London: English Heritage Archaeological Report 17

Woodward, P. (ed.) 1987 *Romano-British industries in Purbeck*. Dorchester: Dorset Natural History and Archaeological Society Monograph 6

Woodward, P., Davies, S. and Graham, A. 1993 *Excavations at Greyhound Yard, Dorchester 1981–4*. Dorchester: Dorset Natural History and Archaeological Society Monograph 12

Yegül, F. 1992 *Baths and bathing in classical antiquity*. New York: The Architectural History Foundation

Young, C. 1977 *The Roman pottery industry of the Oxford region*. Oxford: British Archaeological Reports British Series 43

Young, C. J. 1980 The pottery. In B. Cunliffe Excavations at the Roman fort at Lympne, Kent 1976–78. *Britannia* 11, 274–283

Yule, B. 2005 *A prestigious Roman building complex on the Southwark waterfront: Excavations at Winchester Palace, London, 1983–90*. London: Museum of London Archaeology Service Monograph 23

Yule, B. and Rankov, B. 1998 Legionary soldiers in 3rd-C. Southwark. In B. Watson (ed.) *Roman London recent archaeological work*. Portsmouth, Rhode Island: Journal of Roman Archaeology Supplementary Series 24

Zienkiewicz, D. 1986 *The legionary fortress baths at Caerleon: Volume 2, the finds*. Cardiff: CADW

Index

Page numbers in *italics* denote illustrations. All streets and locations are in London unless specified otherwise.